INTERNATIONAL HUMAN RESOURCE MANAGEMENT

EDITED BY **MIGUEL MARTÍNEZ LUCIO**

INTERNATIONAL HUMAN RESOURCE MANAGEMENT:

AN EMPLOYMENT RELATIONS PERSPECTIVE

Los Angeles | London | New Delhi
Singapore | Washington DC

Los Angeles | London | New Delhi
Singapore | Washington DC

SAGE Publications Ltd
1 Oliver's Yard
55 City Road
London EC1Y 1SP

SAGE Publications Inc.
2455 Teller Road
Thousand Oaks, California 91320

SAGE Publications India Pvt Ltd
B 1/I 1 Mohan Cooperative Industrial Area
Mathura Road
New Delhi 110 044

SAGE Publications Asia-Pacific Pte Ltd
3 Church Street
#10-04 Samsung Hub
Singapore 049483

Editor: Kirsty Smy
Editorial assistant: Nina Smith
Project manager: Cenveo Publisher Services
Marketing manager: Alison Borg
Cover design: Francis Kenney
Typeset by: Cenveo Publisher Services
Printed and bound in Great Britain by Ashford Colour
Press Ltd

First published 2014

Library of Congress Control Number: 2013940262

British Library Cataloguing in Publication data

A catalogue record for this book is available from the British Library

ISBN 978-0-85702-975-1
ISBN 978-0-85702-976-8 (pbk)

Contents

Notes on the editor and contributors

Miguel Martínez Lucio is Professor at the Manchester Business School, University of Manchester, UK. After starting his career at Keele University as a lecturer, he worked at various universities such as Leeds University and Cardiff. He holds a doctorate from Warwick University and previously studied politics at Essex University. He has published various texts and is involved in research on the subject of regulation and representation in relation to work and employment. The focus of his work has been the manner in which regulation (state intervention, trade union engagement and joint regulation) has been the focus of ongoing change in a context of globalization, commercialization and managerialization within the firm and society. He has studied and written on a range of sectors such as airlines, postal services, car manufacturing, food processing and manufacturing, public services and construction. His work also looks at the way internationalization has created new sets of tensions and possibilities within the arenas of worker representation. More recently, he has examined the question of migration and change in terms of comparative employment relations. He is a founder member of the Critical Labour Studies network and has been engaged with a wide range of work with social and public bodies in terms of research and education.

Phil Almond is Professor of Comparative Employment Relations at Leicester Business School, De Montfort University, UK. He has published widely on multinationals, with a particular focus on the relations between multinationals and national and regional institutions. He is the editor, with Anthony Ferner, of *American Multinationals in Europe* (Oxford University Press, 2006). He also has published research on comparative industrial relations and human resource management, comparative methodology and the varieties-of-capitalism debate. His current research projects focus mainly on links between multinationals and social institutions at sub-national levels.

Lisa Berntsen is a PhD candidate at the University of Jyväskylä, Finland, and the University of Groningen, The Netherlands, and a guest researcher at the Amsterdam Institute for Advanced Labour Studies. She works on the ERC-funded 'Transnational Work and Evolution of Sovereignty' project. Lisa holds an MSc in International Economics from the Radboud University of Nijmegen and a master's degree in Social and Cultural Anthropology from the Catholic University of Leuven. Her research interests are labour mobility, flexible employment relations, trade union organizing and representation of migrant workers, worker agency and ethnographic research methods.

Erka Çaro was born in Albania in 1979. After completing her bachelor's degree in Human Geography in 2001, she completed a degree in Demography at Cairo Demographic Center in Egypt. In 2004–2005 she gained a master's degree in Demography at the University of Groningen, The Netherlands. From 2007 to 2011 she was a PhD fellow at the University of Groningen working on the topic of migration and the adjustment process of migrants. From February 2011 Erka has been working as a postdoctoral researcher at the University of Jyvaskula, Finland. Her main research interests are migration, gender, integration processes, culture and qualitative methods.

Fang Lee Cooke (PhD, University of Manchester, UK) is Professor of Human Resource Management (HRM) and Asia Studies at the Department of Management, Faculty of Business and Economics, Monash University, Australia. Her research interests are in the area of employment relations, gender studies, diversity management, strategic HRM, knowledge management and innovation, outsourcing, Chinese outward FDI and employment of Chinese migrants. Fang is the author of *HRM, Work and Employment in China* (2005), *Competition, Strategy and Management in China* (2008) and *Human Resource Management in China: New Trends and Practices* (2012). She is a co-author of *New Horizons of Human Resource Management: Models from China and India* (2013). Fang has also published over 100 journal articles and book chapters. She is Associate Editor for *Human Resource Management* and *Gender, Work, and Organization*; Senior Editor of *Asia Pacific Journal of Management* and Co-Editor of *Asia Pacific Journal of Human Resources*.

Carlos J. Fernández Rodríguez is Lecturer in Sociology at the Universidad Autónoma de Madrid, Spain, and has been a Visiting Research Fellow at Manchester Business School. He has a background in economics, sociology and business studies. His research interests are the sociology of organizations, sociology of labour and industrial relations. He has published several books and peer-reviewed articles in those knowledge areas, mostly in Spanish. His latest publication is 'Narratives, Myths and Prejudice in Understanding Employment Systems: The Case of Rigidities, Dismissals and Flexibility in Spain', in *Economic and Industrial Democracy*, co-written with Miguel Martínez Lucio (2013).

Naresh Kumar, PhD, is Associate Professor and Head of Unit, Research, Entrepreneurship Education and Consultancy, at Global Entrepreneurship Research and Innovation Center, Universiti Malaysia Kelantan. His primary area of expertise is human resource management, and his research interests include human capital development, workplace learning, organizational change and development, knowledge management and employee relations. Many students and professionals from both private and public sectors in Malaysia and abroad have benefited from his teaching, training, consulting and coaching.

Nathan Lillie is University Lecturer in the Department of Social Policy at the University of Jyväskylä, Finland, and Principle Investigator of the Transnational Work and the Evolution of Sovereignty project, ERC Starting Grant #263782. He has written extensively on industrial relations and migrant workers. His current project deals with the regulation of labour mobility in the European Union.

Robert MacKenzie is Professor of Work and Employment at the Leeds University Business School, University of Leeds, UK. His research interests are concerned with the regulation of the employment relationship and industrial restructuring. The role of contracts in the regulation of employment, and their relationship to the wider labour market, have also been key themes within his work. His work has explored the growth of subcontracting as an organizational form and as a means of regulating the supply of labour. This work focuses on the implications of contingent employment forms for skills and labour reproduction and has a comparative dimension. The impact of industrial restructuring in terms of the social and economic impact of redundancy, labour market change and contingent employment practices and the economic social experience of migrant workers and refugees is an increasingly prominent feature of his recent work. He has published extensively in leading journals.

Leo McCann is Senior Lecturer in International and Comparative Management at Manchester Business School, University of Manchester, UK. His research focuses on the impact of globalization and restructuring on national economies, large-scale organizations and individual workers. He has written widely on the subjects of international business, organizational restructuring and white-collar work in journals such as *Journal of Management Studies*, *Human Relations* and *Organization Studies*. He is the author of *International and Comparative Business: Foundations of Political Economies* (Sage, 2013) and co-author of *Managing in the Modern Corporation* (Cambridge University Press, 2009).

María C. González Menéndez is Associate Professor of Sociology at the University of Oviedo, Spain. Her research interests include workers' participation, gender and employment, labour management, and the role of sub-national socioeconomic governance systems in the attraction and retention of multinational firms. Recent publications include the book *Women on Corporate Boards and in Top*

Management. European Trends and Policy (Palgrave, 2012), co-edited with Colette Fagan and Silvia Gómez, and the handbook on HRM in Spain *Gestión de Recursos Humanos: Contexto y Políticas* (Thomson-Civitas, 2011), co-edited with Rodolfo Gutiérrez and Miguel Martínez Lucio.

Dr Stephen Mustchin is a Lecturer in Employment Studies at Manchester Business School, University of Manchester, UK. His research interests focus on industrial relations and human resource management, particularly public sector employment relations and management, changing union strategies, union involvement in learning, vulnerable employment and the role of the state in employment relations. He has published in a range of leading journals and worked on the subject of training for various public bodies.

Óscar Rodríguez-Ruiz is Associate Professor at the Universidad Complutense in Madrid, Spain. He holds a doctorate in Economics and Management and has been a Visiting Fellow at Bradford University School of Management (2006) and the Manchester Business School (2008). He was a researcher in the Business Administration Institute in the Universidad Autónoma de Madrid (1998–2006). His research interests include theories and policies relating to human resource management and industrial relations. He has published his work in peer-reviewed journals such as *International Journal of Human Resource Management* and *Management Research*. Dr Rodríguez-Ruiz teaches both under-graduate and graduate courses on organizational design and human resource management.

Paul Stewart is Professor of the Sociology of Work and Employment at the University of Strathclyde, UK. He is Coordinator of the Marie Curie programme 'Changing Employment'. He has been researching the impact of lean production on auto workers for over two decades, working with assembly workers and the union UNITE. He is also currently working on projects assessing the impact of sectarianism on Polish and Lithuanian migrant workers living in the north of Ireland and Scotland. He is a member of UNITE and the Independent Workers' Union in Ireland. He is also a member of the Critical Labour Studies network, an alternative critical labour studies forum. He is co-author of *We Sell Our Time No More*, a critical sociology of the struggles of car workers against lean production in the UK automotive industry. He was Editor of the journal *Work, Employment and Society* (2001–2004) and *Capital and Class*.

Jeremy Waddington is Professor of Industrial Relations at the University of Manchester, UK. His research interests focus on trade union structure, organiza-tion and activity; employee participation; and comparative industrial relations. Jeremy has worked closely with trade unions and institutions of worker represen-tation in undertaking his research, which is available in a wide range of journal articles. Jeremy's recent book publications include *European Works Councils: An*

Industrial Relations Institution in the Making and *A Comparison of the Trade Union Merger Process in Britain and Germany*.

Ines Wagner is a PhD candidate at the Department of Political Sciences, University of Jyväskylä, Finland, and at the Department of Global Economics and Management, University of Groningen, the Netherlands. Her research on the politics of posted migrant work in Germany and the European Union is part of the project Transnational Work and the Evolution of Sovereignty.

Dr Steve Walker is currently a Senior Lecturer in the Department of Computing and Communication at The Open University, UK. He was one of the founders of the Poptel communications service for trade unions, NGOs and co-operatives during the 1980s, and involved in a number of significant community informatics initiatives. Since returning to academe his research has focused on the use of information systems in non-commercial organizations. This has included the evaluation of several large-scale transnational trade union education projects.

Preface

Miguel Martínez Lucio

When Sage approached me to write or edit a teaching text on International Human Resource Management (IHRM), I was uncertain about doing so owing to the number of books that have already been written in the area. However, as someone who had been teaching the international and comparative dimensions of both Human Resource Management (HR) and Industrial Relations (IR) for over 20 years, I felt that the focus of some IHRM texts was generally too managerial and/or focused on managers and less on workers. This contrasted with the teaching of IR and even HRM, which spends more time on broader questions of work. I also felt that the internal environment of the firm was the primary focus of study in many texts, with the environment of IHRM understood mainly in terms of culture, markets and some minor aspects of international regulation. I therefore took on the challenge and started to craft an outline of a proposal in 2007. I decided to develop an edited IHRM text that drew inspiration from an employment relations perspective; and the Introduction to this book develops the rationale for this in greater detail.

The aim was to discuss globalization, work and multinational corporations (MNCs) from a different perspective. This opens new possibilities and, although not all areas are covered, it does allow for a more progressive and nuanced approach to the comparative and international study of such subjects. Chapters on the Internet and non-governmental organizations, the experience and reality of migration and not just management mobility, the role of consultancies and business schools, the development of lean production as an ideology and problem for workers and a more critical view of globalization would be included. The aim was to broaden the remit of the book. Furthermore, the need to connect with students by using new materials and arguments was something I felt was pressing and challenging. By developing cases that present the dilemmas and real challenges MNCs bring to our lives, we could provide a basis for a more ethical and informed dialogue. The issue of teaching and learning in a business school is also a focus of the book: these institutions have become problematic and themselves embody the tensions that pervade globalization. Business schools link diverse people in organizational and management education, but their education and cultural practices are increasingly based on particular political and economic views which tend toward a more neoliberal agenda.

The book has a secondary purpose as well: to act as a bridgehead for those studying industrial relations – or what is now commonly called labour and employment relations – into the debates on globalization and work. There are many *comparative* industrial relations textbooks that compare and contrast the nature of national systems and deal with new forms of international regulation, but the aim of this textbook would be to also contribute in some way to teaching in the area of *international* labour and employment relations. In this way, it would be of value to those studying in universities and beyond, especially trade unionists and policy-oriented individuals.

Many people have helped me in this endeavour, and I would like to sincerely thank Kirsty Smy and Nina Smith at Sage who helped and inspired me. They have been important navigators for the book. In addition, Natalie Aguilera from Sage was my initial contact, I am grateful to her for this and her confidence in the project. The anonymous reviewers (the army of individuals who silently guided my work and that of my colleagues) played a very important role; they were like a Greek chorus who showed the way ahead.

I would also like to thank my colleagues who contributed to the book and had the time and energy to engage in this project. Without them, this text would not be in your hands today.

Then there are friends and colleagues who encouraged me and who spent time discussing aspects of the book with me. Paul Stewart's strong encouragement and comments on some of the chapters were very important, as was Robert MacKenzie's insight and belief. My Manchester-based colleague, Arjan Keizer, needs special thanks as he read the book in its entirety and was very helpful and frank in his feedback: I will repay him during our ongoing visits to the Sandbar in Manchester. In addition, I would like to thank Keith Povey for checking the style of a selection of the chapters: Keith has been important for much of my work and that of my colleagues. Devanand Srinivasan also needs to be thanked for his work on the style and layout. Needless to say, any shortcomings are all of my making.

Finally, my partner and my daughter (Rosa and Elisa) kept me hopeful in this endeavour, so much is owed to them. They have kept me in good spirits throughout.

Companion website

International Human Resource Management: An Employment Relations Perspective edited by Miguel Martínez Lucio is supported by a companion website.

Visit **www.sagepub.co.uk/martinez-lucio** to take advantage of the learning resources for students and lecturers.

For students

- Selected SAGE journal articles for each chapter are available free to further develop your understanding of the topics covered.
- Podcasts introduce key topics of each chapter.
- Links to relevant websites for each chapter.

For lecturers

- PowerPoint slides for each chapter for use in class.
- Extra case studies provide further examples to use in class.

Introduction:
An employment relations perspective to IHRM

Miguel Martínez Lucio

The challenge of globalization

The way people work, the character and nature of their workplaces, the manner in which they are managed and the mechanisms by which they are recruited into these jobs have to a great extent reflected the economic, political and cultural characteristics of their national economies and specific sectors of employment. A national economy may be more or less developed, the technologies used may vary, and there may be customs and practices that have shaped the way people work and how they value or view the management of their work and themselves as workers. The laws that govern their work may also differ. For example, the rights they have may vary in terms of how they may express their views at work, argue for a safe environment to work in and are compensated when their employment is terminated.

Within capitalist societies, workers have to sell their labour in the labour market and thus enter into a contractual relationship of some form with organizations and other individuals. The nature of this contract, the expectations of each party regarding the contract and the manner in which rights and obligations on either side are understood and operationalized often tend to diverge.

The study of work and employment has become more challenging in a context where the boundaries of labour markets and national economies have been changing. There has also been a restructuring of national spaces around which work and employment are experienced, managed and regulated. These changes have brought new challenges to the ways that companies manage their workforce, be they multinational corporations (MNCs) or local firms.

One of the main sources for change has been *increasing levels of internationalization of investment*. The emergence of a greater intensity of international trade has meant that national systems of employment and management have been subject to greater instability and a range of increasingly diverse influences and pressures. Overseas competition and the ability to compete in international markets mean increasing the pressures on firms to find more productive and cost-efficient ways of employing workers and managing their work.

Globalization and the movement of people and resources across boundaries, between and within firms, brings to the fore the problems of dealing with different approaches to representation and systems of rights and customs in relation to work and employment. Operating across countries, both directly and indirectly – through subcontracting work to a range of smaller firms, for example – brings a degree of complexity which needs ongoing attention from management to detail of contracts and product quality. Different organizational and management approaches and the responses to them have to be taken into account.

For *the workforce itself, changes are emerging* from the opportunities and challenges that globalization brings in one form or another. In many industrial sectors, we may see decline in one country as a result of competition and the undermining of traditional industries in costs and even quality (e.g., the impact of China on steel manufacturing and toy production in Europe). However, there may also be opportunities for new sectors in, for example information technology (IT) or service sectors, or the growing emphasis on high-quality tourism. Globalization also brings with it the adoption of new practices and new ways of working, which may vary in their impact but which begin to alter patterns of work and employment (e.g., a greater emphasis on working in teams or a greater number of workers employed on new types of temporary contract). What is more, the very boundaries of national labour markets may be challenged as people migrate in search of better employment and work (e.g., the use of overseas professionals in the medical sector in the United Kingdom, or the inflow of African migrant workers into the Spanish construction industry in response to local shortages in the 1990s). One could argue that there is nothing new in such changes, but their intensity and regularity across a broader space does appear to be increasing. Multinational corporations (MNCs) now deploy managers and professionals across wider geographical areas.

As a consequence of these changes, *governments are now under pressure to balance a new set of roles in the way they manage work and employment*. They need to ensure that their workforce is 'attractive' in skills and/or costs to those investing or proposing to invest in their country, but they must may also have to deal with the after-effects of the changes outlined above in terms of declining industrial areas, mass mobility across regions (e.g., the move from west to east in China) and the possible exit of key workers and professions from their labour markets.

Globalization, as Chapter 1 will outline, is therefore a complex development bringing various types of change and contradictory outcomes. It is not simply a case of there being winners and losers, because even those gaining from increasing their external trade, and developing new dynamic industrial sectors, face new challenges and objectives in relation to worker expectations and new social needs, such as health services and education. For example, we may see the growth of employment in the IT sector in developing countries, but with that may come new ways of working and new types of control at work, which can unsettle relationships and expectations and generate new ones that are themselves challenging to manage.

The enigma of IHRM

The widening spaces within which leading firms operate globally, and their own widening remit and greater scale, mean that the question of managing and regulating work and employment generates new challenges. International Human Resource Management (IHRM) is one area of study that has addressed this challenge by focusing on the way that MNCs attempt to change the way people work in their operations across different boundaries. Much depends on the type of MNC and whether it wishes to have – or whether it *can* have – an integrated and coherent form of management across a number of countries, and much also depends on the type of business and corporate strategy a company follows.

IHRM emerged initially from a focus on the management structures of MNCs and the problems of organizational control brought by operating in different countries. The focus at first was on the challenge to American multinationals during the late 20th century in adapting to different national contexts and attempting to change them; sustaining a coherent management elite in personnel and strategic terms was a priority, but this reflected an almost colonial perspective where the problem was ensuring order and supporting managers travelling overseas (Scullion 2005: 3–21). Yet this focus on management has led to a range of limitations on the priorities of IHRM. First, the focus has been in the main 'internal'; that is, it has been concerned chiefly with the internal environment of the firm and the manner in which it manages and develops its resources (especially human resources).While the external environment of national cultural factors, different national HRM contexts and the challenge of creating synergies between national contexts in terms of personnel and strategies has been discussed, the focus has been primarily on the internal structures and strategies of the firm, albeit in relation to the external. The MNC is thus the principal focus for much of this debate about creating effective and coherent strategies, structures and personnel deployment across diverse operations. Second, a concern with strategy has predominated. That is, the emphasis has been on the need to create increasingly integrated approaches that allow the MNC to control its environments and manipulate them. At the heart of this concern is the stress on *control*. How people within an MNC – especially management – are rewarded, developed, promoted and supported is considered to be the primary concern of the strategy proposed. In this respect, unlike HRM,

IHRM is more insular in its concerns, which is ironic, given that it is meant to be about globalization. The development of globalization and its impact on various organizational levels is of concern primarily as a test for senior managers and executives in ensuring the success of their MNC.

Increasingly, texts have widened the sphere of engagement by taking an interest in regulation and dealing with international concerns about the behaviour and business ethics of MNCs. In the European context – and the British context in particular – publications have begun to engage with these topics. However, the subject of IHRM remains a challenge because it has no real indigenous theory or focus beyond that mentioned earlier. In part, this is because HRM theories continue to focus on the internal sphere of the firm and management responses to external factors instead of taking a broader view of the political and economic environment. There may be perspectives which concern themselves with the internal politics, diverse stakeholders and competing strategies within a firm (Beer et al. 1985; Blyton and Turnbull 2008; Legge 2005), but these only feature briefly in most IHRM textbooks when they are addressing strategy-related issues. In the US literature, this is a lower priority, though the situation is different in the United Kingdom (see Edwards and Rees 2006).

Broader HRM theories and debates do not always seem to be reflected in IHRM textbooks. The question of a choice between control or cooperative strategies for firms is not an explicit aspect of many managerial texts. Whether an MNC adopts a 'hard' or 'soft' approach in its attitude to its workforce, and the associated ethics and challenges, is more a leitmotif than an explicit subject of concern. At a time when there is concern about the 'dark side' of HRM such as the development of surveillance and tighter performance management, and the ambivalent impact of MNCs on the quality of people's lives, these issues appear to form a small part of the backdrop to the discussion in management texts. Ultimately, Scullion's (2005) concern is correct, and the colonial heritage of management theory seems – unfortunately – to be alive and well in many of these texts. Many publications also pay very little attention to broader questions of organizational theory, as can be seen by constant references to national cultures as opposed to competing organizational cultures. In the main, globalization is seen in terms of the challenge of cultural differences or different systems of management.

There is a need to introduce a broader perspective (Delbridge et al. 2011), as IHRM is not an academic discipline with a clear theoretical basis, but rather an area that derives much from a limited study of organizational behaviour and human resource management. Yet the object of IHRM is – in reality – the management of work and employment: this means that the dynamics that constitute these in terms of representation, worker development, the working environment and regulation need to move into the centre to provide a wider academic and teaching agenda. One area in particular that can greatly benefit this exercise is employment relations, or labour and industrial relations, as some prefer to call it. This is an area that approaches the subject from the perspective of those on the outside who are most affected by the actions within MNCs, that is: workers, national contexts, and national systems of representation and regulation of economies and societies. What is more, labour and employment relations studies have, broadly speaking, also been mapping these subjects in terms of their international dimension (e.g., the mobility of workers internationally, and the changing nature of international systems of regulation). In many ways the aim of this book is to shift the gaze of the reader and start from 'the ground up', seeking to put MNCs in a more dynamic context and a contested space.

An employment relations perspective

This book therefore adopts such a perspective, because it takes a broader approach to work and employment by drawing on the study of employment relations. This perspective is implicit in some of the leading texts (Edwards and Rees 2006; Harzing and Pinnington 2011). The aim here is to ground our approach in the politics of globalization and MNCs in relation to work and employment thus building on the insights of a range of scholars who share this agenda (Morgan and Kristensen 2006; Edwards and Bélanger 2009; Ferner et al. 2012).

First, an employment relations perspective focuses on *the tensions that exist in the employment relationship*. It views these as being the outcome of the nature of the capitalist employment system, which is based on a market where people buy and sell labour. It is important to acknowledge that there is an uncertainty and instability within employment relations and modes of representation (Hyman 1975). This is a radical perspective that sees management initiatives on behalf of employers as being focused on gaining the consent of workers for the purpose of production and effective activity, and worker commitment to their jobs, through the use of consensual (e.g., participative schemes) or controlling mechanisms (e.g., performance management and surveillance) (Friedman 1977). This assumes that there is no real common interest between employers and workers. Some see this as the conflict of interest between labour and capital, given the ownership of the means of production and the alienation of labour from its work (Hyman 1975). Others have elaborated on this arguing that there is a 'structured antagonism' between employer and worker. (Edwards 2003: 17).

> This term is used to stress that the antagonism is part of the basis of the relationship, even though, on a day-to-day level, co-operation is also important. It is important to distinguish this idea from the more usual one of a conflict of interest. The latter has the problem of implying that the real or fundamental interests of capital and labour are opposed, and hence that any form of participation scheme is simply a new way of bending workers to capital's demands. The fact that workers have a range of interests confounds this idea. A structured antagonism is a basic aspect of the

employment relationship, which shapes how day-to-day relations are handled, but it is not something that feeds directly into the interests of the parties. Firms have to find ways of continuing to extract a surplus, and if they do not, then both they and their workers will suffer. (ibid.)

Pluralists in general argue that these tensions can be overcome – at least in the short term (see Blyton and Turnbull [2008] for a discussion of pluralism). This can be done through the use of dialogue and mechanisms of representation that allow the different interests to find some common point of reference – for example, seeking to sustain employment activity in one particular location by developing activities such as training to enhance the skills of the workforce to the benefit of both worker and employer. Chapter 3 will provide further details with regard to the way an employment relations framework assists our understanding of work and employment dynamics, and their politics. So the question becomes one of how employers, managers, workers, and in many cases their representatives, engage with each other to further their specific interests or reconcile them in one way or another, and what the mechanisms are for doing so.

Second, an employment relations perspective is one where *rights, and the propagating and management of rights, are significant*. Human resources are not just another 'resource': what is more, many workers seek fair treatment in the way they are employed and deployed. In this respect, we need to understand the question of individual rights at work. Slichter (1941) spoke of systems such as collective bargaining – where managers and unions negotiate a common settlement regarding questions of pay or working hours – being an extension of democratic rights at work and the extension of the democratic space into work. One could argue that this is relevant where individual rights or liberty are of paramount interest and institutionalized politically, but these rights are more or less organized in different contexts and different ways, and even when they are not institutionalized, the principle of *democratic* activity is at the heart of the process of employment relations and the struggle over rights. In fact, as Macpherson (1992[1965]) argued, rights may not always be linked to the question of just political rights, as in some of the more developed nations at the time his work was first published. In developing countries, the right to economic enhancement may be the basis of political and organizational activities and wages and rewards more generally. Social rights may also be seen as important, in that the right to a working environment without serious hazards or risks in terms of individuals' health and safety may also be the basis of demands from workers, and even the interests of particular managers. The desire to push the understanding of rights as far as the questions of *a voice at work* (political rights), *a decent type of work* (social rights) and *employment itself* (economic rights) are at the very heart of the human dimension of work and employment. In this book, the various chapters deal with the question of rights and their development and meaning.

Third, employment relations is about recognizing the tensions and realities of work and employment, including the importance of rights: but it also highlights *the context of their regulation and control*. These can be formal or informal: written or assumed and tacitly accepted. For many, the discipline of industrial relations (or labour and employment relations) is about the regulation of the employment relationship, and this can be developed in formal terms through written rules, contracts and agreements or through informal and unwritten rules and agreements in the form of custom and practice (MacKenzie and Martínez Lucio 2005; see also Chapter 12). This is the political dynamic and interplay that constitutes the relationship between the firm and the workforce: and, in terms of MNCs, these can involve multiple points of regulation and relationships as they criss-cross countries. These are spaces (MacKenzie and Martínez Lucio 2005) where different organizations – especially the representatives of workers and employers – and classes come together in one way or another and establish a series of agreements that allow a consensus on issues such as pay, working hours, particular practices at work and other related activities to be accepted, and for production and service delivery to proceed unhindered irrespective of the different interests that might exist.

Fourth, this means we have to the '*map*' *the broad range of actors in work and employment in a national, and now international, context*. These are not just the employers and their managers, and the workforce and their representatives. For a complete understanding, this political map must recognize internal and external actors. Internal actors would be management and worker representatives, but these might be differentiated internally, with cohorts of managers having distinct different professional backgrounds or organizational interests (and even networks; see Edwards et al. 1999). Worker representatives may also vary in terms of their political allegiances or their relations with employers. There are also external actors who can frame the process of regulation. The state – and the different institutions that constitute it – is an especially important actor, and one that is much ignored in traditional accounts of IHRM: the state attempts to steer labour and employment relations, for example, by emphasizing different forms of worker representation. Political projects may be developed to counter conflict within the workplace and employment relations, albeit with variable outcomes (see Panitch 1981). Moreover, just as the state incorporates social actors it can also coerce them (Hyman 1975: 144), with strategies of containment and control in the regulation of union affairs, giving rise to new tensions and new forms of worker action. Instability and uncertainty are central features of labour and employment relations, requiring ongoing state investment in institutional processes, projects of reform and strategies of change. Yet, the role of the state is almost non-existent within mainstream IHRM texts. What is more alarming is the absence of any discussion of coercion and force – a major moral and ethical dilemma to which MNCs have in many cases contributed in their darker operations, such as the link between American

MNCs and national governments in Latin America in the repression of democratic systems and worker rights.

Yet new discussions on labour and employment relations also point to a broader set of actors including international law firms; transnational consultancy firms propagating new ideas about work; non-government organizations (NGOs) and social movements raising ethical questions in relation to issues such as child labour; new media and virtual organizations linked by the Internet and organizing work-related protest; educational bodies, particularly business schools that are central to the propagation of approaches to HRM; and so on. Work and employment relations, and approaches to these, are influenced by many bodies that may even be beyond the direct remit of the employment relationship (Heery and Frege 2006). This book attempts to open the door to these issues, and some of these actors, in terms of the way they shape strategies and understanding of employment and human resource management.

Fifth, there is *tension and difference over the nature of the economic and social systems themselves*. MNCs are caught between national systems that organize and regulate work in different ways, and they support the systems they see as convenient and useful for long-term economic development and power. MNCs can be drawn to or deterred by such national systems and can sometimes reflect the practices of different national structures in their own approaches. In this text, much is made of the tension between socially oriented and more coordinated systems on the one hand, and more liberal and market-facing systems on the other: the 'varieties of capitalism' debate (see Hall and Soskice 2001). Various chapters will discuss these issues and the debates that have ensued.

By developing such a perspective, we can start to approach IHRM from a broader environmental context and give due respect to the question of politics. This allows us to locate MNCs in the real dynamic of the competing visions and politics of globalization. Perhaps the term IHRM is not appropriate, given this approach, but it has become the byword for the study of transnational work and employment related issues in MNCs.

The structure of the book

This book therefore attempts to link IHRM more closely to the contribution of labour and employment relations. It attempts to open up IHRM to the new influences and schools of thought engaged with its study from a less managerialist perspective.

Chapter 1 engages with the subject of work and employment in the context of globalization. It aims to look at how we understand globalization and how it has changed the way people are employed and the way that they work. The chapter focuses on the competitive dynamics of such developments, and the competing interpretations of what it is changing in terms of the global context, the firm and the nature of work.

The subject of MNCs and HRM is discussed in Chapter 2. The chapter focuses on how HRM strategies are developed by MNCs, and how they attempt to change the contexts within which they are operating. MNCs use a wide range of strategies and techniques as part of their attempt to transfer their practices and broad philosophies of work to subsidiaries and host contexts. The chapter draws from a range of schools of thought, which view MNCs as micro-political organizations using an array of strategies.

Chapter 3 covers employment relations, by looking at the role of regulation in different contexts and how industrial relations theories – both new and old – can be used to understand the differences that exist in relation to the different environments faced by MNCs and other transnational bodies. Different national contexts in terms of employment relations remain, and though these are changing, it is essential to understand the ways in which these differences are sustained.

The second section of the book consists of chapters engaging with what we could call the internal environment of the firm in relation to the external changes taking place. Chapter 4 focuses on pay, which is the quintessential element of the employment relationship. The chapter looks at how rewards depend on national contexts and structures. MNCs try to introduce new or organizationally specific systems in their reward structures, yet find themselves confronting not just locally embedded and established systems of pay but also tensions that arise in the way they implement changes.

In many respects, this issue is picked up by Chapter 5 on equality and diversity. A major development in IHRM and international employment relations is growing concern with equality and fair treatment of staff. Equality and diversity vary across countries and contexts in terms of origins, meaning and impact. The chapter attempts to map the development of diversity management and outlines some of the challenges it brings.

A further feature of the internal environment of the firm is the question of human resource development, and this is dealt with in Chapter 6. Many IHRM texts engage with how MNCs attempt to develop a more consistent and integrated system of training in light of the more global requirements that emerge from the need to communicate and create increasingly 'cosmopolitan' MNC leadership and management. Yet, local systems of training and the way they are managed remain important. Hence, this chapter points to the role of local contexts and differences in influencing strategies related to human resource development, but it also points to how these local environments emphasize the development of a workforce that is adaptable and focused on social and communication skills.

One of the missing features of the study of IHRM has been the way particular dominant strategies have evolved within MNCs. How visions of production and employment are disseminated has been explained in terms of how MNCs develop such visions and strategies, but not always what the politics of the strategies are. In Chapter 7, we focus on the concept of lean production as a dominant ideology and a set of practices that have been part of the transformation of work in many sectors and national contexts. These practices are seen by many to represent a central form of labour exploitation and a dominant transnational paradigm of capitalism, which brings major issues in terms of health and safety for many workers. Its inclusion as a subject in the book aims to bring the politics of organizations to our attention.

The third section of the book seeks to widen the remit of the discussion to include the impact of, and changes in, the external environment. This starts with Chapter 8, which follows on from the topic of lean production in Chapter 7 by emphasizing more broadly the emergence of particular views of economic and organizational change. It centres on the increasing role of the liberal market model and the emergence of Anglo-Saxonization and Americanization as a reference point in the global context. This brings a vision of globalization that is focused on short-term profitability, shareholders as dominant players and a financial and accounting view of the organization and its priorities. There has been great concern regarding these developments for some time, and the chapter updates us on many features of these shifts (see also Djelic 2001).

These changes have not emerged just because they are 'superior' or because of the dominance of US or UK MNCs in the context of globalization. To a great extent, these are driven by a range of 'other actors' who push the relevance and 'sale' of these models – for example, business schools and consultancy firms. Chapter 9 therefore focuses on the role of US-influenced and US-inspired business schools and management education in disseminating these views. This process is supported by a range of consultancy firms, which in effect sell these 'fashions' and encourage a particular political view of how work and employment should be managed. These are central to the apparatus of the dissemination of Americanization and especially neo-liberalism in organizational practices.

These tensions play themselves out in both developed and developing countries, and Chapter 10 focuses on the latter and the challenges they face in the light of such competing and politicized views of management- and employment-related issues. The role of the state in such contexts is pivotal to responses to the benefits and challenges that MNCs bring. Developing countries are not always passive recipients of overseas investment, but in many cases develop the infrastructure necessary to engage with international firms. However, they are caught between the development of a pliable and supportive local environment in terms of workers' skills, on the one hand, and the management of the expectations that emerge and the democratic sensibilities that can evolve within their workforce and labour markets. These tensions emerge because of the inherent contradiction within MNCs of wanting a skilled and educated workforce on the one hand, but often a cheaper and more pliable workforce on the other.

Chapter 11, on international mobility, focuses on migration and the manner in which MNCs utilize and capitalize on the increasing movement of workers across boundaries. In many cases, this is managed in a way that allows MNCs to bypass regulations and laws relating to pay levels and working conditions. The question of migration has been introduced in this book as a result of the way in which IHRM often only discusses mobility issues with reference to middle and senior managers, as if the workforce does not exist. The role of MNCs in manipulating such flows of labour, and in the main downgrading working conditions, is rarely a subject of discussion, yet this raises the serious issue of the unethical behaviour of many international firms.

This leads to Chapter 12, on the way that transnational systems of regulation have had to be developed to create a political environment that can control and condition MNCs in the darker aspects of their development and behaviour. The chapter talks about new forms of regulation across boundaries, such as the use of international law and ethical codes of conduct as a way of influencing the operations of MNCs. This is discussed in light of the debate on regulation that has emerged in the current economic context of crisis and change.

Such developments bring the book to its two final chapters, which map how the voice of workers and of society in general has developed in the face of greater transnational coordination by firms. Chapter 13 outlines the way that trade unions, as the main expression of workers' interests, have developed international organizational structures. These include both official structures and new forms of network-based organizations that exchange information about the nature and content of MNCs and their operations. The chapter also looks at the development of councils and committees that represent workers in specific MNCs, which can influence the nature of decision making and its outcomes.

Chapter 14 covers the role of the Internet and social movements in developing a transnational dialogue on ethics and the behaviour of corporate capital. These developments have created a virtual and social international community which has tracked and questioned many aspects of the internationalization of capitalism and led campaigns and projects to humanize and challenge it.

Conclusion

IHRM is a broad and rich area of study and practice, and the need to uncouple it further from a managerial agenda and open it to the reality of international issues and agents in work and employment is imperative. Balancing the study of IHRM with a more systematic employment relations perspective is of benefit in understanding the nuances and richness of work and employment in a global context. MNCs exist in a complex relationship with the reality of a world they attempt to develop within. It is also a world that is changing (in part as a result of the impact of MNCs) and which presents ongoing challenges: the presence of MNCs in national environments creates economic responses and social changes.

Understanding the political aspects of many of the facets of management, and the ethical traumas MNCs give rise to, needs to be given greater prominence as human beings speak to and engage with each other across the globe in new and more effective ways. The need to place MNCs in the real context of political competition and action, especially the demands of workers and national states, is the challenge we face.

References

Beer, M., Walton, R. E., Spector, B. A., Mills, D. Q. and Lawrence, P. R. (1985) *Human Resource Management: A General Manager's Perspective: Text and Cases* New York: Free Press.

Blyton, P. and Turnbull, P. (2008) *The Dynamics of Employee Relations.* London: Macmillan,

Delbridge, R., Hauptmeier, M. and Sengupta, S. (2011) 'Beyond the enterprise: Broadening the horizons of international HRM'. *Human Relations*, 64(4): 483–505.

Edwards, P. (2003) 'The employment relationship and the field of industrial relations'. In P. Edwards, (ed.), *Industrial Relations: Theory and Practice.* Oxford: Blackwell-Wiley, pp. 1–36.

Edwards, P. and Bélanger, J. (2009) 'The multinational firm as a contested terrain'. In S. Collinson and G. Morgan (eds.), *Images of the Multinational Firm.* Chichester: John Wiley & Sons, pp. 193–216.

Djelic, M. L. (2001) *Exporting the American Model: The Post-War Transformation of European Business.* Oxford: Oxford University Press.

Edwards, T. and Rees, C. (2006) *International Human Resource Management: Globalization, National Systems and Multinational Companies.* Harlow: Pearson Education.

Edwards, T., Rees, C. and Coller, X. (1999) 'Structure, politics and the diffusion of employment practices in multinationals'. *European Journal of Industrial Relations*, 5(3): 286–306.

Ferner, A., Edwards, T. and Tempel, A. (2012) 'Power, institutions and the cross-national transfer of employment practices in multinationals'. *Human Relations*, 65(2): 163–187.

Friedman, A. L. (1977) *Industry and Labour: Class Struggle at Work and Monopoly Capitalism.* London: Macmillan.

Hall, P. A. and Soskice, D. W. (eds.) (2001) *Varieties of Capitalism: The Institutional Foundations of Comparative Advantage.* Oxford: Oxford University Press, p. 1.

Harzing, A.W. and Pinnington. A. (2011) *International Human Resource Management.* London: Sage.

Heery, E. and Frege, C. (2006) 'New actors in industrial relations'. *British Journal of Industrial Relations*, 44(4): 601–604.

Hyman, R. (1975) *Industrial Relations: A Marxist Introduction*, vol. 220. London: Macmillan.

Legge, K. (2005) *Human Resource Management: Rhetorics and Realities.* London: Macmillan.

MacKenzie, R. and Martínez Lucio, M. (2005) 'The realities of regulatory change beyond the fetish of deregulation'. *Sociology*, 39(3): 499–517.

Macpherson, C. (1992) [1965] *The Real World of Democracy.* Toronto: House of Anansi Press.

Morgan, G. and Kristensen, P.H. (2006) 'The contested space of multinationals: Varieties of institutionalism, varieties of capitalism'. *Human Relations*, 59(11): 1467–1490.

Panitch, L. (1981) 'Trade unions and the capitalist state'. *New Left Review*, 125(1): 21–43.

Scullion, H. (2005) 'International HRM: An introduction'. In *International Human Resource Management: A Critical Text*, H. Scullion and M. Linehan (eds). Basingstoke: Palgrave.

Slichter, S. (1941) 'Union policies and industrial management'. *Right to Work Law Issues*, 37: 53–95.

Section 1

Frameworks and context

1 Globalization, organizations and employment: the dynamics of degradation?

Miguel Martínez Lucio

Learning objectives

- To comprehend the way globalization is discussed and what it means
- To link the issue of globalization to the changing nature of work and employment
- To appreciate the way MNCs have evolved
- To comprehend the challenges to workers that globalization brings in terms of precarious employment and work intensification
- To appreciate the new ironies and tensions concerning work and employment brought by globalization

Introduction

The nature of organizations and employment is changing. There has for some time been a belief that stable employment and organizational structures are no longer a common feature of the 'new' global context. To a great extent, this may be a view that has predominated in the more developed (or privileged) parts of the world, where the latter half of the 20th century witnessed more stable and secure systems of work and management in countries such as Japan, the United States, Sweden or Germany. To some extent, various core industrializing sectors in the same period in countries as different as Nigeria, Uruguay or China saw fairly similar developments in respect of stability and security, especially in their modern and manufacturing-based sectors. However, this stability was predominantly experienced in the more developed countries. Nevertheless, with the growing internationalization of business, the emergence of global markets and to some extent global production and service delivery processes, what we have seen is a challenge to this model of employment with its primarily national structures of employment and organizations.

This chapter will therefore, as a first step towards dealing with the nature of the changes, discuss what is meant by the term *globalization*, and will attempt to explain the different views prevailing. Some consider globalization to be a major challenge and catalyst for change in human resource management (HRM) and industrial relations (IR). However, this chapter will show how these developments are variable in their effects. There are many contradictions inherent in globalization: for example, multinational corporations (MNCs) continue to require a set of political and regulatory interventions and support from nations, which they themselves as private organizations cannot supply. The idea that we are seeing the emergence of omnipotent companies such as Apple or Sony ignores the complex reality of globalization and the continuing role of national systems of regulation.

This chapter will also consider the notion that globalization is, in fact, contested, open and complex. Both the negative and positive features emerging from globalization will be outlined here, leading to both optimistic and pessimistic views of globalization stemming from competing perspectives. The chapter draws on a range of classic and historical views of the current changes: these are ongoing debates that shape the understanding of what we are witnessing.

This chapter will study how globalization impacts on organizations and employment. The changing nature of the firm and the impact of globalization on companies will be outlined through a series of themes; for example, their uneven organizational reach, their increasingly complex structures, and the ongoing challenge of operating in different national environments. So, while the role of such firms in driving globalization will be introduced, we must not forget that they are also subject to the challenges that globalization brings. The aim here is to link back to the argument that globalization is both an exogenous and an endogenous phenomenon: that is, the globalization of organizations creates new experiences and outcomes (e.g., greater organizational change in local environments) but in turn these changes bring pressures on the firms themselves as local environments evolve and respond to MNCs. MNCs are trapped within these changes, and the nature of internationalizing and local contexts forces them to play new political games in order to resolve such dilemmas.

So, what does this all mean for employment and work? The third and key part of this chapter will summarize the impact of globalization on employment and work in terms of the increasing level of insecurity, the question of degradation within employment, and the ongoing pressure of continuous change and uncertainty; however, it will also show how these developments have a contradictory effect and generate new forms of politics in work and new patterns of mobility for both workers and managers. Globalization is contested.

What is globalization?

The term *globalization* is the subject of much political debate concerning its impact and how it evolves, and at what cost. We are inhabiting a political and economic context which is no longer anchored in specific territorial spaces but is subject to movements and forces from further afield. The dominance of key MNCs and increasing levels of labour and product mobility suggest that we are now becoming part of a new global economic dynamic. Culturally, we are subjected to visions of a world where nations are considered to be less significant in political terms, and global corporations organize the economic and employment spaces of our lives. Films such as Norman Jewison's *Rollerball*, which was made in the 1970s, presented us with a view of a world dominated by large corporations, where there are no nation-states and where a violent sport is used as an alternative to war between such organizations (see Lillie and Martínez Lucio 2010). In Ridley Scott's film, *Alien*, which was made a few years after *Rollerball* (and in the subsequent films in the series), the audience was presented with corporations within which dark political forces organized major space expeditions and pernicious experiments. These represent a cultural view or fear of the greater distance of power, and the way that elites dominate the economic spaces we inhabit through larger and more distant organizations over which we have limited control.

Increasingly, we see trade and economic relations organized at a more global level in terms of foreign direct investment (FDI) (see Figure 1.1) as well as global companies increasing in size which now account for a quarter of the global gross domestic product (see Figure 1.2). These figures illustrate the extent of the internationalization of investment and the fundamental role of transnational corporations (TNCs). These have been substantial changes, which are reshaping the social and economic landscape.

The consequences of these powerful changes have seen acrimonious debate about the impact of such developments on society and the economy. Key commentators such as

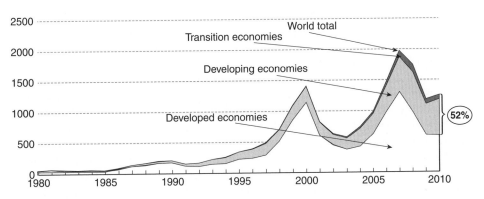

Figure 1.1   FDI inflows, global and by group of economies, 1980–2010 (billions of dollars).

Source: UNCTAD 2011.

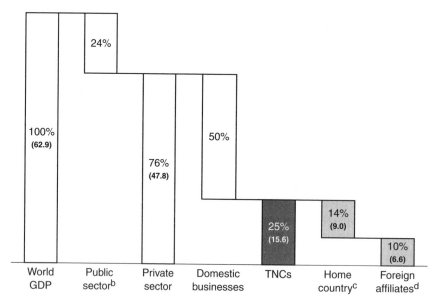

Figure 1.2   TNCs account for one-quarter of the world's GDP, 2010 (percent and trillions of dollars[a]).

Source: UNCTAD 2011.
[a]Current prices, current exchange rates.
[b]ISICL, m, N, Q, X, 92, P (Public administration, Defence, Social security, Health, Sanitation, Community services, Private household employment).
[c]As estimated by the weighted average size of home economies.
[d]See the original Table 1.5 in UNCTAD (2001).

Naomi Klein (2000) argued that transnational corporations have grown in size to such an extent that they dominate political systems and nation-states by virtue of the fact that they can hold them to ransom through investment (setting up workplaces) and disinvestment (closing workplaces down). Using their considerable power, they can undermine the pillars of society and cultural development through a growing emphasis on commercialization and marketing, thus undermining civil liberties, employment and public spaces (ibid.). The ability of MNCs to plunder the scarce resources of the world and to drive down working conditions of many individuals who cannot counter their power means that globalization threatens to undermine the quality and social fabric of all our lives. Local communities and spaces are being undermined by such developments, leaving people with few ways in which to influence the key decisions taken in relation to the economy and employment (Monbiot 2004). In addition, this process of globalization carries with it the semblance of a new world order, managerialist in form, which privileges corporate and market-level values over social ones: for some, this represents an extension of the worst features of the American model of society in respect of its neoliberalism (leaving the more progressive features of its liberal democratic discourse to one side).

There are opponents of such arguments, who suggest that globalization may bring upheaval and much change but that in the longer term there will be a new political space in the form of greater individuality (Friedman 2005). The premise here is that globalization has moved, through stages: nations have faced the challenge of globalization (Friedman's Globalization 1.0, from 1492 to 1800), but so have companies (Globalization 2.0, from 1800 to 2000), as a result of the technological and informational changes that allow individuals to communicate and collaborate on a global scale (ibid.). This latter stage is what Friedman calls Globalization 3.0 – from 2000 to the present. Whether the power of MNCs will have such benign consequences for individuals and facilitate a new form of unhindered and accessible global networking – and hence presumably a new wave of liberal and open behaviour – is another matter, but the discussion continues on the negative and positive features of globalization. Much depends on who will gain and who will lose from the process of globalization and greater free trade.

However, there are other interventions that question the *meaning* of globalization, and the extent and nature of the impact. It is clear that the internationalization of markets and the greater breadth of corporate and economic activity are dis-embedding established relations within local societies, with traditional forms of social action becoming less stable (Giddens 1990). Local political and social relations are stretched, and their ability to influence outcomes is declining, though Giddens (ibid.) would argue that this process has been going on for some time, with the development of capitalism, except that now it has a more transnational dimension. That is not to say the *local* is no longer important, in that much is produced locally and by people whose mobility remains low in relation to that of corporations (Castells 1996). Nevertheless, as Castells argues, these local spaces are dependent on ever more distant and extensive global networks and links, which produce and organize across boundaries (ibid.). It is these 'hubs' within the global network which are the main power centres and which create new systems of power and hierarchy (ibid.). Dickens (2007) elaborated on this point by arguing that these *flows* and the *networks* were the defining features of globalization, and that these could be mapped; but they also become structures, where the participants such as states, MNCs and social organizations take part in unequal exchange relationships by virtue of being fixed within specific spaces. That sportswear is produced by local families in developing countries working in what are less than high-tech workplaces does not mean what they produce is not subject to globalization, because what, how and when the producers make their goods is determined by particular networks of power and interests that link these workplaces together and take the products into richer global markets. There are different experiences and engagements with the processes of change, and in effect there are also winners and losers: the latter are normally those at the end of the line, or on the periphery of the network (Barrientos 2001).

Some observers have stated that such developments of globalization benefit the winners and those already in a privileged position. Hirst and Thompson's (1999) text, for example, argued that core economic flows and activity tended to follow a traditional pattern which privileged specific dominant and developed parts of the globe. Production and distribution remain unequally distributed and shared. Since Hirst and Thompson's book was published, one could argue that the role of India and China has increased within this global space of flows, and within these countries there are privileged internal political and economic hierarchies, and a new type of neocolonial engagement has taken place, as in China's role in Africa. The argument is that globalization follows specific pathways and does not always include all classes and nations equally. Globalization is not something that is to be understood in terms of 'opening up economic borders' but is made and constructed in political, organizational and cultural terms – and therefore with all the tensions these imply.

A growing sense in the debate on globalization is that while there are many negative outcomes, it is not a closed and predetermined process that will lead to a final outcome that is stable and progressive. Instead, there are many possible outcomes. Much depends on the main players and how a language of globalization is constructed, and in what image. Politically, there are greater calls for regulation and control by transnational governing bodies (see Chapter 12). These developments may be underpinned or supported, as Monbiot (2004, 2006) argues, by new oppositional political networks as globalization provides new technologies of dialogue for those who desire more socially oriented outcomes. The consequences of globalization are visible to many people, and so are the ironies – for example, $300 sports shoes being produced in developing countries for $10. Then there is the question of culture: if we look closely at the process of globalization in terms of international management, we are struck by the preponderance of new neo-liberal American management concepts and ideologies coming from business schools and consultancy firms (see Chapters 8 and 9). This is what we call political and ideological constructions. This 'American' hegemony is reinforced by the geopolitical and corporate dominance during much by the 20th century by the United States in key parts of the globe, and as Panitch and Gindin (2012: 223) have argued, this has been reinforced:

> It was one of the hallmarks of the centrality of the American empire in the making of global capitalism that the multilateral and bilateral treaties that established the regime of free trade and investment in the final two decades of the 20th century were deeply inscribed with long standing US legal and juridical rules and practices. The wide international range of US firms, as well as the relative size and importance of US markets … gave rise to extensive coordination of national regulations through international institutions like the newly created WTO, the World Bank, the Bank of International Settlements and the IMF.

Even particular models of production, such as *lean production*, are conflated with the new global agenda by promoting specific processes that infuse globalization with an approach to work based on labour intensification influenced by specific views of economic development (see Chapter 7). Furthermore, global corporations are caught in an ambivalent relationship with local spaces, in that their power derives in part from playing one nation off against another in terms of lower rents for factories, greater public subsidies and lower wages through rules allowing for such developments, as in so-called *special enterprise zones* (Lillie and Martínez Lucio 2010). The global is not 'global' per se: it is about globally located organizations manipulating the 'local'. In this respect, we need to be cautious about viewing the process of globalization as something that has emerged and that represents a new and superior stage: it is something that is manufactured and like all things that are manufactured, it carries the hallmark of the makers.

Organizations and globalization

We need to ensure that we do not fall into the trap of overstating the power of MNCs. Perlmutter (1969), nearly a half a century ago, urged us to classify carefully when it comes to what were called at that time multinational corporations. Such organizations tend in one form or another to evolve from being companies with just a series of international satellite operations in a range of countries directed from the original country of origin. There were, in effect, three types of companies, which reflected the different ways in which they engaged with their environment. *Polycentric* firms were those that fitted effectively into their new foreign environments, and would use local managers and work within the culture and working practices of the host country. This sometimes reflected the nature of the product, which may not require complex supervision, and the culture of the firm, which may have had less evolved structures. This contrasts with *ethnocentric* firms, which were more focused on using management and control systems from their home environments, insisting on a direct form of control through ethnically closed networks and hierarchies. To a great extent, this reflected the nature of the product in question, as well as reflecting the nature of the firm and the manner in which it controls operations. However, Perlmutter began to see the emergence of firms and overseas practices where the management teams did not consist entirely of specific ethnic groups but which were more open and drew from a more cosmopolitan culture: these were *geocentric* forms. This typology helps us to explain the different ways that companies globalize and relate to national contexts; the manner in which they steadily move away from their original home-based practices and body of staff is something that is clear from his understanding of change.

Others, such as Bartlett and Goshal (1998), have shown how international firms have developed since the start of the 20th century from what were in effect polycentric forms through to more geocentric ones. Beginning with what were *multi-domestic*, *multinational* and *decentralized* forms, limited in respect of their spans of control, the 20th century witnessed more multinational forms which were, in fact, *global*, using expatriate managers, and more centralized and coordinated systems of control. This was driven very much by the age of American capital and companies such as General Motors, Ford and IBM and other manufacturing-related enterprises that were using Taylorist forms of capital based on mass and standardized production as well as bureaucratic organizational forms. These enterprises played a major role in propagating particular views of organizational processes and brought with them modern forms of management. These forms are sometimes seen as an *international* form. More recently, according to these authors, a new *transnational* structure of a geocentric nature has emerged, based on networking across sites, more systematic approaches to learning through these networks by exchanging practices, and the adoption of a more cosmopolitan culture. In discussing new and flexible organizational forms in the context of information technology and the software industry, Bharami (1992) pointed to the role of key factors in the new form of international organizational culture: a multi-polar organizational structure with greater collaboration within and across firms, greater synergies between formal and informal structures within the workforce and management, greater autonomy for those managing on the frontline, and a cosmopolitan mindset that incorporates different cultures and diverse viewpoints. The assumption is that these new forms place a greater emphasis on building capabilities within the workforce. These new forms constitute the backbone of such transnational and innovative structures in a global context. However, the problem with such views is they often ignore the political and other realities of governing MNCs, and the motives behind such support for supposedly flexible forms.

More recently, the seminal work of Anthony Ferner and his colleagues (see below) has further developed this form of analysis, and built on the work of Perlmutter. The basis of much of this analysis has been an engagement with the work of DiMaggio and Powell (1983) on the question of how organizations evolve their structures in terms of isomorphism – the process by which two units such as companies or workplaces evolve in terms of their identity, culture and structure and begin to resemble one another due to the nature of their organizational fields. According to them organizations change because of a range of pressures, and they begin to resemble others because of these factors:

- Coercive isomorphism: Changes within organizations or across them occur because of pressures from other organizations or units, which can use resources or disciplinary mechanisms to force change (e.g., threatening to withdraw investment).
- Mimetic isomorphism: Here, change comes through the role of imitation and through internal (managerial fashion) or external (education, consulting) processes, which shift the culture and procedures of a firm (e.g., through the emergence of dominant firms that are seen to be key references for change).
- Normative isomorphism: In this case, the business adopts organizational forms because professional groups or organizations claim they are superior (e.g., management bodies or international agencies pointing to superior or essential norms, and here business schools play a key role).

Ferner and Quintanilla (1998) developed this approach to power and combined it with Perlmutter's to construct a new typology of international firms which looks at the way they control their subsidiaries across various countries:

- Local isomorphism: Subsidiaries of MNCs fit into local cultures and HRM practices – the coercive, mimetic and normative isomorphism is host based.
- Cross-national isomorphism: In this case, MNCs have to conform to the home country in adapting to the structures embedded in the country where the firm originated or has its headquarters; there are many isomorphic qualities emerging from the home country and its MNC elites/senior management.
- Corporate isomorphism: Here, the MNC has a strong, universal approach and is influenced neither by home or host country effects. In this case, a national model may have converged and developed into a particular set of corporate practices and cultures.
- Global inter-corporate isomorphism: The reference points for managers are a process of mimetic isomorphism between corporations, which can be sustained through internal (HRM departments) and external (consultancies) learning processes.

The relevance of such approaches is that constructing a global firm is not straightforward and involves multiple sets of activities. The use of a diverse set of isomorphic processes is essential in the development of international structures. Ferner and Edwards (1995) pointed to a range of practices or relations that could assist MNCs in changing HRM practices in any context: the use and role of resources and their strategic deployment (e.g., investment or disinvestment); the role of authority relations (e.g., the use of leadership structures and the prerogative to push for change); the importance of negotiation and exchange at key points (e.g., bargaining over questions of investment and concessions with workers in a specific site); and the overarching importance of cultural and ideological processes (e.g., establishing 'visions' and 'missions' within organizations that can legitimate change and undermine opposing views). These can be deployed to change the local environment of management and work relations. These relations emerge and are used at different times, depending on the context. It is for this reason that we must ensure that we do not forget that, just as globalization is constructed and sustained in a variety of ways, so the organizational structures of MNCs themselves require political processes for their *sustainability*.

Hence, MNCs are subject to globalization and relate to the external environment in complex ways; therefore, it is important not to play down the fact that many of these organizations are subject to the complexities of globalization in respect of their internal governance and management systems. Globalization challenges the ability of these organizations to govern their management and workforce internally in a coherent manner within the cultural, political and operational contexts in which they operate. This means that, while they influence developments in a host country, they can only normally do so in alliance with other firms, political actors and social forces. MNCs are part of a process of globalization and international forms of political intervention that facilitate their development precisely because *on their own* – no matter how large the MNC happens to be – they cannot easily exercise control over their host and home environments but require external support from public and other bodies. The idea that management strategies in isolation can actually change work and employment relations is questionable.

Globalization and changes in employment and work

The impact of globalization in the broader sense has had a deep and far-reaching impact on the way people work. While the way that people have worked within their companies and the manner in which they are employed in terms of length of contract, for example, varies across different national contexts, there is a realization that, in broad terms, we are seeing a wave of significant changes. It is important that we locate discussions of globalization and work within a historical context because this allows us to observe the contradictory nature of change in a world where work processes are connected through new, but as yet unstable, processes.

The dark side of globalization

In relation to developed countries, there is now an established debate and discussion about the way 'traditional' forms of working and employment have changed. In the 1970s, in developed countries, we began to witness the first cracks in the system of stable employment that had been based mainly on an industrialization model. The notion of 'post-industrial society' alerted individuals to a crisis in the method of standardized and hierarchical forms of work in industrial contexts. Daniel Bell, in his book *The Coming of Post-Industrial Society* (1973), argued that the importance of innovation, a new technical and professional class, and a move away from an engineering/industrial perspective, were emerging in countries such as the United States. The factors for change were complex, combining social changes in the nature of the workforce and the emergence of a strong female presence in the labour market; vigorously expanding service-sector-based organizations; the emergence of the widespread use of computers; and new forms of competition from the Far East (in this context, Japan, with its newly emerging global companies such as Sony, Toshiba and Toyota). These views of change reflected reality but were based on a binary view of change, with the industrial working class being replaced by a new technical middle class, machinery becoming subservient to computers, and the traditional factory culture of work being replaced by new forms of learning. Others began to outline the impact of the industrial crisis and changes of the 1970s and 1980s by drawing attention to the end of the centrality of a traditional work ethic and work based on traditional manufacturing, and a decline in labour organizations such as trade unions (see Touraine 1971 and Gorz 1980). The argument was that the traditional working class was changing and in decline, though many years later others, such as Panitch and Gindin (2012), have pointed out that with the extension of American imperial globalization, the size of the working class has actually expanded if one were to take a world view, as opposed to a European-centric one.

In the 1980s, we began to see a perspective that pointed to the decline of a Fordist model based on standardized mass production, cost reductions through wage control, a high degree of labour specialization and mass consumption (Swyngedouw 1986). This model began to give rise to a series of changes and a steady move to new forms of flexible production, smaller workplaces and flexible forms of working, as workers were deployed across various aspects of the production process: the emphasis was being placed on the quality of the product, and a more fragmented and niche-based product market (ibid.). The changes were driven by more demanding and fragmented consumers, and the development of new technologies and forms of production. Once more, these views were focused on developed countries and the perceived exhaustion of their traditional methods of working (see Harvey 1989: 173–88). Hierarchical and centralized systems of management and labour regulation, which had been dominant during the middle and latter half of the 20th century, were not seen to fit such changes.

New forms of decentralized and flexible forms of organizational practices would prevail: *information* would be the key asset alongside *knowledge* (hence the current fascination with learning), and this would necessitate greater collaboration between workers, managers and sets of new professionals within the firm, and between the different firms themselves. Yet there has been a steady realization that all is not turning out as people imagined. The utopian and positive images of change gave rise to a growing awareness that work was becoming challenging in new and highly problematic ways. The 1990s began to see a new wave of social concerns about the new work regime and its consistency and stability. Various authors began to define this reality, as discussed below.

In his prophetic book *The End of Work*, first published in 1995 (and updated in 2004), Jeremy Rifkin pointed to issues of worker burnout, increasing stress and growing insecurity on a global scale:

> The new information technologies are designed to remove whatever vestigial control workers still exercise over the production process by programming detailed instructions directly into the machine, which then carries them out verbatim. The worker is rendered powerless to exercise independent judgement either on the factory floor or in the office … Before the computer, management laid out detailed instructions in the form of 'schedules', which workers were then expected to follow. Because the

> execution of the task lay in the hands of the workers, it was possible to introduce a subjective element into the process. In implementing the work schedule, each employee placed his or her unique stamp on the production process. The shift from scheduling production to programming production has profoundly altered the relationship of workers to work. Now, an increasing number of workers act solely as observers. (Rifkin 2004: 182)

This has led to unprecedented levels of burnout and stress as workers try to cope with the changing nature of their work (Rifkin 2004). Richard Sennett, in his text *The Corrosion of Character: The Personnel Consequences of Work in the New Capitalism* (1998), explained how new forms of flexibility and of uncertainty at work were eroding workers' sense of purpose and trust in others. The 1990s therefore saw a growing debate about the new work and new global contexts in relation to individual workers and managers, which pointed to the problems of stress, social fragmentation and increasing risk at work. These developments have been paralleled by increasing insecurity and changes within labour markets, leading to what some have described as a new precarious class, that is, the *precariat* (Standing 2010).

> It consists of a multitude of insecure people, living bits-and-pieces lives, in and out of short-term jobs, without a narrative of occupational development, including millions of frustrated educated youth who do not like what they see before them, millions of women abused in oppressive labour, growing numbers of criminalized tagged for life, millions being categorized as 'disabled' and migrants in their hundreds of millions around the world. They are denizens; they have a more restricted range of social, cultural, political and economic rights than citizens around them. (Standing 2011)

Driven further into precariousness by the crisis that has emerged since 2008, these individuals face a changing world owing to the growing absence of long-term and stable employment:

> The precariat has no control over its time, and no economic security. Many in it suffer from what I have called in the book, a *precariaty* trap. This is on top of the familiar *poverty trap* created by the folly of 'targeting' the poor via means-tested social assistance. The precariaty trap arises because it takes time for those on the margins of poverty to obtain access to benefits, which means their hardships are underestimated, while they have no incentive to take low-income temporary jobs once they are receiving benefits. (Standing, 2011)

While some have questioned the extent of such changes and the cohesive nature of the new 'class' discussed, let alone the nature of its politics (Conley 2012), the reality is that globalization has led to change and crisis, which has in turn brought a new degradation within employment paralleling that of the new intensification of work.

In developing countries, these changes can create even greater forms of exclusion and fragmentation. An argument commonly heard is that globalization can create 'hard-to-reach' workers, as in the high-quality footwear industry, where ongoing internationalization of production and outsourcing leads to a workforce in developing countries that is unprotected and easily exploited: the global system is linked by brands that invade social and private space on the one hand, yet shield the exploitative working patterns they develop on the other (Klein 2000). The use of child labour and unpaid female work, for example, has emerged as a major transnational focus of debate because of the way the complex production networks of many MNCs rely on such forms of labour at various points.

> For many women, unpaid work in and for the household takes up the majority of their working hours, with much less time spent in remunerative employment. Even when they participate in the labour market for paid employment, women still undertake the majority of the housework ... When women work outside the household, they earn, on average, far less than men ... They are also more likely to work in more precarious forms of employment with low earnings, little financial security and few or no social benefits ... Women not only earn less than men but also tend to own fewer assets. Smaller salaries and less control over household income constrain their ability to accumulate capital. (UNICEF 2006: 36–7)

Many of these workers are also beyond the reach of regulation, working for small-scale employers, but many of these employers may be linked indirectly to MNCs through their complex chains of command and involvement in developing countries. How can we trace such changes back to a notion of globalization based on an opening of national markets, the greater mobility of capital and the changing orientation of governments in relation to MNCs? There are many factors, such as technological developments and political changes, which may be as important in driving change as some generic economic notion of globalization. First, we could argue that, in the case of the post-industrial narrative discussed earlier, the greater competition from the developing world and countries such as Japan and South Korea played a part in undermining traditional industries, such as manufacturing in developed countries, as did the expansion of labour markets in India and China.

Second, changing markets and new product-based competition in the context of what some call post-Fordism has further undermined a reliance on standardized and centralized forms of production and stable employment patterns. Third, greater uncertainty in a more 'open' world has led to a fundamental insecurity at work and a decline in long-term stable employment contracts. Growing tensions at work and problems in individuals' social lives are related to many factors, but the pressures from greater innovation through the 'cross-pollination' of management ideas, obsessive organizational change and constant transformation in the nature and ownership of firms play a key role. Added to this is the pressure on workers for mobility, as well as changes in their own national contexts, which might force them to seek better employment as a result of social and economic disruption brought about by globalization. Pressures in managerial work may mean that travel becomes a central feature because of the need to control and engage on an ongoing basis with geographically distant clients and groups of workers through the growing internationalization of the firm. Furthermore, globalization is not only a matter of employer mobility, economic change and new workplace practices but of a new informational economy which brings a new spatial set of relations: it coincides with a series of technological developments, especially in information technology and the emergence of the Internet, which creates new spatial and temporal bridges between groups of individuals in distinct geographical spaces (Castells 1996). These break down traditional ways of balancing communication exchange and forms of working. They can provide many possibilities for new forms of political and social action, as outlined in Chapter 14, but at an individual level the benefits can also bring new pressures. Hence, there are a range of factors that can contribute to change at work which emerge from a growing trend towards globalization, and which, once combined, create possibilities for advancement, challenges and dilemmas at both the macro-economic and individual levels. The following short case studies outline some of the social and human dilemmas that are emerging owing to globalization.

Case study: Lost in space – Managers and workers in a global maze

The reality of globalization can be seen in terms of the way it impacts workers and managers (who are also employees and workers). In the case of globalization, a romanticized view of travel as an exotic and somewhat liberating activity has always existed. The positive features associated with being able to work in a range of countries and of developing one's prospects in a new country is one of the attractive features of studying at a business school. Yet the reality of travel and mobility is problematic. In many cases, there is the problem of alienation and social isolation, as well as being vulnerable to the activities of employers. In the United Arab Emirates (UAE), for example, workers have been exposed to a range of problems stemming from workplace politics and social isolation. High levels of suicide among staff led to campaigns such as Mission Zero Suicide, set up to respond to the increasing number of suicides in the UAE related to employment, financial and psychological issues. The press relayed the work of the strategy developed by this project, quoting key exponents:

'Expatriates leave their homeland in search of better options for livelihood. Though foreign land promises prosperity back home, it also offers loneliness and unnecessary indulgences for an expatriate, who takes the path to depression, ultimately taking that extreme step. As per various surveys, this tendency was more prevalent among distressed expatriates in the UAE ...', added Mr. Sudhir Shetty. Mission Zero Suicide campaign was initiated in answer to the rise in the expatriate suicide rate in the UAE ... [through] a signature campaign in which over 200,000 people, including celebrities and eminent personalities, participated by signing up their support to this unique initiative which reached over 1,000,000 people. As part of the campaign, inspiring videos were screened in 4,800 labour camps, 8,000 shops, 380 corporate offices reaching its 16,000 staff members, public gatherings, etc., bringing awareness on personal finance management and stress management.'

Albawaba Business 2012: http://ww.albawaba.com/business/pr/
uae-exchange-mission-zero-suicide-451324)

Second, there is the case of undocumented migrant workers and the physical risks to which they are exposed. Workers who migrate in difficult circumstances are highly vulnerable and face many risks. In 2004, 21 Chinese workers died harvesting cockles in Morecambe Bay in England as the tide rose, and they had not been aware of the dangers. Many of these workers were there at the behest of small employers who did not regulate and support the terms and conditions of employment, such as health and safety:

'The tragedy highlighted the risks and dangers of clandestine migration into the British economy. While the law has changed [since 2004] on gangmasters – the agents who control casual workers in the food industries – there remain wider concerns about what is happening to those Chinese workers, and others, whose presence in the UK may be completely unknown to the authorities'. (Casciani 2005)

Questions

1. What does the first case study tell us about the new ways of working in global corporations?
2. Why do international travel and overseas assignments sometimes create major personal problems for both managers and workers?
3. What do you think are the main responses organizations can develop in relation to such problems?
4. In the second case study, how has globalization contributed to these tragedies?
5. In relation to the second case study, how can governments protect such vulnerable workers?
6. What does this tell us about globalization and its impact?

Contradiction, ironies and new agendas in the changing nature of work

The main concern in many of the discussions is that globalization could be driving down labour standards and undermining rights at work. This is a major issue which is of concern for ethical and social reasons: in effect, there are many more losers than winners as we count the cost of a more unregulated context based on excessive labour intensification.

However, just as we were able to observe earlier with the globalization debate, there are curious ironies. Globalization does not only remove barriers and boundaries, and open up spaces to competition; there are also some curious developments in the way it interacts with the *local environment*. The role of the local environment and the importance of how local developments may reconstruct 'traditional' models of production that were once seen as antiquated in some contexts illustrate the contradictory nature of globalization.

First, globalization works through local structures and can actually enhance differences. Products may be increasingly global, but they sometimes have to adapt to local circumstances, and many global networks have strong local (national and regional) hubs. However, in the areas of management and employment relations, it can also mean that many companies create complex local networks of suppliers and support firms through sub-contracting (Barrientos 2001). This means that a manufactured good may be assembled in one place but emerge from a complex set of smaller companies and firms which specialize in specific regional contexts in particular parts of the world; and pressure is placed on local workers to benchmark their wages locally and not look to higher levels for comparable work elsewhere in the global production process (see Swyngedouw 2004). In one sense, this points to the power of capital to dissect, and fragment, as a form of control, but the irony is that capital has to work through ever more fractured systems of production and employment, which brings inevitable transaction costs and bureaucratic dilemmas around control (MacKenzie 2002).

Second, not only do we see the *international* working through the *national* – the global through the local – but there are also developments which suggest what was left behind (recall the narrative of post-industrialism and its views of manufacturing and traditional industry) resurfaces in various other contexts. As far as sectoral developments are concerned, in countries such as China there are fast-growing manufacturing and traditional industries such as shipbuilding and steel production. Many of these are leading sectors in global terms and form the basis of China's emergent leadership in economic and global terms as a result of the significance of such products to the global economic infrastructure. In quantitative terms, globalization may be a case of rearranging relations within economies and sectors in new spatial terms rather than moving to a new 'higher', virtual and service level of economic activity.

In fact, one could also suggest that this 'return to the industrial' is the case not solely in economic and sectoral terms but in terms of management and employment practices too. Let us take the case of traditional forms of direct control, standardization and surveillance – known to some as scientific management, or Taylorism. These practices are a growing or persistent feature of many aspects of work in developing countries, such as manufacturing in Malaysia, but also – and hence the irony – a feature of work in the more developed nations in the service sector (Bain and Taylor 2000). The use of surveillance, performance monitoring and direct forms of control in call centres in countries such as India and Britain have been the focus of many studies (Taylor and Bain 2005). In other words, the idea of globalization leading to a transformation of work into some new form of post-industrial, post-Fordist – and new HRM – context needs to be approached with a good deal of caution.

Such developments indicate that globalization is not an all-encompassing process, as it gives rise to a range of concerns and political responses from individuals and organizations. The steady move to a new concern with the questions of dignity, decency and fairness at work is in great part driven by the negative developments outlined above – for example, the use of child labour, work intensification, excessive differences in wealth exposed by the strategies of MNCs, and the uneven inclusion of women in the labour market. Management is also deeply affected by the growing intensification of managerial work and the social pressures placed on individuals. Yet the shift in global-level concerns with the social consequences of globalization has begun to open up the discussion in terms of the contingencies and complexities of international economic activity and the handling of its management processes.

Conclusion: shared miseries and possibilities

The way we work and the way we are employed changes as a result of a range of factors. We work within specific spaces, with specific technologies, in relation to different supervisory systems, and within different cultural and organizational contexts. Work remains uneven in respect of its quality, reward and meaning within and between countries. Yet there is a sense that the way we are internationalizing – the growing presence of large corporations, the greater mobility of capital and labour between countries, and the sharing of new ideas about work and employment – is leading to a fundamental shift. This chapter has argued that such shifts can be seen in both negative and positive terms, and that these changes bring many difficult outcomes. There is a sense that globalization is bringing as many challenges as benefits. The construction of a new global space is creating a new set of tensions that are lived on a day-to-day basis by individuals and their families.

The once-hoped-for utopian idea that work will improve and our condition in social terms will be enhanced through the greater convergence of humanity is being questioned. The global order appears to be emerging framed by values and economic relations which appear to enhance market capitalism and a particularly neoliberal and 'Americanized' view of social life that is atomized, fragmented and 'gated'.

Yet these changes are unstable and complex, and rely on broad institutional networks and alliances of players and politics. Both management and workers try to prosper in this situation, but in most cases only just survive these developments. This is a dis-embedding of the traditional way of working that is not necessarily leading to social and economic enhancement. This experience of globalization, the way we work and manage within this context, and the way that corporations are structured are becoming topics of increasing concern. In debating globalization, we therefore have to look carefully at the way it is driven, shaped, managed and *distributed* or *shared* by structure and outcomes.

Reflective questions

1. What are the main causes of globalization?
2. Why are there are different views of globalization?
3. What are the different elements of the optimistic and pessimistic views?
4. How have MNCs developed as a consequence of globalization, and how do they promote its further development?
5. What main concerns has globalization given rise to in terms of the impact on work and employment?
6. What are the main arguments put forward by Sennett and by Standing with regard to changes in terms of work and employment? Are their arguments applicable in most countries?
7. Is there really an end to the industrial and manufacturing pattern of work, or are we overstating this?

Recommended reading

- Ferner, A. and Edwards, P. (1995) Power and the diffusion of organizational change within multinational enterprises. *European Journal of Industrial Relations*, 1(2): 229–257.
- Ferner, A. and Quintanilla, J. (1998) 'Multinationals, national business systems and HRM: the enduring influence of national identity or a process of "Anglo-Saxonization"'. *International Journal of Human Resource Management*, 9(4): 710–731.
- Lillie, N. and Martínez Lucio, M. (2010) Rollerball and the spirit of capitalism:competitive dynamics within the global context, the challenge to labour internationalism and the emergence of ironic outcomes'. *Critical Perspectives on International Business*, 8(1): 74–93.

References

Albawaba Business (2012) 'UAE Exchange Mission Zero Suicide Campaign Ends on a Successful Note', 18 November. Available at: http://www.albawaba.com/business/pr/uae-exchange-mission-zero-suicide-451324; accessed 10 March 2012.

Bain, P. and Taylor, P. (2000) 'Entrapped by the 'electronic panopticon'? Worker resistance in the call centre'. *New Technology, Work and Employment*, 15(1): 2–18.

Barrientos, S. (2001) 'Gender, flexibility and global value chains'. *IDS Bulletin*, 32(3): 83–93.

Bartlett, C. and Goshal, S. (1998) *Managing Across Borders: The Transnational Solution*. Boston: Harvard Business School Press.

Bell, D. (1973) *The Coming of Post-Industrial Society*. New York: Basic Books.

Bharami, H. (1992) 'The emerging flexible organisation: Perspectives from Silicon Valley'. *California Management Review*, 34(4): 33–52.

Casciani, D. (2005) 'Morecambe Bay: One Year On'. BBC News Online, 5 February. Available at: http://news.bbc.co.uk/1/hi/uk/4238209.stm; accessed 10 March 2013.

Castells, M. (1996) *The Rise of Network Society*. Oxford: Blackwell.

Conley, H. (2012) 'Book review symposium: Guy standing, *The Precariat: The New Dangerous Class*, reviewed by Hazel Conley'. *Work, Employment and Society*, 26(4): 686–688.

Dickens, P. (2007) *Global Shift*. London: Sage.

DiMaggio, P. J. and Powell, W. (1983) 'The iron cage revisited: Institutional isomorphism and collective rationality in organizational fields'. *American Sociological Review*, 48: 147–160.

Ferner, A. and Edwards, P. (1995) 'Power and the diffusion of organizational change within multinational enterprises'. *European Journal of Industrial Relations*, 1(2): 229–257.

Ferner, A. and Quintanilla, J. (1998) 'Multinationals, national business systems and HRM: the enduring influence of national identity or a process of 'Anglo-Saxonization'. *International Journal of Human Resource Management*, 9(4): 710–731.

Friedman, T. (2005) *The World is Flat: The Globalised World in the 21st Century*. New York: Allen Lane.

Giddens, A. (1990) *The Consequences of Modernity*. Cambridge: Polity.

Gorz, A. (1980) *Farewell to the Working Class*. London: Pluto Press.

Harvey, D. (1989) *The Condition of Post-Modernity*. Oxford Blackwell.

Hirst, P. and Thompson, G. (1999) *Globalisation in Question*. Cambridge: Polity Press.

Klein, N. (2000) *No Logo*. New York: Taylor & Francis.

Lillie, N. and Martínez Lucio, M. (2010) Rollerball and the spirit of capitalism: Competitive dynamics within the global context, the challenge to labour internationalism and the emergence of ironic outcomes'. *Critical Perspectives on International Business*, 8(1): 74–93.

MacKenzie, R. (2002) 'The migration of bureaucracy: Contracting and the regulation of labour in the telecommunications industry'. *Work, Employment and Society*, 16(4): 599–616.

Monbiot, G. (2004) *The Age of Consent*. London: Harper Perennial.

Monbiot, G. (2006) *Heat: How to Stop the Planet Burning*. London: Allen Lane.

Panitch, L. and Gindin, S. (2012) *The Making of Global Capitalism: The Political Economy of American Empire*. London: Verso.

Perlmutter, H. V. (1969) 'The tortuous evolution of the multinational corporation'. *Columbia Journal of World Business*, 4: 9–18.

Rifkin, J. (2004) *The End of Work*. London: Penguin.

Sennett, R. (1998) *The Corrosion of Character: The Personnel Consequences of Work in the New Capitalism*. New York: W. W. Norton.

Standing, G. (2010) *The Precariat*. New York Bloomsbury Academic.

Standing, G. (2011) 'The Precariat—The new dangerous class'. *Policy Network*. Available at: http://www.policy-network.net/pno_detail.aspx?ID=4004&title=+The+Precariat+%e2%80%93+The+new+dangerous+class.

Swyngedouw, E. (1986) *The Socio-spatial Implications of Innovations in Industrial Organisation*. Centre Européen John Hopkins.

Swyngedouw, E. (2004) 'Globalisation or "glocalisation"? Networks, territories and rescaling'. *Cambridge Review of International Affairs* 17: 1 April.

Touraine, A. (1971) *The Post Industrial Society*. Wildwood House.

UNCTAD (2011) *World Investment Report*. Geneva: United Nations.

UNICEF (2006) *The State of the World's Children*. New York: UNICEF.

2 The changing nature of HRM, organizational change and globalization

Phil Almond and María C. González Menéndez

Learning objectives

- To understand the HRM strategies of TNCs
- To comprehend the ways in which TNCs engage with their environments in terms of HRM
- To outline the nature of change and the ways in which TNCs develop HRM strategies in their operations

Introduction

This chapter looks at the role of international firms as vehicles for change in the management of human resources.[1] Transnational corporations (TNCs) are among the most visible manifestations of economic interconnectedness within globalization, with the growth in foreign direct investment (FDI) comfortably outstripping that in trade between nations in most years. In advanced economies, free trade areas such as NAFTA and the EU have eased cross-border investment, whether through new, 'greenfield' investment, or through mergers and takeovers. The fuller entry of the former Soviet-dominated nations into the global market economy, and the internationalization of Asian economies, particularly China and India, have opened up new potential places of production for firms with global reach. More recently, China and India have also become substantial sources of FDI, through the foreign expansion of their own firms. There now remain few parts of the globe where TNCs are not significant employers.

To their host countries, TNCs have long been seen as a transmission belt for novel ideas about management and employment relations (see Flanders 1964; Enderwick 1985), particularly when they originate from countries with a degree of economic and/or political dominance in the global system. Over the past 30 years, this has meant particular attention has been paid to HRM in US and Japanese TNCs (Almond and Ferner 2006; Doeringer et al. 2003). Importantly, the effects of the process of transmission of novel forms of HRM in which TNCs engage extend beyond their directly owned subsidiaries, into their supply chains and other local firms.

Our starting point is the argument, common within comparative HRM and IR, that how firms in general coordinate and control human resources is likely to be shaped by a range of institutions in areas such as industrial relations, training and education, finance, and arrangements governing inter-firm relations (Whitley 1999; Hall and Soskice 2001), in which national systems have been and remain important. Within this perspective, TNCs are actors of particular interest as, by definition, they operate across a range of different national business/employment systems, often with substantially different national patterns of organizing capitalism in general, and the employment relationship in particular. From a managerial perspective, this produces both challenges and opportunities: challenges because features of national host systems sometimes mean that it is difficult to replicate a uniform system of HRM across the international firm; opportunities because, as we explain in detail below, TNCs often, through their mobility as investors, have the capacity to engage in various forms of 'regime shopping' (Streeck 1991), through which they seek to ensure that their foreign production is conducted in countries where the labour market environment is most favourable.

From a host country point of view, TNCs produce challenges. Foreign TNCs 'inhabit' host systems, but often 'have neither been party to nor have any real interest in the forms of social compromise that have underpinned the joint development of employment and welfare systems' (Rubery 2011: 517). This lesser commitment to host national systems, combined with their potential mobility, may mean that they are particularly likely to challenge parts of host systems which are seen as 'constraints', either through outright resistance or through attempts to shape existing institutions, such as those of worker representation, to their own ends (Almond and Ferner 2006: 4).

In other words, TNCs do not have a binary choice between a passive acceptance of a particular host country system, on the one hand, and deciding to invest elsewhere, on the other. Through their presence in host economies, they participate in the reproduction and/or change of those systems, and in Streeck and Thelen's terms (2005), can be seen as 'institution makers', attempting to adapt elements of host systems to their own ends. That is, they draw on managerial repertoires and rationalities developed elsewhere in the world, rather than behaving as simple 'institution takers', passively accepting host country systems. More broadly, in recent years, TNCs have been important agents in normalizing ideas about the restructuring of employment under the banner of competitiveness.

How these various processes of adaptation and challenge might occur, and with what consequences for national IR systems and patterns of HRM, is the subject of this chapter.

TNCs and strategies of change

TNCs have a number of tools which they use, to varying extents, in order to ensure that, from their perspective, the global workforce is managed as 'efficiently' and profitably as possible (see Edwards and Kuruvilla 2005). These range from simple financial targets, to very direct prescription of HR policy through bureaucratic controls, to the extensive expatriation of home country managers in order to control foreign subsidiaries (Harzing and Sorge 2003). In more sophisticated cases, the latter may be associated with the development of an international internal labour market for senior managers, which among other things represents an attempt to align managerial culture across the international firm. Rather than dealing in detail with these and other micro-level tools, though, we concentrate here on what, broadly, TNCs are trying to achieve in their global HRM systems, and how these interact with national employment systems.

In considering how TNCs interact with national systems, it is important to remember that TNCs are not a homogenous group of enterprises. They differ enormously in their overall HR strategies, not just from firm to firm, but also from place to place. In order to discuss how they seek to change HRM, particularly but not only in foreign host countries, it is first necessary to discuss their overall HR strategies in terms of how much they seek global uniformity of policies, or to adapt to specific national host country conditions.

There are several schools of thought on how TNCs manage their international workforces, and 'international HRM', which in practice largely focuses on HRM within TNCs, is now a substantial field of academic endeavour with its own journals and conferences. The most orthodox approaches, based originally on transaction cost theories of the economics of the firm, try to understand the conditions under which FDI is a better strategy for the firm than trade (i.e., better than simply exporting its production, or, in some cases, licensing production by third parties in foreign countries). From this perspective, which is uncritical of management, the management question in TNCs is largely one of balancing the advantages of (international) integration with those of 'responsiveness' – that is, adaptation to host country conditions (Prahalad and Doz 1999). 'Integration' within international HRM mostly means establishing uniformity, or at least compatibility, of HR systems across the firm's different international operations. This is partly driven by the search for economies of scale and the reduction of transaction costs: one major advantage of operating the same system in different national operations is that the unit costs of running the system, should, all other things being equal, be reduced. Introducing common systems of management across countries also aids firms to achieve standardization of production processes, and facilitates bureaucratic, cultural and financial control over managers and workers in foreign subsidiaries.

On the other hand, some form of 'responsiveness' to host systems is often necessary or useful. Responsiveness can broadly be categorized in two groups, which we will label as 'defensive' and 'offensive'.

(i) *'Defensive'* responsiveness occurs where there are elements of the firm's home country HR system that are impossible or excessively expensive to replicate in a given foreign subsidiary. This may occur for one of several reasons.

First, some HR policies may be allowable in a firm's home country, but illegal in specific host countries. This probably most commonly occurs in the sphere of collective industrial relations: non-union approaches to HRM are commonplace among large firms in the United States, for example (Jacoby 1997), but are not compatible with labour law in some European countries. However, it also occurs in other spheres of HRM; for example, the performance management systems of large US TNCs have sometimes been contested in labour courts in EU countries (Muller-Camen et al. 2001).

Second, policies might also be difficult to export because the host country employment system fails to provide the infrastructure to support them. For example, participatory forms of work organization developed in the home country operations of German TNCs may depend on that country's system of vocational training and social partnership, and be difficult to export to countries lacking these types of institutional arrangements (Tempel 2001).

Finally, responsiveness might also be necessary or useful because home country practices, though legal, are seen as undesirable by host country managers or workers. For instance, it has frequently been questioned whether Chinese managers are motivated by the performance management systems prevalent among large western firms (e.g., Jackson and Bak 1998). It is very common, within mainstream IHRM, to ascribe firms' difficulties in achieving cross-national uniformity to 'cultural differences', typically drawing on the work of Hofstede (1980). However, this research generally has no purchase on (or interest in) the power relations inherent in either the employment relationship or the international firm. In considering processes of transfer/non-transfer of HR practices, it is clearly important to consider what actors in the TNC think of as fair, equitable or justifiable. These 'rationalities' about what is fair are subject to national differences. However, as we will see below, the power of TNCs to overcome problems arising from different national understandings should not be underplayed (see also Almond 2011).

(ii) *'Offensive'* forms of responsiveness are those inspired, not by the 'constraints' presented by subsidiary workforces and employment systems, but rather by the *opportunities* that they offer. They are likely to occur where there are, from the perspective of headquarters managers, advantages to differentiation that outweigh the advantages of uniformity.

Mainstream approaches are notably quieter on these forms of responsiveness than they are on defensive responsiveness. Work that takes more account of how national business systems shape forms of comparative advantage, meanwhile (e.g., Kristensen and Morgan 2006), implies an argument that, if a particular host system presents specific advantages (e.g., Germany's strengths in engineering, derived from some of the institutional resources mentioned above), it may not make economic sense to try to impose a system designed for a workforce lacking these strengths on a German subsidiary, even if there are no particular institutional 'barriers' to doing so.

On a somewhat less benign level, critical approaches to labour markets have long explored how firms in general 'segment' labour markets, offering relatively good employment conditions to 'core' or well-organized groups of workers at the expense of less favoured groups (women, ethnic minorities, etc.) (see Wilkinson 1981). Internationalization, particularly where subsidiaries are situated in significantly poorer countries, presents substantially extended opportunities for firms to act in this way. In other words, where TNCs from the global North choose to locate in lower-cost countries, they have opportunities not only to save on wage costs, but also to impose working conditions that would not be feasible in their country of origin.

Broad orientations of TNCs towards IHRM

Taking into account the variety of motivations for integration and responsiveness, a number of broad orientations towards the coordination and control of international workforces can be portrayed. While these are not necessarily all mutually exclusive, they nevertheless form a basis for discussing TNCs' likely strategies in relation to national employment systems.

a) Integration through the replication of country of origin policies

Here, firms simply seek to export their home country HRM policies abroad. This is characterized in the IHRM literature as an *ethnocentric* approach. The economic logic behind 'country of origin effects' (Ferner 1997) is that TNCs compete internationally on the basis of competitive advantages that they have acquired through the resources of their domestic economies (Doremus et al. 1998; Porter 1990). Or, from a somewhat more sociological perspective, 'firms are likely to be influenced in their international operations by the strategies, ways of doing things, and shared understandings as to appropriate behaviour that they have developed in response to the institutional constraints and opportunities of their home business system' (Ferner and Tempel 2006: 13).

b) Integration through the creation/replication of a 'global best practices' system

For the sake of simplicity, we have so far assumed that where integration occurs, this means that a TNC's various global operations are expected to converge on its domestic practices. This is not necessarily the case, however. The top managers of TNCs may (normally) be socialized within the home country system, but that does not mean that they regard it as 'ideal'.

Firms may therefore seek to set up internationally uniform policies, but inspired by what senior managers believe to be global 'best practices', rather than using country of origin policy as the basis for global policy. This is often referred to as a 'geocentric' approach.

This form of integration is seen as increasingly common, as top corporate decision makers are influenced by common understandings of what constitutes global 'best practice' (for a convincing argument on how good practice ideas shape managerial choices, see Woywode 2002: 501–502). This is often seen as leading towards a tendency to deracination, with country of origin ideas becoming supplanted by global repertoires (see Hayden and Edwards 2001; Pudelko and Harzing 2007; Brewster et al. 2008).

While managers of all TNCs are likely to be influenced to some extent by global best practice messages, these effects may be stronger in TNCs from smaller economies, or those whose regimes are difficult to export. Broadly, liberal market ideas about management are easier to export than those emanating from more coordinated and institutionally dense national systems where home country management models are highly dependent on home country institutions. This is one reason why corporate internationalization poses challenges to more coordinated industrial relations systems, and creates pressures towards convergence on a liberal model of employment.

Cross-national learning on what constitute good HR strategies for international competitiveness is often derived externally to the firm. This includes models of global best practice inculcated in business schools, in the managerial literature, from consultants, or from scanning the policies of competitors or other comparable firms which are successful.

However, TNCs also have the opportunity to engage in active cross-national learning, through their internal corporate networks. In other words, some TNCs may take the 'best practices' from their various national operations, and attempt where appropriate to internationalize them. Thus, if the performance management practices of the British operations of a German TNC are seen as successful (and internationalizable), then the TNC might seek to introduce a global performance management strategy, including in the home country, based on the British rather than German system. This process is sometimes referred to as 'reverse diffusion' (Edwards 1998).

c) Active differentiation

Active differentiation follows the logic of 'offensive' forms of responsiveness, or of strategic segmentation, introduced above. This includes approaches which attempt to exploit the better *quality* of human resources in some foreign subsidiaries. More negatively, it also includes the exploitation of low labour *costs* and/or lax labour *regulation*, particularly in the Global South.

The availability of cheap and less regulated labour elsewhere in the world is obviously one reason for establishing international subsidiaries. Not only might this lead to reduced employment in the country of origin, but the threat of relocation also weakens the bargaining power of labour. Worker-friendly aspects of country of origin employment systems may be challenged if cheaper production facilities exist elsewhere. In the United States, threats to relocate to, or increase investment in, Mexico are commonplace during union organizing campaigns, for example (Logan 2002; Godard 2004). These threats are more realistic given Mexico's presence in the NAFTA trade bloc.

The potential for this 'whipsawing' depends on the extent to which the international division of labour within the firm's production system is fixed or changeable. Workers in TNC operations in high-cost countries are considerably more vulnerable where they are directly competing against investments in low-cost countries, rather than being involved in different parts of the production/ service provision process.

d) Passive differentiation

Finally, we should not neglect the continued existence of TNCs which, for most parts of HRM – certainly as they affect ordinary workers – essentially conform to host country patterns of management. One important facet of wider globalization in recent years has been the creation and internationalization of monopolistic regulated firms, often arising from the privatization of state-owned firms, in such areas as utilities. Such firms do not internationalize in order to integrate their production systems, but to conquer new markets. They may therefore not perceive it as in their interests to internationalize much of HRM.

Strategies vis-a-vis national employment systems

This section examines what strategies TNCs employ when engaging with national employment systems. In broad terms, as argued in the introduction, TNCs are, through the power of mobility and through their knowledge derived from operating in multiple geographies, in a stronger position than purely national firms to 'exploit the indeterminate "spaces" around even the most highly regulated business systems' (Almond and Ferner 2006: 2). While firms that seek to integrate their management internationally probably engage more, overall, in trying to shape the host country employment systems they face, the position of this chapter is not to draw sharp distinctions between the four approaches outlined above (in reality, the same firm may be following different broad orientations to different extents in different parts of its operations). Because of this, although some of the strategies below are a closer match to some of the orientations above than others, there is not likely to be any neat correspondence.

a) Regime shopping

The term 'regime shopping' (Streeck 1991) relates to the leverage that mobility of investment gives to TNCs with regard to national employment systems. Simply put, unless the location of investment is tied to markets, TNCs are likely, all other things being equal, to locate in those countries where the employment system is most amenable. Presuming sufficient quality and productivity of labour can be found in places where labour is cheap and regulation is favourable to employers, this on the face of it poses a threat to more labour-friendly employment systems. First, they are likely to receive less FDI, and large national firms may export employment, with consequent effects on employment levels. Second, as governments, employers' organizations and trade unions are aware of this threat, it is likely to be one source of pressures for employer-friendly 'reform'.

A variant of this sometimes occurs where individual new FDI projects are being negotiated. Host governments – sometimes as much at local and regional as at national levels – and trade unions may come under pressure to develop firm-level systems that might not be so open to domestic firms, in order to secure investment. No-strike agreements in Japanese transplants in the United Kingdom in the 1980s were an example of what might be called negotiated deviation (see Innes and Morris 1995; Ackroyd et al. 1988).

TNCs following a variety of the broad approaches above are likely to indulge in regime shopping to some extent, at least where firms have genuine choices of location. It is likely to be least prevalent in firms following the passive differentiation approach, where internationalization typically has more to do with access to product markets than to labour markets.

b) Replication through functional equivalents

Following an integration approach – whether based on the country-of-origin system or on some kind of global system – does not always mean directly copying HRM policies in each and every host country. Where senior corporate managers have a strong belief in the superiority of a particular system of management, but its details are difficult to export, they may seek to export their overall philosophy of management rather than simply reproduce individual practices.

Again, the large Japanese TNCs have provided examples here. While the Japanese company union system (Kawanishi 1992) is not directly translatable into European employment systems, a number of the Japanese auto manufacturers have sought to reach single-union 'sweetheart' deals (Innes and Morris 1995), or to engage moderate unions in multi-union systems in continental Europe. The idea here is to replicate the company union idea of providing an employee voice without the potential for disruptive industrial conflict. Equally, Elger and Smith (2005) provide a number of examples of Japanese firms seeking to find variants of the harsher employment systems typically used in subcontractors, using aspects of the UK employment system as resources.

c) 'Buying out' the host country system

As one of the current authors has previously argued (Almond 2011), workers do not compare MNC systems with an idealized, textbook presentation of the host country system. Rather, they typically compare the wages and working conditions on offer in TNCs with others available in local labour markets. As many TNCs, through their size, have the capacity to pay higher wages than their local labour market competitors, it is possible to use this labour market power effectively to buy acquiescence to elements of the firm's 'global' system that might otherwise be seen as undesirable. In particular, paying wage premiums at least partly to avoid trade unions has historically been used by some of the largest US-owned TNCs.

d) Embedded reformer/innovator

Some, usually large, TNCs may choose to actively engage with host country systems on an institutional level in an attempt to reform them, or at least try to control their perceived negative effects. IBM, for example, while retaining a strict non-union approach where possible, has historically often sought to take senior positions in host country employers' associations. In highly internationalized sectors, foreign TNCs collectively may come to dominate host country sectors – for example, the UK or Spanish auto sector is almost entirely dominated by foreign-owned firms. In some smaller open economies such as Ireland, the weight of TNCs in the national productive economy means that they become powerful institutional as well as micro-level actors.

This type of approach requires substantial resources, and is therefore likely to be followed mainly by very large TNCs with substantial sunk costs in particular national markets, and perhaps with localized supply chains within host economies.

e) Host system rebellion

A less sophisticated practice is simply to ignore perceived negative aspects of host employment systems. It is not difficult to find examples of TNCs that are prepared to break host country employment or labour law, often in the expectation that any financial punishment for legal infractions is likely to be relatively trivial. Tony Royle's (1998, 2004) work on McDonalds and other low-end service sector TNCs gives a number of examples in Europe. Even less obviously low-end TNCs have been known to export elements of HR systems without, at least initially, paying much regard to the niceties of host country employment law (see Muller-Camen et al. 2001).

Far worse has frequently occurred in the developing world, particularly with regard to union organization. Aside from moral reservations, such an approach obviously carries reputational risk, not only in host countries but also in some cases among consumers. This can be seen, for example, in the pressures on Nike (Locke et al. 2007) and more recently Apple (*New York Times* 2012) to improve the factory regimes among their Asian subcontractors.

f) Whipsawing

Whipsawing has several dimensions. Often, it represents a form of 'home system rebellion' as opposed to the host system rebellion above; firms threaten to invest in lower-cost countries if home country regulations are unfavourable, or if trade unions organize. As mentioned above, this is particularly likely in US firms, partly because of the problematic nature of trade union recognition campaigns in the US industrial relations system.

Whipsawing is, however, also used as a term to describe the more general process by which TNCs play different national subsidiaries off against each other, making 'coercive comparisons' (Marginson et al. 1995) and threatening plant closures if productivity fails to reach the levels achieved elsewhere in the firm's global network. Here, pressure may not be directly on worker-friendly elements of host practices, but rather represent attempts at an international 'speed-up' of production. This process also occurs at very micro-levels, with workers often being made very aware of the perceived advantages of individual production lines elsewhere in the TNC (Almond and Ferner 2006).

It is plausible to argue that whipsawing, as well as a specific strategy, is a more general leitmotif of contemporary corporate internationalization. Particularly, narratives around global competitiveness within, as well as between, TNCs, have been widely deployed as means of justifying forms of corporate change of otherwise questionable legitimacy. Vaara and Tienar (2008), for example, explore how plant shutdowns are justified by reference to share prices, 'overcapacity', and the quasi-scientific term of 'restructuring'. It is notable that, in many countries, widespread deployment of such narratives has led to a degree of acceptance of large firms reducing employment, or closing units down completely, despite the fact that they remain profitable. As Vaara and Teinari note, such moves were not always previously within the realm of acceptable corporate behaviour. Equally, managers often seek to change subsidiary employment relations settlements with a view to 'securing' (not increasing) employment.

Case study: Performance management and industrial relations at AJB Inc.

AJB Inc. is a US-owned TNC in the heavy engineering sector. It has manufacturing operations in the United States, Mexico, Slovakia, China and India, as well as the United Kingdom, where it has two plants. Its US operations were originally established in the North of the United States, but for some time it has been moving operations to the Southern United States, owing to lower wage costs and weaker trade unions in that part of the country. More recently, it has also moved to extend its Mexican operations. The firm has a history of conflictual industrial relations in the United States. Abroad, it has a corporate guideline of attempting to follow non-union HRM strategies where possible. Within the last ten years, it has also moved towards tougher forms of performance management: individual performance-related pay makes up an increasing proportion of salaries, following a forced distribution method which forces appraisers to rank 20% of their employees in a 'poor' performing group. This group is, in countries where labour law permits it, eventually liable to dismissal.

The UK operations consist of one large plant, established in 1946, and a newer, 'greenfield' site, opened in the late 1980s. The larger plant, which also has an R&D facility, has always been strongly unionized, and retains collective bargaining for shopfloor workers. This has been questioned by HQ managers, but has been tolerated due to relatively high productivity levels. The newer, smaller plant is non-union. Managerial employees are part of a global managerial HRM system. A number of senior UK HRM managers objected to the new performance management mechanism, and have attempted to get around it by giving low performance rankings to individuals who were in any case about to leave the firm.

The UK operations have always served the European market. For many years, the UK subsidiary was the only plant servicing this market. The Slovakian plant, launched in 1994, originally handled the assembly of a different product range. More recently, however, the UK operations have had to compete with the Slovakian plant for replacement investment; wage costs in Slovakian manufacturing are 37% of those in the United Kingdom. Additionally, reduced transportation costs mean that it is now possible to undertake some production aimed for the European market in China.

Leading subsidiary managers are partly remunerated on the global performance of the firm. Additionally, the US HQ has in recent years become more open to recruiting senior managers from overseas, and subsidiary managers compete intensely for these high-profile, well-paid posts. At the same time, for many managers, and all non-managers, their fortunes remain tied to those of the UK operations. The need to increase productivity levels in order to compete with other subsidiaries with lower labour costs has been a constant feature of collective bargaining for some years. An enthusiastic pursuit of lean production has led to a significant reduction in the size of the manual workforce.

Questions

1. Why would the TNC seek to have a single global performance management system? What might be the barriers to its success?
2. What are the likely implications for industrial relations in the UK subsidiary of internal competition with the Slovakian plant?
3. What might be the implications of the firm's global non-union guidelines on collective negotiations in the United Kingdom?
4. To what extent would you say the firm is 'responsive' to different host country conditions?
5. Why would the TNC retain any production facilities in the United States or the United Kingdom, given the existence of nearby low-cost alternatives in Mexico or Slovakia?

Implications for employment relations and the role of context

It should be clear from the previous sections that TNCs present a clear challenge to labour and to employment relations. It is not difficult to find cases of super-exploitation in developing countries, or of pressures for work intensification and against collective worker organization under the threat of offshoring or outsourcing to cheaper and/or less regulated national destinations. Equally, as argued above, the substantial presence of mobile foreign-owned firms in host economies can threaten the national solidarity on which more social-democratic industrial relations systems depend. It is important to properly situate and qualify this picture though. First, we look at the relationship between corporate and other forms of globalization and national employment systems. Second, we look at factors internal to the TNC itself.

National employment relations systems

First, for those interested in national employment relations systems rather than only in firm-level HRM, it is sometimes difficult to disentangle the specific effects of TNCs from the wider pressures of the neoliberal form of globalization. Workers, managers, and ultimately trade unions, employer organizations and the state, have increasingly been subject to internationalization in the contemporary period of globalization, in ways that go far beyond the direct effects of the increasing proportion of paid workers who are employed by foreign firms. In particular, we have seen a rapid diffusion of ideas about what constitutes global 'best practice' in management. In HRM, such ideas typically constitute a combination of individualist market-oriented management ideas originally inspired by large non-union firms in the United States, and an interpretation of the lean production ideology of Japanese manufacturers (while the latter concept originated in manufacturing, it has since expanded to the service sector, including to areas of activity as far removed from auto assembly as tax collection and enforcement; see Carter et al. 2011).

While the international travel of management ideas is not in itself new, the contemporary period has seen a rapid diffusion of such ideas, both through business schools and through global consultancies. While one may legitimately question how closely most firms' HR systems approximate to well-known best practice models, elements of the current global HRM orthodoxy have clearly extended beyond TNCs to domestic firms (the spread of appraisal-based performance management systems is an example here).

At a micro-level, this means that managers and workers are often relatively familiar with 'foreign' ideas of management, even if they have no direct experience of working for TNCs. At a macro-level, it has caused pressures on national employment systems to find ways of accommodating contemporary ideas of what constitutes good practice. This can be seen in widespread pressures to modify industrial relations systems in ways that make it easier to reduce demarcations between groups of workers, and more broadly to give individual firms increased autonomy over wage determination and other areas of HR practice through the decentralization of industrial relations systems (Glassner et al. 2011). Equally, the current economic crisis has been used to challenge worker-friendly elements of national labour market systems, particularly in Europe.

More broadly, one of the consequences of neoliberal globalization, sometimes neglected in the conventional discussion of home and host country effects in international HRM, is that host country institutions are changing in nature. While employment regulations, particularly in the older industrialized economies, once had as a primary function the preservation of a sometimes fragile peace between capital and labour, the increasingly open nature of economies means that the focus of national economic policies has for some time been increasingly around ensuring international competitiveness (Jessop 1993; Cerny 2000). This has created, and continues to create, further pressures on national business systems to recast themselves in the image of what might best attract the lead firms in global production networks.

This should not always mean convergence, however. This is in part because national employment regimes are to some degree 'path-dependent'; that is, the possible decisions available to contemporary policy-makers and industrial relations actors are to a considerable extent shaped by decisions made at an earlier point in history (see Hyman 1999). Additionally, where nations have advantages in particular areas of production that are institutionally derived – such as institutions that create high-skilled, adaptable and participative workforces – it is not logical to erode these advantages through deregulation (Sorge 1991; Hall and Soskice 2001). Whether social actors in individual countries are able to find ways of creating competitiveness that avoid a 'race to the bottom' is contingent on national politics and the power resources of social actors (Almond and González Menéndez 2006).

Equally, a discussion on TNCs and their employment practices should not neglect the efforts of global trade union alliances, and consumer groups, to prevent the worst cases of 'super-exploitation' through mechanisms such as global framework agreements (Telljohann et al. 2009) and other means by which TNCs can be encouraged to develop at least some degree of corporate social responsibility as concerns labour (see Chapters 12, 13 and 14).

Finally, it is important to avoid exaggerating the power of TNCs in each and every case by assuming that all location decisions are primarily made according to factors relating to human resources and industrial relations. This is very far from the case. First, the availability of natural resources remains key to the location of some TNCs, the energy sector being perhaps the most obvious example. Equally, the presence of infrastructure such as transport and communications, while declining as a factor owing to technological advances, remains significant in many cases. Third, and more generally importantly, it is often necessary to be physically in a particular place to serve a market. While we are familiar with the fact that even service sector markets can now often be serviced from overseas, with potentially negative consequences for labour in high-cost countries (Holtgrewe et al. 2009; Flecker and Meil 2010), this is not universally the case. For example, it is often not possible to access particular segments of health or defence markets in particular countries without operations in those countries. Fourth, although no less worrying from a social point of view, location decisions are often made in response to other elements of national regulation, such as planning and environmental laws, or corporate taxation. In other words, in discussing how TNCs interact with national business and employment systems, their degree of locational flexibility should properly be seen as a variable, not as a given.

The TNC and micro-politics

Both those using orthodox economic perspectives on TNCs, and their more radical critics, are often guilty of treating TNCs as monolithic entities with the power to make economically rational decisions from corporate HQ and to impose them on a global basis. While it is obviously true that the top corporate executives of TNCs generally have enormous power over strategic decision making, the working out of HR policies and practices across global enterprises is in reality somewhat more complex than that.

As a number of authors have pointed out, an analysis of the power of the TNC needs to be complemented by the recognition that the TNC is a negotiated system. In other words, how global HR policy translates into practice is the result of processes of 'interpretation' between actors within and around the global firm. Local managers and local workers, of course, have radically less power than global managers. However, to varying extents, they retain the power to interpret, accept, reject and through their own choices to modify policy shaped abroad. To the extent that the corporate centre retains the power to shift or close production in a specific national operation, this power is inherently less than in purely national firms. However, this power is not entirely absent (indeed, if it were, there would be no need for business schools and consultants to profit from teaching TNC managers how to conduct international HRM).

What is accepted, rejected or modified is, as mentioned above, likely to depend partly on domestic ideas as to what is 'good' or 'fair' practice. For example, European managers are often highly resistant to forms of performance management currently practised in many US firms, particularly where these lead to either very large pay gaps between employees at the same hierarchical level, or to the threat of dismissal for those at the wrong end of 'forced distributions' (for a discussion of forced distributions, see Blume et al. 2009). Almond and Ferner's (2006) case studies of American firms in Europe show managerial resistance to these ideas, which was sometimes successful either in modifying the policy or ensuring that its full effects were not felt in particular national subsidiaries.

Managers at corporate HQ do not always have the information-processing capacity to know what will work, or what will be interpreted as acceptable, in different national operations. This can give subsidiary managers some power as 'interpreters' of the meaning and implications of local rules, and some degree of leverage in negotiating how 'global' policies will operate within their national operations. This 'negotiation' may be explicit; that is, national subsidiary managers may openly argue their case within the global enterprise. This, however, is a fairly risky strategy for subsidiary managers to take. Often, and particularly where workplace issues are concerned, it may be simpler for local managers and workers to reach local accommodations, or local interpretations of global systems, where a literal interpretation of global policy might be either inefficient or seen as unacceptable.

In other words, subsidiary managers are not necessarily simple automatons for the global enterprise (for a discussion, see Kristensen and Morgan 2006). This extends to contests for repeat investment. Not all subsidiary managers and directors are part of a transnational internal labour market; for many, their own careers and job security are intrinsically linked to the survival and success of their own national subsidiary unit(s). They will therefore seek to ensure that the national subsidiary is successful against its 'competitors' – which may be other national subsidiaries, including the home country operations, of the TNC, rather than other firms. In doing so, to the extent that the various monitoring and control tools of the corporate HQ permit them to, they are likely to do whatever they think is likely to contribute to the success of the national operations. This may well include the use of practices and policies which are outside the scope of the global system.

Conclusion

This chapter serves as an introduction to analysing how TNCs, as powerful actors within global capitalism, interact with national systems of employment to provide pressures for change in HRM.

TNCs cause such pressures both through the specific ways in which they manage their international workforces, and through the more general pressures which can be seen to emerge from international firms competing within neoliberal globalization. Here, we have primarily concentrated on the former, in order to provide a concrete basis for understanding the decisions and power relations in individual firms' international HRM.

We have argued that, in the first place, when analysing specific TNCs, while mainstream approaches are not incorrect in analysing international HRM strategies in terms of the contrast between 'integration' and (host) 'responsiveness', such analysis often remains fairly superficial, and in particular tends to downplay or ignore power dynamics. The first part of the chapter attempts to go further than such work in highlighting what exactly TNCs might choose to be 'responsive' to. We would highlight in particular that much more attention should be paid to the various forms of 'offensive' responsiveness, that is, how TNCs seek to exploit differences in host employment systems.

We then outline various broad approaches that TNCs may have towards IHRM. These include integration on the basis of country of origin practices, integration through global 'best practices', active (or strategic) differentiation of practices between places, or more passive differentiation. While, again unlike much of the conventional literature, we are not arguing that TNCs necessarily fit neatly into only one of these categories (probably most large TNCs follow more than one of these approaches for different operations, or with regard to different areas of policy), it is nevertheless important to be able to distinguish what particular TNCs are attempting to do with regard to specific policies.

When examining specific strategies concerning interactions with national employment systems, we highlight the importance of a number of corporate methodologies. These include regime shopping, the use of functional equivalents, 'buying out' host systems, assuming governance roles in host countries, host system rebellion, and whipsawing. Again, these should not be interpreted as mutually exclusive. The chapter then examines how some of these methods play through in national employment systems, and in the micro-politics of the firm itself.

Broadly, it is difficult sensibly to argue with the proposal that TNCs act, as a whole, in ways that are challenging to the more labour-friendly elements of national employment systems. However, this has to be seen alongside other pressures for change in the global political economy, and should not be seen as eliminating social and political choices at national and international levels.

This chapter is deliberately somewhat particularistic, arguing that it is important to look at the circumstances and strategies of individual TNCs. This is because actors representing the social in and around TNCs need to be able to distinguish between general justificatory discourses of neoliberal globalization, and the actual margins of manoeuvre available in specific cases.

Reflective questions

1. Why might TNCs try to follow uniform HR policies across different national subsidiaries? Are there circumstances in which firms are more likely to want to differentiate policies between subsidiaries?
2. What pressures does the increased internationalization of production and service provision generate for a) workers' representatives, such as trade unions, in subsidiary operations, and b) national industrial relations systems?
3. What options are available to high-cost countries seeking to attract foreign direct investment?
4. Consider a national business and employment system with which you are familiar. How is it likely to shape the HRM strategies of foreign-owned TNCs?
5. What managerial mechanisms might a TNC need to have in place if it wanted to learn from its overseas operations on a global basis?
6. What kinds of firms have high levels of locational flexibility, and which have less? How might this affect the employment relations strategies of local management and trade unions?
7. What is meant by 'regime shopping' and what forms might it take?
8. The internationalization of production is often used as a resource by those arguing in favour of more liberal employment systems in high-cost countries. What kinds of counterarguments can be made against this type of argument?

Recommended reading

- Bélanger, J., Edwards, P. and Wright, M. (1999) 'Best HR practice and the multinational company'. *Human Resource Management Journal*, 9(3): 53–70.
- Edwards, T. and Kuruvilla, S. (2005) 'International HRM: National business systems, organizational politics and the international division of labour in MNCs'. *International Journal of Human Resource Management*, 16(1): 1–21.
- Elger, T. and Smith, C. (2005) *Assembling Work: Remaking Factory Regimes in Japanese Multinationals in Britain*. Oxford: Oxford University Press, especially Ch. 1.
- Ferner, A. M., Edwards, T. and Tempel, A. (2012) 'Power, institutions and the cross-national transfer of employment practices in multinationals'. *Human Relations*, 65(2): 163–187.
- Kristensen, P. and Morgan, G. (2006) 'The contested space of multinationals: Varieties of institutionalism, varieties of capitalism'. *Human Relations*, 59(11): 1467–1490.
- Woywode, M. (2002), 'Global management concepts and local adaptations: Working groups in the French and German car manufacturing industry'. *Organization Studies*, 23: 497–524.

Note

1. Different authors use the terms multinational corporations (MNCs) or transnational corporations (TNCs) to denote international firms, while others use 'multinational' or 'transnational' as particular corporate strategies used by different types of international firms (e.g., Bartlett and Ghoshal 1998). Here, we simply use TNCs to refer to firms that have direct employees in more than one country, through foreign direct investment (World Investment Report 2011).

References

Ackroyd, S., Burrell, G., Hughes, M. and Whitaker, A. (1988) 'The Japanization of British industry?'. *Industrial Relations Journal*, 19(1): 11–23.

Almond, P. (2011) 'Re-visiting "country of origin" effects on HRM in multinational corporations'. *Human Resource Management Journal*, 21(3): 258–271.

Almond, P. and Ferner, A. (2006) *American Multinationals in Europe*. Oxford: Oxford University Press.

Almond, P. and González Menéndez, M. (2006) 'Varieties of capitalism: The importance of political and social choices'. *Transfer*, 12(3): 407–426.

Bartlett, C. and Ghoshal S. (1998) *Managing Across Borders: The Transnational Solution*, 2nd edition. London: Hutchinson.

Blume, B., Baldwin, T. and Rubin, R. (2009) 'Reactions to different types of forced distribution systems'. *Journal of Business and Psychology*, 24(1): 77–91.

Brewster, C., Wood, G. and Brookes, M. (2008) 'Similarity, isomorphism or duality? Recent survey evidence on the human resource management policies of multinational corporations'. *British Journal of Management*, 19(4): 320–342.

Carter, B., Danford, A., Howcroft, D., Richardson, H., Smith, A. and Taylor, P. (2011) '"All they lack is a chain": Lean and the new performance management in the British civil service'. *New Technology, Work and Employment*, 26(2): 83–97.

Cerny, P. (2000) 'Political globalization and the competition state'. In R. Stubbs and G. Underhill, eds., *Political Economy and the Changing Global Order*. Oxford: Oxford University Press, pp. 300–309.

Doeringer, P., Lorenz, E. and Terkla, D. (2003) 'The adoption and diffusion of high-performance management: Lessons from Japanese multinationals in the West'. *Cambridge Journal of Economics*, 27(2): 265–86.

Doremus, P., Keller, W., Pauly, L. and Reich, S. (1998) *The Myth of the Global Corporation*. Princeton, NJ: Princeton University Press.

Edwards, T. (1998) 'Multinationals, employment practices and the process of diffusion'. *International Journal of Human Resource Management*, 9(4): 696–709.

Edwards, T. and Kuruvilla, S. (2005) 'International HRM: National business systems, organizational politics and the international division of labour in MNCs'. *International Journal of Human Resource Management*, 16(1): 1–21.

Elger, T. and Smith, C. (2005) *Assembling Work: Remaking Factory Regimes in Japanese Multinationals in Britain*. Oxford: Oxford University Press.

Enderwick, P. (1985) *Multinational Business and Labour*. London/Sydney: Croom Helm.

Ferner, A. (1997) 'Country of origin effects and HRM in multinational companies'. *Human Resource Management Journal*, 7(1): 19–37.

Ferner, A. and Tempel, A. (2006) 'Multinationals and national business systems: A "power and institutions" perspective'. In P. Almond and A. Ferner, eds., *American Multinationals in Europe*. Oxford: Oxford University Press.

Flanders, A. (1964) *The Fawley Productivity Agreements: A Case Study of Management and Collective Bargaining*. London: Faber & Faber.

Flecker, J. and Meil, P. (2010) 'Organisational restructuring and emerging service value chains: Implications for work and employment'. *Work Employment and Society*, 24(4): 680–698.

Glassner, V, Keune, M. and Marginson, P. (2011) 'Collective bargaining in a time of crisis: developments in the private sector in Europe'. *Transfer: European Journal of Labour Research*, 17(3): 303–322.

Godard, J. (2004) 'Trade union recognition: statutory unfair labour practice regimes in the USA and Canada'. *Employment Relations Research Series No. 29*. London, DTI.

Hall, P. and Soskice, D., eds. (2001) *Varieties of Capitalism*. Oxford: Oxford University Press.

Harzing, A. and Sorge, A. (2003) 'The relative impact of country of origin and universal contingencies on internationalisation strategies and corporate control in multinational enterprises: worldwide and European perspectives'. *Organization Studies*, 24(2): 187–214.

Hayden, A. and Edwards, T. (2001) 'The erosion of the country of origin effect: A case study of a Swedish multinational company'. *Relations Industrielles/Industrial Relations*, 56(1): 116–140.

Holtgrewe, U., Longen, J., Mottweiler, H. and Schonauer, A. (2009) 'Global or embedded service work? The (limited) transnationalisation of the call centre industry'. *Work Organisation Labour and Globalisation*, 3(1): 9–25.

Hofstede, G. (1980) *'Cultures Consequences: International differences in work related values'*. Newbury Park, CA: Sage

Hyman, R. (1999) 'National industrial relations systems and transnational challenges: An essay in review'. *European Journal of Industrial Relations*, 5(1): 89–110.

Innes, E. and Morris, J. (1995) 'Multinational corporations and employee relations: Continuity and change in a mature industrial region'. *Employee Relations*, 17(6): 25–42.

Jackson, T. and Bak, M. (1998) 'Foreign companies and Chinese workers: Employee motivation in the People's Republic of China'. *Journal of Organizational Change Management*, 11(2): 282–300.

Jacoby, S. (1997) *Modern Manors: Welfare Capitalism since the New Deal*. Princeton, NJ: Princeton University Press.

Jessop, B. (1993) *Towards a Schumpeterian Workfare State? Preliminary Remarks on Post-Fordist Political Economy*. Lancaster: University of Lancaster.

Kawanishi, H. (1992) *Enterprise Unionism in Japan*. London: Kegan Paul.

Kristensen, P. and Morgan, G. (2006) 'The contested space of multinationals: Varieties of institutionalism, varieties of capitalism'. *Human Relations*, 59(11): 1467–1490.

Locke, R., Qin, F. and Brause, A. (2007) 'Does monitoring improve labor standards? Lessons from Nike'. *Industrial and Labor Relations Review*, 61(1): 3–31.

Logan, J. (2002) 'Consultants, lawyers, and the "union free" movement in the USA since the 1970s'. *Industrial Relations Journal*, 33(3): 197–214.

Marginson, P., Armstrong, P., Edwards, P. and Purcell, J. (1995) 'Extending beyond borders: multinational companies and the international management of labour'. *International Journal of Human Resource Management*, 6(3): 702–719.

Muller-Camen, M., Almond, P., Gunnigle, P., Quintanilla, J. and Tempel, A. (2001) 'Between home and host country: Multinationals and employment relations in Europe'. *Industrial Relations Journal*, 32(5): 435–449.

New York Times (2012) In China, Human Costs are Built into an iPad, 25th January. http://www.nytimes.com/2012/01/26/business/ieconomy-apples-ipad-and-the-human-costs-for-workers-in-china.html?_r=1&pagewanted=all.

Porter, M. (1990) *The Competitive Advantage of Nations*. Basingstoke: Macmillan.

Prahalad, C. and Doz, Y. (1999) *The Multinational Mission: Balancing Local Demands and Global Vision*. New York: Free Press.

Pudelko, M. and Harzing, A (2007) 'Country-of-origin, localization, or dominance effect? An empirical investigation of HRM practices in foreign subsidiaries'. *Human Resource Management*, 46(4): 535–559.

Royle, T. (1998) 'Avoidance strategies and the German system of co-determination'. *International Journal of Human Resource Management*, 9(6): 1026–1047.

Royle, T. (2004) 'Employment practices of multinationals in the Spanish and German quick-food sectors: Low-road convergence?' *European Journal of Industrial Relations*, 10(1): 51–71.

Rubery, J. (2011) 'Institutionalizing the employment relationship'. In G. Morgan, J. Campbell, C. Crouch, O. Pedersen and R. Whitley, eds., *Oxford Handbook of Comparative Institutional Analysis*. Oxford: Oxford University Press, pp. 497–526.

Sorge, A. (1991) 'Strategic fit and the societal effect: Interpreting cross-national comparisons of technology, organization and human resources'. *Organization Studies*, 12(2): 161–190.

Streeck, W. (1991) 'More uncertainties: German unions facing 1992'. *Industrial Relations*, 30(3): 317–349.

Streeck, W and Thelen, K. (2005) *Beyond Continuity: Institutional Change in Advanced Political Economies*. Oxford: Oxford University Press.

Telljohann, V., da Costa, I., Rehfeldt, U. and Zimmer, R. (2009) 'European and international framework agreements: New tools of transnational industrial relations'. *Transfer: European Review of Labour Research*, 15(3–4): 505–525.

Tempel, A. (2001) *The Cross-National Transfer of Human Resource Management Practices in German and British Multinational Companies*. Munich: Rainer Hampp Verlag.

Vaara, E., and Tienar, J. (2008) 'A discursive perspective on legitimation strategies in multinational corporations'. *Academy of Management Review*, 33(4): 985–993.

Whitley, R. (1999) *Divergent Capitalisms: The Social Structuring and Change of Business Systems*. Oxford: Oxford University Press.

Wilkinson, F. (1981) *The Dynamics of Labour Market Segmentation*. Cambridge: Academic Press.

World Investment Report (2011) *World Investment Report 2011: Non-Equity Modes of International Production and Development*. New York: UNCTAD.

Woywode, M. (2002) 'Global management concepts and local adaptations: Working groups in the French and German car manufacturing industry'. *Organization Studies*, 23: 497–524.

3 National labour and employment relations systems and the impact of globalization

Miguel Martínez Lucio

Learning objectives

- To understand the nature of labour and employment relations and their relevance to a discussion of work, employment and management in a global context
- To understand the different tensions that underlie employment relations
- To appreciate the different reasons why systems of labour and employment relations vary by country
- To understand the changing nature of labour and employment relations due to the development of globalization
- To appreciate the ways that regulation continues to play a role
- To understand innovative developments in the role of the state

Introduction

This chapter looks at how the national level of state intervention in employment relations and its general regulation by national bodies such as trade unions is changing, and with what consequences (for a definition of trade unions, see the Introduction to Chapter 13). The way employment relations have been regulated varies by country and depends on a range of factors. These factors will be discussed in relation to some of the leading (and seminal) work in the area of labour and employment relations. This is a discipline with a long history. The chapter will therefore start by referencing some classic texts before it looks at more contemporary approaches.

The form of our employment and the way we work within organizations are influenced by a range of factors such as the sector in which we work, the level or part of the organization we work in (e.g., local plant or national offices) and the type of job we do within that context. However, the place where we work and its specific geographical location also play a fundamental role in terms of the rights and regulations that govern our employment. *This chapter will outline how these differences are explained within the academic community that studies them.* National systems and contexts range from those that have more stable employment and emphasize the rights of workers in determining and influencing the nature of their work and how they are remunerated, through to those where work is more volatile and where workers are more vulnerable to being mistreated and denied basic employment and even human rights.

Having discussed the factors that lead to these differences, we will then move on to discuss *how national systems of labour and employment relations are being put under pressure by the process of globalization yet continue to evolve and play a role.* Changes such as globalization are placing significant pressure on the more organized and worker-oriented systems of employment relations because of their supposed costs and rigidities (an issue that is the subject of heated discussions). The ability of capital and employers to relocate to low-cost and more 'amenable' systems places a strain on the more organized and regulated systems of employment and work. The chapter will next proceed to argue that *these developments are not capable of straightforward interpretation, and that governments, state agencies and trade unions remain important in mediating and shaping the way that these changes take place.* In addition, governments and trade unions as organizations, while having primarily been locked into national systems of industrial relations, are actually creating new global links and share a range of practices across borders to engage with and challenge increasingly internationalized capitalist processes. The chapter will end by focusing on these dynamics and new forms of transnational learning by workers and the organizations linked to them.

In understanding why labour and employment relations systems differ, we therefore need to work at a range of levels: economic, political, industrial and institutional. We need to be sensitive to the ways in which systems are coordinated and how the different spheres link together. We also need to be aware how individuals and collectives within these different national contexts understand the processes of change and tradition, and how they consider these in terms of risks and challenges. Throughout the chapter, we shall use the term *labour and employment relations system*, although occasionally we use the classic term *industrial relations* when focusing on regulation in particular.

Types of national labour and employment relations systems and state intervention at work

The way we work and are employed involves rules and obligations for both the employer and the worker. The nature, extent and effectiveness of these rules and obligations vary in relation to their context and the different legacies of struggle over worker rights. Why these have evolved the way they have is the subject of discussion, and the reason for their ongoing change is often the subject of significant argument. Why are some workers paid according to collective agreements agreed by trade unions and their employer when in another national context or sector working conditions are imposed by employers alone? What determines how working conditions are affected by legal frameworks developed by governments, and why do they vary greatly?

There is no doubt that the extent of economic development is a factor. There is a strong correlation between the economic status and development of a country and the role of negotiations, dialogue and state enforcement of the social features of work (Kerr et al. 1960). The process of industrialism and development was once seen as an inevitable development that would lead to a unified or homogenous model of economic activity and regulation. At the heart of these general theories is the assumption that a move to common organizational structures and processes, driven by technological developments, will lead to a homogenous set of outcomes (see Lane 1989 for a discussion). While this may seem a dated idea, given the diversity of employment systems, it is still current in various managerial views such as that of lean production, which see a 'one best way' for managing and developing organizations through the use of common techniques (see Chapter 7 for a critique).

Yet this simple link – between economic and technological development, on the one hand, and the evolution of employment systems, on the other – may not always be enough to explain the factors leading up to a situation where a country 'can afford' social rights. First of all, the manner in which a nation has developed may have involved the subjugation of rights of other nations in its imperialist past. For example, the United Kingdom developed in the 19th century not just because of its industrial progress and 'innovative' culture, but also as a result of its exploitation of its colonies, such as India, and their human and non-human resources. Many industrial relations and HRM studies ignore this colonial and historical legacy, which explain there being very different sets of resources underpinning the development of countries and their systems of labour and employment relations. In fact, these racial and national differences are clear within international organizations, where European ethnic groups remain dominant, such as in the trade union movement or international regulatory bodies. Relations between countries and the way they have developed will influence the contours of national systems.

Second, there are significant levels of variation between countries with broadly similar economic levels, in terms of the extent of worker rights and forms of representation in relation to their work and employment. The United States has less collectivist traditions and weaker trade unions than Germany, for example, yet both are located in a superior position in global economic terms. In Latin America, regulation in terms of collective bargaining is more significant in Argentina compared with its neighbour Chile (Ugarte 2012), but both share a fairly similar economic heritage. Hence, political and historical factors and not just economic ones may explain the differences between national systems.

Understanding regulation and rule making: consensus and conflict in labour and employment relations

The institutionalist and pluralist tradition of academic research in the area of employment has focused on the role of explicit rules and regulations that evolve over time and play a part in establishing a framework of expectations and behaviour. The argument here is that collective bargaining – the joint regulation through processes of negotiation between stakeholders of employment conditions – is the main focus of industrial relations (see Poole's (1981) discussion of Clegg 1976). Variations in factors such as the extent of collective bargaining (how many workers are covered), its scope (what is negotiated and dealt with), the nature of trade union involvement (the precise role of worker representatives) and the main level at which agreements are signed (at the national or local level, for example) are seen to be a major influence on trade union behaviour and wider industrial relations outcomes (Poole 1981). However, these are also the outcome of employer and management attitudes as well as of state intervention, which play a part in shaping the nature of employment regulation in the face of worker representation (see Clegg 1976). Much of this tradition draws in part from the work of the American labour economist, John Dunlop, who emphasized the role of rule maintenance and order within industrial relations as Rogowski (2000) described:

> Dunlop's own theory is based on four 'elements' ... actors, contexts, ideologies, and rules. The separate existence or 'autonomy' of industrial relations systems is shaped by ... [these] four 'elements'. Dunlop discusses them separately in his theoretical outline, in which he characterises the 'elements' as follows: the three main *actors* are management, workers and government agencies; *contexts* consist of technology, market constraints, and the power distribution in society; and the *ideologies* of the actors must resume around a common set of ideas that guides the allocation of acceptable roles to the actors. The last, and most crucial 'element' in Dunlop's theory of autonomous industrial relations, is the concept of *rules* governing the relations of industrial actors. This body of rules, which includes rules on procedures for the establishment and administration of substantive rules, constitutes 'the center of attention in an industrial-relations system' (Dunlop 1958: 13). (Rogowski 2000; 100–101 emphasis in original)

In Dunlop's view, the specific character of industrial relations systems derives to an extent from rule making independently of decision making in the economic system. While environmental factors such as the nature of the economy, society and polity contribute to the development of industrial relations, one must also appreciate that the processes of rule maintenance may become autonomous over time. Hence, countries may differ in part as a result of the nature of economic development but – presumably – the evolution, stability and complexity of rules and traditions governing relations between unions and managers, for example, take on a life of their own (suggesting that political relations must be considered in the context of how consensus is forged around the nature of regulation). So the way bargaining develops and impacts may be due to a range of factors and traditions.

Broader political perspectives within political science and industrial relations have looked at the role of national negotiation structures as key factors in shaping the nature of industrial relations. Such approaches have been dominant in the debates on corporatism that are concerned with macro- and national-level negotiations between governments (and their state agencies), and employers and trade unions. Some of the more rule-based and negotiation-based systems of industrial relations tend to include significant dialogue at the national level, which frames local discussions in terms of the content of bargaining and its general spirit. The role of the state can be such that it is able to create a national framework or degree of coordination regarding how industrial relations are conducted locally: it does this by establishing initiatives on pay, training, and health and safety, for example, through legislation to some extent, but it can also accomplish it through some form of political exchange and bargaining that allows unions and employers' associations to be represented and interact with governments (Schmitter 1974). Some of the strongest systems of employment relations in terms of the roles of unions and employers and the extent of collective bargaining, appear to be linked to and combined with strong systems of state-level dialogue (commonly called societal corporatism). Lehmbruch (1984) argued that one could detect stronger systems of such corporatist engagement in Nordic European countries; in many other countries they are weaker, with dialogue being more sporadic, associated with key crisis-related issues, as in the case of Italy. In some cases, the state has created a more authoritarian form of corporatism, as in a one-party system such as China's or during the Francoist dictatorship in Spain (1939–75), where government or government agencies 'negotiate' with national employers and trade unions that are controlled politically and are not independent of the state. In such cases, industrial relations processes are contained, controlled and driven by singular political interests, normally the state and dominant economic elites.

It is partly because of such instances of authoritarian domination in some instances that Marxist and other radical, critical academic strands argue that the pluralist- and institutionalist-oriented view of work and employment can some-times ignore the fact that there may be an inherent instability within employment relations because of the nature of power and the imbalances between actors and classes. Employers and the state, it is argued, are trying continuously to limit or condition the development of unions and worker rights, or to contain them in a variety of ways. In citing Allen (1966), Hyman argued that pluralist industrial relations can therefore be seen as resulting in piecemeal gains for workers that do not question the nature of power relations (Hyman 1975: 192). Hence, framing the agendas of trade union demands and activities is a curious and complex process:

> The union official, in other words, experiences a natural commitment to the existing bargaining arrangements and the terms of existing collective agreements. This commitment, moreover, is attributable less to any personal characteristics of the official than to his function: the negotiation and renegotiation of order within constraints set by a capitalist economy and a capitalist state. (Hyman 1975: 91)

These 'games' may institutionalize and bureaucratize labour organizations, yet they cannot always contain the tensions between workers and management as workers and activists try to better their working conditions and at times circum-vent these agreements. There is no state of rest in such relations, as workers and managers struggle with the limits of institutional arrangements and competing interests. The Marxist contribution explains this instability and the dynamics of industrial relations in a way that pluralists fail to grasp.

In terms of corporatism, Panitch (1981) discusses this instability of the corpo-ratist arrangements of the 1970s in some European cases by referring to how such national strategies of incorporating unions and workers are themselves limited because of the way workplace-based trade union activists may challenge con-straints on wage rises. Thus, national institutional arrangements may cause ten-sions within unions between their leaders and activists on the ground. These contradictions and outcomes are, in turn, a source of, and a focus for, responses and engagement by the state. The attempt to frame and institutionalize industrial relations is therefore never complete and stable. Hence the state attempts to build a political shell around labour and employment relations by emphasizing the control of worker representatives through national leaders, and constrained col-lective bargaining, for example: it solicits hierarchical approaches within both organizations and civil society. National interest and non-class referents are developed to counter conflict and generate a 'common interest' between workers and employers in regard to workplace and employment relations, as seen in the context of corporatist discourse. Thus, some Marxists consider such common interests to be illusory and a smokescreen that hides class conflict (see Panitch 1981). Moreover, just as the state incorporates social actors, it also coerces them at certain moments in time (Hyman 1975: 144). Differences between national forms of industrial relations may therefore be explained in terms of the nature of these ongoing struggles between capital and labour, the balance of forces between them, and the way that the state intervenes and tries to control the rule-making processes through ideologies (e.g., through an emphasis on the notion of social dialogue) or through coercion (e.g., the use of the police or even the armed forces). Hence, there may be strategies of incorporation into passive rule making as trade unions are tied into a system of dialogue through material or ideological incentives, or unions may be coerced through laws restricting their right to strike and even their presence in extremely authoritarian cases. The heritage of Marxism not only emphasises the inevitable 'instability' within employment relations but also the political, coerced and even ideologically driven nature of 'stability'.

Difference and variety in labour and employment relations: institutions in context

While we can outline the general developments and variations in terms of the balance between consensus and coercion, between union-oriented and employer- or state-led industrial relations, and between centralized (corporatist) and decentralized systems of industrial relations, there is still much more that defines differences in terms of the nature of industrial relations. There are qualitative differences in the extent of worker influence on the social and economic relations of a society (welfare approaches versus more economic/wage driven ones), and in the manner in which industrial relations actors have a broader social and political role. Even within what appear to be common national contexts at similar stages of development, historical factors and the nature of political development may provide different patterns of representation and regulation. Since the early 1990s – especially with the impact of the comparative research agenda and a growing realization that the British and US models are quite exceptional and not representative as models of industrial relations – a new focus on attempting to understand how industrial relations systems develop has emerged.

A dominant stream of analysis is the 'varieties of capitalism' debate, which has been a pivot of contemporary understanding of why systems of employment relations and regulation in general vary (Hall and Soskice 2001). This has become an important addition to the debate on comparative industrial relations and the context of various student textbooks (see Hyman 2004; Wailes et al. 2011). The argument rests on the assumption that there are significant variations within capitalism, and that we need to be aware of the different dimensions constituting patterns of regulation and economic management. It is argued that history and the role of institutions are fundamental to the development of capitalist systems of regulation, and that the different dimensions of these systems link and relate to each other in ways that create a consistent system and pattern of development. The dimensions the model refers to are the nature of corporate governance and its structure; how traditions of cooperation and competition have developed; the role of voice mechanisms and industrial relations processes; the role of vocational training and education as a key feature of the labour market; and various other factors.

These have been developed and linked in two different patterns of development: the liberal market economy (LME) and the coordinated market economy (CME). The attraction of such theories is that the nature of industrial relations regulation is sustained by – and sustains – different ways in which capitalism is coordinated: hence, centralized and worker-oriented systems of industrial relations with stronger trade unions fit in with long-term, training-oriented, participative and welfare-driven economies such as Sweden (see Chapters 4, 6 and 8). On the other hand, liberal market economies such as the United States tend to link a profit-driven, shareholder and low-regulation culture with a more individualized and less trade-union-oriented system of industrial relations. Put simply:

- LMEs are market- and competition-oriented with a weaker state role and set of regulatory structures, with an emphasis on risk taking and a less regulated system of firms.
- CMEs have a greater state role and greater degree of regulation, whether joint regulation with organized labour, association-based regulation in employers associations and similar bodies, and/or a greater role for public and quasi-public bodies in areas such as training.

There is also a political attraction to such a model for those who question the neoliberal and right-wing approach which suggests that the market, deregulation and possessive individualism are the only way forward, or the only successful form of capitalism. The varieties-of-capitalism approach allows for a social capitalism and a more regulated system of worker rights to exist within a capitalist context. However, while highly attractive to many commentators, some question the relevance of the model to developing countries and tend to view the model as being more relevant to developed OECD countries. There is also concern with its institutional determinism and obsession with questions of coordination and institutional relations (Kang 2006). Furthermore, organizations such as trade unions in developing countries may be prohibited by the economic and political context from entering into meaningful dialogue with the state and employers because of weaker levels of independence and support for worker representation. In such contexts, coordinated features of a market economy may be based on powerful elites that limit and constrain social rights and engagement. So while the concept of CME is of limited use on occasion, the varieties-of-capitalism approach seems to have become dominant in the study of labour and employment relations.

Similar approaches have emerged in discussions of national business systems (Whitley 2007), which also see relations within and across organizations and broader institutions as key. These focus on the nature of ownership structures, non-ownership relations, and employment relations generally:

- Ownership relations: The means of ownership, the nature of ownership integration and production chains, ownership in relation to sector boundaries and the extent of coordination.
- Non-ownership relations: The extent of alliances and coordination across and within production chains, the extent of collaboration and support between competitors, the extent of alliance coordination across sectors around common interests.
- Employment relations and the management of work: Employer–employee relations and interdependence, the extent of mutual trust, and the delegation of work and decision making.

These systems will vary across countries and types of capitalism, as the ownership of firms may be more coordinated, less restricted by short-term financial interests, built on a complex and mutually beneficial and sustained network of alliances and interests, engaged more fully in a dialogue with stakeholders, such as trade unions, or built on 'trust', as some would argue in the German case. One interesting point to note is that the varieties-of-capitalism debate and the national-business-systems approach do not merely locate labour regulation more generally as an important set of features within any understanding of capitalism (and economic systems); they also note the significant role of employer cultures (whether there is a proclivity towards collectivism, labour representation and an acceptance of social rights and collective welfare), and the centrality of how people are trained, how significant training is within the system, and how stakeholders such as trade unions become involved in training. The argument is that more regulated systems of industrial relations have training at the heart of the system in terms of the quality and not just the cost of labour, as well as the role of negotiation in its development. The emphasis is on the relational features and links that sustain a system, and how these have developed over time through either cooperative or competitive forms.

Ideology and context: national sensitivities and politics

National systems of industrial relations vary, as we have seen above, providing a variety of constraints and possibilities in terms of those who participate in the representation and management of work. We cannot ignore the significance of specific and context-related issues and how they evolve over time (see Hyman 2001, and his discussion of Ross 1981). Hyman (2001) argues that this is a major dimension that has often been ignored by analysts. The reason why some issues are significant in one context and not in another could be because political debates and national discussion viewpoints and sensitivities arise that are particular to a national or local context (Locke and Thelen 1995). The argument we have to appreciate is that certain issues related to work and employment may be viewed and understood as a specific constraint or challenge in one context but not in another. Job controls in Britain, in terms of how local trade unionists forged ways of controlling aspects of work, were seen by the right of the political spectrum to be a major obstacle to economic development (e.g., the deployment of individuals at work), though trade unionists argued that they were important to allow a more controlled and less stressful experience of work. In France, working time, and debates on its link to a much broader view of how workers are meant to work and live, means that the arena of struggle has been less about job control as in the United Kingdom but more focused on the limits employers can place on working time. In addition, certain reforms may be seen as 'positive' or 'negative' by different groups, given their sensitivity and importance within political discourses. For example, in Spain the cost of dismissal of workers has been seen by employers to be prohibitive and has limited their hiring of workers. However, trade unions have argued that such costs have not in fact stopped employers from creating one of the highest levels of unemployment in Europe since the early 1980s, so the idea that they cannot easily fire people is questionable (Fernandez Gonzalez and Martínez Lucio 2013). This is what Locke and Thelen (1995) labelled 'contextualized comparisons', and in discussing national systems we must be aware of these 'national concerns and debates' that frame the ways that issues and themes characterize national systems of industrial relations.

MacKenzie and Martínez Lucio (2005, 2014) have argued that regulation and its politics is underpinned by cultural and ideological factors. In the case of the United Kingdom, during the 1950s and 1960s the popular cinema was important in portraying industrial relations as an archaic and conflict-ridden feature of British society through comedies that often stigmatized trade unionists. These images were also present in a range of cartoons, especially in the right-wing press, which would mobilize opinion against trade union rights. The Glasgow Media Group (1976) studied the way that work-related and trade union issues were covered by the media in the United Kingdom, pointing to the bias against trade unions, which was used by right-wing political interests during the 1980s and 1990s when they were in power. They passed labour legislation making it difficult for trade unions to take strike action, for example.

Hence, in understanding why systems differ, we need to work at a range of levels: economic, political, industrial and institutional. We need to be sensitive to the ways that systems are coordinated and the different spheres link together. We also need to be aware of how individuals and collectives within these different national contexts understand the processes of change and tradition, and how they consider these in terms of risks and challenges. The way that interests are represented is central, and this can be done through a variety of institutional and cultural forms. There are, on the one hand, elements of continuity in the institutions and customs that provide national systems with traditional and established ways of managing and regulating issues related to work. However, on the other hand, there are ongoing tensions and sources of change because of the nature of the employment relations – that is, the way that workers remain dispossessed of a more organic and meaningful role and influence, and the way employers regardless of a rhetoric of participation protect their material interests. The following case study shows how national contexts of labour and employment relations influence specific features of employment and HRM development, in this case it concerns teamwork in Germany and the United Kingdom.

Case study: Teamwork in Germany and the United Kingdom – Two tales of innovation and context

The emergence of teamwork was seen as a major feature of the new wave of managerial innovation in work organization during the 1980s and 1990s (Garrahan and Stewart 1994). These developments built on the popularity of the Japanese model of success, which was seen to involve workers in decision making about how they worked through dedicated teams and team leader structures. However, some raised concerns that this could increase work intensification through peer pressure and management surveillance by members of the team (ibid.).

In the case of the United Kingdom and Germany, the implementation of teamwork in sectors such as metal manufacturing varied considerably, and a range of literature engaged with this issue pointed out that the national industrial relations context had much to do with the way that teamwork was introduced (Murakami 1999). The importance of national systems of industrial relations was highlighted as contributing to different types of work organization and changes within it.

First, in terms of the context, the German system tends towards the CME model, as described by Hall and Soskice (2001), hence the emphasis on developing a more embedded and skills-driven vision of worker participation operating over a longer time frame. The nature of corporate governance was such that long-term qualitative visions of production were sustained. This contrasted with the United Kingdom, where the shift has been towards soft skills, such as communications skills, as a way of creating forms of team based organization where peer pressure was used to increase productivity beyond the reach of union controls and regulation (Garrahan and Stewart 1994). Hence, for some there was a perceived shift to a competitive strategy based on low-cost advantages as in the United Kingdom (see Chapter 7), while a relatively high-quality approach was maintained in core parts of German manufacturing. Teamwork was thus introduced or developed in very different contexts in relation to skills (Wergin 2003).

Second, the nature of trust within each system varied. In the German context, dialogue and negotiation based on a degree of mutual trust between management and the trade unions has been core to industrial relations. This has been an outcome of a state-led post Second World War consensus. This is different in the United Kingdom because of the move away from consensus politics in the 1980s under the neoliberal Conservative regime of Margaret Thatcher, the aim of which was to limit trade union influence. These political contexts meant that the basis for an inclusive dialogue on work organization and teamwork varied.

Third, these political contexts and regulatory environments gave rise to different sensitivities regarding teamwork and changes in work organization. In the United Kingdom, teamwork was considered to be undermining trade unions, as direct forms of representation and control were linked to management, thus bypassing the role of trade unions in the workplace (Garrahan and Stewart 1994). Trade unions saw such practices in part as a politics of creating a system of industrial relations based on individualized relations or managerially oriented worker interests, as teams discussed efficiencies at work but not necessarily social rights (Martinez Lucio et al. 1999). In Germany, teamwork for many – though not all – trade unionists did not pose a threat because of the stronger legislative context that guaranteed trade union rights, but also because trade unions had seen teamwork in the form of 'group work' as a way of enhancing work and creating a greater role for the workforce in workplaces that often involved monotonous and repetitive labour.

Hence, teamwork in very general terms was seen to vary according to its extent in terms of actual/real teamwork (Germany) and symbolic/limited teamwork (the United Kingdom). The nature of skills was such that in Germany it was associated with multi-skilling, while in the United Kingdom it was associated with multi-tasking or job loading (i.e., just combining more lower-level tasks). In addition, leadership of teams was rarely a subject for discussion in the United Kingdom, unlike in Germany. Hence, a very concrete form of working is in fact variable and dependent on the nature and variety of capitalism, business cultures, systems of regulation and innovation, and traditions of struggle. Even so, the extent of difference should not be overstated, as the degree of autonomy workers have in self-management in relation to teamwork within a capitalist enterprise is limited, as research has shown (Murakami 1997, Wergin 2003).

Questions

1. In what ways do you think corporate governance and the involvement of stakeholder interests can influence the development of HR practices?
2. What role does trust play in the workplace?
3. How can trade unions influence the development of management strategies and new forms of working?
4. Why and how does training differ between countries (for example, the emphasis on hard skills or soft skills, and the roles of trade unions and other bodies), and what difference can this make?

The fall and rise of regulation in national systems: globalization, the crisis of industrial relations at the national level and the reinvention of the state and regulation

Irrespective of the differences we seek to understand in the rich tapestry of work and industrial relations, there is a belief that the regulatory capacity of national systems of labour and employment relations (or industrial relations) is declining. According to some observers, the role of the state at the national level has been diminishing because of the impact of transnational corporations (TNCs) and the 'forces' of globalization (Hyman 2001). Chapter 12 outlines how systems of regulation have been placed under pressure, and how the state-regulated and welfare models of employment and work management have been undermined. These changes emerge as a result of a range of developments that are challenging joint regulation, worker representation and nationally embedded systems of regulation. These have been outlined in a seminal and prophetic text which nearly 30 years ago foresaw the process of disorganization confronting the once-organized and regulated system of industrial relations of the late 20th century in developed countries. The nature of the changes, seen through the eyes of Lash and Urry (1987: 5–6), were as follows:

- The decline of closed national economies that are not exposed to competition, which undermines the institutional patterns within national systems of industrial relations.
- The changing nature of the workforce in terms of new, individualized interests and new forms of social organization beyond traditional trade unions.
- The decline in effectiveness of collective bargaining and traditional forms of regulation as pressures emerge to increase efficiencies and undermine costs such as labour costs.
- Increased competition worldwide, leading to greater cost pressures and a downward effect on worker rights.
- A decline in traditionally organized systems of political and employer organization.
- A decline in the scale of capitalist operation in productive terms with a move to smaller and more decentralized systems of service delivery/production.
- Greater social fragmentation and a decline in large working class communities (changing working class districts).
- A change in traditional class cultures, making societies more unstable and less class conscious.

The argument in the current context would be that, regardless of the debate about coordinated versus liberal market economies, the pressure on coordinated and regulated systems has been increasing: that there has been a shift from an interventionist and collective system of capitalism to a more market-oriented, flexible and unstable context. However, the march to a new market and neoliberal world was in Lash and Urry's (1987) view not without problems. The argument and the evidence they presented was premised on the opinion that the new, disorganized capitalism would vary, or could only make sense, if viewed in relation to how national systems had initially been organized in terms of, for example, the structure of capital, the role of the state and regulation, and the nature of management systems. The character of organization would be significant to the nature of disorganization, what its drivers would be, and how it would be moulded. And therefore the character of change in Germany and Sweden would be different from that in the United Kingdom or the United States. In some cases capital would oversee the process; while in other contexts it would be overseen perhaps by the state or even by labour. One can quibble about whether this has been the case – though to a large extent, certain trends have been maintained within many developed countries. Furthermore, Lash and Urry's (1987) argument about trade unions sees a more open set of possibilities for them, depending on their strategic responses and resources. These authors called for unions to lead and shape changes work organization, quality, participation, and so on. In fact, some prophetically took the concept of disorganization to be a new logic that had the potential to mobilize a new, open form of socialism and labour politics based on a more open and flexible approach (Daly 1991), as in the Occupy movements of the post-2008 crisis. What is more, historical frameworks may still shape the nature of change and the values to which it aspires: key aspects of CMEs remain vibrant in some cases such as in Germany and Denmark. The state and various labour and employment relations related bodies such as unions are not the recipients or victims of the changes listed above; they can actually shape them.

If anything, we have seen national states moving to new forms of intervention (Martínez Lucio and MacKenzie, 2004 and Chapter 12). The state, even when it is 'falling over backwards' to attract international investment and to 'prepare' local contexts for further involvement from TNCs, has to consider matters of infrastructure and to ensure a regulated orderly space (Panitch 1994). This may mean it rethinks the system of rights and regulations that exist, putting it on a collision course with social movements and trade unions in some cases; but the state does not evaporate as such, as it has to ensure that the labour market supports development (see Chapter 10).

In addition, the state may reinvent itself in terms of industrial relations in a variety of ways (Martínez Lucio and MacKenzie 2006) by working alongside other 'social partners' around competitive strategies, or ensuring that they are compliant in some manner. It is for this reason that students of the subject must never forget the political dimension of these questions (Jessop 2002). We have seen a move to what Jessop (2002) called Schumpeterian workfare post-national regimes: that is, contexts where the state uses its authority and resources to ensure that labour markets and their workforce are 'supplied' through a 'market mediated exploitation' (ibid.: 276). Hence, governments are caught in the dilemma of either negotiating and consensually developing the labour skills and 'pliability' of workers, or using more directive means – such as welfare to work programmes and other disciplinary approaches – to ensure a workforce that can be utilized by international capital. Yet, whatever the dilemma, the state and regulation remain important (Ritchie 2002) and the state's co-ordination of different regulatory processes is significant (Torfing, 1990).

The state thus begins to play new roles, and sometimes these are discreet and based on coaxing organizations towards certain ends and also 'prompting' management into these new models and approaches (Martínez Lucio and Stuart 2011: 3661–3671):

> First, the state has invested in *networking and the development of new forms of knowledge sharing and collaboration* between managers and between unions, and between both ... This 'governance' perspective of the state pays attention to the nature of joint working across the public, private and social sectors (Kooiman 2003). Second, there is the role of the state in *developing benchmarks and standards* through its conciliation bodies and learning agencies. The state establishes forums, research, consultancy and communications aimed at prompting change and new forms of HRM ... Third, the state also *sets targets and objectives* – political mission statements are developed alongside numerical targets such as the employment of minority groups or satisfaction rates ... This dovetails with the development in corporate social responsibility and the role of a new interest in business ethics within the state. In effect, the state provides support for actors to assimilate some of its roles and to work in partnership with it in a new strategic manner. (Kooiman 2003; emphasis as in original)

So the state plays a variety of direct and indirect roles. In some cases, as in China (Cooke 2011), the state has a directive and centralized approach: it still is compelled to propagate and disseminate practices and ideas about new ways of working or new forms of management. In effect, the state and regulation remain (see Chapter 12). What is more, even trade unions engage in such practices as networking, benchmarking and shared learning as a way of responding to the impact of globalization and change. New practices, such as organizing workers through new forms of mobilization, have been disseminated by alliances between American, Australian and British trade unions. Initiatives around learning and training in the context of the European Union have seen new forms of representation and training programmes that are often led by trade unions (see Chapter 6). In addition, the Internet has facilitated a greater degree of grass-roots dialogue between trade unionists and workplace representatives across the world (see Chapter 14) and labour campaigns coordinated through such forms of new media and communications (Hogan et al. 2010). The future will be about how national systems of regulation and national social organizations, such as trade unions and social movements related to work, link the national contexts together and create synergies and networks in an ever more globalized world.

Conclusion

This chapter links to the book's opening discussion of globalization by focusing on the changing roles of labour and employment relations. National spaces remain an important dimension, continuing to refract and provide meaning to the processes of globalization and change as a result of the balance of forces between capital and labour; the way that institutional relations have been constructed; and practices of engagement, such as bargaining, have been established and developed.

First, we need to be alert to the basic tensions and relations that exist in regard to work in a context where employers and workers are divided by the fact that the latter are forced to sell their labour to the former. This basic tension and how it is resolved must always be present in any analysis. Second, we need to understand how interests and organizations have evolved, and created more cooperative cultures in some contexts than others through the establishment of longer-term perspectives and common interests, such as training and skill formation. Yet even then, these can be established in ways that can veil realities of power, or can be imposed through various political means. However, how systems cope with such differences and antagonisms through complex institutional processes is an important dimension in explaining their diversity. Third, it is this history of conflict, compromises and reflection that also contributes to understandings and cultures of regulation. We have seen how issues may vary across countries, and why. This forms part of the consensus-generating process and the way compromise is forged; it also frames the possibilities and limits of change and the nature of that change.

Furthermore, the chapter has pointed to the fact that the state and regulation remain, and that institutions and organizations can reinvent themselves significantly in a context where new economic demands are made. Even where market relations and greater employer flexibility have emerged, the state and social organizations such as trade unions or similar bodies are still vital to the development of supportive infrastructure, long-term prospects for sustainable development, and – ironically – dealing with the fallout and problems that emerge from the processes of disorganization outlined above (Rubery 2011). The nature of regulation may shift, but it will not disappear. Globalization is not a clear trajectory which somehow disembeds all that exists in terms of national traditions. It is a fact that it brings new pressures and new organizations and bodies into the arena of industrial relations and employment more generally. However, it is also shaped by the way established institutions in the form of the state or within the economy and society, such as trade unions and even employer organizations themselves, respond and develop reflexive policies and strategies. This corresponds to the views on globalization of Hirst and Thompson (1999, 2009), which show how globalization has developed in relation to established hierarchies and power relations. Hence, the idea that globalization and increasing marketization give rise to an 'Americanized' and 'marketized'/ 'neo-liberal'system of industrial relations and work organization is not a given (see Chapter 8). What we see is a new transnational politics and engagement with regulation (a theme picked up in Chapters 12, 13 and 14).

Reflective questions

1. Why is there a tension between employers and workers?
2. What are the ways in which such tensions have been responded to and what roles do collective bargaining and state legislation play?
3. Why are national systems of labour and employment relations different?
4. What are the ways in which these systems are changing and why?
5. What are the main ways in which the state influences the conduct of labour and employment relations and how are these state roles changing?

Recommended reading

- Cooke, F. L. (2011) 'The role of the state and human resource management in China'. *International Journal of Human Resource Management*, 22(18): 3830–3848.
- Hogan, J., Nolan, P. and Greco, M. (2010) 'Unions, technologies of coordination, and the changing contours of globally distributed power'. *Labour History*, 51(1): 29–40.
- MacKenzie, R. and Martínez Lucio, M. (2005) 'The realities of regulatory change: Beyond the fetish of deregulation'. *Sociology*, 39(3): 499–517.

References

Allen, V. (1966) *Militant Trade Unions*. London: Merlin.

Clegg, H. (1976) *Trade Unionism under Collective Bargaining*. Oxford: Oxford University Press.

Cooke, F. L. (2011) 'The role of the state and human resource management in China'. *International Journal of Human Resource Management*, 22(18): 3830–3848.

Daly, G. (1991) 'The discursive construction of economic space'. *Economy and Society*, 20(10): 79–102.

Dunlop, J. T. (1958) *Industrial Relations Systems*. New York: Holt.

Fernandez Gonzalez, C. J. and Martínez Lucio, M. (2013) 'Narratives, myths and prejudice in understanding employment systems: The case of rigidities, dismissals and flexibility in Spain'. *Economic and Industrial Democracy*, 34(2): 313–336.

Garrahan, P. and Stewart, P. (1994) *The Nissan Enigma*. London: Mansell.

Glasgow Media Group (1976) *Bad News*, vol. 1. London: Routledge & Kegan Paul.

Hall, P. and Soskice, D. (2001) 'Introduction'. In P. Hall and D. Soskice (eds.), *Varieties of Capitalism*. New York: Oxford University Press.

Hirst, P. and Thompson, G. (1999) *Globalization in Question*. Oxford: Wiley-Blackwell.

Hirst, P. and Thompson, G. (2009) *Globalization in Question*. Cambridge: Polity Press.

Hogan, J., Nolan, P. and Greco, M. (2010) 'Unions, technologies of coordination, and the changing contours of globally distributed power'. *Labour History*, 51(1): 29–40.

Hyman, R. (1975) *Industrial Relations: A Marxist Introduction*. London: Macmillan.

Hyman, R. (2001) 'Trade unions and cross-national comparison'. *European Journal of Industrial Relations*, 7(2): 203–232.

Hyman, R. (2004) 'Varieties of capitalism, national industrial relations systems and transnational challenges'. In A.-W. Harzing and J. Van Ruysseveldt (eds.), *International Human Resource Management*. London: Sage.

Jessop, B. (2002) *The Future of the Capitalist State*. Cambridge: Polity Press.

Kang, N. (2006) A Critique of the "Varieties of Capitalism" Approach. Research Paper Series No 45, International Centre for Corporate Social Responsibility, Nottingham University Business School, Nottingham.

Kerr, C., Dunlop, J. T., Harbison, F. H. and Meyers, C. A. (1960) *Industrialism and Industrial Man*. London: Penguin.

Kooiman, J. (2003) *Governing as Governance*. London: Sage.

Lane, C. (1989) *Management and Labour in Europe*. Aldershot: Edward Elgar.

Lash, S. and Urry, J. (1987) *The End of Organised Capitalism*. Cambridge: Polity Press.

Lehmbruch, G. (1984) 'Corporatism in decline?' In J. H. Goldthorpe (ed.), *Order and Conflict in Contemporary Capitalism*. Oxford: Clarendon Press.

Locke, R. M. and Thelen, K. (1995) 'Apples and oranges revisited: Contextualised comparisons and the study of labour politics'. *Politics and Society*, 23(3): 337–367.

MacKenzie, R. and Martínez Lucio, M. (2005) 'The realities of regulatory change: Beyond the fetish of deregulation'. *Sociology*, 39(3): 499–517.

MacKenzie, R and Martínez Lucio, M (2014) 'The colonisation of employment regulation and industrial relations? Dynamics and developments over five decades of change' *Labor History* (forthcoming).

Martínez Lucio, M., Jenkins, S. and Noon. M (1999) 'The question of teamwork and union identity in the Royal Mail: Beyond negotiation?.' In F. Mueller and S. Procter (eds.), *Teamworking* London: Macmillan

Martínez Lucio, M. and MacKenzie, R. (2004) 'Unstable boundaries? Evaluating the "new regulation" within employment relations'. *Economy and Society*, 33(1): 77–97.

Martínez Lucio, M. and MacKenzie, R. (2006) 'Developments in patterns of regulation in employment relations: Re-appraising views of the state in industrial relations analysis'. Paper presented to *Industrial Relations in Europe Conference*, Ljubljana, Slovenia, 31 August–2 September.

Martínez Lucio, M. and Stuart, M. (2011) 'The state, public policy and the renewal of HRM'. *International Journal of Human Resource Management*, 22(18): 3661–3671.

Murakami, T. (1997) 'The autonomy of teams in the car industry: A cross-national comparison'. *Work, Employment and Society*, 11(4): 749–758.

Murakami, T. (1999) 'Works councils and teamwork in a German car plant'. *Employee Relations*, 21(1): 26–44.

Panitch, L. (1981) 'Trade unions and the capitalist state'. *New Left Review*, 125 (January–February): 21–43.

Panitch, L. (1994) 'Globalisation and the state'. In R. Miliband and L. Panitch (eds.), *Socialist Register 1994: Between Globalism and Nationalism*. London: Merlin.

Poole, M. (1981) *Theories of Trade Unionism*. London: Routledge & Kegan Paul.

Ritchie, B. K. (2002) *Foreign Direct Investment and Intellectual Capital Formation in Southeast Asia*. Paris: OECD Development Centre, pp. 4–41.

Rogowski, R. (2000) 'Industrial relations as a social system'. *Industrielle Beziehungen*, 7(1): 97–126.

Ross, G. (1981) 'What is progressive about unions?' *Theory and Society*, 10: 609–643.

Rubery, J. (2011) 'Reconstruction amid deconstruction: Or why we need more of the social in European social models'. *Work, Employment and Society*, 25(4): 658–674.

Schmitter, P. C. (1974) 'Still the century of corporatism?' *The Review of Politics*, 36(1): 85–131.

Torfing, J. (1990) 'A hegemony approach to capitalist regulation'. In R. B. Bertramsen, J. P. Thomson and J. Torfing (eds.), *State, Economy and Society*. London: Unwin Hyman.

Ugarte, S. (2012) 'Women's relative position in the labour market segment of Argentina and Chile'. Paper presented at the *Fairness at Work Research Centre Conference*, University of Manchester, 6–7 September.

Wailes, N., Bamber, G. J. and Lansbury, R. D. (2011) 'International and comparative employment relations: An introduction'. In G. J. Bamber, R. D. Lansbury and N. Wailes (eds.), *International and Comparative Employment Relations: Globalization and Change*. London: Sage.

Wergin, N. E. (2003) 'Teamwork in the automobile industry – An Anglo-German comparison'. *European Political Economy Review*, 1(2), 152–190.

Whitley, R. (2007) *Business Systems and Organizational Capabilities: The Institutional Structuring of Competitive Competences*. Oxford: Oxford University Press.

Section 2

The internal environment

4 Pay and remuneration in multinationals

Óscar Rodríguez-Ruiz

Learning objectives

- To understand the nature of payment systems and their development
- To comprehend the development of payment systems in the context of MNCs
- To engage with the problems and challenges of reward systems in relation to IHRM
- To explain some of the ongoing issues in relation to globalization

Introduction

Pay is a central element in labour relations, and one of the most important human resource management (HRM) activities. It plays a key role in organizational functioning, determining the success of the whole human resources (HR) system. The effectiveness and fairness of the management of people is dependent to a great extent on reward policies. The wage relation significantly affects attitudes, work behaviours and organizational events. For employees, compensation is a source of monetary value, benefits and job satisfaction. For employers, it is a payment for a service delivered and a cost of doing business in emerging global markets. Decisions on pay also have political and social implications. In this context, payment systems that define small differences in earnings have been considered egalitarian. Conversely, systems that fix a hierarchy of wages based on large differentials are labelled inegalitarian. With the globalization of markets and the development of multinational companies (MNCs), it is increasingly necessary to understand pay in an international context. Governments compete hard to attract foreign direct investment (FDI), and global firms play an important part in this, being a source of capital, employment, know-how and managerial philosophies. According to Fenwick (2004: 308), international compensation is 'the provision of monetary and non-monetary rewards, including base salary, benefits, perquisites, long- and short-term incentives, valued by employees in accordance with their relative contributions to MNCs' performance'. International reward policies must be adapted to the 'needs and expectations of very different groups of subsidiaries and employees located in different countries with different legal systems' (Hiltrop 2002: 330). Thus, pay is administered differently in organizations, depending on business strategy, economic environments, institutional frameworks and cultural factors. MNCs manage an international workforce from different cultural backgrounds and deal with multiple employment relations frameworks. Their location in different national business systems leads to different attitudes towards pay. As a result, international operations can generate differences in the levels and types of compensation provided in each country or region. The challenge of creating a fair pay system in countries with different cultures and legal frameworks raises serious issues in terms of internal and external equity. Internal equity demands consistency regarding the way that employees doing equal jobs are paid. External equity requires the matching of the organization's pay rates with those of other firms. This chapter provides a general view of the main frameworks, controversies and shortcomings of the compensation policies of MNCs. It attempts to cover the diverse developments that are affecting global wage relations at the beginning of the 21st century. The next section of this chapter presents the general background of payment systems and pay determination. It looks at the different approaches to determining compensation in the countries in which international companies operate. The third section discusses inegalitarian and egalitarian systems as competing forms of pay regulation. Specifically, it explores how wage bargaining in MNCs can take place at different levels. The fourth section describes recent developments in payment systems, noting that the pressures towards standardization and cost reduction can undermine equality and labour standards. Some final thoughts are discussed in the last section.

To paint a comprehensive picture of global compensation issues in MNCs, some preliminary observations are necessary. Historically, the vast majority of international compensation literature has been marked by three characteristics: emphasis on the debate about the centralization or localization of pay in international companies; disregard of the study of reward policies for non-managerial workers; and lack of attention to equality and fairness issues.

The first major characteristic is that, traditionally, *the central debate about compensation in MNCs has been focused on the influence of national factors and strategic alignment in the design of pay systems*. As Bloom et al. (2003) point out, managers have a strong preference for aligning the design of compensation criteria with the organizational context. The companies that follow this approach look for the reproduction of headquarters' remuneration schemes in all locations ('one pay system all over the world'). Conversely, other businesses try to create as many compensation systems as the host contexts in which they compete ('many countries, many compensation systems'). This controversy reveals a confrontation between markets and nations as competing forms of determination of the compensation system. MNCs such as IBM judge that aligning pay policies with business strategy and corporate culture is more important than adapting to local customs and idiosyncrasies. However, practices regarding pay levels, forms of pay and pay structures differ across countries. For example, while European firms have a long tradition of offering non-cash benefits, American companies use more intensively cash-based compensation. Unlike Japanese MNCs, which link pay to seniority, US international firms trust firmly in pay based on individual performance. These facts reinforce the idea that international compensation must be tailored to fit national cultures and variations in contextual factors. Nevertheless, in recent years, with shifts in the power of capital relative to states, many MNCs only adapt themselves to the national structures of collective bargaining after being compelled to do so. As a consequence, friction between company practices and local prevailing conditions in terms of national culture and business systems is growing all over the world. Local institutions, such as governments, trade unions and consumer groups, are warning about the dangers that globalization entails for labour standards and industrial relations traditions (Martínez Lucio 2009).

Second, *international HRM has concentrated mainly on remuneration for international managers, disregarding non-managerial workers* (Lowe et al. 2002; Almond 2004; Almond et al. 2006). However, compensation in MNCs is more than merely fixing sophisticated remuneration packages for expatriate elites isolated in upper-class dwellings in which they do not have contact with the local culture of the destination country. The study of reward management of the entire workforce reveals that MNCs today use pay determination systems that differ significantly between manual and managerial job holders. A thorough analysis of pay and remuneration needs to take into account the full range of workers employed by international businesses, distinguishing between the compensation schemes of managerial and non-managerial employees. This is a key distinction, as there is great variety in the amount of compensation offered by MNCs to their employees. In fact, strong criticism has arisen about the overpayment of executives in comparison to rank-and-file employees. For example, in Switzerland, where managers are the highest paid in Europe, different groups collected signatures to call for a national vote to change Swiss law to increase transparency and accountability in executive pay. Lower wages and poorer working conditions often seem to be associated with blue-collar positions, while upper-level managers benefit from individualized packages ('cafeteria approach') which include a company car, club membership, insurance, educational tuition, and so on (Wentland 2003).

Recent debates about global compensation show that there is great disagreement about 'what represents best practice in compensation management' (Guthrie 2007: 345). Specifically, issues such as *fairness and equality are not sufficiently addressed*. In the context of international business, the application of the principle of equal pay for work of equal value is especially complex. Reward policies cannot be 'informed by business strategy in isolation from considerations of internal and external equity' (Perkins and White 2008: 364). This means that consistency and fairness have to influence reward management within and across the organizations. Apparently, the MNCs' expertise allows them to pay higher wages than local competitors in many countries (OECD 2008). Equality of pay could be insurance against worker turnover and industrial unrest. Nevertheless, wage dispersion is growing between companies and within organizational units.

The general background of payment systems and pay determination

To address the complexities of pay in MNCs, it is necessary to clarify the differences between the concepts of pay structure, pay systems, pay criteria and pay levels. The *pay structure* is the pattern of pay relations in a company that is determined by both internal factors (culture, strategy and structure) and external factors (national idiosyncrasies, legislation, market characteristics and so on). It involves an ordering of pay rates for jobs or groups of jobs, and deals with issues of internal equity of the salary. The processes involved in remunerating employees within the pay structure constitute the pay form or *pay system* (Lowry 2002; Guthrie 2007). There are four types of system: time-based pay; competence- and skills-based pay; individual-performance-related pay; and organizational-performance-related pay. The first type rewards employees for the amount of time they spend at work. In this case, compensation is based on the job position. Competence-based remuneration is not based on the job but rather on the skills of the individual. The third category rewards individuals according to some measure of their performance, such as output or service quality. Finally, the fourth type consists of group-based pay systems that reward teams or organizational subunits or entire organizations according to the firm's performance. *Pay criteria* represent the basis on which organizations determine and distribute rewards. The concept of *pay level* refers to the average compensation paid by a particular firm relative to that paid by its competitors. The salary levels are the outcome of corporate pay policies and determine the external equity of the wages. Sometimes it is possible for similar pay policies to result in very different levels of salary (Fay 2008).

The design of the structure and systems of pay in MNCs is a central issue affected by a wide range of influences. Among these influencing factors, Edwards and Ferner (2002) have identified country of origin effects, host country effects, dominance effects and pressures for international integration. *Country of origin effects* can be perceived in the extension of the basic principles of work organization of the MNC's home country to its international operations. Japanese companies follow this form of reward strategy, 'transplanting' the HR system of the parent company to the subsidiaries. There are also *influences of the destination country on the pay policies of global companies*. For example,

McDonald's included overtime pay in its reward system to adapt to Japanese regulations (Royle 2010). At the same time, the determination of pay can be affected by the *imitation of the HRM practices of the dominant states*. American firms are perceived as being innovative in their management of pay and performance, introducing forms of rewards that have become commonplace in other industrialized countries (Muller-Camen et al. 2001). This trend has led to an Americanization of compensation schemes, considered to be global best practices. Thus, companies such as Toshiba are abandoning traditional Japanese reward forms and increasing pay for performance. Finally, it is possible to note *pressures for international integration* when MNCs apply similar pay systems across their subsidiaries to reinforce uniformity and control. This is the case with Walmart and its low wages policy. Country of origin and host country pressures have generated two methods of compensation: home country based or host country based. The first involves exporting the pay schemes of the nation of the parent company, with minimal adjustment, to the destination country. Host-country-based compensation attempts to adapt reward practices to the destination country's culture and standards. The underlying philosophy of this view is that 'differences in national cultures call for differences in management practices' (Newman and Nolen 1996: 753). According to this perspective, cultural norms 'of fair treatment within countries act as foundations for employee expectations for their pay' (Graham and Trevor 2000: 136). Thus, we can observe that, in cultures with high individualism, there is a greater use of performance-related pay linked to formal appraisals of individual effort (Cleveland et al. 2000). In general terms, the companies that follow the host country approach are adapters that try to design pay systems matching as closely as possible the local cultural preferences, economic conditions and social constraints. In this vein, it is curious that sometimes even local competitors set the institutional parameters for employment relations in multinational subsidiaries. For example, the Spanish-owned retail store El Corte Inglés has used its power and influence to fix pay and working conditions in the Spanish supermarket sector, which also determines the behaviour of the French MNC Carrefour in Spain (Royle and Ortíz 2009).

Obviously, there are hybrid systems combining elements of home and host approaches in many MNCs. For example, regional approaches are applied when an expatriate makes a commitment to work within a particular region of the world. Then a benchmark of wages is fixed for the operations throughout this cluster of countries with similar values. In line with this approach, the EU as a whole can be considered as a destination country for MNCs. In recent times, the formation of trade blocs is 'pushing the trend toward regional executive compensation plans' (Gross and Wingerup 1999: 31).

In any case, whether or not MNCs develop global HR policies is shaped by the extent and nature of their international integration (Edwards 2011). There are a great variety of MNCs, and each has different incentives for implementing homogeneous pay practices. Companies that provide standardized goods and services, such as UPS, enjoy benefits from making their HR practices uniform. Conversely, firms with an internationally fragmented production process, such as the leading American IT companies, do not need major commonalities in their employment relations. Following Perlmutter (1969) (see Chapter 1), it is possible to distinguish three types of MNCs: ethnocentric, polycentric and geocentric. Ethnocentric MNCs have a centralized structure, and subsidiaries follow the practices of the parent company. Their business approach is global, providing standardized goods and services. Polycentric MNCs develop a local adaptation strategy based on decentralization and autonomy for affiliates. In these firms, the management practices of the subsidiaries conform to the local practice of the destination country. Finally, geocentric MNCs combine characteristics of both global and multi-domestic companies, balancing global efficacy and national responsiveness. Logically, each category of MNC has a different approach to compensation and benefits. For example, polycentric companies show the greatest interest in localizing pay policies.

The pressures to develop globally standardized pay policies are strong, but the diversity of socioeconomic paradigms and the heterogeneous nature of MNCs at the same time cause convergence and divergence in reward practices. While internationalization has become a driver towards greater consistency (Chiang 2005: 1548), differences are unavoidable among culturally sensitive areas. In this global scenario, the MNC can reinforce the symbolic value of compensation policies (Zajac and Westphal 1995) by accepting the demands of the institutional environment.

The duality of home country–host country reflects the need to achieve a balance in MNCs between global integration and local responsiveness. The first studies of this issue supported the idea that international firms tend to adapt to local practices rather than exporting their own HRM policies (Marginson and Sisson 1994; Rosenzweig and Nohria 1994). However, in recent times many international companies have adopted a global element in the way they manage their international workforces. They make important investments in technology to standardize reward management practice and want to follow a common recipe for compensating workforce members irrespective of the operating environment (Perkins and White 2008). Many of them have adopted a 'quick-fix' philosophy, moving, hiring, paying and firing people around the world without much advance reflection. A few are concerned with the implementation of 'global compensation systems that allow the organization to maintain the flexibility and ease of transfer between countries and regions while providing employees a just wage' (Watson and Singh 2005: 33). It is significant that, in the past, global pay programmes for executives were defined at the corporate level, while strategies for other employee groups were determined either regionally or locally. But now, as employers want to facilitate mobility and reinforce organizational culture, they are attempting to globalize reward schemes below the executive level (Mercer 2007). MNCs try to somehow define an international employment system where the wage relation is mainly determined by cost containment criteria.

Competing forms of pay regulation

As Bloom et al. (2003: 1364) point out, 'compensation is embedded in many nations' social contracts'. This means that the national realities of industrial relation systems condition the salary structures. There are national business systems that differ in terms of labour relations, regulation and patterns of education and training (see Chapters 3, 6 and 9). Thus, in liberal market economies, such as the United States or the United Kingdom, the weakness of the institutions of wage determination above the firm level has led to a consolidation of inegalitarian/decentralized/individual systems of pay. Conversely, in countries such as Sweden or Denmark, where there are social market economies, government regulations have standardized employment conditions, thus promoting more egalitarian/centralized/collective systems of pay (Sánchez Marín 2008). Inegalitarian and egalitarian systems represent competing forms of pay regulation in MNCs. The former are associated with large differentials in earnings. The emphasis is on variable pay and external equity. Compensation administration is flexible, and parties are allowed great freedom to settle working conditions. Government intervention is minimal. By contrast, egalitarian systems promote shared incentives and small differences in wages. Pay is based on professional categories, and internal equity is important. Compensation procedures are formal, and control is exerted by collective bargaining and the state. In recent years, international companies seem to be moving from 'paying the job' to 'paying the person'. Nations with an individualistic culture have emphasized inegalitarian/decentralized/person-based pay, and their MNCs have tried to customize executive salaries at the individual level. This vision is coherent with the American ideal of 'employment at will', in which pay determination involves only agreement between the firm and the wage earners. The emphasis on individual employee contributions, usually associated with a lean workforce constantly adapted to changing markets and organizational demands, does not work well in many countries (Newman and Nolen 1996). It seems clear, for example, that the use of 'forced distributions' in MNCs to rank employees according to their level of performance has been a failure in some European nations. In countries with egalitarian/centralized/collective systems, the politics of wage distribution involves negotiation between unions and employers, and firms and sectors are included in a single wage settlement. The governments usually extend union-negotiated wage contracts to non-union members. Within these systems, collective sectoral bargaining has a number of effects on the management of pay. This is the case in Germany, where work councils co-determine bonus rates and performance-related remuneration. Traditionally, pay systems were 'collectivistic in nature', involving 'natural incremental progression along the pay structure' (Lowry 2002: 158). Nevertheless, this collectivistic approach has been steadily replaced in recent decades by a more individualized focus in which moving up the corporate ladder allows for the negotiation of customized compensation packages. The extension of individual performance-related pay for managers and non-unionized workforces has been widespread. In this process, Western Europe's stronger labour regulation and more influential trade unions represent a major challenge for MNCs (Royle 2010).

Developments in payment systems

It is possible to identify different trends in the compensation policies of MNCs in recent years. The concentration of capital has stimulated the centralization of pay and the implementation of cost-reduction initiatives. At the same time, international companies have adopted avoidance strategies to promote control of their workforces. The asymmetric development of globalization has also provoked wage dispersion and a growth in inequities. The main features of these developments are explained below.

Centralization and standardization

Increasingly, MNCs are standardizing reward policies worldwide following headquarters' guidelines (Mercer HR Consultancy 2007). With the aim of achieving internal consistency, international firms are defining rules and procedures for uniform salary decisions and applying them throughout their organizations. The main purpose is to establish compensation systems based on the principle of flexibility for the employer (Milkovich and Bloom 1998) rather than matching local conditions. This flexibility is conceived as the ability to change wage conditions arbitrarily while allowing some 'cherry-picking' approaches for top executives who are sent overseas. The centralization of pay practices is particularly strong considering the autonomy that headquarters permit among subsidiaries in other areas of HRM (Almond et al. 2006). Key strategic salary decisions are taken in the home country by nationals of the home country which determine the behaviour of the firm at the international level. It is significant that few organizations have compensation professionals based outside of their headquarters (Mercer HR Consultancy 2007). Thus, corporate HR specialists 'adopt the role of corporate policy integrity guardians' (Perkins and White 2008: 373), imposing uniform practices and avoiding the need to analyse each location on a case-by-case basis. Obviously, this orientation towards standardization does not mean an exactly identical approach in all the company's subsidiaries, but rather the adoption of a firm-based system of pay with uniform grading policies and similar criteria for measuring individual performance and bonus payments. Indeed, as Pudelko and Harzing (2008) remark, the standardization of personnel practices in general, and of compensation in particular, can gravitate towards two different poles: towards headquarters and towards global best practices. In the latter case, it must not be forgotten that corporate HR is the department responsible for collecting examples of best practice and disseminating them from its central position. The degree of centralization varies over time and is subject to negotiation at the subsidiary level, though subsidiaries have to justify deviations from central policies. Furthermore, head office permission is required for major expenditure. The central administration of the reward and incentive system has a number of advantages. First, it makes the determination of salaries a simpler process defined by the global labour market (Phillips and Fox 2003). This simplicity mitigates the risks derived from operating in multiple and diverse economic environments, and employment and taxation regimes. Second, the centralization of data enables headquarters to gain a global view of pay across the organization. Processes can be benchmarked to the industry (Solomon 1995), and cutting costs is easier, because compensation packages are seen in a company-wide context. Under these circumstances, differential compensation strategies are deemed unnecessary, and companies can concentrate on the definition of common job descriptions to achieve economies of scale. In general terms, development of a centralized policy has brought more management control and pressures for efficiency.

In conclusion, it seems that while the HRM function is under pressure to adapt to local labour markets, pay policies in MNCs are increasingly centralized in corporate HR departments. Executives at the head office possess resources and technologies to apply the pay practices with which they are most familiar. Compensation policies are intimately linked to financial control, a competence retained by the corporative centre. A culture-free approach to compensation is steadily being promoted and applied almost universally. A good example of this trend is Compaq, a company that has been a pioneer in introducing corporate global pay.

Avoidance of national regulations

MNCs are political systems in which different organizational actors seek to extend the application of global policies (see Chapter 2). They develop a number of avoidance strategies to overcome the national regulations that make the implementation of homogeneous practices difficult. Since the 1980s, there has been extensive evidence of the progressive growth of these avoidance strategies, particularly among US MNCs (Muller-Camen et al. 2001). National tax and employment relation systems function as equalizing factors in many countries. This protection is deemed by MNCs to be an impediment to the globalization of pay criteria. To achieve flexibility, they try to avoid mandatory and customary pay practices, seeking alternatives in terms of response to governmental action. Thus, salary conditions are often presented as something non-negotiable, reducing the claims of both workers and states. The avoidance of national regulations is reinforced by the 'structural bargaining power' of MNCs (Phillips and Fox 2003: 465) that allows them to place workers and countries in competition for the available jobs on offer. This power has increased in recent years as MNCs have the 'weapon of offshore investment' (McMichael 1999: 31). In the context of recession, global firms exploit the internal heterogeneity of national business systems by locating units in less developed areas, and areas of high unemployment and/or low union organization (Royle 1998: 1042). Over the years, some MNCs have moved their production lines to developing countries with non-unionized workforces to take advantage of low wages. This is a strategy aimed at extracting value by underpaying workers in environments that can easily be entered and exited. McDonald's represents another example of a MNC that has been able to avoid local conformance pressures by taking advantage of weaknesses in regulations. In recent times, US global firms have been promoting low-labour-regulation approaches to impose management prerogatives. International compensation within these large organizations represents an attempt to move away from systems of collective bargaining. The general 'anti-union animus' of some firms (Almond et al. 2006) reveals a desire to avoid the pay constraints of the standard sectoral system of collective agreement considered as an 'additional hurdle' (Gross and Wingerup 1999: 28). Obviously, overriding local norms has consequences such as penalties or losing the goodwill of the local actors. Nevertheless, some MNCs carry on improving their profits by extracting concessions from the workforce. The following case study outlines some of the issues that emerge in relation to how MNCs move and use workers around different national contexts within their operations, and the implications such a strategy has for payment systems. This was a very high-profile case in the European Union.

Case study: The Lindsey Oil Refinery

The profound metamorphosis that the global economy is experiencing frequently shows how MNCs can use the mobility of capital and labour to challenge nationally managed employment systems and local forms of administration of wages. In January 2009, the Lindsey Oil Refinery, located in North Lincolnshire (United Kingdom), was the 'epicentre' of an industrial relations dispute that is indicative of the connections between the management of people in MNCs and the broader processes of globalization in a context of economic downturn and fear of unemployment. The site, operated by the French multinational Total S.A., was the third-largest refinery in Britain, processing 10 million tons of crude oil per annum. When additional work was needed on the construction of a desulphurization plant, Jacobs Engineering Group Inc., an American multinational that was carrying out the expansion of the refinery, switched work from a British subcontractor to IREM, an Italian company, which brought in 200 Italian and Portuguese platers, welders, electricians and pipefitters (The *Guardian* 2009a). Despite assurances from Total that these foreign workers were being paid at UK national rates and had identical conditions to their British counterparts, regional officials from the unions accused the French company of discriminating against host country nationals by undercutting their pay and labour conditions (World Socialist Website 2009). In the utilities sector, it is very common for MNCs that own and operate facilities to bring in foreign workers for large construction projects (Immigration

Watch Canada 2009). The freedom of employers and their subcontractors to decide whom to hire, the freedom of EU nationals to work abroad and the power of unions to enforce national agreements on pay and conditions are at stake in these cases. Essentially, at the heart of the dispute in Lindsey the use of the EU Posted Workers Directive (96/721/EC) (IDS 2009). This norm requires that the minimum terms and conditions of employment set down by national law or 'universally applicable' collective agreements are extended to posted workers. According to the management of some MNCs, the UK National Agreement for the Construction and Engineering Industry (NACEI) is not a 'universally applicable' agreement. Therefore, they consider that it is not a requirement to pay workers from other EU states rates settled by employers and trade unions, the only limit being the host state's minimum wage. Major MNCs such as Shell, BP, E.ON and EDF are members of NACEI, and they routinely subcontract parts of their work to other companies. The agreement determines the actual rates of pay for workers at all major sites. In the case of the Lindsey refinery, unions argued that non-unionized foreign workers were employed at Grade 3, getting lower rates of pay than British employees employed at Grade 5. Whether this happened or not, it is difficult to be precise about the situation because of a lack of information about the full details of the contractual arrangements (IDS 2009). However, what is clear is that the problems at Lindsey could be attributed to poor industrial relations (The *Guardian* 2009b). The main issue is not to do with xenophobia or economic nationalism. It is about big global employers taking advantage of the ambiguities in the regulations to impose their pay systems and depress wages where possible. The Posted Workers Directive does not identify clearly how mandatory standards can be guaranteed through collective bargaining. As a result, workers can see their individual rights eroded by free movement of labour and work. To the extent that global capital and labour are not going to go away, it is necessary to watch subcontracting chains that undermine social regulation. The Lindsey episode could be an example of the increasing latitude that MNCs have to challenge European labour and social protection.

Questions

1. Do you think that it is easy to determine who the employer was in the construction of the desul-phurization plant in Lindsey? What are the consequences of this in terms of pay management?
2. Is Total S.A. following an avoidance strategy to impose a global pay policy? Is the company following a host country approach? Justify your answer.
3. What equality problems in terms of pay do you perceive in this case? Explain.
4. What are the implications of the Posted Workers Directive? Look for decisions of the European Court of Justice that deal with this norm and analyse them. Discuss in groups.
5. Do you consider that there is a need for defining international labour standards in order to govern the behaviour of MNCs? How could these standards be protected?

Cost containment

MNCs have been putting a great emphasis on cost control in recent years. Managing populations across borders is a big investment, and there is a need for 'doing more with less and better people' (Swaak 1995). The first manifestation of the cost containment trend has been *MNCs' business expansion, motivated to a great extent by the cost of labour*. Developing countries have generally been considered as sources of cheap workers. This is the case among the Asian-Pacific states that do not mandate pay increases. Their productivity and low wages have provoked an exodus of industrial companies to enclaves of low-cost manufacturing. Simultaneously, *the mobility of the international workforce has brought 'increased capabilities and often lower costs to multinationals'* (Lowe et al. 2002: 46). It is interesting that companies are curtailing sharply the high costs associated with expatriate compensation packages. Foreign assignments are increasingly considered to be part of a normal course of career development for the employee (Sims and Schraeder 2005; Watson and Singh 2005) and a cost-sensitive investment for the company. Consultants are hired to design compensation solutions, and expatriates are recommended to use 'efficient shopper indexes'. The intensive scrutiny of accommodation and education expenses, and a reduction in the use of cost of living allowances are some of the measures oriented towards cost containment. There has also been an *intense movement towards variable pay*. This means a subtle introduction of pay at risk, because an important portion of the employees' compensation is uncertain and depends on individual, group or organizational performance. Muller-Camen et al. (2001) mention as an example IBM's attempt to introduce a worldwide bonus system which reduced guaranteed monthly salaries and increased flexible pay. *The standardization of pay policies is also justified for reasons of cost and economies of scale* (Almond et al. 2006). As getting timely information about each country's employment laws, tax regulation and market conditions is difficult and expensive, MNCs provide elements that are uniform around the world. By using easily available enterprise software, companies can track and compare labour costs, facilitating the role of managers who have bonuses tied to their success in cutting the personnel payroll.

Growth of inequities

The rule of fair and effective remuneration has been considered a basic principle of the design of compensation systems. However, *the inegalitarian effects of international compensation are growing in the global context (see Chapter 5)*. Preserving equality in MNCs is difficult because of geographical and cultural differences and the mix of home, host and third-country nationals (Fenwick 2004). To promote fairness, employees at the same organizational level and performing an identical level of tasks must have similar rewards. Nevertheless, because international businesses operate across nations at different levels of economic development, 'disparity in compensation is unavoidable' (Chen et al. 2002: 807). The increasing contact between employees from different countries has made salary and grading differences more obvious, leading to problems of internal equity. For this reason, MNCs have attempted to incorporate national cultural norms into their pay programmes to receive favourable assessments of fairness (Graham and Trevor 2000: 142).

Equality problems show that traditional forms of compensation are required to change. The balance sheet approach, based on a salary in line with compensation in the home country, results in clear inequities between local and expatriate employees. In the host country approach, there can be notable differences in pay between workers performing similar jobs in different countries. Paradoxically, the recent trend towards the standardization of pay has increased inequality, provoking a loss of work arrangements and social standards. At the same time, *the sky-high growth of executive compensation has also exacerbated the lack of equity*. It is significant that the higher an employee's organizational level, the more likely he or she is to be included in a profit sharing scheme. Egalitarian systems of pay are being replaced progressively by the American model, which promotes large differences in compensation between top managers and average workers. In a context where pay levels trend downwards, exceptional treatments are eroding trust in the reward systems and employees' perceptions of fairness.

Final thoughts

This chapter has reviewed the key topics and emerging issues that are shaping the compensation polices of MNCs in the global economy of the beginning of the 21st century. It has explored the complexities of the pay systems of international firms and their major implications in terms of inequality and erosion of the national basis of the wage relation. We round off with some final considerations.

In theory, ethnocentric exporting of reward practices and the 'locally responsive' response are considered extreme positions in the management of pay in MNCs. The *long debate around centralization–local responsiveness cannot be resolved by declaring one position more important than another* (Pudelko and Harzing 2008). Nevertheless, some global firms have a 'strong interest in establishing common reward structures worldwide where possible' (Almond et al. 2006: 126; Mercer HR Consultancy 2007). They try hard to develop common elements in pay policies with the aim of reinforcing their organizational competences and original national base. The motor company Toyota, for example, has used compensation policies to emphasize its Japanese identity. Frequently, the management of pay is considered to be a core competence that cannot be decentralized. As a consequence, many international firms regard compensation as an essential element of HR practice and try to prevent host-country effects imposing a global reward strategy in local markets. This involves a certain standardization of work, grade of jobs and appraisals. For the managers of large corporations, a global mindset creates cross-border comparability and the consolidation of an internal labour market. In this sense, we can say that *international compensation has been 're-centralized' in recent years as 'home country effect has become stronger'* (Muller-Camen et al. 2001: 36). A common approach to pay is understood as a sort of 'global glue' (Gross and

Wingerup 1999), and companies such as Unilever, which have traditionally had a decentralized structure, are no longer allowing autonomy to subsidiaries to develop their HR policies. Basically, the home-pay management system is conceived as an organizational capability that can be replicated in other places. Because of this, reverse knowledge transfer from the affiliates to the corporate office barely occurs in the area of pay. There are international companies that maintain communities of practice devoted to compensation at the regional and local level, but they constitute an exception. The 'one size fits all' approach, supported by compensation-consulting firms, eventually shapes the nature of institutional frameworks (Edwards and Kuruvilla 2005).

However, if we *take into account the importance of local pay drivers, 'it is impossible 'to pretend that pay globalization is ever purely global'* (Gross and Wingerup 1999: 29). For this reason, in some circumstances, MNCs do not impose a homogeneous set of practices in all their foreign subsidiaries. The home-country influences, therefore, cannot be automatically assumed. As a general rule, MNCs export their compensation practices in countries with weak legislation and unorganized unions (Cleveland et al. 2000). When union affiliation is low, global companies can operate outside of national agreements and determine pay at the individual level. However, if there is a high level of regulation, they implement host country schemes. It seems that MNCs only accommodate to national arrangements when institutions set limits to what is feasible on the part of actors. If firms are not able to avoid collective bargaining, they initiate cooperative relations in an attempt to improve their image and reflect the norms of the host country. Thus, in strong institutional contexts, international firms are pragmatic in following the legal requirements to negotiate wages and working time with trade unions. However, when local norms are broad and diffuse, large firms find room to manoeuvre. This fact demonstrates that MNCs take advantage of what countries offers in terms of organizational consistency and minimization of costs. *The standardization towards head office and global best practices is limited by differences in national, cultural and institutional characteristics, which force MNCs to localize pay management.*

In other cases, MNCs do not derive benefits from standardizing HR policies. This happens in international companies that follow a local adaptation strategy with employees from very diverse cultural backgrounds. When the workforce presents multiple cultural influences, a local responsiveness strategy is justified. Conversely, the use of this strategy is deemed a 'waste of resources' when there is cultural similarity. In this case, adherence to parent company practices does not mean indifference to local practices. In the end, *the balance between globalization of pay and local responsiveness is mediated by pressures for the minimization of costs.*

As mentioned earlier, *the management of the international workforce is contingent on the nature and form of the international integration of the firm.* Different types of MNCs will have different incentives to build global HR policies. Edwards (2011) has distinguished four types of MNCs with different approaches to HRM. With respect to compensation, we can say, first, that MNCs looking for financial economies through unrelated diversification are not likely to implement global reward policies, because they have a wide range of different goods and services. Second, the division of labour between subsidiaries can generate another exception to the principle of global pay. There are MNCs that carry out different aspects of their production across their various sites. If there is segregation between labour-intensive locations and knowledge-based locations, firms have little incentive to implement homogeneous pay policies (Edwards and Kuruvilla 2005). Frequently, policies focused on cost minimization are applied in countries that do not constitute a source of competitive advantage, while more sophisticated approaches to pay are used in other places. A third category of global firms is formed by MNCs diversified into related areas. This is the case, for example, where pharmaceutical companies replicate the production process at different sites. These businesses have significant scope to implement a global pay policy, but this is constrained by the need to adapt to the different host countries. Finally, there are MNCs with a high level of international integration that are producing standardized goods and services – such as Starbucks, for example. These kinds of companies develop a common element in relation to how they pay their workforce across countries. Within these global industries, forces for worldwide integration are strong, and subsidiaries have little room to shape specific HRM practices.

As a final reflection, it is essential to consider that often corporate decisions about pay are not the product of rational calculations, but rather the result of political factors. Political behaviour complements the economic behaviour of MNCs. In this vein, actors at corporate headquarters see global policies as a way of extending their influence and authority within the firm. At other times, corporate priorities around the rationalization and standardization of pay cannot be implemented because subsidiary management has considerable power because of their knowledge of local markets. Different subsidiaries are exposed to different pressures to conform to parent practices. As Edwards (2011) admits, the form of international integration shapes the firm's approach to HRM but, it is 'the ideological commitment on the part of senior management' that ultimately determines the management of people. In recent decades, the managerial strategy of 'minimizing differences' to remain profitable (Perkins and White 2008) seems to have been adopted by many global companies. While in the past subsidiaries had scope to influence and reinterpret pay policies, now headquarters impose their reward programmes increasingly across the different operating environments. However, MNCs' power to execute their strategies can be moderated by 'localized points of resistance' (Phelps and Waley 2004: 19) and governmental and regulatory bodies.

Reflective questions

1. What are the main factors that form the basis of national payments systems?
2. In what way are such systems different?
3. What are the major changes taking place and why?
4. What are the consequences of such developments and what new tensions may they bring?

Recommended reading

- Baeten, X. (2010) 'Global compensation and benefits management: The need for communication and coordination'. *Compensation and Benefits Review*, 42(5): 392–402.
- Nuti, M. D. (2011) 'Industrial relations at FIAT: Dr Marchionne's class war'. *European Review of Labour and Research*, 17(2): 251–254.
- Watson, B. W., Jr. and Singh, G. (2005) 'Global pay systems: Compensation in support of a multinational strategy'. *Compensation and Benefits Review*, 37(1): 33–36.

References

Almond, P. (2004) 'The management of pay, wage classification and performance in the UK subsidiaries of US MNCs'. Paper presented at *2nd Conference on Human Resource Management in Multinational Corporations*, Barcelona, July.

Almond, P., Muller-Camen, M., Collings, D. G. and Quintanilla, J. (2006) 'Pay and performance'. In *American Multinationals in Europe: Managing Employment Relations across National Borders*, edited by P. Almond and A. Ferner. Oxford: Oxford University Press, pp. 119–145.

Bloom, M., Milkovich G. T. and Mitra, A. (2003) 'International compensation: Learning from how managers respond to variations in local host contexts'. *International Journal of Human Resource Management*, 14(8): 1350–1367.

Chen, C. C., Chui, J. and Chi, S. (2002) 'Making justice sense of local–expatriate compensation disparity: Mitigation by local referents, ideological explanations and interpersonal sensitivity in China–foreign joint ventures'. *Academy of Management Journal*, 45(4): 807–817.

Chiang, F. (2005) 'A critical examination of Hofstede's thesis and its application to international reward management'. *International Journal of Human Resource Management*, 16(9): 1545–1563.

Cleveland, J. N., Gunnigle, P., Heraty, N., Morley, M. and Murphy, K. R. (2000) 'US multinationals and human resource management: Evidence on HR practices in European subsidiaries'. *Journal of the Irish Academy of Management*, 21(1): 9–27.

Edwards, T. (2011) 'The nature of international integration and HR policies in multinational companies'. *Cambridge Journal of Economics*, 35(3): 483–498.

Edwards, T. and Ferner, A. (2002) 'The renewed "American challenge": A review of employment practices in US multinationals'. *Industrial Relations Journal*, 33(2): 94–111.

Edwards, T. and Kuruvilla, S. (2005) 'International HRM: National business systems, organizational politics and the international division of labour in MNCs'. *International Journal of Human Resource Management*, 15(1): 1–21.

Fay, C. H. (2008) 'The global convergence of compensation practices'. In *Global Compensation: Foundations and Perspectives (HRM)*, edited by L. Gómez-Mejia and S. Werner. London: Routledge, pp. 129–141.

Fenwick, M. (2004) 'International compensation and performance management'. In *International Human Resource Management*, edited by A. Harzing and J. Van Ruysseveldt. London: Sage, p. 308.

Graham, M. E. and Trevor, C. O. (2000) 'Managing new pay program introduction to enhance the competitiveness of multinational corporations'. *Competitiveness Review*, 10(1): 136–154.

Gross, S. and Wingerup, P. L. (1999) 'Global pay? Maybe not yet'. *Compensation and Benefits Review*, 31(4): 25–34.

The Guardian (2009a) 'Mandelson to examine UK engineering in light of strikes', 16 February. http://www.theguardian.com/business/2009/feb/16/mandelson-strikes-uk-engineering

The Guardian (2009b) 'Wildcat strikes spread as Acas fails to end oil refinery dispute', 18 June. http://www.theguardian.com/politics/2009/jun/18/wildcat-strikes-oil-refinery

Guthrie, J. P. (2007) 'Remuneration: Pay effects at work'. In *The Oxford Handbook of Human Resource Management*, edited by P. Boxall, J. Purcell and P. Wright. Oxford/New York: Oxford University Press, pp. 344–363.

Hiltrop, J. M. (2002) 'Mapping the HRM practices of international organizations'. *Strategic Change*, 11(6): 329–338.

IDS (2009) 'Briefing note: Lindsey oil refinery dispute'. *IDS Pay Report*, February: 23–25.

Immigration Watch Canada (2009) 'Wildcat strikes over foreign workers spread across Britain', 30 January. http://www.immigrationwatchcanada.org/2009/01/30/wildcat-strikes-over-foreign-workers-spread-across-britain/

Lowe, K. B., Milliman, J., De Cieri, H. and Dowling, P. J. (2002) 'International compensation practices: A ten-country comparative analysis'. *Human Resource Management*, 41(1): 45–66.

Lowry, D. (2002) 'Reward management'. In *Human Resources in Organizations*, edited by J. Leopold. Harlow: Pearson Education, pp. 147–160.

McMichael, P. (1999) 'The global crisis of wage labour'. *Studies in Political Economy*, 58: 11–40.

Marginson, P. and Sisson, K. (1994) 'The structure of transnational capital in Europe: The emerging Euro-company and its implications for industrial relations'. In *New Frontiers in European Industrial Relations*, edited by R. Hyman and A. Ferner. Oxford: Blackwell, pp. 15–51.

Martínez Lucio, M. (2009) 'The organization of HR strategies: Narratives and power in understanding labour management in a context of fragmentation'. In *The Sage Handbook of Organisational Behaviour*, edited by S. Clegg and C. L. Cooper. London: Sage, pp. 323–339.

Mercer HR Consultancy (2007) *Global Compensation Strategy and Administration Survey*. Louisville, KY: Mercer.

Milkovich, G. T. and Bloom, M. (1998) 'Rethinking international compensation'. *Compensation and Benefits Review*, 30(1): 15.

Muller-Camen, M., Almond, P., Gunnigle, P., Quintanilla, J. and Tempel, A. (2001) 'Between home and host country: Multinationals and employment relations in Europe'. *Industrial Relations Journal*, 32(5): 435–448.

Newman, K. L. and Nolen, S. (1996) 'Culture and congruence: The fit between management practices and national culture'. *Journal of International Business Studies*, 27(4): 743.

OECD (2008) 'Do multinationals promote better pay and working conditions?'. *OECD Employment Outlook*, Paris.

Perkins, S. J. and White, G. (2008) *Employee Reward: Alternatives, Consequences and Contexts*. London: CIPD.

Perlmutter, H. (1969) 'The tortuous evolution of the multinational corporation'. *Columbia Journal of World Business*, 4(January–February): 9–18.

Phelps, N. A. and Waley, P. (2004) 'Capital versus the districts: A tale of one multinational company's attempt to disembed itself'. *Economic Geography*, 80(2): 191–215.

Phillips, L. and Fox, M. A. (2003) 'Compensation strategy in transnational corporations'. *Management Decision*, 41(5/6): 465–476.

Pudelko, M. and Harzing, A. W. (2008) 'The golden triangle for MNCs: Standardization towards headquarters practices, standardization towards global best practices and localization'. *Organizational Dynamics*, 37(4): 394–404.

Rosenzweig, P. M. and Nohria, N. (1994) 'Influences on human resource practices in multinational corporations'. *Journal of International Business Studies*, 2(25): 229–251.

Royle, T. (1998) 'Avoidance strategies and the German system of co-determination'. *International Journal of Human Resource Management*, 9(6): 1026–1047.

Royle, T. (2010) 'Low road Americanization and the global "McJob": A longitudinal analysis of work, pay and unionization in the international fast-food industry'. *Labor History*, 51(2): 249–270.

Royle, T. and Ortíz, L. (2009) 'Dominance effects from local competitors: Setting institutional parameters for employment relations in multinational subsidiaries—a case from the Spanish supermarket sector'. *British Journal of Industrial Relations*, 47(4): 653–675.

Sánchez Marín, G. (2008) 'National differences in compensation: The influence of the institutional and cultural context'. In *Global Compensation: Foundations and Perspectives (HRM)*, edited by L. Gómez-Mejia and S. Werner. London: Routledge, pp. 18–28.

Sims, R. H. and Schraeder, M. (2005) 'Expatriate compensation: An exploratory review of salient contextual factors and common practices'. *Career Development International*, 10(2): 98–108.

Solomon, C. M. (1995) 'Global compensation: Learn the ABCs'. *Personnel Journal*, 74(7): 70.

Swaak, R. E. (1995) 'Expatriate management: The search for best practices'. *Compensation and Benefits Review*, 27(2): 21.

Watson, B. W., Jr. and Singh, G. (2005) 'Global pay systems: Compensation in support of a multinational strategy'. *Compensation and Benefits Review*, 37(1): 33–36.

Wentland, D. M. (2003) 'A new practical guide for determining expatriate compensation: The comprehensive model'. *Compensation and Benefits Review*, 35(3): 45–49.

Word Socialist Website (2009) 'Report exposes false claims of British unions' "Britons First" campaign', 21 February. http://www.wsws.org/en/articles/2009/02/ukbf-f21.html?-view=print

Zajac, E. J. and Westphal, J. D. (1995) 'Accounting for the explanations of CEO compensation: Substance and symbolism'. *Administrative Science Quarterly*, 40: 283–308.

5 Equality, diversity and fairness as a new politics in multinational corporations

Fang Lee Cooke

Learning objectives

- To understand the notions of equality, fairness and diversity management in the context of human resource management
- To identify individual, organizational and institutional barriers to implementing equal opportunity regulations and diversity initiatives in an international environment for multinational firms
- To highlight tensions and the politics of equality and diversity initiatives at the organizational and national level
- To familiarize readers with organizational practices in different parts of the world
- To prepare readers for designing diversity initiatives in multinational operations

Introduction

The notion of fairness and justice is central to the academic debate and government policy orientation on equal opportunity and diversity/inclusiveness. The meaning of fairness, equality and diversity is socially constructed and embedded in a specific politico-historical context. Equal opportunity (EO) and diversity management (DM) have emerged as two related and important elements in human resource management (HRM). This is largely owing to the changes in the demographic makeup of the workforce and the internationalization of firms.

The emergence of *equality* and *diversity* policies in international HRM reflects not only the importance of a more transnational and multinational/cultural dimension to the workforce, but also the complex role of multinational corporations (MNCs) as political and economic actors and the opportunities and constraints they face in the global economy. In this chapter, we assess the equality and diversity policies and practices of MNCs by examining the internal management of these issues as well as the role of the broader institutional environments in shaping organizational practices.

This chapter consists of four main sections, in addition to the Introduction, Case Study and Conclusion. The first main section highlights the societal contexts in which equality and diversity issues manifest themselves. Within this broader context, the second section examines challenges facing MNCs in managing a diverse workforce. The third section contemplates sources of political pressure on equality and DM from the macro level, including the enactment of national regulations and the role of international regulatory bodies and voluntary global initiatives. In the fourth section, we analyze discourses of equality and diversity, their competing meanings, and the role of the institutional and organizational actors through a critical lens.

Equality and diversity in the international context

The term *equal opportunities* is associated with employment equity legislation related to discrimination as a result of individuals' characteristics, such as gender, age, ethnicity, religion, physical ability and sexual orientation. Many national governments have promulgated equal-opportunity-related legislation over the last three decades, although what 'equal opportunities' means and who may be included in the category for protection vary from country to country. The focus on and pressure to introduce EO legislation is not the same across nations, and its introduction is often a response to the changing political, socio-economic, labour market and employment relations environment.

The promulgation of EO legislation has often been accompanied by the launch of affirmative action (AA) programmes directed by the state. Some organizations have an EO policy in place partly to comply with statutory requirements and partly to portray a positive image that they are an EO employer. Gender equality constitutes a significant part of public debates, EO legislation and AA programmes. Unfortunately, despite the increasing provisions of anti-discrimination legislation and espoused commitment from organizations to equality, gender inequality at various stages of the employment process remains a significant feature in most countries, and is more pronounced in some than others (e.g., Davidson and Burke 2011; Yukongdi and Benson 2006). Other forms of inequality related to, for example, ethnicity, race, religion, age and sexuality, also commonly exist in organizational life, despite the fact that they have increasingly featured in the EO debate and legislation and policy.

Since the 1990s, a complementary, or what some would call a competing, concept to EO has emerged in the HRM literature: DM. The concept of managing diversity has its origin in the United States and emerged as an HR intervention in the mid-1980s. It is primarily a response to the demographic changes (e.g., more immigrants and women) in the workplace as well as in the customer base (Agocs and Burr 1996). It is also a response to the corporate discontent with the affirmative action approach imposed by the US government. Organizations are searching for an alternative to broaden the perceived narrow scope of affirmative action legislation that focuses primarily on recruitment. DM is seen as a way to address retention, integration and career development issues (Agocs and Burr 1996). The growing demands from the ethnic minority, women, older, disabled, gay and lesbian groups for equal rights and the consequent human rights legislation in the 1990s and 2000s gave further momentum to the need to recognize, accept and value individual differences at workplaces and in society more generally (Mor Barak 2005).

The concept of DM began to be propagated in countries outside of North America during the late 1990s. For example, Süß and Kleiner (2007) observed a sharp increase in the use of the concept in Germany since the late 1990s. In the United Kingdom, the concept has undoubtedly become more influential since the mid/late 1990s in part owing to the demographic change of the workforce, but more so because DM is seen as a more comprehensive and sophisticated approach to EO management that adds value to business. The Chartered Institute of Personnel and Development (CIPD) defines diversity as 'valuing everyone as an individual – valuing people as employees, customers and clients' (CIPD 2006: 2).

It is suggested that the objectives of DM are for organizations to increase awareness of cultural differences, develop the ability to recognize, accept and value diversity, minimize patterns of inequality experienced by those not in the mainstream, and modify organizational culture and leadership practices (Cox 1993; Soni 2000). DM is regarded as a better approach than EO because it adopts an inclusive approach that 'focuses on valuing people as unique individuals rather than on group-related issues covered by legislation' (CIPD 2007: 6). More recent DM literature advocates an inclusive approach to managing diversity that goes beyond organizational and national boundaries (e.g., Mor Barak 2005).

The transition from a focus on EO to DM signals a move away from an emphasis on procedural justice to a utilitarian approach that views DM as a means to an end to be managed strategically. In other words, it is a shift away from a negative perspective on staff who are disadvantaged and discriminated against to a more positive perspective of celebrating and valuing the differences among all employees and utilizing them in a creative way to benefit both the organization and individuals (Maxwell et al. 2001; also see Foster and Harris 2005 for key differences between managing EO and DM).

However, the distinction between EO and DM may in practice be far less clear (Foster and Harris 2005). As Ferner et al. (2005: 309) noted, despite growing

academic interest, DM is a poorly understood, increasingly slippery and controversial concept that is used 'in an all-embracing fashion to include not just the social categories of AA such as race and sex but a wide range of personal characteristics'. Consequently, the concept and moral soundness of DM remains a contentious issue (see below for further discussion; also see Lorbiecki and Jack 2000 for an overview of the conceptual premises and a critique of DM). Authors on strategic HRM (e.g., Bowen and Ostroff 2004; Nishii et al. 2008; Purcell 1999) have argued that the way firms adopt HRM practices has a significant impact on employees' perceptions of the intention of these practices. This perception will in turn affect the outcomes of the practices implemented.

It is important to note that the practice of DM may not necessarily lead to enhanced productivity. Academic studies on diversity–performance relationships have so far yielded inconclusive results. While some researchers argue that diversity leads to better group and ultimately organizational performance (e.g., Cox et al. 1991), others contend that diversity leads to a negative organizational performance outcome in part due to intra- and inter-group conflicts and communication deadlock derived from differences (e.g., Lau and Murnighan 1998; Tsui et al. 1992). Moreover, there may be tensions between a collective approach to managing diverse employee groups and a more individualized approach focusing on individual needs and abilities which may actually increase, rather than decrease, inequalities (e.g., Agocs and Burr 1996; Liff 1996). Ali et al.'s (2011) study also suggests that an industry-specific approach is required to manage a gender-diverse workforce to capture the benefits of diversity.

In addition, the utility of this US-originated concept in other societal contexts has been questioned by many researchers (e.g., Agocs and Burr 1996; Ferner et al. 2005; Healy and Oikelome 2007; Nishii and Özbilgin 2007). A number of country-specific studies have revealed unique societal contexts in which diversity issues are embedded. For example, Jones et al.'s (2000) study showed that the language used to describe diversity and the perception of diversity issues in New Zealand are markedly different from those manifested in the dominant discourse of DM embedded with US cultural assumptions. In African countries, politics assumes supreme importance in DM, and ethnicity dominates 'most national debates on diversity' as the central issue (Healy and Oikelome 2007: 1923). This is because some disadvantaged ethnic groups have been oppressed historically, and there are now increasing demands for radical remedial actions to address racial grievances. By contrast, ethnic groups in Japan and Korea are relatively homogenous, and as a result, gender, women's marital status, and their related employment status may be the key source of workforce diversity (Cooke 2010).

In the United States and the United Kingdom, workforce diversity may cover: gender, race, ethnicity, religion, age, disability, immigration status, social class, political association, marital status, parental status, sexual orientation, and ex-offenders, among other categories. Many of these differences are accepted by western societies, protected by law and acknowledged in company policy. Some of these characteristics, however, may not be acceptable socially or legally in Asian countries such as China and India. Furthermore, significant differences may exist within Asian countries. For example, caste, ethnicity, religion and gender are the main sources of diversity in India, whereas age, gender, disability, and place of origin (e.g., rural versus urban background) are the main causes of social inequality in China. India is a democracy in which 'inclusiveness' is the major politico-economic discourse at present. In furtherance of this thinking, talk of empowerment of socially disadvantaged groups is emerging as a powerful weapon for political parties to connect with their constituencies. By contrast, China is a socialist regime with centralized control by the communist party. Elimination of social inequality is intended to be achieved by introducing government policies and regulations through a top-down interventionist approach (Cooke 2011).

Managing an aging workforce is an issue in developed economies, whereas this is largely not the case in developing countries, where the population is relatively young, as is the workforce. In many developing countries, employment insecurity is relatively high and the provision of social security benefits is extended to few. Large groups of poor people are fighting for the very right to a basic living through low-paid employment with long working hours and poor conditions. The fact that they are treated unfairly is much less of a concern for some, and inequality in the workplace and in society generally is often accepted, internalized and unchallenged due to historically deep-rooted discrimination and the evident absence of remedial prospects. For example, Cooke and Saini's (2012) comparative study of DM in China and India revealed that as a strategic HRM concept, DM had been rarely heard of and featured even less in management discussions and presentations. In addition, management's indifferent attitude to DM may well be linked to the lack of voice and bargaining power of the disadvantaged groups in these countries.

In the European continent, the dissolution of the former communist countries, such as the Soviet Union and Czechoslovakia, and the increasing level of inter-country migration among the Central and Eastern European Countries (CEECs) have led to heightened tensions and sensitivities regarding the issues of national and ethnic identity, employment rights and protections. This is partly a consequence of the different policies adopted by the Central and Eastern European states in granting citizenship to the former Soviet Union citizens and the immigration status of migrants, with some governments being more inclusive than others. National or ethnic identity is thus based on the value attached to the membership of one or another national group. For Russian speakers in the Baltic republics, this is a rather complicated issue (Vedina and Vadi 2008). These enduring cultural heritage, social and political identities manifest themselves in the workplace through organizational policies, managerial preference and peer relationships. This poses further difficulties for foreign MNCs operating in CEECs because ethnic minority employees not only have to identify themselves with the host country's culture but also that of the MNCs.

MNCs and the management of equality and diversity

MNCs face a diverse set of incentives and pressures to adopt equality and diversity initiatives in their parent as well as host country operations (see Chapter 11). These incentives and pressures exist at the macro and micro level, and emanate from home and host countries (see Figure 5.1 and more discussion later). Efforts to manage equality and diversity are often marred by institutional challenges and societal tensions, as described in the previous section. In this section, we look at some of the tensions and challenges encountered by MNCs in managing a diverse workforce.

Existing studies on DM in MNCs have found that attempts to roll out US domestic diversity programmes globally often fail to achieve their objectives and/ or meet with strong resistance in the host country operations (e.g., Ferner et al. 2005; Nishii and Özbilgin 2007). This is mainly because the US-specific programmes fail to reflect the specific demographic profile and the legal, historical, political and cultural contexts of equality in the host countries. Many US-owned MNCs studied in fact made little attempt to adapt their US-designed diversity programmes to capture local characteristics (Nishii and Özbilgin 2007). As a result, MNCs may encounter 'regulatory, normative and cognitive challenges' when designing and implementing their global DM initiatives (Sippola and Smale 2007: 1895). While the diversity philosophy may be accepted globally within the corporation, a more multi-domestic approach has been found necessary to implement the diversity initiatives, as was revealed in Sippola and Smale's (2007) study.

Company-based case studies of DM in various countries have further revealed the gap between the reality and the aspiration projected in the rhetoric of DM. For instance, Dameron and Joffre's (2007: 2053) study of the integration team established to manage the post-merger integration of France Telecom Mobile and Orange UK found that the coexistence of the French and English cultures was 'never seen as an opportunity, a differentiation, and a source of creativity.' Rather, 'cultural diversity was always experienced by the members of the integration team as a difficulty to overcome' (Dameron and Joffre 2007: 2053; also see De Cieri 2007 for a more detailed discussion on cultural diversity). Subeliani and Tsogas's (2005) study of DM in a large bank in the Netherlands showed that diversity initiatives were designed and implemented in large cities where a large ethnic market existed from which the bank could benefit. Employees with immigrant backgrounds were mostly recruited for lower positions, where they could be visible to customers, but promotion for them was very difficult, if not impossible. They were trapped at the lower end of the organizational hierarchy, with little freedom to express their cultural and religious views. In this case, it was clear that business motives had taken precedence over moral concerns when adopting the DM programme.

The deployment of expatriate employees poses another DM challenge to MNCs whose subsidiaries span across western and eastern geographic and cultural boundaries. Existing studies have highlighted the tension created by differential

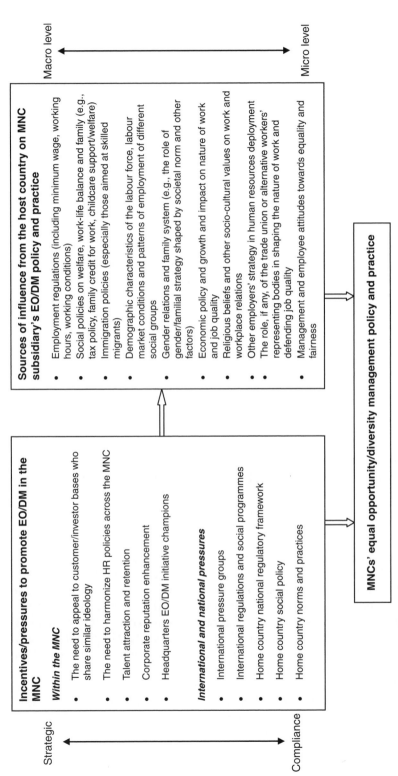

Figure 5.1 Factors influencing the equal opportunity and diversity management policy and practice of MNC subsidiaries.

Source: Author

remuneration packages awarded to expatriates and local managers in developing countries (e.g., Bonache et al. 2009; Chen et al. 2011). An attractive compensation package is often a key mechanism to attract expatriate talent from developed home countries to work in host countries where both working and living conditions may be less favourable than in the former. However, such expatriate–local compensation disparity not only causes resentment from local managers, leading to organizational conflicts, but also raises broader issues regarding fairness and distributive justice (Chen et al. 2011).

In Muslim countries, the gender norms and other cultural values may differ fundamentally from those prevalent in western societies. The transplantation of the Anglo-Saxon-originated DM concept to Muslim majority countries may be met with strong challenges and require adaptation (Syed and Özbilgin 2009). For example, according to Paetkau (2009), a large US-owned MNC set up a joint venture in Saudi Arabia and strongly encouraged certain employees to relocate there for three to four years. This expatriation was promoted as a smart career move providing enriching professional and personal experience. The Saudi Government, however, refused to issue work visas for young single women, those openly homosexual, Jews, the disabled, and employees over the age of 50. As a result, the 'Congress created a "foreign laws" defence or exception, which permits a covered US employer to participate in otherwise discriminatory action to avoid violating the laws of a foreign country' (Paetkau 2009: 93).

Equality politics and international regulatory bodies

Two driving forces motivate firms to adopt EO and DM policies: legal and moral obligations and competitive advantage (the business case). Commitment to equality and DM is an important indication of a firm's commitment to its corporate social responsibility (CSR). Legal compliance and social justice are the primary concerns of employment ethics (see Chapter 12). The business case perspective, which appears to be the dominant discourse of CSR and diversity, advances the argument further by suggesting that implementing labour standards, EO legislation and DM programmes not only fulfils firms' legal and social justice obligations, but also creates business benefits through ethical behaviour and valuing people (Cooke 2011). These two lines of argument reflect two distinct perspectives and different levels of politics at play (see Table 5.1). In this section, we focus on the politics of equality regulations and policies at the macro level by examining the background and impacts of some of the EO laws and regulations at the national level, as well as the role of some of the international initiatives aimed at enhancing labour standards.

The elimination of inequality requires state intervention through legislation and affirmative action policies to provide at least a basic level of protection in principle. However, slippage in policy implementation appears to be common across countries, albeit to varying degrees. Some national legal systems are impeded by

Table 5.1 The politics of equality and diversity management

Level	Focus/Approach	Mechanisms	Actors
Macro politics	Socially driven (social justice and workforce well-being)	Social policies and regulations	Institutional (e.g., policy makers, employers, trade unions, NGOs, international regulatory bodies and pressure groups)
Micro politics	Managerial driven (business case)	Organizational initiatives	Organizational (managers, employees, trade unions and DM consultants)

Source: Author

the complexity and multiplicity of employment-related laws, directive regulations and administrative policies issued at different administrative levels. Others lack clear enforcement channels and support through which workers can seek to secure compliance with the law. In some cases, government determination to advance social equality may be compromised by its economic agenda.

For example, it was reported that despite the promulgation of the Equal Employment Opportunity Law (EEOL) in 1986, Japan had a much lower proportion of women managers in government organizations than it had in its corporations in the early 1990s (Steinhoff and Tanaka 1993). The introduction of EEOL was controversial among the legislators, employers and the state from the outset and 'produced few gains in employment opportunities for women' (Gelb 2000: 385). There is a widespread consensus among scholars in Japan that the government passed EEOL more as a response to international pressure than as an acknowledgement of changing social values in Japan (Gelb 2000). EEOL has been criticized for its 'over-reliance on voluntary compliance' with 'little government enforcement power', although it is recognized that 'it has led to renewed efforts at litigation, increased consciousness and activism among women, and amendments to the law, passed in 1997' (Gelb 2000: 385).

Similarly, although the Constitution of India 'allows affirmative action through reservations in education and employment' (Venkata Ratnam and Chandra 1996: 85), the enforcement of the constitutional rights of Indian women is uneven owing to 'the lack of a uniform civil code in India' (Ghosh and Roy 1997: 904). In the Republic of Korea, the Gender-Equal Employment Act of 1987 'stipulates that employers can be imprisoned for up to two years if they pay different wages for work of equal value in the same business; but few, if any, employers have actually gone to jail' (van der Meulen Rodgers 1998: 746). By condoning employers' discriminatory practices, the state is actually 'perpetuating gender norms and stereotypes that disadvantage women' (Seguino 2000: 34). In China, state intervention as part of its socialist campaign of gender equality during its state-planned economy period (1949–1978) had led to significant advances in pay and social equity for female workers. This achievement, however, has been eroded by ensuing efforts towards marketization and integration with the global economy, partly as a result of the loosening of state control of business affairs.

Legislation that is intended to provide an enhanced level of equality may actually prove to be counterproductive, especially when effective enforcement remains problematic. For example, India's labour regulations are considered to be 'among the most restrictive and complex in the world' and 'have constrained the growth of the formal manufacturing sector where these laws have their widest application' (The World Bank 2006: 3). This discourages employers from creating employment with a better job quality in the formal sector and traps millions in poor-quality jobs in the informal sector. Mandatory maternity leave and the requirement for breast-feeding breaks and crèches at workplaces where the majority of workers are women are often perceived by employers as liabilities and discourage them from employing women (Venkata Ratnam and Jain 2002).

The effective implementation of employment equity legislation may yield positive psychological and employment outcomes for those who were previously disadvantaged. For example, in South Africa, the Constitution of South Africa (1996) and the Employment Equity Act (1998) were introduced to, through affirmative actions at the workplace level, promote the constitutional rights of equality, eliminate unfair discrimination in employment and achieve a diverse workforce broadly representative of its people. These regulations are said to have led to positive outcomes for some employees. However, this positive effect may simultaneously be accompanied by a higher level of turnover or intention to quit by incumbents as a result of their improved labour market position (e.g., Wöcke and Sutherland 2008). Therefore, where employers' efforts to build workforce relationships are undermined by labour market conditions, as is the case where employment laws are not effectively enforced, employers may have less incentive to observe regulations and adopt EO policies.

The political ideal of equality may be hijacked by politicians to serve their purposes. In democratic countries, it is not uncommon for politicians to adopt DM language to appeal to voters (e.g., in India). In China, where the political regime is less challenged, the notion of equality conforms to its ideological rhetoric: enhancing social harmony. By contrast, Australia, a country that relies heavily on the immigration of skilled labour, has witnessed a 'multicultural roll back', 'despite official rhetoric about the business benefits of cultural diversity' (Syed and Kramar 2010: 99). According to Syed and Kramar (2010: 99), 'mainstream Australian media and politics evince to varying degrees a visible resentment against multiculturalism'. Organizations are given freedom as to how they manage the cultural diversity of their ethnically diverse workforce.

EO legislation and administrative regulations are often enacted as a remedial action to create a level playing field for politically and socially disadvantaged groups. The design of these laws and regulations is conditioned by a state's legislative ability and enforcement capacity, as well as its political agenda and societal cultural norms. Some of the laws and regulations may be discriminatory, intentionally or unintentionally, real or perceived. As we have noted earlier, certain countries' immigration laws may restrict the types of workers entering the country as expatriate employees, putting the MNC in a legally challenged position unless the home country provides specific legal exemptions to the MNCs should their discriminative actions be imposed upon them by the host country's legislation.

Nation-states' legislative power may be challenged by international pressure groups and groups of workers with substantial bargaining power. In China, foreign workers, including those hired locally and expatriates, have reacted negatively to the new Social Security Law enacted in 2010 and have lobbied hard for exemption. The law is aimed at tightening social security provisions for workers in China (after years of criticism of the lack of such provisions). It requires both employers and employees to contribute to the social security premium. However, foreign workers, backed by some foreign media outlets, protested that the law is unfair because, they argued, they are less likely to benefit from the social security provision since they are not permanent residents of the country (the law specifies that they can get a partial refund when they leave the country) (Towers Watson 2011). It is worth noting that in developed countries with well-established social security systems, it is often compulsory for individual workers to make a contribution to their social security fund. Few countries will refund this when foreign workers decide to leave the country.

In situations where the coverage of local/national laws is not extended to foreign workers, employers may take advantage of this legislative loophole to avoid compliance. For instance, frustrated by the local workers' work attitude and industrial actions that demanded acceptable wages and working conditions, Chinese MNCs are exporting workers from China to work in some African and southeast Asian countries, particularly in the mining and construction industry. Employing Chinese workers also enables the Chinese MNCs to overcome language and cultural barriers as well as ignore local trade unions' demands for unionization. This strategy causes outrage among the local institutional actors such as opposition parties and trade unions, who exert pressure on the government to introduce regulations that would prohibit foreign firms from bringing in their own labour and force them to hire local workers instead (e.g., Cooke and Lin 2012; Jansson et al. 2009). Host country governments are faced with the dilemma of creating favourable conditions to attract foreign direct investment for development on the one hand, and the pressure to create jobs that offer decent terms and conditions on the other.

National legislation on equality may be supplemented by international regulations and global initiatives that are voluntary and have limited enforcement power. These include, for example, the International Labour Standards and Decent Work initiative issued by the International Labour Organization (ILO), Fair Trade, International Framework Agreement, and United Nations Global Compact. Although led by different international organizations and pressure groups, a common objective of these initiatives is to raise the labour standards and therefore living standards in the developing world, especially in the poorest countries. Employers are required to provide decent working conditions, fair wages, and freedom of association for workers. An emphasis of these regulations and initiatives is human rights through the elimination of discrimination and unfair practices. MNCs from the developed world are urged to take the lead and participate in the programmes associated with these regulations and initiatives, for example, through paying sustainable prices for products purchased from poor farmers and producers. Despite the high-profile campaigns of these organizations and some positive results, the effects of these initiatives are not universal and are not always positive. MNCs may join the programmes for reputational reasons and to avoid sanctions rather than to make a genuine effort. Their site inspection trips may actually add costs for the local suppliers. Local employers may find ways to overcome the constraints of international inspection, for example, through subcontracting (e.g., Cooke 2012; Harney 2009).

Case study: Diversity management at PharmaCo (India)

The Indian pharmaceutical industry is one that is heavily populated, and in fact was dominated until the 1980s, by foreign-owned MNCs. Owing to India's large population, low-cost production and research base, and the enormous scope for medical development, the pharmaceutical market in India not only offers strong growth potential but also triggers fierce competition between foreign-owned and domestic pharmaceutical firms.

PharmaCorp, a Fortune 500 US-owned MNC, first entered the Indian market in the mid-1990s and subsequently set up its subsidiary PharmaCo (India) in 1997. PharmaCo (India) has several manufacturing plants in India and enjoys a high level of operational autonomy from the headquarters (HQ). Most of the senior managers are Indian nationals, as are the majority of the workforce. As a result, the culture of PharmaCo (India) is heavily influenced by the Indian ethos, and the management practices are a blend of international practices that emphasize performance on the one hand, and an Indian approach to handling HR issues discreetly on the other.

PharmaCo (India) adopts a rigorous recruitment process to ensure that only top performers are hired. According to the managers, PharmaCo (India) adopts an innovative '11 by 11' strategy to recruit managerial and professional/technical staff. That is, recruiting from the top 11 companies in the pharmaceutical sector for the top 11 regions in India. The intention is to ensure that the new recruits are already trained and possess the skills needed by the company. At the graduate recruitment level, PharmaCo (India) mainly targets the second-tier higher education institutes because it cannot afford the employment packages expected by graduates from the top-tier colleges.

In some of the PharmaCo (India) plants, a large proportion of female employees are employed. They are recruited mainly from the tailoring institutes/sewing schools because these students have the precise hand movements and accurate eye–hand coordination that are required for certain production processes. Since these institutes/schools tend to have more female than male students, the company ended up recruiting more female than male employees. The high proportion of female employees enables PharmaCo (India) to satisfy the minimum gender ratio in the workforce imposed by the HQ.

Interestingly, most of the heavy manual work that is traditionally done by male workers is outsourced. Though strongly denied by management, it is believed that the reason for employing a female-dominant workforce is to avoid unionization and union demands on behalf of its members. Traditionally, female Indian workers do not get involved in a union and its politics. By contrast, manual male workers are more heavily unionized or demand unionization and collective bargaining on terms and conditions.

Despite the existence of high-profile DM propaganda at the HQ, there is no formal DM policy in PharmaCo (India). Its management believes that the country has a diverse population and the Indian workforce is tolerant in general. There is, therefore, no need for a formal DM policy. Instead, any issues raised can be addressed at the monthly management meeting. In addition, the company is said to have an established culture which encourages employees to discuss their problems with their line managers. In general, employees feel that the work environment is free from discrimination as all employees are treated alike.

The company does have a number of policies in place that are aimed at accommodating the work–life commitment of its (female) employees. For example, in general, women are allocated the day shifts, whereas men work the night shifts. Crèche, maternity leave and career breaks are available to help female employees meet their child-rearing responsibilities. It is reported that the crèche facilities are seldom used by the working mothers because the high workload makes it impossible for them to visit their children during the working hours. They prefer to use domestic childcare support drawn from family networks, which is believed to be more reliable.

Like many other firms in India, PharmaCo (India) suffers from a high staff turnover rate. In order to combat retention problems, a flexibility policy, together with other HR initiatives, has been introduced to accommodate the diverse needs of the workforce. For example, shift adjustments are made to enable young employees to study part-time at the college. At times when the staffing level is low on the shop floor, managers may physically fill the staffing gaps to maintain the production level.

Apart from the gender ratio in the workforce and the accommodation of women workers' childcare needs, there are no specific practices regarding caste, creed, colour and religion beyond the legal requirements.

Source: Compiled based on data from a research project on DM led by the author

Tensions and issues of diversity: some critiques

Studies on DM can be categorized into two broad strands. One comes from policy circles, professional association outlets, consultancy promotions and elementary strategic management textbooks. These publications focus on the perceived benefits of DM programmes and provide practical advice on effective implementation. They are often prescriptive in advice and simplistic in analysis. Presuming consensus, they focus primarily on the cognitive ability of individuals and organizations rather than on the nuances of organizational politics and the hegemonic power of certain groups over other groups of actors (Zanoni and Janssens 2004). The other body of literature on DM consists of the more scholarly studies published in academic journals and research volumes. They are more critical in analyzing the tensions and issues that exist on both the conceptual and practical fronts of DM as well as the methodological challenges (e.g., Boxenbaum 2006; Ferner et al. 2005; Healy et al. 2010; Kamenou 2007). Some of these studies have been discussed in the previous sections. In this section, we devote more space to this second strand of the literature to understand the role of managers and consultants as micro-institutional actors in shaping the DM agenda at the organizational level (see Table 5.1).

Critics of the rhetoric of DM and the array of DM programmes in the HRM context have pointed out a number of tensions and issues. First, DM is seen as a managerialized discourse, the language of which is constructed in ways 'that are functional to maintaining [the managers'] privileged rights at the expense of other organizational actors' (Zanoni and Janssens 2004: 58). In particular, '[all] employees are solely constructed as members of a group, to which a certain work attitude is ascribed' (Zanoni and Janssens 2004: 65). According to Zanoni and Janssens (2004: 57), the rhetoric of valuing individual 'differences' in DM masks the presence of power in diversity and portrays organizations 'as arenas where differences and competences are valued and individuals receive the same opportunities'.

Empirical research on the implementation of DM in different parts of the world revealed that DM was primarily used to fulfil organizational goals. As such, socially disadvantaged groups, such as migrants and women, may be used strategically to curtail the power of traditionally dominant groups, such as male workers, rendering them powerless vis-à-vis management and disadvantaged in the labour market (see Chapter 11). For example, Zanoni and Janssens' (2004: 65) study in Belgium found that 'migrant workers are valued for their willingness to take jobs that require great flexibility, are badly paid, and socially devalued'. In the case study of PharmaCo in this chapter, women are preferred for their skills, mentality and obedience. Flexible working time is only implemented for retention purposes.

Second, key organizational actors, such as managers and trade unions, are political actors in the organizations who manipulate the DM initiative to defend and advance their own interests, as was observed by Ferner et al. (2005) and Poster (2008) in the parent–subsidiary negotiations among key groups of organizational actors in the MNCs they studied. Similarly, Boxenbaum's (2006) study revealed how subsidiary managers in Denmark strategically reframed diversity policy from the United Sates to appeal to regional funding agencies for support.

Third, managers are not the only political actors who shape the diversity agenda. In North America, where DM has become a 'fashionable' business, independent consultants and their associations play a crucial role in shaping the diversity agenda and the perceived outcome for their client organizations (Prasad et al. 2010). Prasad et al.'s (2010: 703) study of six firms in the Canadian petroleum and insurance sectors found that these firms 'were manipulated by an institutional field of consultants and experts into adopting relatively superficial initiatives that lacked local relevance, and produced a high level of organizational cynicism regarding diversity'. For example, American-based consultants were providing DM workshops to their Canadian corporate clients based on the American history of discrimination against African Americans and professional white women rather than tailoring the workshops to reflect the local diversity issues. However, these organizations gained legitimacy for their DM programme by remaining fashionable, which 'mostly implied hiring the reputed US-based consulting firms and regularly changing diversity initiatives at the workplace' (Prasad et al. 2010: 715). Prasad et al.'s (2010: 712) study further revealed that:

> Major suppliers of diversity management products and tools regularly interacted with each other, and closely followed each other's activities in diversity conferences and other professional forums. Diversity consultants and practitioners were also institutionally linked through their memberships in professional organizations such as the American Society for Training and Development and the Conference Board. We also found considerable movement and circulation of diversity management experts (a) across different consulting firms, (b) across different corporations engaged in managing diversity, and (c) between consulting firms and their corporate clients.

Conclusion

'The spread of corporate diversity programs in the past decade has meant renewed attention to the rhetoric of fairness in employment relations' (Poster 2008: 307). Within this context, we have, in this chapter, examined the conceptual ambiguity of the notion of equality and diversity and the practical challenges to the implementation of DM programmes. We have explored the diverse national contexts in which equality and diversity issues arise. We have also discussed tensions and dynamics related to the politics of some of the regulations that are aimed at enhancing equality and social justice at the national and international level on the one hand, and the manipulation of the managerialized diversity discourse at the organizational level on the other.

For organizations, issues related to diversity are manifold. One is that the concept of diversity is subject to the interpretation of organizational actors, often in ways that advance their interests. As Poster argued, 'the term *diversity* in organizations implies a commitment to social justice and respect for disadvantaged workers, yet it can be interpreted in different ways by corporate actors' (2008: 307 original emphasis). The discourse of diversity is socially constructed and embedded in power relations that serve to entrench the power imbalance across class, gender, race and organizational positions (Ferner et al. 2005; Zanoni and Janssens 2004). Inequality at workplaces is an outcome of unequal power relations at the individual, group and business unit levels. So is the design and implementation of DM initiatives that are aimed at dealing with inequalities. As we have seen, management may choose to employ certain socially disadvantaged groups of workers not because of the former's commitment to equality and social justice, but precisely because of the lack of voice and power of the latter. Disparity of power also exists between the headquarters and subsidiaries. The very fact that the former is able to set the agenda of DM for the latter reveals this uneven relationship (Ferner et al. 2005; Poster 2008).

Another issue is that the internationalization of firms and the greater mobility of labour associated with it have led to a rising level of ambiguity, and on some occasions, conflicts, with regard to the applicability of host country labour regulations to expatriates. Host country regulations and other labour market conditions may discourage MNCs from deploying local workers, and instead they may choose to export workers from their home country. This staffing strategy may cause political and organizational problems which have yet to receive much more academic attention than granted thus far.

A third issue is the utility problem of DM. For MNCs, initiatives designed within the North American context, which tend to be more business case driven, may not be well received in European countries whose ideology of diversity may be more informed by social values and expectations and is underpinned by public policy such as parental leave and benefits. Similarly, European-based DM programmes that aim to provide a better work–life balance for the workforce may not be adequate in developing countries like China where for many workers the need to enhance their purchasing power outweighs their desire to have a more balanced family life. In addition, authoritarian management may not entertain the notion of flexible working time to accommodate workers' work–life demands (Xiao and Cooke 2012). Although the notion of equal opportunity informed by the Marxist perspective is well understood, if less practised, in the politically unitaryist China, the concept of DM premised on a pluralistic view of society remains novel to most Chinese managers and workers who are unaccustomed to a pluralistic view, despite the increasingly liberal political environment of the country.

For DM professionals from consultancy firms or professional associations, there may be a vested interest in the way they promote equality and diversity. For policy makers, commitment to upholding the ideology of fairness and social justice may be undermined by the need to provide a 'business-friendly' environment for economic growth. The enforcement of national laws is by no means guaranteed, whereas soft regulations and voluntary initiatives developed at the international level that are aimed to provide extra sanctions in the weaker states may lack appeal or enforceability at the local level.

In short, DM is a contentious area underpinned by macro and micro politics through the involvement of institutional and organizational actors (see Table 5.1). Issues related to equality and diversity for MNCs are made even more complicated owing to the pressures from home and host countries and the involvement of a diverse range of actors at various levels, with some being more powerful than others. When contemplating EO and DM issues, it is therefore important to adopt a broader and multi-level analytical framework (see Figure 5.1; also see Syed and Özbilgin 2009 for their relational analytical framework of DM) informed by political and social perspectives as well as that of strategic management.

Reflective questions

1. What are the characteristics of the approach to DM in PharmaCo (India)? In what ways may the HRM practices adopted by the company clash with the principles espoused in the American approach to DM, at least in rhetoric? What are the politics at play?
2. Imagine that you are the equal opportunities officer of an American-owned international law firm that is expanding its operations in the Middle East. A small number of US-based single female lawyers who have strong career potential raise their concerns with you that they are being discriminated against by the Middle Eastern host country's working visa restrictions that may disadvantage foreign single women. What solutions would you propose to the firm to (a) prevent the firm from being sued for discrimination by the women lawyers; (b) provide an international development opportunity for the women lawyers which will benefit their career advancement; and (c) take broader action to avoid incidents like this in the future?
3. You are the chairperson of a trade union in the mining industry in an African country where the Chinese mining firms are bringing in their own miners from China in order to maintain control of the workers to secure productivity at the expense of local jobs. What would you do to persuade the Chinese firms to abandon the labour-import practice and hire local workers instead? How would you work with other institutional actors, such as the government and (international) NGOs, to achieve this goal? How would you engage the local workers in the process?
4. You are the HR Director of a UK-based MNC in the telecommunication industry. You have been asked by the CEO to develop a global work–life balance programme as part of the corporation's DM initiative. The aim of the programme is to attract and retain talent in the corporation's various subsidiaries in Europe, North America and Asia. What are the key factors you would be considering when designing such a programme?

Acknowledgement

Part of this chapter draws from Cooke, F. L. (2011) 'Social responsibility, sustainability and diversity of human resources'. In A. Harzing and A. Pinnington (eds), *International Human Resource Management*, 3rd edition. London: Sage, pp. 583–624.

Recommended reading

- Ely, R. J. and Thomas, D. A. (2001) 'Cultural diversity at work: The effects of diversity perspectives on work group processes and outcomes'. *Administrative Science Quarterly*, 46(2): 229–273.
- Houkamau, C. and Boxall, P. (2011) 'The incidence and impacts of diversity management: A survey of New Zealand employees'. *Asia Pacific Journal of Human Resources*, 49(4): 440–460.
- Githens, R. P. (2011) 'Diversity and incivility: Toward an action-oriented approach'. *Advances in Developing Human Resources*, 13(1): 40–53.

References

Agocs, C. and Burr, C. (1996) 'Employment equity, affirmative action and managing diversity: Assessing the differences'. *International Journal of Manpower*, 17(4/5): 30–45.

Ali, M., Kulik, C. T. and Metz, I. (2011) 'The gender diversity-performance relationship in services and manufacturing organizations'. *International Journal of Human Resource Management*, 22(7): 1464–1485.

Bonache, J., Sanchez, J. I. and Zárraga-Oberty, C. (2009) 'The interaction of expatriate pay differential and expatriate inputs on host country nationals' pay unfairness'. *International Journal of Human Resource Management*, 20(10): 2135–2149.

Bowen, D. and Ostroff, C. (2004) 'Understanding HRM-firm performance linkages: The role of the "strength" of the HRM system'. *Academy of Management Review*, 29(2): 203–221.

Boxenbaum, E. (2006) 'Lost in translation: The making of Danish diversity management'. *American Behavioral Scientist*, 49(7): 939–948.

Chen, C. C., Kraemer, J. and Gathii, J. (2011) 'Understanding locals' compensation fairness vis-à-vis foreign expatriates: The role of perceived equity'. *International Journal of Human Resource Management*, first published on: 05 April 2011 (iFirst).

CIPD (Chartered Institute of Personnel and Development) (2006) *Diversity: An Overview*. CIPD factsheet, Internet source: http://www.cipd.co.uk, accessed on 20 August 2007.

CIPD (2007) *Diversity in Business: A Focus for Progress*. London: Chartered Institute of Personnel and Development.

Cooke, F. L. (2010) 'Women's participation in employment in Asia: A comparative analysis of China, India, Japan and South Korea'. *International Journal of Human Resource Management*, 21(10–12): 2249–2270.

Cooke, F. L. (2011) 'Social responsibility, sustainability and diversity of human resources'. In A. Harzing and A. Pinnington (eds), *International Human Resource Management*. 3rd edition. London: Sage, pp. 583–624.

Cooke, F. L. (2012) *Human Resource Management in China: New Trends and Practices*. London: Routledge.

Cooke, F. L. and Lin, Z. H. (2012) 'Chinese firms in Vietnam: Investment motives, institutional environment and human resource challenges'. *Asia-Pacific Journal of Human Resources*, 50(2): 205–226.

Cooke, F. L. and Saini, D. (2012) 'Managing diversity in India and China: Implications for western MNCs'. *Journal of Chinese Human Resource Management*, 3(1): 16–32.

Cox, T. (1993) *Cultural Diversity in Organizations: Theory, Research and Practice*. San Francisco: Barrett-Koehler Publishers.

Cox, T., Lobel, S. and McLeod, P. (1991) 'Effects of ethnic group cultural differences on cooperative and competitive behaviour on a group task'. *Academy of Management Journal*, 34(4): 827–847.

Dameron, S. and Joffre, O. (2007) 'The good and the bad: the impact of diversity management on co-operative relationships'. *International Journal of Human Resource Management*, 18(11): 2037–2056.

Davidson, M. and Burke, R. (eds) (2011) *Women in Management Worldwide: Progress and Prospects*. Oxford: Ashgate Publishing.

De Cieri, H. (2007) 'Transnational firms and cultural diversity'. In P. Boxall, J. Purcell and P. Wright (eds), *The Oxford Handbook of Human Resource Management*. Oxford: Oxford University Press, pp. 509–532.

Ferner, A., Almond, P. and Colling, T. (2005) 'Institutional theory and the cross-national transfer of employment policy: The case of "workforce diversity" in US multinationals'. *Journal of International Business Studies*, 36(3): 304–321.

Foster, C. and Harris, L. (2005) 'From equal opportunities to diversity management'. In J. Leopold, L. Harris and T. Watson (eds), *The Strategic Managing of Human Resources*. Essex: Pearson Education Ltd., pp. 116–139.

Gelb, J. (2000) 'The equal employment opportunity law: A decade of change for Japanese women'. *Law and Policy*, 22(3&4): 365–407.

Ghosh, R. and Roy, K. (1997) 'The changing status of women in India: Impact of urbanization and development'. *International Journal of Social Economics*, 24(7/8/9): 902–917.

Harney, A. (2009) *The China Price: The True Cost of Chinese Competitive Advantage*. Penguin Books.

Healy, G. and Oikelome, F. (2007) 'A global link between national diversity policies? The case of the migration of Nigerian physicians to the UK and USA'. *International Journal of Human Resource Management*, 18(11): 1917–1933.

Healy, G., Kirton, G., Özbilgin, M. and Oikelome, F. (2010) 'Competing rationalities in the diversity project of the UK judiciary: The politics of assessment centres'. *Human Relations*, 63(6): 807–834.

Jansson, J., Burke, C. and Jiang, W. R. (2009) *Chinese Companies in the Extractive Industries of Gabon and the DRC: Perceptions of Transparency*. Centre for Chinese Studies, University of Stellenbosch.

Jones, D., Pringle, J. and Shepherd, D. (2000) 'Managing diversity meets Aotearoa/New Zealand'. *Personnel Review*, 29(3): 364–380.

Kamenou, N. (2007) 'Methodological considerations in conducting research across gender, "race", ethnicity and culture: A challenge to context specificity in diversity research methods'. *International Journal of Human Resource Management*, 18(11): 1995–2010.

Lau, D. and Murnighan, J. (1998) 'Demographic diversity and faultlines: The compositional dynamics of organizational groups'. *Academy of Management Review*, 23(2): 325–340.

Liff, S. (1996) 'Two routes to managing diversity: Individual differences or social group characteristics'. *Employee Relations*, 19(1): 11–26.

Lorbiecki, A. and Jack, G., (2000) 'Critical turns in the evolution of diversity management'. *British Journal of Management*, 11, Special Issue, S17–S31.

Maxwell, G., Blair, S. and McDougall, M. (2001) 'Edging towards managing diversity in practice'. *Employee Relations*, 23(5): 468–482.

Mor Barak, M. (2005). *Managing Diversity: Towards a Globally Inclusive Workplace*. Thousand Oaks: Sage.

Nishii, L., Lepak, D. and Schneider, B. (2008) 'Employee attributions of the "why" of HR practices: Their effects on employee attitudes and behaviors, and customer satisfaction'. *Personnel Psychology*, 61(3): 503–545.

Nishii, L. and Özbilgin, F. (2007) 'Global diversity management: Towards a conceptual framework'. *International Journal of Human Resource Management*, 18(11): 1883–1894.

Paetkau, T. (2009) 'When does a foreign law compel a U.S. employer to discriminate against U.S. expatriates? A modest proposal for reform'. *Labor Law Journal*, 60(2): 92–103.

Purcell, J. (1999) '"Best practice" and "best fit": Chimera or cul-de-sac?'. *Human Resource Management Journal*, 9(3): 26–41.

Poster, W. (2008) 'Filtering diversity: A global corporation struggles with race, class, and gender in employment policy'. *American Behavioral Scientist*, 52(3): 307–341.

Prasad, A., Prasad, P. and Mir, R. (2010) '"One mirror in another": Managing diversity and the discourse of fashion'. *Human Relations*, 64(5): 703–724.

Seguino, S. (2000) 'Accounting for gender in Asian economic growth'. *Feminist Economics*, 6(3): 27–58.

Soni, V. (2000) 'A twenty-first-century reception for diversity in public sector: A case study'. *Public Administration Review*, 60(5): 395–408.

Sippola, A. and Smale, A. (2007) 'The global integration of diversity management: A longitudinal case study'. *International Journal of Human Resource Management*, 18(11): 1895–1916.

Steinhoff, P. and Tanaka, K. (1993) 'Women managers in Japan'. *International Studies of Management and Organizations*, 23(2): 25–48.

Subeliani, D. and Tsogas, G. (2005) 'Managing diversity in the Netherlands: A case study of Rabobank'. *International Journal of Human Resource Management*, 16(5): 831–885.

Süß, S. and Kleiner, M. (2007) 'Diversity management in Germany: Dissemination and design of the concept'. *International Journal of Human Resource Management*, 18(11): 1934–1953.

Syed, J. and Kramar, R. (2010) 'What is the Australian model for managing cultural diversity?' *Personnel Review*, 39(1): 96–115.

Syed, J. and Özbilgin, M. (2009) 'A relational framework for international transfer of diversity management practices'. *International Journal of Human Resource Management*, 20(12): 2435–2453.

Towers Watson (2011) 'China: New law in China will create a more unified nationwide social security system'. Internet source: http://www.towerswatson.com/newsletters/global-news-briefs/4873, accessed on 7 July 2011.

Tsui, A., Egan, T. and O'Reilly, C. (1992) 'Being different: Relational demography and organizational attachment'. *Administrative Science Quarterly*, 37(4): 549–579.

Van der Meulen Rodgers, Y. (1998) 'A reversal of fortune for Korean women: Explaining the 1983 upward turn in relative earnings'. *Economic Development and Cultural Change*, 46(4): 727–748.

Vedina, R. and Vadi, M. (2008) 'A national identity perspective on collectivistic attitudes and perception of organisational culture'. *Baltic Journal of Management*, 3(2): 129–144.

Venkata Ratnam, C. and Chandra, V. (1996) 'Source of diversity and the challenge before human resource management in India'. *International Journal of Manpower*, 17(4/5): 76–108.

Venkata Ratnam, C. and Jain, H. (2002) 'Women in trade unions in India'. *International Journal of Manpower*, 23(3): 277–292.

Wöcke, A. and Sutherland, M. (2008) 'The impact of employment equity regulations on psychological contracts in South Africa'. *International Journal of Human Resource Management*, 19(4): 528–542.

World Bank, The (2006) *India Country Overview 2006*. The World Bank, Internet source: http://worldbank.org, accessed on 16 March 2007.

Xiao, Y. C. and Cooke, F. L. (2012) 'Work-life balance in China? Social policy, employer strategy and individual coping mechanisms'. *Asia-Pacific Journal of Human Resources*, 50: 1.

Yukongdi, V. and Benson, J. (Eds) (2006) *Women in Asian Management*. London: Routledge.

Zanoni, P. and Janssens, M. (2004) 'Deconstructing difference: The rhetoric of human resource managers' diversity discourses'. *Organization Studies*, 25(1): 55–74.

6 Training and workplace skills in the context of globalization: new directions and discourses in skills

Miguel Martínez Lucio and Stephen Mustchin

Learning objectives

- To outline the reasons why training varies across countries
- To understand the changing approaches to skill formation
- To comprehend the impact of MNCs on the development of a nation's skills
- To appreciate the economic and political significance of the development of soft skills
- To understand the role of soft skills in management development
- To outline the role of trade unions in such matters as skills in a global context and describe new progressive ways of approaching training and learning

The aim of this chapter is to outline the subject of training and development in relation to the growing internationalization of the firm and the changing nature of employment relations. The development of work-related skills is a vital feature of economic and social development. It is seen by many to be pivotal to the resources of a firm and a country in relation to their strategic market position. The ability to work within certain organizational environments, with specific technologies and within a climate of continuous innovation is held to be one of the defining features of leading-edge competitors. A range of developing countries at a more advanced state of their development emphasize the need to develop a nation's skills, especially those of its core workforce and its management. These countries set targets for their education systems; alongside a desire to promote economic growth is an obsession with meeting education and learning targets, from higher education through to workplace qualifications. These developments are also shaped by fundamental changes in the nature of education:

> Higher education today is characterised by massive expansion and wider participation; the emergence of new players; more diverse profiles of HEIs, programmes and their students; broader adoption and more integrated use of communications and educational technologies; greater internationalisation, competition and signalling mechanisms; growing pressures on costs and new forms of financing; as well as new modes and roles of governance, including increasing emphasis on performance, quality and accountability. (Tremblay et al. 2012: 16)

However, the question of skills and the development of skill formation is political (Heyes and Stuart 1998). The level of resources and the level of political commitment to skills formation and vocational education are key factors in this political process, along with the role and capacity of governments and their broader public bodies. Much also depends on the commitment of employers and their representative associations (and the effectiveness of these associations), alongside the role of worker's organizations in their involvement and commitment to training. In addition, the political focus of skill formation can vary: in some cases, training can be a matter of providing new technical abilities that are essential to particular jobs, but on the other hand, training may focus on attitudinal issues and on changing the 'mindsets' of workers in relation to new forms of work. Certain 'skills' may also be developed with a view to enhancing the further exploitation of workers, as we discuss later. There is therefore the fundamental question of what types of skills are being focused on in any one context. Is it hard technical and industrial skills are that are being pushed or softer, social and communications skills? Are specific types of skills being used to develop a more adaptable and harmonious workforce in the knowledge that much of the new work associated with MNCs in a developing country may be of a highly intensive nature? In the case of Indonesia or Malaysia, for example, has the development of learning been driven by the objective of enhancing real skills and technical knowledge that allows people to 'do their jobs effectively' or is it also about 'westernizing' and 'creating a more flexible workforce' for new overseas investors?

The reality is that nation-states develop different approaches to the resourcing, organizing and development of training programmes for their workforce, and the first part of this chapter will discuss this: the difference between coordinated and liberal market approaches in terms of regulated and state-led approaches in the former and more market- and employer-oriented approaches in the latter. This is not just about the difference between developed and developing countries; there are also differences within the 'developed' world, where we see that there is a tension between two different views of skills formation which are central to the future paths others take. MNCs engage with, and can shape and influence, these regimes and approaches, hence their own role will be discussed: while they can provide new job opportunities, they do not always provide consistent and meaningful processes of skills development.

Central to these discussions are notions of 'soft skills'. These skills are seen as important for dealing with a greater level of organizational change and continuous improvement and innovation. For some, this is central to the new, post-bureaucratic age; however, for others this represents a move to greater exploitation of workers (see Chapter 1). The chapter will also focus on the question of alternative and more emancipatory views regarding skills and training. Trade unions have begun since the late 20th century to develop a more engaged approach to worker education – although some would argue that this was always the case in terms of supporting free education and accessible learning. However, we have seen a greater interest in workplace learning and the ongoing development of workers that builds not just those features of the workforce that are relevant to their job and employer, but the broader capacities of individuals (Cornelius et al. 2008) as both workers and as active citizens within society. The chapter focuses on the broader workforce and not just a select elite minority of managers, which is often the way IHRM approaches the subject.

Context of skills: national systems and different approaches

In a classic study of management and labour in Europe, Lane (1989: 63, 64) pointed to the importance of recognising differences in emphasis in terms of public policy and employment relations and how they influenced the way management and employers responded to the question of skills. In Germany, general and vocational education have been equally developed, through a strong role for the state, the establishment of a system of social dialogue and highly structured approaches to skill formation. This contrasts with Britain, where there has been a more decentralized approach with an unclear – if not confusing – set of bodies dealing with learning. There has been a move to systematically create national vocational standards, but the level of investment and engagement remains uneven. The United Kingdom contrasts with the more centralized, institutionally embedded German system.

This fundamental difference between the more voluntarist and market-based learning contexts of the United Kingdom on the one hand and state-oriented and social-dialogue-based systems on the other hand, such as in Germany, has been explored in studies on the redesign of work:

> Workplace innovation has come to mean a broader process of organisational renewal consistent with, high quality, high skill, high trust, business approaches. An important question is the extent to which publicly supported

programmes aimed at supporting and resourcing this kind of development are able to achieve success. (Payne and Keep 2005: 148)

In a study of Finland and Norway on the one hand and the United Kingdom on the other, Payne and Keep (2005) argued that while changes to skills and worker roles were not always that easily measurable in the former two countries as a consequence of such developments, in the case of the United Kingdom the decline in bargaining, the lack of state regulation and resourcing and the absence of a high trust relation between workers and managers meant that workplace redesign and change were often concerned with cutting labour costs and a tokenistic approach to re-skilling workers. Grugulis (2007: 36–39) sees such differences in training – in terms of resourcing, coordination and creating a culture of worker involvement – as depending on the nature of state intervention with some relying more on public funding and intervention while others rely more on voluntarist employer-led systems. To this extent, the role of worker participation at the national and/or the workplace level is one dimension that seems to configure the politics and approaches to training.

Much of the employment relations literature is therefore concerned with how skills and their development vary greatly according to the nature of the employment system and its regulation (see Chapter 3). The level of state resourcing may also vary, as will the role of employer organizations and worker representatives in participating in training systems and their input into work. In some cases, one may see a more organized and bureaucratic approach to skills with clear definitions in terms of skill differences, classifications and their development from – for example – an apprentice level through to a qualified full-time employed worker.

In the past ten years, such an approach to the study of training has been further underpinned by a deeper interest in the *nature* of capitalist systems. This work, pioneered by Hall and Soskice (2001), looks at capitalism more broadly and not solely at systems of regulation in terms of who drives training and skill formation. By focusing on the nature of relations between different sets of capitalist interests and the role of ownership structures, this approach locates training in the nature of political and economic relations that exist in any one context (see Chapter 8 and Chapter 3 on national systems of employment relations for a discussion of coordinated market economies (CME) and liberal market economies (LME)). According to Kaufman (2011: 49, 50), this approach has become a major pivot of the study of labour and employment relations. It allows for different approaches to capitalism to be wedded to an understanding of the nature of training and learning across different contexts. In LMEs, the emphasis is on lowering costs, less government intervention and a more flexible approach to skills: this is linked to a short-term approach to investment and the pursuit of higher profitability with skills developed in a more ad hoc manner. Within this context, employers are a clear driver with less state and union involvement. The United Kingdom and the United States are seen as examples of LMEs. CMEs are different as there is a greater attempt to organize skill formation through longer-term apprenticeships and more systematic and technical approaches to skills, based on a labour relations systems driven by dialogue and trust, with unions and government sometimes even leading discussions. The focus is on the long term and investment in deeper skill formation, in part due to there being less of an emphasis on short term profits among shareholders. Germany is seen as an example of a CME. Analysis of how training opportunities are distributed within the relatively liberal context of the United States indicates that those with a higher level of educational attainment are more likely to get further opportunities to train (Lillard and Tan 1992: 46), thus limiting opportunities to access training among a significant part of the population.

In terms of management development, we can also see such differences reflected in the way managers are trained. Handy et al. (1988), in a dated but highly significant and pioneering report on the way managers were trained and developed during the latter half of the 20th century, pointed to similarities and differences between countries such as Japan, the United Kingdom, France, Germany and the United States. There were many similarities: (i) it was large firms that tended to set the management development agenda, (ii) university-based education was pivotal in the early stages (apart from the United Kingdom), (iii) continuous management education was common, and (iv) greater levels of organizational change were requiring and bringing forth a broader approach to management learning based on understanding different types of management. However, there were differences that reflected some of the features outlined earlier: continuous learning in relation to managers was more structured and formal in Germany and Japan compared with the relatively opportunistic approach of the United States and the United Kingdom; management and business education was more pronounced in the United States, whereas in Germany the sciences, engineering, law and economics were the basis of management background; and in Japan the company and its internal practical spaces were important for on-the-job training, while the French and British tended to recruit from elite educational institutions for their management elites with less emphasis on internal progression. In the United Kingdom, accountancy has been a more dominant route into management compared to Japan or Germany. A further study has reinforced this view that there are curious differences between management cultures in relation to training and development. Evans et al. (2002) pointed to how German firms emphasized having stable development programmes based on strong internal labour markets, while the UK and the Dutch models were driven by a market-based approach and less internal development. Many management studies are replete with simplistic stereotypes of nations – so caution is needed with such generalizations – but the point we need to consider is that regardless of such typologies, differences between the more coordinated and liberal market approaches in general terms tend to hold even for these types of studies on management.

MNCs are confronted with very different contexts of training in terms of how it is financed, how skills are classified, and how managers and workers are involved in the development of learning agendas. Nevertheless, MNCs can have an influence on these contexts, as we discuss later. The increasing pace of globalization and the greater movement of capital in order to exploit labour costs and skills have placed increasing pressures on systems with a high resource investment level. Hence, we are witnessing changes. There is a tension at the heart of developed countries with a significant broader relevance in that two quite different models of learning are emerging as transnational points of reference. Within the European Union, there has been a growing interest in propagating some of the more flexible features of the LME model (Greenwood and Stuart 2005). In a wide-ranging study of the European context, Stuart (2007) argued that there were pressures to shift to new approaches:

> In the context of heightened global competition and economic uncertainty, economies and firms need constantly to upgrade their skills base to remain competitive and, in the case of the EU, respond to the challenge of cheap-wage, low-skill competitors through upgrading strategies based on high skills and quality products. Given the imperatives of capitalist firms constantly to restructure their operations and increase the adaptability and flexibility of labour, workers (and citizens) are exhorted to take increased responsibility for their learning, training and skills development, so that they can remain employable. (Stuart 2007: 269)

In addition, there has been a growing emphasis on new types of skills and learning – commonly called soft skills (see below). At the heart of this approach is a supply-side emphasis which highlights flexibility and adaptability as key features of the learning agenda (Stuart 2007), which is problematic as this may represent a more neoliberal and liberal market approach involving changes in policy in more coordinated economic contexts (Greenwood and Stuart 2005). Implementing these changes when systems of skills regulation remain focused around complex relations and traditions, and involving actors such as employer bodies and trade unions to implement and sustain developments, is difficult (Martínez Lucio et al. 2007), especially when in the key nation-states within the European Union, training budgets have been challenged in the past few years. However, in Europe political and social dialogue around learning and training remains a major feature of policy involving public bodies, employers and trade unions, although this varies in intensity across countries (Heyes 2007).

These complex dynamics and changes are apparent in developing- or emerging-state contexts. In such contexts, the role of the state is central in distributing funding for training and its implementation (see Chapter 10). Governments play a key role; however, their limited resources, the problem of an undeveloped national employer class, reliance on lower labour costs and limited or constrained social dialogue on such issues with employers and unions means that they cannot adopt the CME approach with consistency. The relationship between the state and employers, and the extent to which they involve unions, varies and often reflects ideology, power structures and traditions. Further problems arise when MNC demand for higher skills is mainly met by those within developing countries with enough wealth to access the education system, potentially reinforcing existing inequalities (Kapstein 2001: 10). However, the state remains one of the few actors capable of sustaining a vocational training strategy in the absence of strong national capitalist enterprises and effective 'peak' organizations such as employer associations and trade unions:

> Rather than simply retreating to the sidelines to function as the game's referee, the state must strategically co-ordinate the interaction between key economic actors in a way that will stimulate deep and crosscutting developmental linkages. These linkages are necessary to facilitate information flow, increase vested interests through participation (as opposed to simply consultation), and improve cross-checked monitoring and implementation ... But this new role for the state is also dramatically different from the theoretical role of the developmental state. Instead of simply directing investment and ameliorating risk, the state must now encourage, facilitate, and co-ordinate the formation of *intangible* assets, which often requires more private-sector leadership. (Ritchie 2002: 32)

Part of this more 'facilitative role' is a growing interest in a more market-oriented and neoliberal view of skills, and a general institutional mimicking of 'Americanized' approaches such as the emphasis on soft skills (see below). This can lead to a tendency to reproduce the rhetoric but not always the realities of the developed state (see Chapter 10).

Training in both developed and developing countries therefore can be measured across various dimensions: we may find some countries tending to emphasize formal skills and a more industrial, state-driven agenda, while others may emphasize the service sector and new understandings of skills (as discussed later). In many cases, some will aspire to the former, but owing to the absence of resources and the earlier stages of their economic development, are driven to develop a workforce which is more amenable to a low-cost approach and lower skills base to attract MNCs.

Globalization and change in training and skills

The question of MNCs and their roles

An important view within many international bodies and governments is that MNCs are keenly attracted to areas where there are high levels of human capital and a strong infrastructure of technological capabilities (Noorbakhsh et al. 2001 as quoted in Ritchie 2002). This is one reason why governments see their education strategies as essential to the development of their countries through greater foreign direct investment (FDI). Hence, MNCs can in many cases be free-riders by 'shopping around' not just for cheaper labour costs but a workforce that has already been trained up for their organizational needs. Yet this would be only one side of what MNCs do. The counterargument suggests that MNCs in developing countries in South East Asia such as Malaysia have added to the skills stock by providing more training than local employers (Abdullah 1994, as quoted in Ritchie 2002); however, the comparison may not be a fair one as local firms may not have a strong training tradition or access to state resources to start with. The focus of such inward investment is often on relatively low-skilled manufacturing processes, and thus the types of skills needed may be of a routine, assembly-oriented nature, centred on short-term commitments based on 'kit' production – putting manufactured components together but not actually making them. In a classic study of MNCs and FDI in the United Kingdom during a period of de-industrialization, Knell (1993) argued that overseas companies may just bring specific low-skill aspects of their work, exploit lower wage costs and take a narrow view of training.

Much depends on the sector which is being discussed, as some will lend themselves to a lower skills approach (as in much manufacturing and many service industries), while others (such as medical research, engineering and IT) may not. However, one thing that does emerge from these studies is that the interaction between national state bodies and MNCs is a key factor in enhancing longer-term development in terms of skill. The way the state intervenes in a wide manner of ways – not just in terms of resourcing but in terms of creating alliances between firms and public bodies, creating spaces for dialogue about training and in creating benchmarks and best practices – is of fundamental importance (Martínez Lucio and Stuart 2011). In Chapter 10, we note how the Malaysian state built a longer-term view of training with levies on employers for resourcing with an attempt to use inward investment to create a longer-term legacy. However, in the case of the United Kingdom, from the 1990s onwards the government viewed specific sectors such as manufacturing as representing a declining feature of the economy – and thus did not invest substantially in technical and manufacturing skills – which only worsened the problems in relation to skills shortages for those manufacturing firms still contributing to the economy. Underinvestment in technical skills leads to shortages, weakening of domestic industry in relation to competitors, and a greater reliance on migrant or posted workers to source particular skills, as can be seen in the cases of the construction and engineering sectors, among others. In many respects, the national political approach of the British state was driven by a liberal market economy perspective – see above – which was more short-term and service-sector driven in its view of skills and their formation and development. Given this, it can be seen that exporting a coordinated market economy approach (Hall and Soskice 2001) is difficult due to the nature of long-term, stable and embedded relations which are required in CMEs.

The age of soft skills?

Hence, while we see very different approaches to skill formation and its context, there is a view that soft skills are crucial to the way workers are developed. The dominant skills models of LMEs are framing the development of global 'skill sets' at work in the form of soft skills (Shakir 2009). What are soft skills and why are they seen as being fundamentally important to training for future forms of work? Grugulis (2007: 72–79) draws together a range of positions and argues that there are various factors that constitute and drive the development and use of soft skills:

1. There are sectors such as hospitality and retail that require a type of employee with certain social and communication skills.
2. This links to a more positive attitude to work and life – working as a team and behaving socially towards an economic end.
3. This in effect is based on a range (and sometimes complex understanding) of personal traits and attitudes which are seen as being cohesive and engaged with a market approach.
4. Hence, technical skills have to be supplemented by soft skills that engage the customer and place an emotional element within the relationships between workers and their clients. This is relevant for dealing with external customers but also for seeing your own work colleagues as internal customers.
5. This has led to a growing debate about 'emotional labour' – a new type of labour based on the use and portrayal of one's emotions in a positive light.

It is not hard to see the ideological dimension of these characteristics and preferred skills as they are clearly linked to a market economy and a focus on customer relations as a primary concern for HRM. They are about sustaining a more adaptable workforce which is positive in their engagement with organizational change. In some respects, it is an extension of the 'Americanization' of workplace relations (see Chapter 8). The aim is to continuously engage in a positive manner and to not exhibit criticism at work (Hughes 2005) and to be conformist with organizational needs in terms of appearance and even dress code, which is a feature of aesthetic labour (Nickson et al. 2005). In addition, much of the soft skills agenda is also about basic self-management and creating a vision of a reliable and manageable individual which in some contexts is seen as vital even for national development (Baharun et al. 2012).

However, the idea that we need to view each other as customers can ironically undermine open discussion and genuine and authentic interaction (Ritzer 1997). There are concerns that the development of soft skills can be a conduit for a new form of exploitation and work intensification.

First, the increasing emphasis on the needs of the customer creates new forms of labour control and further pressures on workers (Bain and Taylor 2000). In viewing students as customers and trying to satisfy their needs, academics, for example, may lower standards and change the way they assess students so that more pass their modules. Student complaints and student surveys can be used to humiliate and even discipline academics. In call centres in India, workers have to tolerate a range of bullying behaviour from UK callers, given the imperative to engage positively with such callers (Taylor and Bain 2005). In some cases, such behaviour may be racist; this puts the worker in a difficult position as they have to 'please the customer'.

Second, call centre customer interactions may be scripted with workers having to follow certain protocols and standard phrases, which undermines their ability to work autonomously. This scripting of work can create a pressurized environment which inhibits displays of emotion and which can create tensions between workers attempting to do the work in a meaningful manner or just doing the work to get through as many customers as possible (Korczynski 2003). The emphasis on soft skills and new forms of work may obscure the routine and repetitive nature of much service employment (Ritzer 1997).

Third, many governments now push the development of such skills as the basis of development, sometimes to the exclusion of more technical forms of skill formation. Such skills are seen as being important to the attitudinal restructuring of the workforce: creating a culture of work which is more flexible and adaptable. In various developing economy contexts, soft skills are viewed as a key dimension of the changes required for a more 'western', 'developed', and market-facing culture. Some MNCs such as McDonald's have been major drivers of such developments in the same way that Ford was a major pioneer of the assembly line approach to production in the early 20th century.

The move towards soft skills can create a dimension of work where skill is more symbolic than formal and driven by new forms of control. In some developing countries, such developments may create a policy discourse of skill formation and a set of policy objectives that emphasizes soft skills with notions of social dialogue and associated institutional arrangements often excluded from the policy discourse for ideological reasons.

Management development and soft skills

In many respects, this dimension of skills is becoming significant to the area of management development too. In quoting and building on Sparrow (1996), Mabey and Finch-Lees (2008: 192) argue that British approaches to management development are 'preoccupied with "soft" skills, especially the ability to motivate, lead and get the best from teams …' The view that management needs to think more in terms of the qualities of leadership and thus a range of interpersonal skills which allow for a more socially engaged approach in ethical, visionary and, personal terms (Alldredge and Nilan 2000) is becoming increasingly important; although that does not mean management attitudes and approaches to the rights of workers may be softer or more socially oriented. In effect, the training of management is partly being driven by an emphasis on soft and not just technical skills: this is clear from the emphasis on socialization in business schools in terms of networking, communication skills and social skills becoming almost as important as acquiring substantive knowledge. Managing from a neoliberal and marketized perspective (see Chapter 8) is an ideological development, and this is enshrined in the role of consultancies and business schools in the way they drive cultures of management (see Chapter 9). This raises some difficult ethical issues, as we will discuss later on.

However, there are other drivers to such developments as well, not just the process of Americanization and the nature of neoliberal management education (which takes much of its cue from the United States through accreditation bodies). The nature of work within MNCs means there are likely to be real pressures on management in terms of coping with an array of cultures and ethnicities in their workplaces and especially on international assignments (see Colling et al. 2007). By their very nature, international assignments and ongoing cross-national and cross-ethical project-based work, for example, bring together a range of individuals where communication, cultural adaptation and awareness, and sensitivity to ethical differences and behaviour moves increasingly to the forefront of the work of managers at all levels. That many are still closeted within a specific social and elitist space – especially at the highest levels within the enclosed and 'gated' spaces of expensive hotels and VIP airport lounges – does not detract from the ever-increasing social and economic pressures that bring to the forefront a need to engage with new approaches to management learning. It is for this reason that diversity management, for example, is seen as central to the new skills portfolios of management (see Chapter 5). The problems begin when soft skills are seen as more important than having a systematic understanding of the cultures and values of the people management deals with (Sippola and Smale 2007). For example, forms of courtesy and social engagement need to be underpinned by a real understanding of national contexts and history if the former are not to be viewed as tokenistic. Hence, the question of soft skills is an important feature of the debate on learning and can on occasion become an end in itself at the expense of detailed knowledge and awareness.

Furthermore, in an age of continuous communication and with the impact of the Internet, the need to modify and control communication at a range of levels brings a new set of pressures on managers as employees. Expectations of constant accessibility and accountability mean that social interactions are increasingly scrutinized. The need to develop forms of leadership around notions of transparency and openness may clash with and slow down decision-making processes. Hence, management development increasingly focuses on the modification of management work with an emphasis on the processes of communication and not just the content. Writing e-mails is one area where there has been greater attention to detail owing to the problems of misinterpretation and litigation. However, to what extent this is more a matter of controlling risk than engendering transparent management is questionable. MNCs therefore increasingly engage with the development of soft skills in a range of work groups as an essential aspect of their expansion, and this is often reflected in the approach to skills taken by states that receive FDI (Shakir 2009). The following set of short case studies illustrates some of the issues that can emerge in relation to soft skills; it uses the example of changes in higher education.

Case studies: Soft skills, organizational politics and learning in higher education

It is argued that for a country to develop further, it is essential that potential graduates are taught a range of new skills which are central to what many perceive to be at the heart of recruitment practices within MNCs and large, organized companies in general, and which dovetail with developments in contexts such as the United States. These skills, according to Baharun et al. (2012: 8795) in the Malaysian case, for example, entail that

> graduates must change their attitude when entering the job market as employers placed greater emphasis on the ability of graduates to fulfil their responsibility and keep appointments. On the other hand, based on experience, employers found graduates to be lacking in this positive attitude. The present findings indicate that undergraduates reported a relatively lower ability to fulfil responsibility, manage time and the inability to improve knowledge after graduation. This suggests that skills development opportunities during their study in university is a key issue that needs to be addressed.

The Ministry of Higher Education has announced that the development of soft skills was a high-priority issue and objective in Malaysia in the past few years (Shakir 2009). Key personal attributes in terms of organization, communication skills and general presentation have also been seen as essential for potential employees in various parts of the South Pacific as well (Bhanugopan and Fish 2009).

It is therefore suggested by various experts that there is a need for formal educational processes to be supplemented with the learning of such soft skills. In India, the investment in soft skills was seen as essential if the nation was to draw in investment in such key service sectors as call centres, as this would facilitate the development of a more proactive customer service orientation and attract overseas investors in financial services, for example (Crome 1998). Many such developments are driven by a view of learning which is influenced by liberal market economic approaches (see above and Chapter 8).

However, the development of such types of skills can present a series of dilemmas, as we have outlined earlier. Within a UK business school, for example, the introduction of soft business skills modules into the curriculum was viewed with uncertainty as it would mean that soft-skills-related modules would take up a sizeable portion of the teaching that students received. The only way that such a focus on soft skills could be achieved would be by removing other modules which covered more substantive issues. For example, it was proposed to remove a business and management law module in order to accommodate the soft skills modules being proposed. This raised concerns among some of the academic staff, who argued that the removal of the law module would weaken the knowledge required to work in the ever more litigious arena of modern management. Issues of contract law, corporate governance, employment law, branding, and other topics needed to be part of the knowledge sets of students, they argued. It was deemed important to have law wedded to the degree programme as a compulsory module with the aim of sensitizing student understanding of 'the real politics of businesses'. Some of those advocating the business skills module argued that students 'needed to be able to develop social and communication skills' instead to avoid organizational problems and that there was also government interest in developing soft skills more systematically. Those defending the law module responded by arguing that such skills were better embedded in the tutorial work of various modules (e.g., assessment of presentation, time-keeping) and should never be at the expense of core organizational knowledge. The exponents of law pointed to declarations by national employer bodies, who were worried that student recruits needed to understand the legal environment and the extensive risks associated with this. There was also concern among some academic staff that the use of soft skills in other contexts was being used to lower standards and undermine a systematic knowledge of management and its environment, sending signals about higher education which were problematic.

The United States has seen real issues in the transformation of education standards in universities:

> Even though a higher percentage of Americans are attending college, they are not necessarily learning more. An increasing number are unqualified for college work, many leave without completing their degrees, and others receive degrees reflecting standards much lower than what a college degree has usually been understood to mean. (Muller 2013: 47)

Questions

1. What are the key elements of soft skills and why are they important?
2. In a development context, why would soft skills be important and not just technical skills?
3. Should soft skills be the basis for a deeper development of our emotional attachments to work and our customers?
4. What do the cases suggest are the issues in relation to the way soft skills are embedded in learning?
5. How can we develop a view of soft skills which is more than just working in teams, being organized, and engaging positively with others in our organization but which has a meaningful basis?
6. What are the costs of over-emphasizing soft skills and how is this agenda open to abuse?

Employment relations and learning: questions of rights and emancipation

The question of learning is a broad issue involving various organizations, institutions and movements. Within the European Union (EU), for example, there has been increasing interest in expanding the role of trade unions in relation to learning and training. With the increasing realization in the past 20 years that the quality of skills and the adaptability of workers in a more fragmented and ever-changing labour market – where long-term jobs are increasingly less likely – has come an agenda to develop 'human resources'. The delivery of new forms of training in terms of basic skills and soft skills, for example, has been a major part of this agenda (Greenwood and Stuart 2005) linked to the social dimension of the EU that is meant to act as a counterweight to economic and market priorities (Mathers 2010). Faced with these challenges, training, skills development and certification have become increasingly prominent issues for unions as they aim to ensure their members are appropriately rewarded for their skills and are able to adapt to labour market change (Cooney and Stuart 2012).

In addition, the intensification of migration has meant that there is a perceived need to engage large groups of migrants who may be excluded from accessing learning and skills development, especially at the lower skills end (see Mustchin 2012; Perrett et al. 2012). Trade union presence in workplaces and communities allows them to be a vehicle for offering such learning in some cases. In Spain, for example, the trade unions during the past 20 years received and managed a range of state funds to offer training to workers in their workplaces and in the local community. In other contexts such as the United States, learning and the development of basic skills is an important feature of local community worker centres, which involve unions and community groups (Fine 2006). While state funding varies across these different contexts, the new learning agenda is more expansive than some management focused academics would have us believe, and within this unions play a role (Heyes 2007; Heyes and Rainbird 2011).

There have been concerns that many of these union-led initiatives may sometimes simply focus on low-level technical, basic or soft skills, but there is an increasing realization that such initiatives can contribute to the development of a more engaging and independent learning agenda (Ferus-Comello and Novelli 2010). Additionally, the way learning is provided is important, especially given the way it is can sometimes be focused on simply adjusting workers to new forms of exploitation and acceptance of low-skilled jobs (Verger and Novelli 2010). Fusing the learning agenda into a broader development agenda for workers has been the basis of discussions within trade unions and social movements. Learning has the potential to support individuals in shaping their careers and social communities in positive ways as opposed to attempting to create passive individuals who are pliable and easily controlled. Hence, as mentioned previously, learning and skills development is clearly a political issue (Heyes and Stuart 1998). Many social organizations such as charities and NGOs view learning as a major vehicle for political and economic development. However, training is partly driven by the perception of some development agencies that training is a less problematic and less challenging issue for involving employers, governments and unions in capacity building and the policy process (Polidano 1999).

The concept of capabilities is therefore becoming important to various alternative approaches to skills and a person's development (Sen 2005). The argument is that we need to look across a person's ability to be autonomous, creative, socially engaged, reasoned, and their capacity for self-development and even play (Nussbaum 2000). The problem is that the skills agenda may be fragmented, uneven and skewed to specific narrow interests if it is primarily driven by MNCs or a market-driven policy agenda (see Knell 1994). Hence, we see a broader politics of skills driven by trade unions and social movements as a way of building on the more limited views inherent in the soft skills debate. International Labour Organization programmes such as Decent Work place a strong emphasis on the right of workers to be developed and trained in a more systematic and meaningful manner. These initiatives are meant to frame a global response which places worker rights at the heart of the employment and training agenda.

Conclusion

When we think in terms of training and development in relation to systems of work, it is clear that there are various dimensions to this discussion. The way skills are developed is both complex and nuanced. This chapter has pointed out how skills can be developed in a systematic manner on the one hand but also in a more ad hoc and symbolic manner on the other, with approaches often determined by institutional contexts and the role of the state. Students at universities are constantly being told that the substantive content of their degrees is only one part of their development, and that they also need communication, team working and emotional skills to be able to utilize their technical knowledge. However, to what extent this secondary feature begins to replace the first in terms of emphasis is a matter of conjecture. This chapter has also noted that different national contexts present varied responses to training in terms of the extent of resourcing, social participation, the focus of policy and the nature of skills developed. There are different regimes and traditions across the globe. However, as stated earlier, 'soft skills' have become an important feature within the arena of training and development, often with negative implications. Global organization, mobility and production bring a second tier and set of issues to the forefront in terms of cultural training, ethical awareness and emotional labour. These are the fundamental skills supposedly needed within global organizations and a global workforce, yet this can sometimes become an end in itself and be abused as a way of creating a more adaptable and therefore exploitable workforce and management (see Chapter 7).

The chapter has pointed to the way MNCs have an uneven impact on the development of skills. The nature of the context in which they operate is important, the way in which state agencies respond to and facilitate MNC investment is also significant and the nature of change within these institutional contexts – partly driven by the presence of MNCs – is another salient factor. However, the impact of MNCs does not ensure any deep or lasting commitment to the development of the skills of workers and managers, especially in an age of pliable and flexible production (an age when capital moves in and out of countries and regions at ever greater speed, thus not allowing jobs and skills to be embedded) (Knell 1994). Hence, the emphasis is on adaptability to change and a pliable workforce and not necessarily a stable and highly skilled one.

The chapter ends with the new social and inclusive agenda for skills and learning which has emerged. The increasing engagement with learning and skills by trade unions and NGOs presents us with a new alternative to short-term and narrow skill formation, although much will depend on the levels of resourcing and political commitment from governments. In addition, the United Nations and many other bodies are taking a deeper interest in the question of *capabilities*. The aim is to provide a learning agenda and context that depends on engaged, socially oriented, autonomous and capable individuals within a broader social context. Whether MNCs engage with this agenda is a matter of concern, but the future of learning and development at a global level is very much dependent on the ongoing development of a corporate social responsibility (CSR) agenda (see Chapter 12), the greater coordination of organized labour and NGOs around such agendas, and the emergence of a transnational system of regulation concerned with workplace rights but also broader understanding of a person's development and a deeper engagement with the meanings of skill. As Heyes and Stuart (1998) pointed out: skills and their development is a political matter.

Reflective questions

1. What are the principal differences between national approaches to training and why are they important?
2. How do governments try to ensure they are attractive to overseas investors in terms of skills?
3. What are the positive and negative impacts of MNCs in terms of skills development within countries and what do you think explains this?
4. What are soft skills and how are they linked to globalization?
5. What benefits do such developments bring for workers and managers?
6. What are the possible issues that emerge in relation to soft skills in terms of (a) work intensification, (b) the development of your skills and (c) the position and role of more technical skills formation?
7. How can learning be linked to a broader development of individuals and what role can an understanding of capability theory provide?

> **Recommended reading**
>
> - Abdullah, W. A. W. (1994) 'Transnational corporations and human resource development'. *Personnel Review*, 23(5): 50–70.
> - Hughes, J. (2005) 'Bringing emotion to work emotional intelligence, employee resistance and the reinvention of character'. *Work, Employment and Society*, 19(3): 603–625.
> - Knell, J. (1993) Transnational corporations and the dynamics of human capital formation: evidence from West Yorkshire. *Human Resource Management Journal*, 3(4): 48–59.
> - Ritchie, B. K. (2002) *Foreign Direct Investment and Intellectual Capital Formation in Southeast Asia*. Paris: OECD Development Centre, pp. 4–41.
> - Shakir, R. (2009) 'Soft skills at the Malaysian institutes of higher learning'. *Asia Pacific Education Review*, 10(3): 309–315.

References

Abdullah, W. A. W. (1994) 'Transnational corporations and human resource development'. *Personnel Review*, 23(5): 50–70.

Alldredge, M. E. and Nilan, K. J. (2000) '3M's leadership competency model: An internally developed solution'. *Human Resource Management*, 39(2–3): 133–145.

Baharun, R., Suleiman, E. S. and Awang, Z. (2012) Changing skills required by industries: Perceptions of what makes business graduates employable. *African Journal of Business Management*, 6(30): 8789–8796.

Bhanugopan, R. and Fish, A. (2009) 'Achieving graduate employability through consensus in the South Pacific island nation'. *Education + Training*, 51(2): 108–123.

Bain, P. and Taylor, P. (2000) 'Entrapped by the "electronic panopticon"? Worker resistance in the call centre'. *New Technology, Work and Employment*, 15(1): 2–18.

Collings, D. G., Scullion, H. and Morley, M. J. (2007) 'Changing patterns of global staffing in the multinational enterprise: challenges to the conventional expatriate assignment and emerging alternatives'. *Journal of World Business*, 42(2): 198–213.

Cooney, R. and Stuart, M. (2012) *Trade Unions and Workplace Training: Issues and International Perspectives*. Abingdon: Routledge.

Cornelius, N., Todres, M., Janjuha-Jivraj, S., Woods, A. and Wallace, J. (2008) 'The social enterprise and capacity, capabilities and quality of life'. *Journal of Business Ethics*, 81(2): 355–370.

Crome, M. (1998) 'Call centres: Battery farming or free range?' *Industrial and Commercial Training*, 30(4): 137–141.

Evans, P., Pucik, V. and Björkman, I. (2002) *The Global Challenge: International Human Resource Management*. Boston: McGraw-Hill Education.

Ferus-Comelo, A. and Novelli, M (2010) 'Creating the space for optimism through popular education'. In A. Ferus-Comelo and M. Novelli (eds.), *Globalisation, Knowledge and Labour*. London: Routledge.

Fine, J. (2006) *Workers Centers*. Ithaca, NY: Cornell University Press.

Greenwood, I. and Stuart, M. (2006) 'Employability and the flexible economy: Some considerations of the politics and contradictions of the European employment strategy'. In L. E. Alonso and M. Martínez Lucio (eds.), *Employment Relations in a Changing Society: Assessing the Post-Fordist Paradigm*. London: Palgrave.

Grugulis, I. (2007) *Skills, Training and Human Resource Development: A Critical Text*. London: Routledge.

Hall, P. A. and Soskice, D. (2001) *Varieties of Capitalism and Institutional Complementarities*. Oxford: Oxford University Press, pp. 43–76.

Handy, C., Gordon, C., Gough, I. and Randlsome, C. (1988) *Making Managers*. London: Pitman.

Heyes, J. (2007) Training, social dialogue and collective bargaining in Western Europe. *Economic and Industrial Democracy*, 28(2): 239–258.

Heyes, J. and Rainbird, H. (2011) 'Mobilising resources for union learning: A strategy for revitalisation?' *Industrial Relations Journal*, 42(6): 565–579.

Heyes, J. and Stuart, M. (1998) Bargaining for skills: Trade unions and training at the workplace. *British Journal of Industrial Relations*, 36(3): 459–467.

Hughes, J. (2005) 'Bringing emotion to work emotional intelligence, employee resistance and the reinvention of character'. *Work, Employment and Society*, 19(3): 603–625.

Kapstein, E. (2001) Virtuous Circles? Human Capital Formation, Economic Development and the Multinational Enterprise. OECD Development Centre Working Paper No. 191.

Kaufmann, B. (2011) 'Comparative employment relations: Institutional and neo-institutional theories'. In M. Barry and A. Wilkinson (eds.), *Research Handbook of Comparative Employment Relations*. Cheltenham: Edward Elgar.

Knell, J. (1993) 'Transnational corporations and the dynamics of human capital formation: evidence from West Yorkshire'. *Human Resource Management Journal*, 3(4): 48–59.

Korczynski, M. (2003) Communities of coping: Collective emotional labour in service work. *Organization*, 10(1): 55–79.

Lane, C. (1989) *Management and Labour in Europe: The Industrial Enterprise in Germany, Britain and France*. Aldershot: Edward Elgar.

Lillard, L. and Tan, H. (1992) 'Private sector training: Who gets it and what are its effects?' *Research in Labor Economics*, 13: 1–62.

Mabey, C. and Finch-Lees, T. F. (2008) *Management and Leadership Development*. London: Sage.

Martínez Lucio, M., Skule, S., Kruse, W. and Trappmann, V. (2007) 'Regulating skill formation in Europe: German, Norwegian and Spanish policies on transferable skills'. *European Journal of Industrial Relations*, 13(3), 323–340.

Martínez Lucio, M. and Stuart, M. (2011) 'The state, public policy and the renewal of HRM'. *The International Journal of Human Resource Management*, 22(18): 3661–3671.

Mathers, A. (2010) 'Learning across borders: A European way?' In A. Ferus-Comelo and M. Novelli (eds.), *Globalisation, Knowledge and Labour*. London: Routledge.

Muller, J. Z. (2013) 'Capitalism and inequality: What the right and left get wrong'. *Foreign Affairs*, 92(2): 30–51.

Mustchin, S. (2012) 'Unions, learning, migrant workers and union revitalization'. *Work, Employment and Society*, 26(6): 951–967.

Nussbaum, M. C. (2000) *Women and Human Development: The Capabilities Approach*. Cambridge: Cambridge University Press.

Nickson, D., Warhurst, C. and Dutton, E. (2005) 'The importance of attitude and appearance in the service encounter in retail and hospitality'. *Managing Service Quality*, 15(2), 195–208.

Noorbakhsh, F., Paloni, A. and Youseef, A. (2001) 'Human capital and FDI inflows to developing countries: New empirical evidence'. *World Development*, 29(9): 1593–1610.

Payne, J. and Keep, E. (2005) 'Promoting workplace development: Lessons for UK policy from nordic approaches to job redesign and the quality of working life'. In B. Harley, J. Hyman and P. Thompson (eds.), *Participation and Democracy at Work: Essays in Honour of Harvie Ramsay*. Basingstoke, UK: Palgrave, pp. 146–166.

Perrett, R., Lucio, M. M., McBride, J. and Craig, S. (2012) 'Trade union learning strategies and migrant workers policies and practice in a new-liberal environment'. *Urban Studies*, 49(3), 649–667.

Polidano, C. (1999) 'The new public management in developing countries'. *Institute for Development Policy and Management Working Paper No.13 November 1999*. Manchester: Manchester University.

Ritchie, B. K. (2002) *Foreign Direct Investment and Intellectual Capital Formation in Southeast Asia*. Paris: OECD Development Centre, pp. 4–41.

Ritzer, G. (1997) *The McDonaldization Thesis: Explorations and Extensions*. London: Sage.

Sen, A. (2005) Human rights and capabilities. *Journal of Human Development*, 6(2): 151–166.

Shakir, R. (2009) 'Soft skills at the Malaysian institutes of higher learning'. *Asia Pacific Education Review*, 10(3): 309–315.

Sippola, A. and Smale, A. (2007) 'The global integration of diversity management: A longitudinal case study'. *The International Journal of Human Resource Management*, 18(11): 1895–1916.

Sparrow, P. R. (1996) 'Careers and the psychological contract: Understanding the European context'. *European Journal of Work and Organizational Psychology*, 5(4): 479–500.

Stuart, M. (2007) 'Introduction: The industrial relations of learning and training: A new consensus or a new politics?'. *European Journal of Industrial Relations*, 13(3): 269–280.

Taylor, P. and Bain, P. (2005) '"India calling to the far away towns" the call centre labour process and globalization'. *Work, Employment and Society*, 19(2): 261–282.

Tremblay, K., Lalancette, D. and Roseveare, D. (2012) 'Assessment of Higher Education Learning Outcomes Feasibility Study Report: Volume 1 – Design and Implementation'. OECD.

Verger A. and Novelli, M. (2010) '"Education is not for sale": Teachers' unions multi-scalar struggles against liberalisation the education sector'. In A. Ferus-Comelo and M. Novelli (eds.), *Globalisation, Knowledge and Labour*. London: Routledge.

7 Lean production and globalization: a 'revolutionary' management agenda and the re-making of labour intensification?

Paul Stewart

Learning objectives

- To engage the reader in the debate on lean production in relation to globalization
- To explain the meanings of lean production and the consequences for workers and managers
- To outline the relation between lean production and neoliberalism
- To outline the consequences of lean production in terms of health and safety

Introduction

When we discuss the question of globalization in relation to work and employment, we should be mindful that the issue is not solely about the development of transnational corporations and transnational forms of regulation. Important though this is, it is only part of the story. This is because globalization is just as much concerned with the power of new ideas and views about how the employment relationship and work are organized: in other words, it is also about ideology and the fact that ideologies have a very powerful role in defining the nature of the implementation of work, including how it is organized. We write 'should' because what typically occurs in the employment relationship is that the dominant force, typically management, insists that this or that way to work must be followed: that 'there is no alternative'; that there is 'one best way'.[1] What is more, whatever the ideology states, the actual organization of work will be mediated by the interactions between workers and employers. It is in this light that lean production can be seen as, whatever else is said about its actual technical characteristics, a powerful contemporary management ideology. Its origins can be said to lie with the rise to prominence of what for some were perceived to be distinctive forms of work organization and firm strategy. These, it is argued by some commentators, originate in the Japanese firm Toyota's production system, thereby offering, as a mirror of the automotive manufacturer's success, a way out of the late 20th and early 21st century western capitalist crisis.

Characteristically, when describing what they take to be lean production, managers and some academics refer only to a number of associated organizational techniques and processes, including just-in-time (JIT) delivery systems; a quality and product check inventory system known as *kanban* (assessing the quality and authenticity of up-stream product delivered by your co-worker who is also to be seen as a 'business partner'); team working and team meetings, whose main role is to encourage and deliver continuous improvement (*kaizen* is the Japanese word); and reduce waste in the system (*muda*, another Japanese word).

The advent of neoliberal economic strategies (see Chapter 8) has been characterized by what at first glance appears to be a paradox – less external (state) regulation of business, but at the same time tighter regulation of peoples' actual work by myriad forms of monitoring and surveillance. However, the actual paradox is not that of less external regulation and greater internal regulation since, after all, it stands to reason that the greater the degree of external unpredictability, the more a firm will want to tighten up its internal life, including the actual work that is carried out. While lean production is thus very well suited to such circumstances and especially neoliberal capitalist societies in which the external business environment has become especially febrile, if not in crisis, the significant paradox is that lean production was born in the more highly regulated economy of post 1945/Second World War Japan. Indeed, one might argue that the lessons of what are termed lean production manufacturing techniques and organizational practices have been used to greater effect in a neoliberal business climate. Moreover, perhaps this also serves to highlight some of the false juxtapositions in the typology of neoliberalism (liberal market economy) and state regulation (coordinated market economy). The issue as to whether lean can resolve the problems of economic crisis *within* the firm (manufacturing or otherwise) has not been proved in any research, and so we must be extremely sceptical of any claims by soothsayers of neoliberalism who see crisis resolution in the extension of lean to the wider society in respect of the way our non-work lives are organized.

Nevertheless, this belief does not prohibit lean 'evangelists' from trying to extend more widely what they take to be lean's various truths. And while it is no doubt the case that society, and not only employment, is becoming more stressful, again whether we label the causes of this as deriving from the effects of lean production is open to question. While the advocates of lean will see its extension as an inherent good with any downside attributed to poor and inadequate implementation, nevertheless, a number of commentators argue that it is lean that is implicitly responsible for increasing levels of stress in society and that this needs to be challenged, not by making lean work more efficiently but, on the contrary, by rejecting lean in its entirety. From this perspective, lean production is taken as an indication of broader changes not just to society-in-work per se, but also to the idea of capitalist society in general. *Flux tendu* is the term introduced by the French sociologist Jean-Pierre Durand (*The Invisible Chain*, 2007) to account for the seeming encroachment of more than simply the techniques of lean production into our everyday lives and society. While his argument centres on the manner in which lean production changes the ways in which we work, together with a focus on the nature of the wider employment relationship, he is also concerned to highlight how lean impacts the wider society: the whole of our lives, and not just the time spent at work, is increasingly being affected by the imperatives (and the philosophy) of lean. Perhaps we are on the brink of the lean capitalist society? (Durand, 2007:1–26, 199–208.)

Advocates of the verities of lean production argue that its assumed approach to the management of company resources, including human and physical capital, was developed by the Toyota automobile company. Their view is that this lay behind Toyota's subsequent success beginning in the 1980s. Of dispute, however, are not only a number of key accounts of the way in which Toyota achieved its success but also the sometimes overly optimistic interpretation of the term itself.

In this chapter, first we set the context (the crisis of Fordism) for the rise of the concept of lean production. Second, we examine several ways in which the concept of lean production has been used to account for developments of work, labour and the corporation in the light of the evolutions of the last 30 years. Many profound changes have occurred in the world of work and employment during this time, and just because these have been described as leading towards the inevitability of lean and lean production, we need to be cautious about simply taking for granted how the enthusiasts of lean themselves explain change. We explore three ways in which lean production has been understood both in the academy and in business. Thus, ways of considering lean production include:

1   'Lean' as a description of taken-for-granted modern management practices whose origins, supposedly, account for Japan's post Second World War economic success. Often, this view is put forward by managerial advocates (who sometimes seem almost evangelical in their enthusiasm) who see lean as in

some sense revolutionary. There is another strand to this 'lean-as-wholly dis-tinctive' view which is critical of lean's impact on work and employment. This is a view, broadly stated, held by some critics of management and capitalism.

2   In substance, a number of significant features such as time management and stock and quality control (including JIT) notwithstanding, lean is not so differ-ent from existing management practices. If anything, lean is largely the same but with more *enforced* and 'controlled' employee involvement than previous or other forms of management control.

3   Lean is seen as fundamentally important for the new political economy of capitalism, and as such while it is principally concerned with work, it also has implications for the wider society. This position critiques the first two (i.e., lean as distinctive/lean as continuity). It challenges those in both strands by arguing that their accounts of what is termed lean production are neither accurate in explaining new management practices nor in what it is these new practices (which they term 'lean') actually achieve. Whether we can describe the nature and importance of lean as heralding a new type of society or merely a new development *within* existing capitalism is a question to which we return in the conclusion to the chapter. Moreover, thinking of the latter, it could arguably be a new development not just *within* capitalism but a new form *of* capitalism itself.

Our objective then is to understand more accurately the developments and raison d'être of this late 20th century and early 21st century form of management both at the level of the work place but also in society. Thus, we seek to highlight the manner in which the breakdown in the late 1970s and early 1980s of the post Second World War consensus based on Fordist production and consumption strategies in the Keynesian era made it possible to restore profitability. This was seen to lay the basis for a new dominant management paradigm seeking to shift the burden of risk onto non-core businesses (second- and other-tier suppliers) and subordinate social groups and the workforce in general. The burden of what we term *the accumulation strategy* (how capital and labour interact in the creation of profit) has fallen significantly upon labour, and lean production has been the mechanism by which the workforce has been controlled. In recent decades, the rationale of reducing costs and enhancing productivity through organizational changes and the development of new forms of human resource management (HRM) have had a tendency to become universal (both nationally and globally) across all sectors, including the public sector and non-profit organizations (in health and social care, for example).

To sum up, and take the discussion forward, we are asking the following inter-related questions. First, to what extent have the transformations affecting work, labour and the organization been open to discussion and debate owing to their mainstreaming in much of management and political discourse? Specifically for the United Kingdom, how did lean production grow out of the debate about so-called 'Japanization'? Second, to what extent can we say that these transformations remain unchallenged at the level of the workplace and employment relations, never mind more widely? After all, it is only to be expected that attempts to introduce workplace change, however one social group (management in this instance) might try to sell it as being in everyone's interest, will be challenged by others with the inevitable consequence that the outcome will almost certainly differ from the intention. Relatedly, how have trade unions challenged lean production? Third, to what extent is 'lean production' as effective as it is proclaimed to be by its advocates and moreover, what are its limits and contradictions? Specifically, we will here be concerned with what happens to those whose work is affected by what we term a 'regime of lean production'. This will be explored through a case study in the automotive sector, the source of the management strategy known as lean production.

The context: the crisis of Fordism and the rise of lean production

The late 1980s was a watershed for trade unions internationally with the fall of the Berlin Wall – a metaphor and reality for the end of the state communist era – and the crisis in socialist responses to the offensive by capital in countries such as France and Spain. This offensive typically arrived in the form of what have been described as neoliberal economic and political strategies (see Chapter 12). Even though capital's offensive may have drawn succour from the collapse of bureaucratic socialism, the social and economic foundation of its newfound vigour was quite separate and grew out of what we generally understand to be the crisis in its own pattern of capital accumulation and economic organization, Fordism (see Chapter 8).

By Fordism, we are referring to the social and economic context in which the pursuit of profit by means of employment and wider state and social strategies was based upon the incorporation of labour and trade unions (see also Hirst and Zeitlin 1991). Typically, in post Second World War Europe, this necessitated a welfare state supported by general taxation sustained in turn by strong, autonomous trade unions committed to negotiations with management at the company and sectoral level (in some European countries, these amounted to pacts): it was a coming together of mass production and mass consumption. This was a period in which management too was seen to gain, and principally owing to the strength of national trade unions, capable of maintaining workplace peace.

Seen to have generally been weakened and then undermined by the oil, and then more general, crisis in commodities in the early 1970s, Fordism came to be associated with inflexible labour relations, inflexible commodity production techniques and an overregulated economic system (especially by those on the right of the political system though this eventually included those on the social democratic left). The fact that this perception was based on an overgeneralization of the origins of the capitalist crisis in the late 20th century had no bearing on the attractiveness of this view, and it usefully provided the backdrop for a series of attempted prognoses and remedies. If Fordism was seemingly unable to resolve the economic crisis that began in the 1970s, how would the crisis be resolved? Often, the concept of neoliberalism is used to sum up the attack by capital on state regulation and good labour standards, and what some commentators termed lean production arguably became central to the supposedly new phenomenon of globalization.

Yet the specific intellectual origins of 'lean production', though framed in this period, came from an apparently distinctive source seemingly disinterested, at least initially, with state regulation focussing simply upon business success. In the mid to late 1980s, a number of management consultants, policy analysts and a cadre of academics argued that Japan, seemingly immune to the 1970s crisis, could be held up as a beacon of hope for western capitalism. More especially, some argued that the explanation for Japan's post-war economic success lay not only with the structure of its business organization and employment relations, but more decidedly in its internal workplace and labour process relationships. As we shall see below, it is here that the origins of the so-called Japanization debate lay. This debate is important in understanding the nature of the origins of the concept of lean production.

The dimensions of lean production: origins of the lean production agenda

i) Lean as distinctive: a managerialist perspective from an Anglo-Saxon context

The debate in the United Kingdom about the character and significance of lean production first gained prominence with Oliver and Wilkinson's *The Japanisation of British Industry* (first published in 1988 and reference here is to second edition, 1992). It was here that the so-called Japanization school which developed the concept of Japanization from Peter Turnbull (1986) began. The term *lean production* was subordinated to a broader concern with the theme of transfer of what were interpreted as Japanese management practices. The main idea was subsequently refined in 1992 in a sequel to the *Japanisation of British Industry*, subtitled *New Developments in the 1990s*. The main thesis was that the significant and transformative management practices in Britain for the foreseeable future would be *essentially* Japanese. (See Ackroyd et al. 1988, for an alternative reading of the notion of Japanization. For an attempt to operationalize the concept of Japanization in Wales see Morris et al. 1992.) They argued that if they were not identifiably Japanese, then they would act as such, by proxy (in the form of what were termed 'functional equivalents' – a concept also utilized by the lean production school). Japan and Japanese practices would become the benchmark against which the effectiveness of new management practices would be judged so that competitiveness would be ensured. (See also Elger and Smith's introduction to their *Global Japanisation* 1994, in which they spell out the range of interpretations and significance of the term.) While a greater sophistication subsequently infused the Japanization position in the special issue of the *Journal of Management Studies* (vol. 32, no. 6) (JMS) in 1995 (notably, Abdullah and Keenoy 1995; Delbridge 1995; Humphrey 1995; Morris and Wilkinson 1995), in many respects the outcome merely reinforced existing weaknesses in the approach, because here too the specialness of Japan was retained. The debate on so-called Japanization was revisited in a special issue of *Employee Relations* in 1998 (vol. 20, no. 3) and, again, the 2012 British Universities Industrial Relations Association conference research on Japanese inward investment in Poland harking back to the early approach in the United Kingdom was framed within the paradigm of Japanization.

However, the difficulty with the Japanization frame of reference was that an obsession with the Japanese origins of lean production techniques effectively led to a certain inability to think of the techniques as transferable from one place (culture) to another. Or rather, the issue of portability somewhat missed the point. While the issue of transferability is interesting enough, it was unhelpful to management practitioners. Nevertheless, one certainly positive development came out of the JMS papers: a rejection of an explicit genuflection to the work of the IMVP group (1992: 5–9, 15. IMVP: the International Motor Vehicle Program was co-ordinated by the Massachusetts Institute of Technology. IMVP comprised academics and managerial consultants). As a consequence, greater emphasis was placed upon the theme of the 'employee domination', as this now seemed to be inscribed in the very idea of Japanese management practices. On one level, this could be viewed as having led to a more positive emphasis on the independent role of labour because in the 1988 and 1992 Japanization texts, the problem of employee domination tended to be subsumed within a framework emphasizing the creative tension involved in the management of 'high dependency' relationships (1992:82–87). Here, organizational and technical features of the new workplace such as JIT placed employees in a potentially very powerful position – as the system of production became more prone to disruption due to JIT – despite the fact that they rarely sought to realize this power. The answer given by managerialist writers on Japanization as to why workers effectively acquiesced was that the management regime allowed for some element of employee benefit in welfare and involvement programmes in Japan (e.g., stable employment). One important problem with the Oliver and Wilkinson thesis was that it had little direct empirical grounding in terms of workplace research based upon employee responses. The major advance of the research reported in the 1995 *Journal of Management Studies* special issue (vol. 32, no. 6) was that this absence of field research into employee responses was addressed by several of the contributors such that the 'dark side' of this management was stressed – 'the iron fist in the velvet glove', to quote the conclusion's epithet on Japanese management (JMS: Wilkinson et al. 1995). A fatalistic view of labour control was expounded whereby collective, autonomous labour could not develop let alone establish an independent agenda.

With the advance of the lean production paradigm at the end of 1980s, all of these discomforting problems associated with the difficulty of the transfer of what were arguably culturally specific management practices could be laid to rest (so the managerial evangelists hoped). For the first time, the key reference points in the theme of Japanization would be stripped to their bare (technical) essentials. Lean production might well have been invented in Japan, but the conundrum ends there. By concentrating on the de-cultured and de-socialized aspects of things Japanese, management could now, with cautious optimism, apply the lessons of the Japanese way just as they supposedly applied the verities of America's Taylorism in a previous era. For the lean production school, there would be precious little need to worry unduly about difficult issues of cultural transfer. This was not to say that social, cultural and organizational matters did not figure in the account, either in its original version in Womack, Jones and Roos (1990) *The Machine that Changed the World* (a major text on the study of new management practices termed lean production) or in the work of British counterparts, and notably in the writing of Dan Jones and his colleagues working with the Andersen Consulting group; merely that they were seen to be secondary to the overriding technical imperatives of lean production. In a notable exception to the usual technological determinism underlying the assumptions of the lean production school, Oliver et al. (1993) gave some credence to the role of leadership in the implementation of lean strategies. However, even in this instance, social relations were perceived to be significant only in so far as they conformed to the imperatives of 'lean' management behaviour. Technology and its proper implementation (in the right institutional context that included team working and *kaizen*) was the key to the 'one best way' of achieving manufacturing success (in the United Kingdom, this debate was led by Oliver et al. 1994; Jones 1992; Oliver 1991).

The solution to economic failure, according to the IMVP authors Womack, Jones and Roos in *The Machine that Changed the World* (1990), and later developed by Andersen Consulting (Oliver et al. 1994), was to be found by introducing the organization and technical truths of lean production. The main social and employee relations argument put forward by the IMVP team was that trade unions had to adapt to the requirements of international competition or risk becoming obsolete. It must, in other words, give up on what was seen as the old-fashioned nostrums of independent trade unionism – a by-word for confrontation – and the existence of trade unions as institutions set up to protect workers from the consequences of working in a capitalist economy. The hope for advocates of lean production was that lean might oversee the creation of a new form of 'industrial citizenship' (Womack et al. :103 and Jones 1992) based on worker participation linked to the needs of production. In the United Kingdom, there has been an attempt to restore the vitality of the lean prognosis through an internal critique. This has emphasized the way in which the earlier enthusiasts underestimated the obstacles to bringing employees onboard the great new 'enterprise' of lean transformation. The work of Seddon and Caulkin (2007), in particular, has been taken up by a range of public sector organizations seeking to apply the methods drawn from manufacturing to public services (see the critique of this agenda by Mooney and Mooney and Law, eds, 2007). Seddon argues that the interpretation and application of much of the IMVP research, and especially in its popularized versions, such as the one purveyed in Womack et al., derived from a limited understanding of the origins *and meaning* of lean in the Toyota production system. Often, lean-inspired management consultants have reduced the meaning of Ohno's insights (Toyota's key figure in this regard) to a bowdlerized and oversimplified drive to standardization: the very opposite, according to Seddon, of the Toyota philosophy.

If lean's advocates argued that trade unions could be encouraged to see that the interests of capital and labour are reconcilable, conflict and disagreement could be dispensed with. Needless to say, this would allow management to effect change in its own image and on its own terms, specifically by following the Toyota production philosophy – the One Best Way to achieve world-class manufacturing (Womack et al. 1990).[2] We know how limited a view this was as the long-term work of the international network GERPISA demonstrated over the period from the early 1990s until the present (Boyer and Freyssenet 2002; Durand 2007; Charron and Stewart 2004). For these researchers, the variety of practices that could be described as lean and the myriad contexts merely served to illustrate that there that could be no One Best Way (see Jurgens et al. 1993 for the classic empirical rebuttal).

ii) Lean as something distinctive: a Marxist and political economy perspective

While there is a second strand to the view of lean production as distinctive, considering it to be in many respects a break from the past and notably Fordism, the conclusions drawn about its origins, purposes and trajectory are entirely different from those advanced by lean 'evangelists'. Arising from a Marxist and political economy perspective, this approach sees lean as in many ways a revolutionary break from Fordism, in the context of the last 100 years. The view is that it was developed in response to the crisis of Fordism and as such represents a managerialist, or capitalist, agenda for restoring profitability in a post-Fordist context.

For Smith (2000), the rise of lean production should be traced to the 'crisis of the Fordist' pattern of capital accumulation in the last decades of the 20th century (pp. 6–8) expressed in terms of six problematic features of the economy, work and organization of the Fordist era of accumulation:

1. 'Constant capital'. This includes problems of the high costs of raw materials inventory costs and 'inflexibility of machinery'.
2. 'Circulation time', by which he is referring to the rising costs associated with delivery of stock, retooling, bureaucracy and quality.
3. Problems associated with the link 'between science and capital form'. This refers to 'the separation of research and development departments from other divisions in the Fordist corporate structure' (p. 7).

4. Relations between capital and labour in work. These include the increasing costs of a separate cadre of managers, worker struggles against work and wage rates are seen to be out of sync with productivity; perceived problems with quality tied specifically to the separation of quality control from production.
5. The relations between the consumer and capital. Problems here are associated with Fordism in general, that is, massification and standardization of products and services leading to the neglect of consumer desires and interests.
6. The institutional separation of the various units of capital along the supply chain leading to increased expense and unnecessary (in the workplace) investment in planning, tracking and implementation processes.

Lean production responds to these since it significantly links new and information technologies to management and control of labour and capital utilizing both manufacturing techniques and a labour control agenda first developed in Japan (pp. 1–12). The question for Smith is not whether it is everywhere and in all sectors present and dominant, the question is rather the extent to which it can be understood as leading to the development of new patterns of capital accumulation (in both private and public sector organizations). Moreover, lean production leads to the dispersal and integration of new and information technologies around the system that is a highly defining feature of lean as the 'second age of information technology' (p. 13). This is the golden nugget in the ability of lean to deliver considerably higher levels of productivity than was possible under Fordism, much higher levels of quality and more extensive product innovation (pp. 22–23).

Yet, whether by skill we mean the technical complexity inherent in specific activities, or the job and task loading associated with lean assembly routines, Smith confidently cites evidence in favour of new skills for certain categories of worker. If commodity production is carried out in divided labour markets (skilled–less skilled work), what lean has done is to reinforce this characteristic by considerably reducing the condition of labour of many while creating a core of other, more highly skilled workers. On the other hand, all of the negative outcomes associated with lean management processes reinforce the conflict at the heart of workplace relations between managers and workers. Specifically, for Smith, lean recreates and sustains three inherent antagonistic features of the capital–labour relationship: structural coercion, exploitation, and the real subsumption of labour.[3]

Nonetheless, radical though Smith's view is, embracing both an assessment of the strengths of lean and thus a critique (lean attacks many unskilled and unorganized workers), some argue that the account of lean based on what its advocates claim it is overestimates its actual uniqueness and thus scope for solving organizational and economic crises.

For some researchers, lean production is, in fact, restricted as an account of new management techniques (most notably, Berggren 1988, 1993, 1995; Kenney and

Florida, 1991; Milkman 1991). This was argued by the Williams et al. in the United Kingdom ('Against Lean Production' 1992a; 'Ford Versus Fordism' 1992; 'Factories or Warehouses' 1992b; 'The Myth of the Line' 1993). Their argument, derived from a radical tradition in accounting and economics, was that the very term lean production provided an implausible understanding of the nature of new production and management practices, and they challenged the advocates' and propagandists' claims to originality, especially those proffered by Womack et al. For Williams et al., it was Ford's, as opposed to Toyota's, 'lean production' model that was truly revolutionary. The first and major innovation established by Ford, initially at Highland Park between 1909 and 1916, was the ability to strip labour out of the labour process (Williams, Haslam and Williams 1992:522). The significant advance was not in the extension of the principles of mass production; rather, development was established through the creation of what Williams et al. described as a 'proto-Japanese' (ibid.:519) factory. It was with this factory regime that Ford really established the foundations of new production arrangements, the lessons of which were lost over the next 40 or so years, only to be rediscovered by Toyota in the 1950s (ibid.:546).

The meaning of 'lean': society and ideology

While the above two sections outline the debate about lean production with respect to key advocates and critics, there is another set of issues concerning the politics and consequences of what is termed lean production for society more broadly. From this perspective, it is necessary to recognize the extent to which lean production can be understood as an ideology promoting claims to workplace innovation whether or not these are wrapped in the cloak of a 'lean enthusiast'. What we might describe as the 'lean ideology' promotes the belief that there is 'one best way' to improve performance, productivity and the organization of work: this will of necessity depend principally upon JIT, *kaizen*, team working and a form of employee involvement that negates independent worker representation such as trade unions in a variety of ways. For example, management may neutralize a trade union's workplace agenda by tying it up in workplace practices – such as agreeing to sanction the election of team leaders; by excluding them entirely from the company; or, where unions are accepted, by tying them into the company belief system as happened in high-profile cases such as Nissan UK in the 1980s and the American UAW in NUMMI in Fremont, California. There are, it is important to note, a range of interesting examples where trade unions, while being unable to block the introduction of lean practices, continually challenge management and its lean imperatives: see the case study below. Arguably the most powerful trade union response to lean production can be witnessed in the celebrated example of CAMI (a joint venture between Suzuki and GM in Canada) where the CAW (Canadian

Auto Workers) successfully intervened in the implementation of lean production strategies (see Rinehart et al. 1997; CAW 1990).

In other words, while management and management consultants approach workplace change in an ideological fashion, what they are describing, advocating and implementing has very particular consequences even if the account they provide of what it is they are introducing is open to judgement. The ideology reflects at the same time as it reinforces actual concrete change. Lean's advocates believe that if what they see as the lean agenda is pursued, then a win–win outcome is possible for both employer and employee alike. Moreover, and to reinforce the point in contrast to perspectives 1 and 2 outlined above, one can argue that while advocates of lean typically employ a mix of managerialist arguments and weak social science to advance their claims, this does not deny the fact that significant change is occurring within the world of work, many features of which can be attributed to practices that are seen to be central to the operation of what has come to be termed lean production.

However, this is where the question about the nature of lean production becomes even more interesting: the advocates of lean miss the point about what it is that lean represents in their account of workplace and management change. How might we better explain the evident changes highlighted in a range of studies which point to the seriously negative features of lean production? A second closely related question the advocates ignore is, 'Who are the main beneficiaries of these changes to work?' Finally, they also ignore the question, 'What is the link between lean production and neoliberalism today?' We can take these three questions together.

Smith's argument is important since he links together structural coercion, exploitation and the real subordination of employees. This trio of factors belies the rhetorical win–win world of lean production, and for Smith the practical consequences of employee subordination often remain unexamined by researchers. Also, one of the questions we should explore more fully is his view that lean is a more advanced capitalist management approach. We can say that for many in management it is an undoubted advance to be able to micro-manage the production process, and this of course includes the ability to tie labour into the companies' nostrums about work and organization: the company man or woman following the 'one-best-way' and 'working smarter not harder'. However, we also now understand much more about the wider social, economic and ecological inefficiencies attendant on the introduction of what some term 'lean' (see the case study below on GM and BMW). Lean production may be more efficient for this or that particular company, but we also know that it is not only at the expense of workers who carry the cost in terms of the squeeze on their own personal and family time (let us not forget too that many managers also suffer from the pressure to perform lean's sometimes punishing work schedules). Moreover, it also places a weight on suppliers, who must carry the burden of the downward pressure on price (including inventory costs).

Nevertheless, while it is crucial to examine the workings of new forms of management in the realm of commodity manufacture, sometimes overlooked is the spread of lean to other areas of work and employment.

Since structural coercion, exploitation and the real subordination of labour are at the root of any opposition to the world of lean production, what can be argued here is that understanding lean has to begin with recognition of its origins in the wider capitalist political economy together with the political imperatives that drive it. And looking at the nature of employment beyond the realm of commodity production, to forms of work in the public-state sector, we can see the extent to which lean has spread right across the political economy and into the realm of social reproduction (Mooney and Law 2007).

The importance of lean for neoliberals and 'lean capitalists' cannot be overstated since for them is has achieved iconic status: it is taken to represent everything that is the opposite of what they see as the downside of so-called Fordism. For advocates of lean, capital (the employer) in the old system of Fordism bears disproportionate costs in what the employer takes to be high wage rates encompassing good pay and conditions, including pension provision. Under Fordism, the immediate costs of injury and early exit are in the main borne by the employer, the state and the worker by means of the social wage (welfare state provision including a sound deferred wage-pension). However, with early exit increasingly a feature of ever more pressurized work under lean production, the state, as opposed to the employer, bears more of the burden of health and social care and notably where the worker permanently exits employment. In the society dominated by lean production, the employer and advocates of lean argue that it is insufficient to assume that this burden will continue to be met through the social wage (welfare state provision) and the deferred wage (pension) and especially since from their perspective it is certainly not up to the employer to pay. This is a crucial point of principle for those committed (lean evangelists) to the view that others (not the immediate employer) should bear the cost of the new world of lean production. Yet with a rise in early retirement in many sectors and with the acceleration in the concentration of private as against social wealth resulting from the political economy of the contemporary neoliberal state, it has to be asked whether this is fair. In other words, the discussion about the nature of lean-in-the-workplace very quickly becomes a discussion about the relationships between work, employment and the wider social context. Thus, does 'lean working' presuppose the 'lean society'? We leave this question for discussion since it is one thing to argue that lean management strategies are being implemented across society and quite another large step to argue we live in a 'lean society'. Put another way – is the lean society an even more intensive variant of capitalism? If this is so, could one argue that it is in fact a new type of capitalism?

Yet, the extensive nature and implications of this invasion of lean working methods (we might even refer to it as 'lean politics') throughout many societies should not be underestimated. Thus, we only have to consider for a moment that the costs of reproduction in the lean political economy are carried largely by workers when they are in work (see the case study and the impact on health and welfare). Employers' additional costs can be eliminated with the early job exits. After employment, early retirement costs owing to injury or an inability to cope with pressure of lean working routines means that costs are increasingly carried by the state and its agencies – costs, moreover, which lean neoliberal capital and its supporters in government seek to reduce with ever more stringent regulations for unemployment and disability benefit provision. Mooney and Law (ibid.) are concerned with the lean character of work and labour relations for state employees; those confronted by the casualties of the lean accumulation of surplus value, and now the latest to be hit by lean's long march through the various sectors of the economy. These employees work in local government, health and social care, and they are also now finding that lean management practices are being introduced into their workplaces. Mooney and Law place their examination in the intersection between the politics and ideology of the neoliberal state and lean production *within* the state, and this is important. Because they highlight the distinctive nature of state employment from that of workers involved in the creation of surplus value (the production of consumer goods), we would argue that their focus draws attention to the process of the social reproduction of what the cultural critic John Berger describes as 'abandonment'. State employees who themselves are being made to work under lean management regimes are increasingly 'working', as part of their labour process, with those workers who are the inevitable casualties of the paradigm of lean production, or 'management by stress' in manufacturing (Parker and Slaughter 1988). Being pushed out of employment too early is certainly not a problem for a system designed to seek and eliminate weakness from production. It is, of course, a problem for those workers forced out (too soon) and for those (other state) workers who have themselves to cope with the consequences of this aspect of economic exclusion in their role as state employees. So, what kinds of working conditions might lead to circumstances which employees might find increasingly intolerable?

We take as an exemplar excerpts from a recent study of two automotive assembly plants in the UK made by a team of shop floor workers and academics. This study describes what may be termed a 'New Regime of Production'. Another feature of this landmark study is that unlike much pro-lean production research, the study is based upon long-term engagement with shop floor workers by researchers, taking into account the views and experiences workers have of lean production over a 20-year period.

Case study: General Motors (GM) and BMW

'Working Conditions and Workload' taken from chapter 7, pp. 159–200, Stewart et al. 2009.

The dominant managerial discourse governing the labour productivity benefits that accrue from lean production is underpinned by a belief in the potential of a more sophisticated management ... Compared to conventional Fordist work organization, the technological and supervisory architecture of lean production is assumed to engender high trust relations and processes of empowerment on the shop-floor. In the 1980s and 1990s, this was summarized through the trite maxim 'working smarter not harder' and exemplified by the work of [the] IMVP research [team]. In more refined form, it was also embodied in the work of Kenney and Florida (1993) who argued that the competitive edge of Japanese forms of lean production lay in what they termed 'innovation-mediated production'. Essentially, this was a relational framework that attempted to harness the job knowledge of design and production engineers and shop-floor workers.

We provide an alternative – and more problematic – picture to this, an analysis of line workers' own experiences of the automotive lean production line [in specific contexts]. We consider in turn, basic conditions on the line, workload and work speed before moving on to different dimensions of quality of working life, such as employee autonomy, workplace stress and bullying. While it is not difficult to find evidence of work place harassment, or bullying, in the good old, bad old days, there is certainly evidence for its persistence under the various manifestations of lean. As one BMW steward pointed out, the way in which workers cope with it is different today since exit options are limited.

> Well the management styles have changed considerably because twenty years ago things that the management are doing now wouldn't have been tolerated, people, you know, would have just got their coats on and gone home. But now I mean they treat you ... [looks away resigned] I wouldn't treat a dog like some managers treat people. (28/9/00)

In our sample, three-quarters of employees reported that they worked in some form of production team (of which two thirds reported the practice of job rotation). And despite the optimistic claims of those management gurus who proclaim a new, post-Taylorist manufacturing environment, few workers had any delusions over the skill content of work on the new team-based lean production assembly line. At both [GM and BMW] plants, three-quarters of workers felt that it would take less than a month to train someone to do their job and nearly 40 per cent felt it would take a few days or less. According to one body shop worker:

> It's not really skill as such like even with the new car. I mean yea, you do get a lot of different new things to do but taken on their own they're pretty simple jobs. It's not skill it's like you

are really a robot. For me that's easy, I can switch off and I'm sitting on a beach in Barbados. It's bloody boring.

Another facet of the labour process of these employees was the high degree of management surveillance reported ... Again this stands in contrast to the 'independent', 'working smarter' idiom of lean management discourse. 72 per cent of employees indicated that their work performance was either closely or very closely monitored by management ... these associations do suggest that as well as remaining a source of work degradation and a pervasive alternative management strategy to a more enlightened 'responsible autonomy' (Friedman 1977), direct control can also impair the psychological and material well-being of workers who are subject to its managerial gaze.

Significant minorities of employees also reported work overload. Around a quarter of employees felt that their workload was too heavy, although the figure was higher at GM ... We explored the problem of work intensity further by asking employees what proportion of each day they had to work as fast as they could to keep up with the rhythm of production and whether they felt they could maintain their current work pace until the age of 60 ... Not surprisingly, nearly two thirds felt that they would be unlikely to be able to maintain the current pace of work until the age of 60. Arduous, repetitive and monotonous work of the type associated with the automotive production line is always likely to be stressful for workers ... One of the core claims of the IMVP researchers was that lean production offered something better for workers in that 'working smarter' provided them with the space and management techniques to establish a more participative (and less stressful) work environment:

> While the mass-production plant is often filled with mind-numbing stress, as workers struggle to assemble unmanufacturable products and have no way to improve their working environment, lean production offers a creative tension in which workers have many ways to address challenges. This creative tension involved in solving complex problems is precisely what has separated manual factory work from professional 'think' work in the age of mass production. (Womack et al. 1990:101)

There is now a good deal of critical research that refutes this claim. For example, case study work such as Graham (1995) and Rinehart et al. (1997) found that the core features of worker experience involved job rationalization, work overload and constant 'speed-up' of the production line. Survey work has found relatively high level of worker stress in car plants in Canada, Japan and the United Kingdom (Stewart et al. 2004), while multi-sectoral survey work in the United States has found clear evidence that the use of such lean techniques as just-in-time and quality circles increases the risk of cumulative trauma disorders (Brenner et al. 2004).

Although managerial harassment in its different forms has long been regarded as a defining feature of the process of direct management control, it is only relatively recently that this has been problematized as a discrete feature of workplace relations. Moreover, in the new world of lean production, respect is supposed to have superseded condescension. The ILO (1999) defined bullying as a form of workplace violence in which a person is threatened or assaulted and that can originate in customers and co-workers at any level of the organization. According to one worker:

> Managers don't really show a lot respect nowadays. It's a different culture because managers may be under pressure too. I mean I'm not making excuses for them, because they take their pressure out on the shop floor. We've had instances where people have been spoken to in terrible situations where people have got sworn at and, apart from physically hitting somebody, it's the worse kind of abuse that you can get, you know harassment. They don't even get rapped over the knuckles. If it was you or me you'd lose your job. But see it's like a class system.

Questions

1. What would you see as the major problems emerging from this new regime of production?
2. Why do you think these problems are likely to emerge?
3. What changes does it bring in terms of management–worker relations as outlined by the discussion on bullying?

Conclusion

This chapter has considered the three main approaches to understanding the concept of lean production. In the first approach, we examined the claims by those who see lean as in some sense representing a revolutionary break, beginning in the late 1980s, from previous approaches to work often described as 'Fordist'. The advocates here embrace managers, management consultants and a range of pro-management academics. The ideological nature of this view was examined. However, there is also a much more critical current within this approach of lean-as-revolutionary that, while arguing for its innovation and greater efficiency, sees it as having a downside for many workers. In the second approach, a range of critics argue that lean production is to all intents and purposes not in the least revolutionary: more a case of old wine in new bottles. The third approach argues that while there this is something useful to be had in the use of the term lean production, the term itself does not allow for an adequate account of the origins of what is termed lean production nor of what 'lean production' does. To understand what 'lean' is, the protagonists of this approach argue that the best way to interpret lean is to hold up the claims of its advocates to the light of empirical enquiry. Our case study illustrates an attempt to do just this. The essential claims of the proponents of lean – the 'leanistas' – are: lean is more efficient for everyone; it is more democratic and participatory; in allowing people to work 'smarter not harder' it reduces workplace stress and pressure while increasing empowerment.

However, far from the benign workplace regime delivering the empowerment its advocates claim, lean is in fact a new form of 'class struggle from above' assisting, and thereby extending, existing workplace regimes of subordination. Lean is the new means by which the employer seeks to take control of the shop floor and workplace more broadly. Does this mean that greater employee control of society should be a necessary next step? Although the case study does not seek to answer this question, it is certainly a reasonable one to contemplate.

Lean is indeed an innovative form of work for both capitalist firms and other organizations not driven by the profit motive. It represents an evolution of existing means by which the workplace and other forms of social organization are coordinated. Moreover, related to its origins in capitalist production techniques, its principal role is to reduce costs and principally those involving human labour. Lean firms and lean work strategies are therefore concerned with taking labour out of production, increasing labour and other efficiencies at the expense of a firm's own staff and its competitors. Thus, despite the rhetoric from advocates of lean that it represents a win–win strategy, it is in fact management and capital who are the ultimate beneficiaries. Cost is consequently displaced onto others and the wider society which bear the burden in terms of unemployment, employee injury and social and material waste. This is the backdrop to a febrile environment: continual change, continual uncertainty. Lean production does not of itself create the latter, but it does sustain it. This would seem to be paradoxical, especially since it is the professed claim of the leanistas that lean allows for control and long-term planning. However, the paradox exists precisely because lean production cannot determine the cycles of demand (booms and slumps in commodity prices) in the ways its advocates would like. In fact, another way to understand lean and consequently its implication for human resources is to view its obsession with ever-tighter forms of resource (human and technical) management as a response to the impact of neoliberalism in the firm's external economy. That is, the more uncertain the external world, the weaker the forms of labour and commodity regulation, the more individual capital seeks to control the internal life-world of the firm. This is, after all, what lean management of human and other resources is concerned with.

Thus, by overlooking the fact of lean's broader social inefficiencies, its advocates ignore the wider costs to our world of ever-faster conception-to-execution rates as firms chase the next and exciting product. JIT and *kanban* stock control make it possible to enact swift changes that develop and market another product line almost before the previous one has been amortized (costs realized). This is not even to mention the terrifying environmental costs of the mountain of waste created by the seemingly endless drive to find the next new product winner. In other words, while lean has achieved much for the owners of successful companies, the often great cost to others must be added to the social and economic balance sheet. It is important that we recognize the social, economic (and political) factors driving lean in the first place. These are organizational, workplace and economic changes at the heart of the political economy of contemporary capitalism.

To describe lean production simply as a system of organizational and technical variables is unsustainable. To see lean as in some sense transportable to any time, place and social system would be to fail to understand its historical rootedness in the era of contemporary capitalist crises of profitability.

Reflective questions

1. Outline the three main ways in which lean production can be understood. You should also distinguish the variations within approaches 1 and 3.
2. Is lean production an ideology of work put forward by management or is it actually a new innovative form of work? Or is it both? Another way to look at the question is to consider whether lean production is really just a new way of describing the ongoing intensification of existing work and management practices.
3. Referring to the case study, consider how the authors address at least two assumptions of those who advocate the supposed benefits of lean production.
4. What are the differences in perspective between those who see lean production as being just concerned with new forms of work unconnected with wider society, and those who see in lean production the basis of a new type of society embracing our lives within and beyond the world of production?
5. Is there a problem with way in which the term lean production is used as a short-hand for management control throughout this chapter?

Recommended reading

- Kenney, M. and Florida, R. (1991) 'Transplanted organisations: The transfer of Japanese industrial organization to the US'. *American Sociological Review*, 56: 381–398.
- Stewart, P. and Garrahan, P. (1995) 'Employee responses to new management techniques in the auto industry'. *Work, Employment and Society*, 9(3): September.
- Carter, B, Danford, A., Howcroft, D., Richardson, H., Smith, A and Taylor, P. (2013) "Stressed out of my box": employee experience of lean working and occupational ill-health in clerical work in the UK public sector'. *Work, Employment and Society*, 0950017012469064, first published on May 20, 2013. http://wes.sagepub.com/content/early/2013/05/20/0950017012469064. The online version of this article can be found at: DOI: 10.1177/0950017012469064
- Stewart, P., Richardson, M., Danford, A., Murphy, K., Richardson, T. and Wass, V. (2009) *We Sell Our Time No More. Workers' Struggles Against Lean Production in the British Car Industry.* London: Pluto Press.

Notes

1. Coffey's the *Myth of Japanese efficiency. The World Car Industry in a Globalizing Age* is probably the sharpest critique of the lean production-as-ideology approach to understanding the meaning and usages of the concept of lean production (see pp. 1–22).
2. For a salutary critique on the empirical consequences of 'transfer', albeit in a non-automotive sector, see Milkman (1991) and on the logic of transfer more generally, Berggren (1988, 1993).
3. By 'structural coercion' is meant workers non-ownership of the means of production and the consequent economic compulsion to labour which this requires. 'Exploitation' means the intensification of labour, including the extension of working time and the exploitation of social divisions. The mechanisms of social and organizational restraint, which is what is meant by the 'real subsumption of labour', refers, inter alia, to team working principally in terms of peer pressure and surveillance (Fucini and Fucini 1990; Garrahan and Stewart 1992; Graham 1995; Stephenson 1995).

References

Abdullah, S. R. S. and Keenoy, T. (1995) 'Japanese management practices in the Malaysian electronics industry'. *Journal of Management Studies*, 32(6): 747–766.

Ackroyd, S., Burrell, G., Hughes, H. and Whitaker, A. (1988) 'The Japanisation of British industry?' *Industrial Relations Journal*, 19(1): 11–23.

Berggren, C. (1988) '"New production concepts" in final assembly—the Swedish experience'. In Dankbaar B., Jurgens, U. and Malsch, T. (eds), *Die Zukunft der Arbeit in der Automobilindustrie*, Berlin: WZB.

Berggren, C. (1993) 'The end of history?'. *Work Employment and Society*, 7(2): 163–188.

Berggren, C. (1995) 'Japan as number two: Competitive problems and the future of alliance capitalism after the burst of the bubble economy'. *Work, Employment and Society*, 9(1): 53–95.

Boyer, R. and Freyssenet, M. (2000) *The Productive Models: The Conditions of Profitability.* Basingstoke: Palgrave-Macmillan.

Brenner, M., Fairris, D. and Ruser, J. (2004) '"Flexible" work practices and occupational safety and health: exploring the relationship between cumulative trauma disorders and workplace transformation', *Industrial Relations*, 43, 242–266.

Canadian Auto Workers (CAW) (1990) 'Workplace issues, work reorganisation: responding to lean producton.' Willowfield, Ontario: CAW Research and Communications Departments.

Carter, B, Danford, A , Howcroft, D, Richardson, H, Smith, A and Taylor, P (3013) 'Stressed out of my box': employee experience of lean working and occupational ill-health in clerical work in the UK public sector', *Work, Employment & Society October 2013* 27: 747–767, Volume 27 number 5.

Charron, E. and Stewart, P. (eds.) (2004) *Work and Employment Relations in the Automobile Industry.* Basingstoke: Palgrave-Macmillan.

Coffey, D. (2006) The *Myth of Japanese Efficiency: The World Car Industry in a Globalizing Age.* Cheltenham: Edward Elgar.

Delbridge, R. (1995) 'Surviving JIT: Control and resistance in a Japanese transplant'. *Journal of Management Studies*, 32(6): 803–817.

Durand, J.-P. (2007) *The Invisible Chain: Constraints and Opportunities in the New World of Employment*. Basingstoke: Palgrave-Macmillan.

Elger, T. and Smith, C. (1994) *Global Japanization: The Transformation of the Labour Process*. London: Routledge.

Friedman, A (1977) Industry and Labour: class struggle at work and monopoly capitalism, London: Macmillan.

Fucini, J. and Fucini, S. (1990) *Working for the Japanese*. New York: The Free Press.

Garrahan, P. and Stewart, P. (1992) *The Nissan Enigma: Flexibility and Work in a Local Economy*. London: Mansell.

GERPISA (1993) 'Trajectories of automobile firms'. *Proceedings of the Group for the Study of the Auto Industry and its Employees*. Paris: University d'Evry-Val d'Essone.

Graham, L. (1995) *On the line at Subaru-Isuzu: The Japanese model and the American worker*. Ithaca, NY: ILR/Cornell University Press.

Hirst, P. and Zeitlin, J. (1991) 'Flexible specialisation versus post-Fordism: Theory, evidence and policy implications'. *Economy and Society*, 20(1): 1–56.

Humphrey, J. (1995) 'The adoption of Japanese management techniques in Brazilian industry'. *Journal of Management Studies*, 32(6): 767–787.

Jones, D. (1992) 'Lean production (an update)'. Paper presented to the *Lean Production and European Trade Union Co-operation*. TGWU Centre, 6th–11th December 1992. Eastbourne, UK.

Jurgens, U., Malsch, T. and Dohse, K. (1993) *Breaking from Taylorism: Changing Forms of Work in the Automobile Industry*. Cambridge: Cambridge University Press.

Kenney, M. and Florida, R. (1991) 'Transplanted organisations: The transfer of Japanese industrial organization to the US'. *American Sociological Review*, 56: 381–398.

Kenney, M. and Florida, R. (1993) *Beyond Mass Production: The Japanese System and Its Transfer to the US*. Oxford: Oxford University Press.

Milkman, R. (1991) *Japan's Californian Factories—Labour Relations and Economic Globalisation*. Los Angeles: Institute of Industrial Relations, University of California.

Mooney, G. and Law, A. (eds.) (2007) *New Labour/Hard Labour: Restructuring and Resistance inside the Welfare Industry*. Bristol: The Policy Press.

Morris, J., Munday, M. and Wilkinson, B. (1992) *Japanese Investment in Wales: Social and Economic Consequences*. Cardiff Business School, mimeo.

Morris, J. and Wilkinson, B. (1995) 'The transfer of Japanese management to alien institutional environments'. *Journal of Managment Studies*, 32(6): 719–730.

Oliver, N. (1991) 'The dynamics of just-in-time'. *New Technology, Work and Employment*, 6(1): 19–27.

Oliver, N., Delbridge, R., Jones, D. and Lowe, J. (1993) 'World class manufacturing: further evidence in the lean production debate'. Paper presented to the *British Academy of Management Conference*, Milton Keynes, September.

Oliver, N., Jones, D., Delbridge, R. and Lowe, J. (1994) 'Worldwide Manufacturing Competitiveness Study'. The Second Lean Enterprise Report, Andersen Consulting.

Oliver, N. and Wilkinson, B. (1992) *The Japanization of British Industry: New Developments in the 1990s*. London: Blackwell.

Parker, M. and Slaughter, J. (1988) *Choosing Sides: Unions and the Team Concept*. Boston: South End Press.

Rinehart, J., Huxley, C. and Robertson, D. (1997) *Just Another Car Factory: Lean Production and Its Discontents*. Ithaca: ILR Press.

Seddon, J. and Caulkin, S. (2007) 'Systems thinking, lean production and action learning'. *Action Learning: Research and Practice*, 4(1): 9–24.

Smith, T. (2000) *Technology and Capital in the Age of Lean Production: A Marxian Critique of the 'New Economy'*. New York: SUNY Press.

Stephenson, C. (1995) 'The different experience of trade unionism in two Japanese transplants'. In Acker, P., Smith, C. and Smith, P. (eds.), *The New Workplace and Trade Unionism*. London: Routledge.

Stewart, P. and Garrahan, P. (1995) 'Employee responses to new management techniques in the auto industry'. *Work, Employment and Society*, 9(3): 517–536.

Stewart, P., Lewchuk., Yates, C., Saruta, M. and Danford, A. (2004) 'Patterns of labour control and the erosion of labour standards: towards an international study of the quality of working life in the automobile industry (Canada, Japan and the UK)', in Charron, E. and Stewart, P. (eds.) (2004) *Work and Employment Relations in the Automobile Industry*. Basingstoke: Palgrave-Macmillan.

Turnbull, P. J. (1986) 'The "Japanisation" of production and industrial relations at Lucas electrical'. *Industrial Relations Journal*, 17(3): 193–206.

Williams, K., Haslam, C., Williams, J., Cutler, T., Adcroft, A. and Johal, S. (1992a) 'Against lean production'. *Economy and Society*, 21(3): 321–354.

Williams, K., Haslam, C., Adcroft, A. and Johal, S. (1992b) 'Factories or warehouses' mimeo.

Williams, K., Haslam, C. and Williams, J. (1992c) 'Ford -v-"Fordism": The beginning of mass production?'. *Work Employment and Society,* 6(4): 517–555.

Williams, K., Haslam, C., Adcroft, A. and Johal, S. (1993) 'The myth of the line: Ford's production of the Model T at Highland Park, 1909–16'. *Business History*, 35(3): 66–87.

Wilkinson, B., Morris, J. and Mundy, M. (1995) 'The iron fist in the velvet glove: Management and organisation in Japanese manufacturing transplants in Wales'. *Journal of Management Studies*, 32(6): 819–830.

Womack, J. P., Roos, D. and Jones, D. T. (1990) *The Machine that Changed the World*. Rawson: New York.

Section 3

The external environment

8 Economic and social context: Are there varieties of capitalism? what difference does it make to employment relations?

Leo McCann

Learning objectives

- To discuss the broader national and international contexts into which organizations and employment relations are embedded, showing that there are considerable differences across the world in terms of national institutions, practices and traditions of economic governance and work and employment relations.
- To explore the nature of these differences in national business context, such as the differences between so-called 'liberal market economies' (e.g., the United States and the United Kingdom) and 'coordinated market economies' (e.g., Germany and Japan). What are the impacts of these 'varieties of capitalism' on employment relations in firms located in different regions?
- To explore the extent to which national differences in business context and practice might be becoming less significant as the world economy is increasingly integrated under the pressures of globalization and the growth of transnational corporations and 'global best practice'.
- To provide a critical case study which explores the problems of trying to operate internationally when national traditions of business (especially when it comes to work and employment conditions) can be so distinct from, and possibly incompatible with, each other.

Introduction

> We live in a world of transformations, affecting almost every aspect of what
> we do. For better or for worse, we are being propelled into a global order that
> no one fully understands, but which is making its effects felt upon all of us.
>
> (Giddens 1999: 6–7)

> Despite numerous claims of growing convergence and the 'globalization' of
> managerial structures and strategies, the ways in which economic activities
> are organized and controlled in, for example, … Japan, South Korea …, and
> Taiwan differ considerably from those prevalent in the USA and UK.
>
> (Whitley 1999: 3)

These two quotations exemplify positions at either end of a debate that has been
under way for several decades – a debate about globalization and the supposed
'convergence' of business systems. In a context of increasing internationalization
of world business and, crucially, an increasing *awareness and consciousness* among
people that the world is internationalizing (see Steger 2009: 15), one might expect
business, management and labour systems to be *converging*, that is, becoming
more similar to one another. Globalization might also be sweeping away traditional
differences in business, management and organization as businesses interact globally and forms of 'world best practice' become established.

Many, however, dispute the extent of globalization, and instead point to the
continued *divergence* in business systems. In recent years, schools of thought
known as the varieties of capitalism, comparative capitalisms and national business systems approaches have developed rapidly (see McCann 2014). This is not
the place to go into a major interpretation of each of these approaches; for our
purposes, it is simpler and more sensible to refer to the whole paradigm as
'varieties of capitalism' (or VoC). While not tending to deny the existence of
globalizing forces, VoC authors argue that different ways of organizing, financing
and staffing firms across the world remain powerful, and, while changing, seem
unlikely to be fully eroded. In certain ways, national differences are actually reinforced by globalization.

The role of this chapter is to discuss and explain the continuing differences
between national business and employment systems in terms of the economic and
regulatory contexts of capitalism. The relevance of this chapter for the book is that
it will illustrate how the external environment of TNCs and transnational organizations remains complex; distinct national-level entities shape the management of
work in a variety of ways. This is explained by briefly outlining the theoretical
approach of VoC. There are many ways of examining the convergence versus
divergence debate, but for reasons of space the chapter will mostly address it by
exploring how and why ideas of 'global best practice' filter between nations.
Particular attention will be paid to the spread of 'American-style' corporate

governance from the United States to the world, and to the spread of so-called 'lean production' from Japan to the world. The role played by TNCs in spreading global best practice will be discussed. The chapter also encourages students to consider how ideas of global best practice are actually 'received' by host nations, and how they are emulated resisted, translated and often rejected.

What is 'global best practice'?

TNCs play a central role in debates around globalization. Many versions of the globalization story have TNCs as central characters, contributing to the increasing acceleration and integration of cross-border trade and investment, and at the forefront of developing ideologies of globalization that further spread the awareness of people all around the world that they are increasingly being drawn into global relations (Steger 2009: 15). Business schools, MBA programmes, consulting and mainstream business literature (including academic, 'popular' and media sources) develop and spread the ideology of globalization. Excellent examples include the bestselling book *The World is Flat* by Thomas Friedman (2005), or memoirs of high-profile 'global business leaders' such as Jack Welch, formerly of GE (Welch 2001). Such texts promote the idea of a radically globalized economy, of intense competition where the weak go to the wall and 'the status quo is a prescription for disaster' (Taylor and Webber 1996: x). They describe an integrated 'New Economy' – a global economy where TNCs must radically restructure themselves in order to become more competitive, more flexible and more adaptable. Going through painful and dramatic processes of corporate metamorphosis, TNCs emerge as genuinely global firms, operating genuinely global strategies. These strategies include hiring the best 'talent' from anywhere in the world, and undergoing culture change which is designed to obviate the need for employees to be represented by 'old economy'-style trade unions. The concept of a global labour market was famously popularized by the influential McKinsey Consulting study known as the 'War for Talent' (Chambers et al. 1998), in which firms are encouraged to develop 'global talent management programmes' to identify, recruit and retain the 'best and the brightest' staff who have a 'global mindset' and are able to slot seamlessly into any world-class employer with minimal fuss or culture shock. A 'global sourcing' model is adopted in which labour and management are recruited from all over the world and posted to all points globally. One high-profile example of such global sourcing is provided by the British bank HSBC's 'International Manager' programme, a recruitment and employment stream for those prepared to take on extremely demanding roles with regular overseas postings. Persons attached to local culture and home comforts need not apply![1]

Such 'international managers' start to resemble an archetype of the global troubleshooter or special operative who (quite obviously) was born somewhere but has been educated in numerous high-profile, elite and internationalized universities and business schools, and now possesses no obvious home nation or base of operations.

Such a character has probably worked for several high-profile 'global' firms across his or her career, and now spends a great deal of time flying business class, listening to the thoughts of global leadership gurus such as Tom Peters while waiting in airport lounges, dropping in to help 'roll out' a new global performance management system for employees at a semiconductor subsidiary in Vietnam one day, then flying long distance to meet disgruntled French trade union representatives in Paris the next.

While this extreme vision of hypermobile, globalized managers is a reality for a select few, it is hard to reconcile this picture with daily realities for the vast majority of employees and managers. While mainstream business literature emphasizes global uniformity and hypermobility, VoC reminds us that the world system tolerates a wide diversity of organizational and economic forms, and that national, rather than international, forces remain very powerful, restricting the development of the truly 'global' employment practices portrayed in mainstream business sources.

The present chapter argues that many TNCs are attempting to develop genuinely global HRM strategies, and there are clear signs of a globalized ideology of 'best practice' that has its roots in the United States. However, both practice and theory are problematic in several ways because national and regional institutions make it hard for systems designed to be universal to take effect. There are also competing 'models' or forms of 'best practice' from nations such as Japan, Germany and Denmark. I suggest that in order to fully understand the emerging internationalized economy, observers need to sensitize themselves to both local and transnational pressures, forces and institutions that replicate themselves over time. Changes are highly contingent, and care must be taken when asserting the superiority or appropriateness of one model over another, as enthusiasm for, and advocacy of, various models can wax and wane rapidly (see McCormack 2008; Whitley 2009). The following section provides some theoretical backing to these claims, by outlining the VoC approach in more detail.

The 'varieties of capitalism' approach: an introductory background

Academic discussion of national differences in economic structure and conduct has a long history. But the emergence of the VoC literature seems to have been triggered by the avalanche of literature about globalization and convergence that appeared in the 1990s after the collapse of the Soviet Union. Institutionalist authors were keen to offer a more sceptical view, noting change but also pointing to the vital importance of local and regional diversity. VoC as a body of literature is strong when it comes to refuting or rebalancing the wilder claims of the globalization literature. It offers detailed and useful discussions of the wide range of diversity that undoubtedly still exists in the international economy. However, it is a very abstract body of literature, and VoC authors can often be vague in regards to what actually happens inside firms (see, for example, Campbell and Pedersen 2007). It also tends to be rather conservative when it comes to explaining changes to firms and to institutions. Detailed expositions of VoC have been produced by, among others, Hall and Soskice (2001), Whitley (1999), Amable (2003) and Coates (2000). These texts provide great detail on the main claims made by VoC theoreticians. However, the abstractness of this literature can be off-putting, and some find the lack of detail on firms and daily work practices frustrating. Work on core VoC theory tends to focus at an abstract, 'system' or 'model' level, usually aiming to provide overviews which can be helpful for theoretical and conceptual development. There are also many other studies available in the literature which, although not explicitly connected to VoC theory, still have a lot to say about the convergence or divergence of business systems. These are often written by regional experts such as Dore (2000), who is one of the world's foremost experts on Japan, or business or labour historians such as Jacoby (2005) and McCraw (1997), who provide substantial detail on how companies behave 'on the ground'. Findings from company-level studies often reflect what VoC theory predicts, but can just as often contradict VoC. For example, a recent special issue of *British Journal of Industrial Relations* (vol. 48, no. 2) included research papers presenting findings from across numerous countries that both supported and rejected VoC theory; see, in particular, papers by Batt et al. (2010) on call centres, and McCann et al. (2010) on middle managers in the United States, United Kingdom and Japan.

VoC's main contribution to our knowledge – and it is a powerful one – is that the world economy tolerates a wide diversity of national business systems. VoC theorists draw out the similarities and differences in capitalism across the world, pointing to the various ways in which the business environment (in particular, the various *institutions*) in place across nations structure what is possible for economic actors such as managers, employees, bankers, governments and trade unionists. In their analysis of business environments, VoC authors often subdivide economies into several key sectors, effectively into *clusters of institutional phenomena* that have structuring effects on economic action and actors. These clusters provide the 'rules of the game' for economic action across different societies, and they put in place enablements and constraints on economic behaviour. They frame what is possible and what is less possible for firms, unions and other actors, making certain behaviours and outcomes more likely to occur and others less likely to occur (Whitley 1999: 3).

VoC draws much of its influence from *institutional theory*, an approach most widely used in the disciplines of sociology, political studies and organizational studies. Institutional theory argues that economic action cannot be fully understood by the conventions of 'rational-choice' economics, which emphasizes 'universal laws' of supply and demand that apply in essentially the same form across all societies. Instead, institutionalists claim that economic action is simply one form of *social* action, and can therefore only be understood with reference to the broader social structures into which economic action takes place. The academic term often used is *embeddedness* – forms of economic and business interaction and exchange are embedded in social institutions, such as national legal frameworks or social norms of what is morally and cultural appropriate (Hollingsworth and Boyer 1997). These customs, laws and structures differ across nations and regions. VoC theory is, therefore, an important counterweight to neoliberal arguments about the inevitability of western-driven globalization. VoC thus takes a somewhat sceptical approach to globalization (see Giddens 1999: 6–20; Held et al. 1999: 2–28).

Perhaps the most famous distinction between economic models was made by Hall and Soskice in the introductory chapter to their edited volume *Varieties of Capitalism* (2001), which is widely acknowledged as a 'must-read' in the field. They lay out liberal market economies (LMEs) versus coordinated market economies (CMEs) as the two fundamental types of economic model in existence. The binary division of LMEs and CMEs has, however, been challenged by numerous authors for being somewhat simplistic and general (see Whitley 1999; Amable 2003). Recent works by Jackson and Deeg (2006, 2007) provide comprehensive and invaluable analyses of the strengths and weaknesses of the literature on comparative capitalism. They conclude that the split between CMEs and LMEs, while somewhat crude, does make sense empirically and theoretically.

Specifically, the models refer to the features described in the next two sections.

Liberal market economies (LMEs)

These are national economies characterized by a high degree of openness to globalization and world trade, which have been through considerable processes of neoliberal deregulation and privatization since the 1980s (see Dore 2000: 2–19). Fundamental to LMEs are the *processes of marketization and financialization*, the processes by which ever-greater parts of national economies are opened up to market forces, with 'shareholder value preached as the sole legitimate objective of corporate executives' (Dore 2000: 5; Lazonick and O'Sullivan 2000). In other words, LMEs are increasing dominated by financial interests over and above those of other stakeholders (such as government or labour). An excellent overview of the growth of financialization, showing how it is increasingly spreading to CMEs, is provided by Dore (2000), who compares the United States/United Kingdom (paradigmatic examples of LMEs) with Germany and Japan (the most powerful CMEs). Institutions of LMEs have been transformed to facilitate increased marketization, such as changes to corporate and employment law, which have handed more power to fund managers and corporate management, tempting them to take ever-greater risks with the (increasingly globalized) financial markets, which, in the year 2000, reached a combined value of *72 trillion dollars* (Smith and Walter 2006: 23). Under financialization, time horizons for firms are shrunk as executives look to make decisions that will please investors, that is, decisions that will result in a short-term uplift in share prices. Such short-term thinking makes it hard to sustain long-term investment in costly projects, especially in manufacturing sectors. LMEs are, therefore, usually characterized by large services sectors and hugely reduced industrial and manufacturing sectors. In the realm of corporate governance, firms have what is known as an active 'market for corporate control', whereby companies are threatened with hostile takeovers if their share price falls to a level where it might be profitable for outside investors or other firms to purchase the company (gaining 'leverage' from global financial markets to do so). Where markets for corporate control exist, companies can be bought and sold almost at will, and where shareholder value is regarded as the only legitimate purpose of a firm, this is widely seen as legitimate, even something to expect. LME nations such as the United States or the United Kingdom (representative of what is often labelled 'Anglo-Saxon capitalism'), therefore, have a reputation for being ruthless, unstable, ever-changing economies where there is no long term for investors, managers or employees. Just as company ownership is vulnerable to change, people's careers are also disrupted, and staff would be wise not to expect loyalty from their employer, and can expect to have several employers over the course of their working life.

Change can be a good thing, of course. A more positive appraisal of LMEs would point to their dynamic and fast-moving nature, their willingness to shift into new economic sectors and undertake radical innovations, often backed by highly liquid forms of funding, such as venture capital or private equity, which is able to flood in and out of new markets as needed. Perhaps, therefore, LME firms are best exemplified by Silicon Valley high-tech start-ups, initially funded with venture capital, with little prior history but at the cutting-edge of technology and IT product markets. The United States is, after all, the home of dynamic and wildly successful companies which started out this way, such as Amazon, Microsoft, Apple, Cisco Systems, Google and eBay. On the other hand, famous industrial giants such as Ford, General Motors, US Steel and Radio Corporation of America (RCA) have struggled with decline, uncertainty and even collapse in the last three decades.

Coordinated market economies (CMEs)

In terms of ideal types, CMEs are characterized by essentially the opposite of all of the above. Typical CME nations such as Japan and Germany are organized according to quite different principles from LMEs. They have, in general, a much higher role for state regulation (and even ownership) of the economy, and the processes of marketization and financialization have proceeded much more slowly than in LMEs. Large firms in CMEs tend to be much more stable in terms of their organizational, ownership and employment conditions. Stock markets play a much-reduced role in CMEs. There is often little or no market for corporate control: companies are insulated from takeover by purchasing and maintaining mutually defensive blocks of shares in each other and by much stricter legal frameworks which limit the possibilities for leveraged buy-outs. (In Japan, for example, the Ministry of Finance will traditionally not approve bank loans for the purpose of leveraged buyouts.) In France (until fairly recently), the Ministry of Finance had to approve all loans over a certain value, which effectively handed financial control of corporate affairs to the state. French governments used to be big believers in long-range strategic planning, involving state allocation of cheap loans to critical industrial sectors (such as railways and nuclear reactors), and established state-backed 'national champions' in automotive and insurance industries, in common with almost all of the East Asian nations that experienced rapid economic growth from the 1960s to the 1990s.

The great advantage of this less marketized and less ruthless system is that it provides long time horizons for forward planning, which is often regarded as essential for companies to be able to genuinely compete in world-class mass manufacturing sectors such as cars and consumer electronics, where cost-cutting and compensating on quality and reliability are not really viable strategies. Long-range planning also lends itself to *incremental innovation*, whereby firms make steady, continual and small improvements to existing technologies, perfecting them over many years to improve their quality, safety, efficiency and robustness. German machine tools and cars, for example, are widely regarded as the highest quality in the world, based on years of engineering experience built up over the long term. Firms from CME nations also tend to be strong in technologies which require many years to perfect, such as petrol-electric hybrid vehicles (the Toyota Prius has been a runaway success, for example), and Japanese manufacturers are arguably leading the way in the next generation of zero-emissions electric cars such as the Mitsubishi i-MiEV and Nissan Leaf. The archetypal CME firm (such as Bosch or Hitachi) focuses its energies on quality and customer satisfaction, in high-end manufacturing and engineering sectors, and CMEs at large (especially Germany and Japan) tend to be export-led economies. Large firms typically employ their core staff on what are effectively 'jobs-for-life' contracts, and employees enjoy generous terms and conditions in return for hard work and loyalty. In several CMEs (notably Germany), powerful laws exist stipulating that all large firms must have Works Councils and other forms of 'codetermination' whereby employees and unions are properly brought into company decision-making. CME firms tend to be less interested in so-called global best practice as it pertains to employment issues, and instead look internally for staff development, promoting employees gradually after years of service. Firms in CMEs such as Canon or Siemens tend to make a virtue out of employment stability, arguing that genuinely developing and defending their own traditions of corporate culture and of nurturing internal talent over years represent the most effective way of maintaining quality and competing globally (Jacoby 2005: 168).

Employment in CMEs usually reflects at least an implicit promise of a long-term career with one employer. CME firms often have long-term, rather rigid, but generous seniority-based pay, promotion and pension systems. Trade union density and collective bargaining coverage tend to be substantially higher in CMEs than in LMEs, where unions have rapidly declined in influence (see Thelen 2001). Corporate life for those working inside CME firms is often fairly strictly controlled, with the benefit that jobs are fairly secure, worker participation is encouraged and supported, career headroom exists and staff have less chance of being laid off than workers in firms in LMEs. There are fewer reasons for staff to wish to job-hop under CME conditions, and this also applies to managers, even to senior managers; there is a much less developed market for corporate control, and therefore less demand for 'top management talent' to be recruited into senior positions. Compared to LMEs, corporate reorganizations are therefore rarer in CMEs, and there is much less emphasis on radical restructuring or dramatic new 'visions and values' coming down from senior executives.

The weakness of CMEs is that they can be slow to get out of less well-performing sectors and markets, and shareholders' interests are neglected in favour of internal stakeholders such as employees and pensioners; shareholders often receive moderate or poor returns on their investments. The internal, life-time employed engineers and product specialists often dominate company strategy, expending too much capital and labour on making technically highly advanced products that customers do not necessarily want, retailers struggle to sell and stock market analysts do not rate.

Using this basic ideal-type division into two models, VoC authors develop explanations for how these models can be expected to behave across numerous dimensions: typically across their financial, labour and innovation 'systems'. These are the sub-sectors of national economies which, according to VoC, are affected by various institutional structures that, to a large extent, define and shape their behaviours.[2]

Financial system

The ways in which firms are able to gain access to capital under the different institutional regimes of LME or CME plays a hugely important explanatory role in VoC theory. Financial systems under LMEs are described as open, 'arms-length', liquid and competitive, in which 'lenders and users remain relatively remote from one another' (Whitley 1999: 49), and where riskier, more liquid forms of finance are tapped by firms, such as securities traded on stock markets, or private equity financing. Lenders and investors expect firms to deliver returns on these investments in the short term. In CMEs, financial markets are less liquid, and the 'dominant institutions' here are either large, 'universal' banks, as in Germany, or 'a combination of commercial banks and long-term credit banks coordinated by state agencies and ministries, as in France, Japan and some other countries' (Whitley 1999: 49). Under typical CME conditions, lending organizations are much more closely linked to corporations, locked into long-term partnerships that both parties have little incentive to break. Critically, these 'bank-based' or 'credit-based' financial systems typical in CMEs allow firms to develop much longer-term strategies than is usually possible in LMEs. VoC theory tends to suggest that this is the main reason why capital-intensive industries such as manufacturing have survived and prospered in CME nations (especially in the archetypes of Germany and Japan), and declined so drastically in LMEs such as Britain and the United States.

The financial system also lays out the 'rules of the game' for corporate governance. In the liquid, speculative, restless world of LME finance, where short-term returns rule and investors rather than corporate managers call the shots, a very active 'market for corporate control' emerges. This is an absolutely crucial issue. Corporate governance is about the very nature of the firm itself. What are large firms for? Whose interests do they claim to serve: their owners (shareholders), or insider stakeholders (such as employees, the local regional government or business allies)? The Anglo-Saxon approach has, especially since the rise of neo-liberalism in the 1980s, explicitly focused on shareholder returns as the only true purpose of a major corporation. (This view is widely labelled 'shareholder value logic' or SVL). SVL is strongly associated with the decline of postwar 'managerial capitalism', and the rise of 'investor capitalism' (Useem 1996). SVL forces firms to focus much more intently on 'the bottom line', focusing on their quarterly financial statements and constantly looking for areas where they can reduce their costs, and hence boost their stock rating and share price (Lazonick and O'Sullivan 2000). This can make firms ruthless; employees can expect to be worked harder for their wages and bonuses, and they can also expect much-reduced job security. On the positive side, investor capitalism (as exemplified by the LME financial system) is said to be more dynamic and more willing to move into newly developing, often 'project-based', sectors, such as high-tech industries, services, IT, software and the entertainment industry, which are highly dependent on short-term and liquid forms of finance such as venture capital. Firms in LMEs therefore have weak managers and strong owners; shareholders have considerable power to force a replacement of top management if stock market performance is poor. In stark contrast, CME firms tend towards strong managers and weak owners – the model is closer to the classic form of managerial capitalism, as firms are controlled by insiders, often lifetime employees who have worked their way to the top and usually place the firms' interests ahead of those of shareholders.

Innovation system

As hinted at above, the ways in which firms design, launch, develop and maintain their products and services tend to be quite different under the institutional domains of LMEs and CMEs. Hall and Soskice (2001: 39–43) offer a particularly detailed account of these aspects, arguing that different nations develop different specializations according to the institutional structuring of their economies. They note that the kinds of sectors CMEs specialize in (mechanical engineering, consumer durables, machine tools) depend on incremental innovations, and are 'just the reverse' of those that LMEs specialize in (medical engineering, biotechnology, IT), where radical innovations are more important.

In my own experience of research into Japanese firms (Hassard et al. 2009), I was repeatedly struck by employees' obsessive attention to detail, and the way in which Japanese middle managers in industrial corporations wore practical, engineering-style uniforms rather than suits. The entrance lobby to the corporations we visited for our research interviews were practical and humbly furnished, and they invariably featured display cases of the companies' products over time with highly detailed explanations as to how this particular part was progressively reduced in size over many years of research and incremental improvements. They were like exhibits in a museum. This is precisely the image of *kaizen*, or 'continuous improvement', that Japanese firms are renowned for. Theoretically, ideal-typical LME firms tend to specialize in much more radical forms of innovation, enabled by a financial system which embraces entrepreneurship and the risk of failure, as firms try to develop new 'killer apps' that can shift the direction of entire industries. On the other hand, CME firms tend to specialize by making incremental improvements over time to existing technology in order to build up market share by building their products to extremely exacting standards. (In practice, however, this 'radical/incremental' division can be highly artificial.)

Education and labour system

VoC authors have consistently demonstrated that the ways in which states and firms develop employees' skills and how they put these skills to work (i.e., their systems of employment relations or HRM), differ considerably across national business systems. CMEs tend to have relatively strong labour unions, which have a greater say in workplace affairs than they do under the typically 'adversarial' management–labour relationship in LMEs (Hall and Soskice 2001: 59; Thelen 2001). In CMEs, the long-term focused financial systems and incremental innovation systems help facilitate, and are facilitated by, long-term skills development. CME labour markets tend to be characterized by low levels of 'poaching' and job-hopping. CME governments, trade unions and employers traditionally have worked closely together to invest long term in workforce skills development, backed by strong levels of certification and professionalization. In LMEs, by contrast, labour markets are flexible and deregulated, where employers have more of a free hand to 'hire and fire' workers to and from any position (known as 'employment at will' in the United States), and employees, for their part, are much more willing and able to leave companies in search of better opportunities. Hall and Soskice (2001: 19) present a graph which plots stock market capitalization along the x axis and the strictness of labour laws along the y axis, indicating one cluster of countries that exhibits high levels of employment protection and low forms of financialization (namely, CMEs such as Germany, Italy, France, Japan, Finland and Denmark) and another cluster exhibiting low levels of employment protection and high degrees of financialization (namely, the United States, Canada, Australia and Britain). Jacoby (2005), in a powerful and detailed analysis of five Japanese and five US corporations, very usefully links forms of corporate governance with the kinds of employment relations that result. LME firms typically pay less attention to HR matters, and their HR departments are relatively weak and marginalized players in the corporate hierarchy, whereas for CME firms, HR or personnel divisions tend to play central roles in shaping senior company strategy.

Crucially therefore, for most VoC authors, the subsystems of finance, labour/ education, innovation system and others interact and interlock, meaning that continuity of processes over time is likely, making change difficult to achieve. For example, it might be tempting for firms and governments to attempt to liberalize the German labour markets to make them more flexible and to release cost savings. But doing so would disrupt the sophisticated and long-term focused German skills system, which would in turn threaten its incremental innovation system which underpins its leadership in world-class engineering and manufacturing (see below). So perhaps it is best to shelve or abandon plans to introduce Anglo-Saxon-style flexible labour markets. This is the concept of *path dependence*, an important idea in institutional theory which suggests that prior history lays out the tracks for what is possible in the future. The interlocking of institutional subsystems is often described as 'complementarity'. In many ways, the concepts of embeddedness, path dependency and complementarity are the foundation stones of VoC theory. They provide the main conceptual reasons for VoC's sceptical arguments about globalization and convergence. According to VoC, the rules of the game are structured in such complex ways that international pressures for transformation are unlikely to result in radical change.

While the typically more abstract core VoC theoreticians such as Hall and Soskice, Amable and Whitley tend to be agnostic about the ethical and moral value of different systems, regional specialists such as Dore (2000: 219) can be much more explicit in their defence of the traditions of CMEs such as Japan and Germany, claiming that 'the processes of marketization and financialization are a bad thing'. With questions about the moral and ethical value of different models of capitalism in mind, we turn to the next section, which discusses the ways in which models become popular and unpopular, how elements of them spread and diffuse into other nations and what this means for employment relations in large organizations.

The emergence of Anglo-Saxonization and Americanization

Having sketched out the broad ideas of VoC theory and of the main competing models, we can now turn to explore the ways in which different models have increasingly been exposed to each other in an era of rapidly internationalizing economic relations, where ideas of 'best practice' rapidly move across national borders. The chapter demonstrates that there is strong evidence of attempted moves in CMEs toward adopting forms of corporate governance that more closely resemble LME institutions, and that these changes to corporate governance increasingly open the door for the development of LME-style employment relations. However, both of these transformations are far from complete, and there is strong evidence of resistance and translation as the new forms of best practice are developed.

It appears increasingly clear that CME nations are undergoing significant changes towards SVL- and LME-style investor capitalism (Morris et al. 2008). This is in line with a gradual and long-term process of erosion of managerial capitalism in general, and its morphing into investor capitalism. The shift from managerial to investor capitalism has been very pronounced in the United Kingdom and the United States since the 1980s, and is visible in parts in France, Japan, Germany and other CMEs. The pressure for change (both from external and internal actors) is certainly there, but the effects on the ground have not always travelled as far. Some companies domiciled in CMEs have always been western-focused and have long traditions of adopting LME-style features, such as Sony, which is often regarded by western financial observers as having the 'best' (i.e., the most western-looking) corporate governance, auditing, accounting standards and the clearest and most useful annual reports (Roche 2005: 183). Dore (2000) and Jacoby (2005), however, argue that these changes in corporate governance have not necessarily resulted in significant changes to employment practice. Claims about the 'inevitable' erosion of lifetime employment in Japan have circulated for many decades, yet the trends towards flexible labour markets are modest, with many traditional Japanese employment features retained.

It is also important to bear in mind that the flow of best practice ideas is not all one way; it is not simply a case of American ideas flowing to CMEs. Many features of CMEs have been adopted or advocated in LMEs. Perhaps the most notable example is that of 'lean manufacturing', which has spread from Japan to many parts of the world. American, British and European car manufacturing establishments have widely adopted lean concepts, or at least used them as the inspiration for other managerial technologies such as Total Quality Control, continuous improvement and Six Sigma. Interestingly, lean concepts are not always implemented 'properly' in alien environments such as Indiana, USA or South Wales in the United Kingdom (see the excellent workplace studies by among others Graham (1995), and Delbridge (1998)). Lean was developed through many years under CME financial and employment systems that emphasized long-term investment and genuine focus on quality improvement. Lean adoption under the short-term financial imperatives of the LME financial and employment system instead tended to mean that lean adoption was often more rhetorical than real. In recent years, lean has even been taken up as a panacea for public sector organizations such as the United Kingdom's National Probation Service, HM Revenue and Customs and National Health Service. Again, the results are questionable, demonstrating confusion, resistance and a great deal of rhetorical window-dressing about its beneficial effects (Waring and Bishop 2010).

Certain elements of other CMEs have also been favoured over the years as models for LMEs to adopt. LMEs such as the United Kingdom and the United States have struggled for many years with the problem of the growth of poor-quality jobs – so-called 'McJobs' with low pay and skill levels, often in retail and services industries. Many observers have advocated radical reform to education and training provision in the United States and the United Kingdom, to emulate the so-called 'German skills machine' in order to close the gap in skills generation. Classic studies have revealed in the past that on almost every measure (such as labour productivity and the availability of high skills), the labour force of Germany and other Continental nations such as the Netherlands and France was significantly more advanced than the United Kingdom's (see Coates 2000: 115). Another high-profile model is the so-called 'flexicurity' system of Denmark, whereby high levels of labour market flexibility and marketization are combined with strong forms of welfare protection and active labour market stimulation policies, resulting in low unemployment and high levels of labour utilization (Campbell and Pedersen 2007; Zhao 2007). One might say that 'best practice' comes in many forms; strong economic performance is not all dependent on LME-style marketization and financialization.

Nevertheless, it seems that US-style corporate governance is spreading to East Asia (Dore 2000) and has an increasingly large footprint in Europe (Goyer (2007: 200–1). Traditional German systems for coordinating management–labour relationships are arguably crumbling (Kinderman 2005). This is potentially hugely important because corporate governance reform can facilitate changes to employment relations (Jacoby 2005; Dore 2000; Morris et al. 2008; Hassard et al. 2009). Open markets for corporate control provide the legitimacy for shareholder value to be reframed as the central organizational principle for firms, opening the door to American-style employment relations (Smith and Walter 2006: 44). This is certainly the argument of those who accept the globalization and convergence picture. However, in accordance with VoC, the adoption and spread of actual 'best practice' is slow, contingent and contradictory, and faces considerable resistance. In what follows, I attempt to highlight this situation with reference to a case study, in which executives in a US firm consider whether or not to go ahead with the plan to buy up the stock and eventually purchase a rather conservative Japanese firm.

Case study: A difficult phone call

In this fictional case study, a US private equity firm, Reflexus Capital, is pursuing the possibility of investing in small- and medium-sized Japanese technology firms. Mike Gifford is an executive vice president for Overseas Ventures at Reflexus. He has been working in Japan for the last three months meeting various representatives of mid-sized Japanese firms in the fields of consumer electronics, biotechnologies and renewable energy. He has been impressed by the advanced technology being developed in many of these companies, and by the close attention to detail showed by managers and engineers in almost all of the companies he has visited. He was surprised and rather impressed to learn that senior managers in these companies – even their owners – were themselves technically very competent engineers and systems analysts, who seemed passionate about the precise workings of their companies' projects and products.

Over the last few weeks, he had settled on one company as a possible candidate for Reflexus to invest in. The target is Ohmatsu Systems, a company developing some highly specialized materials for use in renewable energy generation. Some at Reflexus are talking about a complete buyout, even about replacing its top management, or at least inserting some new management figures from outside. But the closer Mike got to recommending a go-ahead to senior management, the more worried he was becoming as to whether or not this whole idea was wise. That evening he was due to place a call to Ed McCulloch, global strategy leader at Reflexus. He had not been looking forward to making the call.

The phone is ringing. It is a strange feeling to hear the US ring tone.

- 'Mike, hi! How's it going?'
- 'Yeah, OK, it's ah, going great'.
- 'So what's up with this Ohmatsu thing? Are we going for it or what?'
- 'Yeah, ah, well, you know it's a great company. The guys there, Mr Hatsumano, they are just great guys and some of their products are real exciting, you know?'
- 'Sure yeah. It all looks great. Mike, remind me, what's the story on 'Comp and Bens' out there? How are they all paid?'
- 'It's all salary, mostly. They get a salary with a possible twice-yearly bonus. It's kind of strict, you know, a lot of it seems to be based around your length of service, your seniority. Pensions are Defined Benefit'.
- 'Really? Still? Well, we'd have to sort that out. And what kind of share plan do they all have – you know, the execs, guys like Katayama?'
- 'There isn't one'.
- 'No stock options at all? How are they motivated?'
- 'Its, ah, it's hard to explain. They just don't seem to know the idea or don't really value it. They sort of say, er, "we do things this way", or "it is important to have a hierarchy". They are kind of vague about it, but I sort of know what they mean'.

- 'What do you mean by that, Mike?'
- 'Well, I feel sometimes ... I feel that maybe sometimes it is important to respect the structures they've already got in place. It's like Katayama-san, he's pretty impressive. They seem to respect him a lot, you know. They don't do much without consulting him on everything. He's been there, like forever, since the company started. He knows everything about the product, his whole life is invested in it, you know?'

There is a long silence.

- 'Ed? You still there?'
- 'Yeah. Yeah, I'm just thinking'.
- 'There's something else. This whole thing, they are real tied in with the local mayor's office here. They are all set on Ohmatsu playing a part in this urban redevelopment the're doing. They call it Super Enviro Town. It's all there in the mayor's office, they've got all these plans laid out – models, you know? I hear Katayama and the mayor came through the same grad school together, they go way back'.
- 'Hmm. OK. So let's see. You want to give this a couple more days? I'm getting a bit of heat back here on this, you know? They are all kinda keyed up on this, you know, "give me an answer" sort of thing?'
- 'Yeah, I can imagine'.
- 'OK, Mike. You, ah, you put all this in an e-mail to me, right? OK? Then call me by, uh, let's say Tuesday? Tuesday same time, and then we'll work out what to do. You happy with that?'
- 'Er, that should be OK, yeah'.
- 'Bye, Mike'.
- 'Er, yeah OK, bye. Bye'.
- The line goes dead. Mike replaces the handset in an oddly slow and careful way.

Questions

1. What impression does the case study give as to the employment relations and overall working culture of Japanese companies?
2. To what extent is this traditional Japanese working culture likely to be effective in an increasingly globalized world?
3. Why was Mike becoming sceptical about the prospects for Reflexus to get involved in Ohmatsu?
4. What should Mike do here? What should he recommend to Ed? What options does he realistically have?
5. Does the case study rely on stereotypes? Or is there some accuracy to the way the US and Japanese characters are portrayed?

Conclusion: tensions, issues, alternatives, futures

The above discussion has highlighted the social and political implications of the pre-eminence of LMEs, and the rhetorical dominance of the US-driven model of investor capitalism and shareholder value, arguing that this model has been increasingly ascendant in the last three decades. But it has also widely discussed the powerful and still-existing alternative in the form of the CME model. The years 2007–2009 will long be remembered for the dramatic collapse of confidence in investor capitalism as the subprime mortgage crash deeply tarnished the value (ethically and financially) of the US model (Whitley 2009). This event is likely to reinforce scepticism among managers, workers and unions in CMEs about the motives, knowledge and competence of high-profile, globally educated 'international managers' who 'drop in', lecture the locals about globalization and best practice, then 'fly off' again.

US ideas of best practice in corporate governance and employment relations clearly have a dominant rhetorical force in global capitalism. But these ideas are not simply ported over wholesale to other regions; they are adapted and translated as they diffuse, sometimes replacing, sometimes melding and sometimes clashing with existing practices and institutions. In some cases, western ideas and western business leaders are accepted in CME environments. A famous example is Carlos Ghosn, the highly respected CEO of Renault-Nissan, who is regarded as a celebrity CEO in Japan after a difficult start. Elsewhere, the German New Social Market Initiative is a home-grown movement pressuring German employers' associations to adopt more Anglo-Saxon employment relations, advocating a diminution of the traditional power of German trade unions and codetermination (Kinderman 2005). However, it stills seems clear that the differences in models of capitalism remain powerful and important, and that there are significant institutional barriers to the unproblematic adoption of LME concepts in CME nations. These barriers are unlikely to ever disappear. But it is equally clear that powerful forces of globalization and liberalization also show no signs of declining in importance, and we can probably expect national models to show further erosion, blurring and scrambling in years to come. In such a complex and unpredictable scenario, it becomes more and more necessary for firms, unions and individual workers to develop effective strategies for facing up to increased levels of competition, marketization and uncertainty; to try to prepare for as many eventualities as they can – to work out a core set of ideas and principles about what forms of organization and employment are effective and just, but also the capacity to rethink their assumptions about how markets operate, what customers require, and how competitors are moving. Employees need to develop and retain the right abilities, educational and professional credentials and attitudes, and to nurture an aptitude for critical thinking, to evaluate the effectiveness (or otherwise) of so-called 'global best practice', and of employers, their workplace representatives and themselves as economic actors in a turbulent and difficult era.

Reflective questions

1. To what extent does globalization require firms to radically restructure their people management and corporate governance structures?
2. Can firms genuinely be global in their outlook? Why are they so keen to project this kind of internationalized image?
3. Is there a global best practice for human resource management and the appointment and retention of 'talent'? Or will effective ways of working always be contingent on local histories and structures?
4. Globally speaking, are 'jobs for life' and internal career ladders now things of the past? Why or why not?

Recommended reading

- Campbell, J. L. and Pedersen, O. K. (2007) 'The varieties of capitalism and hybrid success: Denmark in the global economy'. *Comparative Political Studies*, 40(3): 307–332.
- McCormack, K. (2008) 'Sociologists and "the Japanese model": A passing enthusiasm?'. *Work, Employment and Society*, 21(4): 751–771.
- Morris, J., Hassard J. and McCann, L. (2008) 'The resilience of "institution-alization capitalism": managing managers under "shareholder capitalism" and "managerial capitalism"'. *Human Relations*, 61(5): 687–710.

Notes

1. Details on this programme can be found on the HSBC website, accessed July 2011: http://www.hsbcglobalresourcing.com/news.aspx?newsid=11. Thanks to Damian Hodgson, of Manchester Business School, for letting me know of this example.
2. There are many more subsystems identified in VoC texts, such as 'norms and values governing trust and authority relations' (Whitley 1999: 51–54) but I will focus on the three of most obvious importance for our discussion of corporate governance and labour management. A very useful and up-to-date overview of these subsystems or 'institutional domains' is provided by Jackson and Deeg (2006: 12–20).

References

Amable, B. (2003) *The Diversity of Modern Capitalism*, Cambridge: Cambridge University Press.

Batt, R., Nohara, H. and Kwun, H. (2010) 'Employer strategies and wages in new service activities: A comparison of co-ordinated and liberal market economies'. *British Journal of Industrial Relations*, 48(2): 400–435.

Campbell, J. L. and Pedersen, O. K. (2007) 'The varieties of capitalism and hybrid success: Denmark in the global economy'. *Comparative Political Studies*, 40(3): 307–332.

Chambers, E. G., Foulon, M., Handfield-Jones, H., Hankin, S. M. and Michaels, E. G. (1998) 'The war for talent'. *McKinsey Quarterly*, 3: 44–57.

Coates, D. (2000) *Models of Capitalism: Growth and Stagnation in the Modern Era*. Cambridge: Polity.

Dore, R. (2000) *Stock Market Capitalism: Welfare Capitalism, Japan and Germany versus the Anglo-Saxons*. Oxford: Oxford University Press.

Delbridge, R. (1998) *Life on the Line in Contemporary Manufacturing: The Workplace Experience of Lean Production and the 'Japanese' Model*. Oxford: Oxford University Press.

Friedman, T. L. (2005) *The World is Flat: The Globalized World in the Twenty-First Century*. London: Penguin.

Giddens, A. (1999) *Runaway World: How Globalisation is Reshaping our Lives*. London: Profile.

Goyer, M. (2007) 'Capital mobility, varieties of institutional investors, and the transforming stability of corporate governance in France and Germany'. In Hancke, B., Rhodes, M. and Thatcher, M. (eds.), *Beyond Varieties of Capitalism: Conflict, Contradictions and Complementarities in the European Economy*. Oxford: Oxford University Press.

Graham, L. (1995) *On the Line at Subaru-Isuzu*. Ithaca: Cornell University Press.

Hall, P. and Soskice, D. (eds.) (2001) *Varieties of Capitalism: The Institutional Foundations of Comparative Advantage*. New York: Oxford University Press.

Hassard, J., McCann, L. and Morris, J. (2009) *Managing in the Modern Corporation: The Intensification of Managerial Work in the US, UK and Japan*. Cambridge: Cambridge University Press.

Held, D., McGrew, A., Goldblatt, D. and Perraton, J. (1999) *Global Transformations: Politics, Economics, and Culture*. Cambridge: Polity.

Hollingsworth, J. and Boyer, R. (eds.) (1997) *Contemporary Capitalism: The Embeddedness of Institutions*. Cambridge: Cambridge University Press.

Kinderman, D. (2005) 'Pressure from without, subversion from within: The two-pronged German employer offensive'. *Comparative European Politics*, 3(4): 432–463.

Jackson, G. and Deeg, R. (2006) 'How Many Varieties of Capitalism? Comparing the Comparative Institutional Analyses of Capitalist Diversity'. MPIfG Discussion Paper 06/2. Available at: http://www.mpifg.de/pu/mpifg_dp/dp06-2.pdf

Jackson, G. and Deeg, R. (2007) 'Towards a more dynamic theory of capitalist variety'. *Socio-Economic Review* 5(1): 149–179.

Jacoby, S. (2005) *The Embedded Corporation: Corporate Governance and Employment Relations in the USA and Japan*. Princeton: Princeton University Press.

Lazonick, W. and O'Sullivan, M. (2000) 'Maximizing shareholder value: A new ideology for corporate governance', *Economy and Society*, 29(1): 13–35.

McCann, L. (2014) *International and Comparative Business: Foundations of Poltical Economies*, London: Sage Publications.

McCann, L., Hassard, J. and Morris, J. (2010) 'Restructuring managerial labour in the USA, UK and Japan: Challenging the salience of "varieties of capitalism"'. *British Journal of Industrial Relations*, 48(2): 347–374.

McCormack, K. (2008) 'Sociologists and "the Japanese model": A passing enthusiasm?'. *Work, Employment and Society*, 21(4): 751–771.

McCraw, T. (ed.) (1997) *Creating Modern Capitalism: How Entrepreneurs, Companies, and Countries Triumphed in Three Industrial Revolutions'*. Cambridge, MA: Harvard University Press.

Morris, J., Hassard J. and McCann, L. (2008) 'The resilience of "institutionalization capitalism": managing managers under "shareholder capitalism" and "managerial capitalism"'. *Human Relations*, 61(5): 687–710.

Roche, J. (2005) *Corporate Governance in Asia*. Abingdon: Routledge.

Smith, R. C. and Walter, I. (2006) *Governing the Modern Corporation: Capital Markets, Corporate Control, and Economic Performance*. Oxford: Oxford University Press.

Steger, M. B. (2009) *Globalization: A Very Short Introduction*, 2nd edition. Oxford: Oxford University Press.

Taylor, W. C. and Webber, A. M. (1996) *Going Global: Four Entrepreneurs Map the New World Marketplace*. London: Penguin.

Thelen, K. (2001) 'Varieties of labor politics in the developed democracies'. In Hall, P. and Soskice, D. (eds.), *Varieties of Capitalism: the Institutional Foundations of Comparative Advantage*. New York: Oxford University Press.

Useem, M. (1996) *Investor Capitalism: How Money Managers Are Changing the Face of Corporate America*. New York: Basic Books.

Waring, J. J. and Bishop, S. (2010) 'Lean healthcare: Rhetoric, ritual, and resistance'. *Social Science and Medicine*, 71(7): 1332–1340.

Welch, J. F. (2001) *Jack: Straight from the Gut*. New York: Warner Books.

Whitley, R. (1999) *Divergent Capitalisms: The Social Structuring and Change of Business Systems*. Oxford: Oxford University Press.

Whitley, R. (2009) 'U.S. capitalism: A tarnished model?'. *Academy of Management Perspectives*, 23(2): 11–22.

Zhao, J. (2007) 'Danish for All? Balancing Flexibility with Security: The Flexicurity Model'. IMF Working Paper WP/07/36, available at: http://www.imf.org/external/pubs/ft/wp/2007/wp0736.pdf

9 The learning environment and the politics of globalization: consultants and business schools between standardization and rhetoric

Carlos J. Fernández Rodríguez

Learning objectives

- To explain the role of business schools and consultancy for the study of globalization and MNCs
- To outline the importance of such organizations in the transmission of management philosophies and practices
- To conceptualize the link between neoliberalism and market-oriented policies and the nature of management education and learning
- To raise ethical and political issues in relation to the manner in which such bodies have evolved in various contexts

Introduction

Since the 1980s, studies in business and management have become increasingly important in post-compulsory education. There seems to be a strong demand for business education, and management positions are generally considered to be socially desirable jobs. In addition, current organizational values – performance, accountability, empowerment, flexibility and so on – have gained influence in related fields such as politics, the media, or in economic or social policies, helping to develop pro-market attitudes among populations and a general concern for good management. The goal of this contribution is to grasp the issues behind this managerial drive by looking at the institutions that forge the concepts of what we understand by management; that is, the learning environment, which includes business schools and consultancies as key actors and disseminators.

This chapter will focus specifically on the institutions that traditionally have played a key role in the diffusion of management values and knowledge, in order to understand the way they frame what it is commonly understood as good management as well as the socioeconomic and ideological implications of such perspectives. To do so, first, the background in which that dissemination of management takes place will be analysed, highlighting the important role that business schools or consultancies play in such dissemination. The key debate about the Americanization of organizational life – usually linked to any discussion regarding management diffusion – will then be described, followed by a selected case study. Finally, the tensions, issues and future scenarios regarding these actors will be discussed in a brief conclusion.

Background: regulation, institutions and the dissemination of management

To understand the hegemony of managerial and pro-business discourses in our societies, it is important to pay attention to the institutional background behind the business learning environment. In this section, we shall focus on three points. First, the influence of a post-Fordist deregulation – expressed by some authors as the concept of a 'new spirit of capitalism'– in the managerial turn of recent decades will be highlighted; second, it will be argued that the processes of dissemination are complex, confronting theories such as institutional isomorphism with the issues of local and national adaptations and management fads and fashions; and finally, the pivotal role of business schools and consultancies will be discussed, as both are considered to be key actors in the circulation of management theories and knowledge.

According to many authors, since the late 1970s there has been a shift in the regulation of the capitalist system (Lash and Urry 1987; Castells 2000). The postwar period of 1945–1975 featured a regulated model of capitalism (Fordism) through an implicit social pact between capital, labour and the state. It relied on both Keynesian economic policies and mass production processes: these implied long-term investments and strategies, and therefore a need for stability (see Chapter 1). However, since the late 1970s, a new economic scenario (post-Fordism) has emerged, characterized by a shift towards a deregulation of financial and labour markets in order to stimulate free market competition on a global scale (Jessop 1995; Alonso and Martínez Lucio 2006). The inability of Fordism to maintain benefits in a context of increasing competitiveness, more fragmented markets and political and social turmoil led to a shocking economic crisis and the subsequent reaction in the form of a managerial turn (Boltanski and Chiapello 2005). New pro-market discourses became hegemonic and have highly influenced the sphere of the political, with the result that there has been a prioritization of more capital-biased approaches and a decline in social-democratic pacts in favour of neoliberal policies (Harvey 2005). This reaction was fuelled by the globalization of markets and by specific national policies, particularly once neoliberal governments had started to develop their deregulation and privatization agendas – justified on the basis of a quest for better management (Du Gay 1996). In this context, it was foreseeable that managerial discourses would become very important, helping to develop an industry linked to management knowledge.

These new management ideologies are considered by some scholars to be what is justifying people's commitment to capitalism, and rendering this commitment attractive. They represent the *new spirit of capitalism* (Boltanski and Chiapello 2005) since they imply certain moral and ethical values that differ from the ones that were relevant just a few decades ago. For example, in the 1950s and 1960s, long-term planning or bureaucratic organization were considered to be the core values inside an organization, while nowadays new management-oriented discourses and practices highlight the importance of new values such as innovation, flexibility, knowledge or entrepreneurship (Boltanski and Chiapello 2005; Gantman 2005). These values have spread through different organizations largely via specific institutions and channels, making management knowledge very visible in numerous ways, ranging from the production of a specialized literature (either academic or popular) to the implementation of routine organizational practices.

In fact, some scholars, such as DiMaggio and Powell (1983), have pointed out that in many current organizations there is a surprising homogeneity of forms and practices, which they described as *institutional isomorphism*. For example, it is possible to think that in almost every firm (no matter what its geographical location) with a certain number of employees, we are going to find similar departments: marketing, production, HRM and finance. In their classic paper, DiMaggio and Powell argued that organizations suffer different pressures that lead them to adapt themselves to the uncertainties of the surrounding environment. They distinguished three mechanisms through which that institutional isomorphic change would take place: a *coercive* one – pressures exerted either by other organizations on which they are dependent or by cultural expectations from society; a *mimetic* one – where other models are simply followed to provide an answer to uncertainty; and a *normative* one – whose source is professionalization, primarily in two ways: the legitimization of a cognitive framework developed by specialists, and the development of professional networks which help to diffuse innovations through a specific field. In this sense, it would be possible for us to argue that the normative mechanism might be playing a very important role in the development of such an isomorphism in management knowledge inside firms, once some of their managers might have learnt specific managerial skills in a business school, or a consultant might have been hired to develop a strategy of organizational change. Therefore, management ideologies would be contributing towards shaping companies in a similar way – for example, networks, e-business and so on – so that values such as flexibility or empowerment would be embraced in most of them. They provide certainties in a complex environment.

However, management knowledge is also influenced to varying degrees by social, political and economic factors, and can therefore show remarkable differences across national contexts in terms of organization and functioning (Whitley 2008). The diversity of models of capitalism (Hall and Soskice 2001; Amable 2003) also implies that the tendency to isomorphism is limited by contextual approaches and adaptations, particularly local ones. Therefore, while most of the generation of management knowledge originates from Anglo-Saxon culture, the concrete use of the theories produced might differ in places such as Argentina, Turkey, China, Indonesia or South Africa. Besides, many scholars have indicated that while certain motifs such as commitment to work or uncritical views towards firms remain stable, these discourses are also characterized by the constant incorporation of new jargon and managerial tools, to the extent that it is possible to speak of management fads and fashions (Abrahamson 1991; Collins 2000; Gantman 2005). The field of management knowledge is prolific in terms of managerial solutions to common problems of organizations, which means that new concepts will emerge quite regularly, such as quality circles, excellence, business process reengineering, emotional intelligence, balanced scorecard or knowledge management.

Research has indicated that certain institutions and actors are fundamental to the dissemination of different management theories, among them being business schools (Grey 2005) and consultancies (Kipping 1999). If we follow the scheme of Mazza and Álvarez (2000; see also Table 9.1), the creation of management theories and practices as well as their diffusion can be conceptualized as a three-phase process: production, diffusion and legitimization. While Mazza and Álvarez's paper is focused on the third stage (the popularization of management topics via the popular press), the authors also discuss the ways in which business schools (and other educational institutions) and consultancy firms are involved in the first

Table 9.1   Creation and diffusion of management theories and practices

	Actors	**Knowledge**	**Arguments**	**Audience**
Production	Universities Business schools Consulting firms	Formal/scientific	Management as science	Business community Management scholars
Diffusion	Business press Consulting firms Business schools	Scientific/ practical	Management as techniques and rules of thumb	Business community Professionals
Legitimation	Popular press Business press Large firms	Ideological	Narratives of management success	Business community Society at large

Source: Mazza and Álvarez (2000: 572).

two stages of the process. In the production phase, they elaborate on formal managerial knowledge following the rules of academic production, creating new or recycled theories. These theories are spread during the next stage of diffusion by management education institutions and consulting firms, which combine scientific knowledge on management (which would provide academic validation) with a practical knowledge that engages with the more down-to-earth aspects. In this critical phase, social legitimacy and crucial linkages of both educational institutions and consulting firms with key actors in various fields (politics, organizations, and so on) help to build an essential background to extend the diffusion of theories outside the business community. Therefore, it is important to explore the role that business schools and consultancies have played in the development and transmission of managerial knowledge since their creation. To do so, the next section will provide a brief background of both institutions, to assess their influence on the creation of a very specific approach to management problems.

Institutions and ideas: the history of business schools and consultancies and the US influence through research and education

Not surprisingly, the origins of both business schools and consultancies can be traced to the 19th century United States. While there were several institutions in Europe (particularly in France) and America that included commerce as their main programme of studies, it is widely agreed that the Wharton School of Finance and Commerce of the University of Pennsylvania (founded in 1881 by the industrialist and philanthropist, Joseph Wharton; hence the name) is considered to be the oldest collegiate business school in the world. The reason it was founded there illustrates the important links that were established between firms, business schools and the emerging figures of consultants. Joseph Wharton's company, Bethlehem Steel Works, had a famous engineer conducting his research at the shop-floor level: none other than Mr Frederick W. Taylor, originator of Scientific Management, probably one of the first management theories, the impact of which was nothing less than revolutionary as it formed the foundation of the Fordist model (Grey 2005). Soon other schools followed, usually being part of universities despite some objections being raised over the status of business and commerce as scientific disciplines (Engwall 2009). Some of them are still top American business schools, such as Chicago (1898), Columbia (1908) or the Harvard Business School (1908). Meanwhile, schools of commerce were also being founded across Western Europe, though their approaches were slightly different from the American ones as they sprang from different academic traditions, thus leading to different models of management (Guillén 1994).

Business schools continued to grow during the first half of the 20th century, while management knowledge developed through an extensive body of publications, dominated mainly by F. W. Taylor's theory (Guillén 1994). Following in the foot-steps of the Wharton School and others, they offered specialized courses for current or future executives, on topics ranging from accounting to marketing or finance. The first Master of Business Administration (MBA) programme was offered by Harvard Business School in 1910, and some years later their case study approach revolutionized the teaching methods of this type of institution. Despite the severe economic crisis following the financial crash of 1929, new business schools were founded, which helped to establish the foundations of an American dominance in business higher education. The field of management education expanded notably after the Second World War, once fascism had been defeated and Western Europe needed the financial aid of the US Marshall Plan to rebuild the war-damaged economies. The importance of this plan has been discussed by many scholars (Kipping 1999; Schröter 2005), not so much for the financial aid package but rather for the crucial role that the Marshall Plan was to have in terms of assessment and the transfer of managerial knowledge to the countries of Western Europe (this topic will be discussed in the next section). From the 1950s onwards, American business schools became not only the institutions where future top executives received their specialized education and improved their business skills, but also a channel for the transmission of a certain 'American way of business' which spread all over Europe. This was to have indelible consequences, not only for the way that business and organizations were conceived and understood during the following decades, but also on the American cultural hegemony in the capitalist bloc.

During the post-war period, the business school system gradually organized itself. The leading institutions were top American business schools: some had a long tradition, while newer ones were created by Ivy League universities to overcome their lack of specific business degrees. Therefore, institutions such as Chicago, Dartmouth, Columbia, Harvard, Kellogg, Stanford and MIT Sloan became pivotal. It is important to note that most of these are private institutions. European institutions either engaged with the new American approach to knowledge while still keeping their own identities (as in the case of the London Business School (LBS) or the Nordic business schools) or were simply spin-offs from American institutions (the main example of this is INSEAD). Some of the European schools have achieved enormous prestige: INSEAD itself, the Spanish IESE or ESADE, or the British Manchester Business School (MBS), Warwick Business School (WBS) or LSE, some of them with strong American assistance . However, the American schools were considered the most prestigious, attracting foreign students and providing top executives for multinational corporations. They also helped to develop, in many cases with direct assistance, more management schools overseas, not only in Europe but also in other countries and regions that fell under US political influence (e.g., Turkey or the Latin American countries).

Nevertheless, the most important expansion of business schools took place in the 1980s, pushed by several factors: the technological drive of an economy which helps to stimulate enormous growth in the financial markets inside the framework of a new capitalist deregulation (post-Fordism); the rise of neoliberal governance trumpeting the so-called 'enterprise culture', praising business-oriented values such as innovation, competitiveness or entrepreneurship; and economic globalization. Business schools have since then become extremely popular as they provide an education that meets the new requirements of largely deregulated economies: being the holder of an MBA has become the compulsory entry point to the upper echelons of business (Grey 2005). Nevertheless, the roles of these schools are by no means limited to mere transmission of education: they are also the producers and disseminators of managerial knowledge, helping to reinforce the ideological dominance of business-oriented thinking and thus being crucial supporters of neoliberal capitalism. For example, some of the most important management gurus are professors in these top business schools; fine examples are Michael Porter and Rosabeth Moss Kanter at Harvard Business School, and Philip Kotler at Kellogg School of Management, Northwestern University.

The consulting industry has also been a key actor in the dissemination of different waves of managerial expertise during the 20th century (Barley and Kunda 1992; Kipping 1999; Kipping and Engwall 2002). The origins of management consulting are Anglo-American. The founders were US pioneers in the late 19th century, whose main role was to help manufacturers to become more productive and efficient. Some authors (Rassam 1998; Kipping 1999) claim that the first management thinkers were also the first consultants, and names such as F. W. Taylor, Arthur D. Little, Frank and Lillian Gilbreth or Elton Mayo developed their main theoretical contributions directly from their empirical work (in the form of analysis and further assessment) in industrial firms. In the United Kingdom, consulting activities began by the 1920s with leading management thinkers and businessmen such as Lyndall Urwick. Most of these authors were engineers (apart from Mayo, who was a sociologist, among other things), who attempted to provide scientific solutions to the organization of production and the assignment of labour to tasks. Nevertheless, during the 1930s, a new type of consulting firm emerged in the United States that proved to be very influential and was to shape the image of the profession. It was no longer associated with shop-floor or office improvements but rather with wider organizational issues, providing both short-term and long-term strategic business plans, specialized assessment in different departments and activities inside the corporations, and providing a certificate of 'professionalism' that helped to reduce anxiety among managers. McKinsey, founded in 1926, became the blueprint for other consulting firms (Kipping 1999) with their famous dress code, their 'up or out' promotion policy and an image that resembled that of law firms (Kipping 2011). They also tended to hire many of their consultants from a selected number of business schools, forging a strong relationship between both types of institution. Soon, new companies developed consulting services, including some that in the beginning provided mainly auditing and tax services, such as the pioneer firm Arthur Andersen (founded in 1913).

During the 1960s, the consulting industry experienced a boom in response to a rapidly changing industrial and economic structure, and managerial fashions spread rapidly among companies. Consulting companies began to launch services related to products such as MBO (management by objectives) and approaches that emphasized attitudes such as leadership and a more democratic management approach. American consulting firms developed a strategy of internationalization with the beginning of overseas activities and work. McKinsey opened an office in London, and soon other companies established themselves in Europe and began to develop a strong network with local firms and business schools. Later, the strategy of internationalization reached Latin America and, in particular, Asia. During the 1980s and 1990s, there was an expansion in the number of consulting firms. The market environment became more uncertain owing to global competition, and more managers and companies were willing to look for advice. Several mergers also reduced the number of consulting multinationals. Nowadays the structure of the consulting industry is organized around accountancy-based firms (today reduced to a sort of Big Four: Ernst & Young, KPMG, Deloitte Touche Tohmatsu and PwC – PricewaterhouseCoopers); multinational companies whose core business is consulting, such as Accenture (a spin-off of the defunct Arthur Andersen and the largest consulting firm in the world); or well-known medium-sized consultancies such as McKinsey, Boston Consulting Group, Arthur D. Little, Bain and Hay; IT companies and business-school-based consultancies focused on specific niches; and in small firms and sole practitioners at the local level.

The consulting industry has an important role as a channel of diffusion of managerial services and practices. This role cannot be fully understood without noticing the strong connections that these companies have with business schools and management gurus, the source of most of the innovations offered through their consulting services. For example, management gurus such as Tom Peters, Robert Waterman or Kenichi Ohmae were McKinsey employees for many years; many others were also executives or managers for other, less-well-known companies. Other gurus have also created their own consulting companies once their ideas have become popular. Consultants from McKinsey were initially Harvard Business School (HBS) graduates, building a long-lasting relationship between consulting firms and business schools from which employees were recruited (Kipping 2011). Given the global scope that consulting industry activities have, these networks are crucial to the dissemination of managerial practices: students from top business schools receive their education and knowledge from top management gurus; once they get their MBAs, they are hired by top consulting firms; at some point they join new companies, but their background and practices have already been modelled under the influence of these institutions. These processes help to extend the influence of managerial theories; and in addition they contribute to the expansion of a certain analysis style or attitude towards organizational problems from a specific point of view that will be discussed in the next section.

Case study: A Spanish business school

Business studies in public Spanish universities have traditionally been considered to be merely a continuation of the study of economics, and they usually failed to provide an adequate education at the postgraduate level. This gap has been filled by the efforts of a select group of private business schools, which have not missed their chance to provide education for business elites and top managers. Most of them have an unusual common feature: the religious character of their founders. Our selected case study is an initiative undertaken by a religious order in the 1950s that wished to create an institution to train managers, combining the most modern management knowledge with a solid Christian morality. In this case study, three issues will be dealt with: first, the importance of Americanization as a political project; second, how that project evolved over time through specific features; and, finally, how culture helps to shape Americanization, adapting it to the specific interests of the local elites.

During the development period the Spanish economy underwent in the 1960s, several business schools with links to Catholic groups were launched in the private sector. The goal was to 'modernize' management in an economy marred by inefficiencies, backwardness and a corrupt state, and modernization was associated with one significant source: the United States. The school in our case study established a link with a very prestigious American business school, adopted the case study method as a basis for teaching and launched the first MBA studies programme in the 1960s. The very strong relationship between the schools owed much to the closeness between the Spanish Franco regime and the US government during the Cold War, but also to similar views shared by the American business school managers and the religious order members who founded the Spanish school. In fact, both advocated technocracy in terms of economic ideologies and commitment to work, supporting *franquismo* (the dictatorship governing Spain from 1939 to 1975) to turn to a more free market approach in the late 1950s. Democracy was not imported in that move, though. Business schools like this provided an encounter between entrepreneurial ethics and particular views of Christian morality. Their contribution was aimed at shaping Spanish managers' Catholic values towards an attitude of Protestant work ethics, rationalizing the economy but without any critical approach to the political framework. This business school soon gained enormous prestige at the postgraduate level.

The transition to democracy in the 1970s in Spain did not appear to erode this prestige, and the school rapidly evolved through the different stages of the Americanization process. Heavily influenced by American models, its academic programmes have been shaped around a managerial and pro-business approach tied strongly to the relationship between the business school and Spanish firms. The expansion of the Spanish economy during the 1980s and 1990s helped not only to attract students from all over Europe and Latin America, but also to develop strong networks and many subsidiaries in the latter. In a neoliberal scenario, the school abandoned the project of Spanish 'modernization' to compete in the new European market of business higher education. The move has been successful, at least according to international rankings, such as those appearing in the *Financial Times*, *The Economist* or the *Wall Street Journal*, where the school has frequently appeared in top positions. In addition, the school undertook new strategies that followed global trends in the field of higher education. To strengthen the quality of their MBA programmes (e.g., studentships in business schools abroad, visiting professors and so on), some changes have been implemented. The need to hire teaching staff with papers accepted by the Institute for Scientific Information (ISI) journals to cope with the growing influence of a 'publish or perish' mentality in the field has led not only to changes in the profiles and backgrounds of the academics (there is a lesser role for management practitioners, for example, who were key figures in the past), but also to policies in which the school funds the doctoral studies of senior lecturers in prestigious universities. These policies have a contradictory effect: on the one hand, they strengthen the quality of the research and broaden the perspectives on management studies; but on the other hand, they reinforce their technocratic approach, particularly once most of the members have committed to publishing in American top management journals. Thus, the Americanization project is maintained through different stages.

Finally, it is important to highlight the importance of the local culture when looking at business education models. In this case study, it is essential to point out that, despite political changes and economic reorganization, this school has remained faithful to its Christian origins while adapting to a new environment of liberal democracy and post-Fordist market deregulation. There has never been a critical position towards politics in Spain, despite coexisting with a dictatorship for more than 15 years. On the other hand, the school supported every step towards a deregulated free market economy. This is not only because of a limited technocratic approach that despises politics as an obstacle to management performance and the invisible hand of the market, but also because of the critical role that schools like this provided locally through the formation of elites. The extraordinary high fees charged by the school has limited their catchment to the upper and upper-middle classes, who attempt to preserve their social position and wealth, in this case by holding top positions in corporations. Needless to say, the school not only provided their students with skills, but also gave them an important range of contacts and networks that were extremely useful in the context of a Southern European culture. In addition, the religious order behind the school had close links with the right-wing elites of the country. Ironically, while promoting modernization through free market policies and better management, the school's role reinforced elitism and maintained strong class divisions through the transition to democracy. Because of a lack of real meritocracy, it could be argued that this school was actually unable to attract the best students but rather only the younger generations of Spanish elites.

Questions

1. How does the Americanization project evolve through the story of this Spanish business school?
2. Why does it evolve in this way?
3. According to this case study, are modernization and economic liberalism associated with democracy?
4. What does the case reveal about the politics of business schools?

The emergence of Anglo-Saxonization and Americanization as models for dissemination and the role of business schools and management consultancies

The international expansion of both management consultancies and business schools has led recently to an interesting debate about what kinds of managerial practices are disseminated around the world. For example, in top business schools English has become the lingua franca for international business communication, pushing a certain isomorphism in the way that business analyses are developed throughout the world. Scholars such as Tietze (2004) take this argument further and claim that the spread of the English language and the increasing dominance of a management discourse have strong links with tacit assumptions and specific ideologies, encouraging the emergence of identities in line with neoliberal market economies. Moreover, other researchers (e.g., Djelic 1998; Schröter 2005) have argued that business schools and consultancies, among other institutions, might be conceived as vehicles for a process of Americanization of economies and societies all over the world (see Chapter 8).

What does this concept of Americanization mean? According to most of the scholars who have reviewed this issue, this concept expresses the influence that American businesses and managerial ideas have enjoyed in other regions in the world, mainly Europe but also Japan or Latin America, to very different degrees (Djelic 1998; Zeitlin 2000; Rodríguez Ruiz and Martínez Lucio 2010). This process is associated mainly with the post Second World War period and post Marshall Plan American politics, and is deeply interconnected with the development of American capitalism. According to some authors (Kipping and Bjarnar 1998; Schröter 2005), the Marshall Plan set the conditions for a transfer of US management models, exporting American practices and attitudes towards business in European economic life. This transfer would have continued more recently through other countries.

However, it can also be claimed that this process has extended itself far beyond the Marshall Plan. For example, Schröter (2005) indicates that Americanization has tended to occur in waves. The first wave took place in the period 1870–1945, its outcome being the widespread adoption of Taylorism and Fordism by European companies. The next period (spanning 1945–75) represents a post-war boom in which Americanization can be basically understood as a mission. The enlarged role of the economy in society, the efforts to improve productivity, new commercialization techniques, competition as a cure-all and individualization would be the main issues that American experts were interested in transferring. Some countries were excluded from the Marshall Plan (e.g., Spain), but further assistance was provided later. Finally, the third wave of Americanization has been taking place since the 1980s, featuring deregulation, privatization as a policy to help the growth of GDP, and reinforced by globalization. Despite these waves, however, Schröter considers that only the years 1945–55 can properly be labelled as real Americanization, since there was an explicit American project with which to take the US management models to Europe. If there has been more influence from America than elsewhere, that is because the United States is the society of reference for most of the world. Kipping (1999) concurs in pointing at scientific management as the first wave of the internationalization of American managerial ideas. Nevertheless, the influence before the Second World War would have been relatively small, at least until the Great Depression, when European companies began to seek improvements in productivity and performance, and found answers in the more technologically advanced American companies. This process was reinforced during the war, when there were widespread efforts to improve labour productivity. Kipping claims that the influence of American consultancies was not high in the immediate post-war period: the US Marshall Plan administration preferred to employ managers and executives rather than consultants. This situation changed from the late 1950s, however: with the recovery of European industry and corporations, American consulting firms were made welcome and increased their influence to the point that, according to some European analysts, American-style management was the force that was helping to unify Europe (Servan-Schreiber 1969).

Americanization also strongly impacted on European business schools. It is important to note that some of them, particularly in the Nordic countries, had a strong German influence before the Second World War, after which there was a consolidation of American dominance (Engwall 2009). Influence was spread by launching new business schools with American staff and learning methods (the prestigious INSEAD being the most notable example) or at least some kind of assistance (including personnel from American institutions; for example, IESE in Spain had strong ties with Harvard Business School). American business schools also became a magnet for aspiring elites all over the world. The US model has been dominant since then in the field of higher management education (Grey 2005), leaving an indelible stamp on the way curricula, subjects, teaching methods or management problems are designed, selected and presented. Thus, organizations are analysed from a perspective in tune with capitalist values, hiding intrinsic problems within these organizations such as conflicts, exploitation, power relations, authoritarianism, or gender and race discrimination.

Instead, values identified with the American Dream are promoted, emphasizing individualism, self-reliance and free market ethics.

Finally, other authors have pointed out that American business schools have contributed, with other institutional actors, to integrate native elites in developing countries into the international business world through the transmission of hegemonic neoliberal ideologies presented as scientifically validated knowledge. In this regard, and referring particularly to Latin American business schools, Ibarra-Colado (2006) defines the subordination of the latter to their North American peers (expressed by importing management knowledge from the 'centre') as a process of 'epistemic coloniality'. This process would have been assisted by the increased translation and distribution of textbooks by large American and other publishing houses from English-speaking countries. In these textbooks there could be found a well-defined project of dissemination of the principles of hegemonic managerial ideology. This process of epistemic coloniality was to help shape the views of the elites from semi-peripheral and peripheral countries, helping to connect them to the international centres of business while obscuring national peculiarities and struggles. Business schools, in particular, have contributed dramatically to the co-optation of elites, proving that they have an underlying function of providing mechanisms of social selection, particularly in the Latin countries (Schröter 2005). Moreover, they have provided and transferred management knowledge and skills to the dominant classes in certain nations while in the main ignoring social inequalities, structural economic problems or even the lack of political liberty. These cases of epistemic coloniality are not necessarily limited to Latin America, Asia or other continents, however, as not all European countries were world financial centres during the 20th century (Fernández Rodríguez and Gantman 2011).

Tensions, issues and futures: competing cultures and contexts, the politics of consultancy firms, networks and the political dimension

In sum, the narrative of Americanization seems to be a controversial one, but it is only one of the issues affected by polemics and criticism regarding business schools and the consulting industry, once they are subjected to the critical gaze of scholars (Fournier and Grey 2000; Clark and Fincham 2002). This section will give an account of some of the most relevant critics.

The main source of criticism is focused on the type of management knowledge provided by these institutions. It has been claimed that management in itself cannot be labelled as an exact science (Whitley 1984) – it would have a status similar to other social sciences, where the approach to knowledge would be strongly influenced by the ideological values of the researcher. Thus, it is important to point out that there is a clear relationship between how management topics are addressed and the ideological values of the different scholars. For example, schools of thought such as Critical Management Studies make their critical approach to management and organizations very explicit (Alvesson and Willmott 1992; Grey and Willmott 2005). However, most of the so-called mainstream management thinkers have rarely expressed their values in such a clear way, highlighting their compromise with the promotion of free market economics and the support to managers as controllers of rationality inside organizations. Therefore, business schools and consultancies would be responsible for exporting a specific American business model whose theoretical foundations are far from the neutrality they claim to have. Rather than an empirically tested neutral science without values, management is actually greatly influenced by pro-capitalist ideologies and rhetoric (Parker 2002). Apart from the aforementioned Americanization, managerial ideologies emphasize a view, also noted earlier, that hides or denies salient features of organizations such as conflict, collision of interests, discrimination, power games or inner politics. Moreover, they have disregarded ethics (the economic crisis at the time of writing has highlighted reprehensible behaviour by those who were in charge in large corporations), which have been substituted by calls to a morality based on a strange tension between individualization and a strong commitment to the enterprise culture. They have also been accused of being biased towards white American male images (Grey 2005), despite efforts to promote diversity.

In addition, their dual approach to knowledge brings some problems to the fore. On the one hand, a supposedly scientific body of theory is provided by experts, in some cases in the form of a magical solution to companies' struggles; while, on the other hand, cases are explained to illustrate the best decisions that managers are able to take. But where exactly is the link between the two approaches if the practices are based on the charismatic vision of successful managers when theory should be grounded in more serious methodologies and achieve an abstract dimension? It is a complex issue since management knowledge in itself is quite contextual and difficult to grasp compared with other academic disciplines. However, it becomes even more complex when economic interests pervade the whole discipline. Kieser (2002), for example, mentions the marionette theory – developed by the German sociologist, Werner Sombart – to explain the role of consultancies, highlighting that the knowledge being marketed by them is intended to provide a fictitious advantage for products where a real one would not be possible. Consultancy services thus help to build illusions of safety and certainty among managers.

In fact it is noticeable that serious management thinkers have sometimes engaged with so-called 'pop' management. Business schools and consultancies have also been criticized recently because of the role they play in launching and disseminating management fads (Huczinski 1993; Micklethwait and Wooldridge 1996; Clark and Salaman 1998; Collins 2000). According to Mazza and Álvarez (2000), the process of diffusion of these fads resembles the way the fashion industry disseminates its new seasonal collections. Thus, the metaphors of 'haute couture' and 'prêt-à-porter' are used to explain the different approaches towards the creation of management knowledge by distinct actors in the field. According to these authors, since the beginning of the 1980s the 'haute couture' approach (which produces complex theories published in either academic books or peer-reviewed journals and aimed at promoting intellectual discussion) has gradually been turning into a 'prêt-à-porter' approach, which relies on tacit knowledge and experience-based rules, and whose channels of diffusion are bestseller books and the popular press (newspapers and magazines), thus helping to increase the popularization of management issues. The eventual goal is not so much to provide an accurate theory but to sell more books and charge higher conference fees, and theorists finally decide to turn themselves into management gurus. This link between these institutions and fashions in management have led to a growing body of research that questions this relationship and criticizes the link between expertise and profit (e.g., Clark and Salaman 1998; Collins 2000).

This also has a consequence for another issue: the professionalization of managers and consultants, which remains controversial. It is not clear what functions a manager, or a consultant, performs if we compare them with a doctor or an engineer, say. In the case of consultancies, some authors (Kipping 2011) have claimed that there has been excessive importance attributed to 'image professionalism', in which the image of both firm and individual (the 'impression') performs almost a more important role that the quality or definition of the services provided (Clark and Fincham 2002). What in fact exists is a tension between professionalism and market logic that is difficult to solve, so professionalism is defined in a very narrow way, and rhetoric eventually plays a major role. In fact, some authors have labelled consultants as agents of anxiety and sellers of security, and even esoteric experts (Alvesson and Johansson 2002). They argue that there is a permanent tension among the profession of consultants: they claim to work according to principles of professionalism, but then disregard those same principles if it is necessary for business reasons.

Finally, there is an issue related to the influence these institutions also have on the field of education: for example, in its marketing, to the extent that it is possible to speak of 'corporate universities' (Wedlin 2006). The hegemony of management and its emphasis on efficiency have meant the closing of many university humanities departments because they are not profitable, while relocating resources to faculties with a bigger role in producing revenues (such as the business schools). Education is turning into a market, and rankings become important to incorporate otherwise reluctant universities into the neoliberal project. Since the *Financial Times* published the first MBA/business schools rankings in 1998, and one year later their world rankings, the development of these rankings has been astonishing, strengthening rules such as rationalized rituals of inspection, and boundary-work to set limits within the community (Wedlin 2006). Given the fact that the main references in the field represent mainstream thinking, it is not surprising that the remainder of the institutions get their inspiration from them. Recent developments, such as the Research Assessment Exercise (RAE) which has become the Research Excellence Framework (REF) in the United Kingdom, also involve contradictory effects. It would appear that RAE/REF was likely to pursue a fairer distribution of resources across the United Kingdom's academia, but in fact it helps to enhance two contradictory effects: on the one hand, it attempts to stimulate intellectual production, but on the other hand, in the case of management, it promotes publishing in American journals (which are dominated by scholars from top business schools, rewarding managerial contributions over critical ones), so it promotes mainstream thinking. This issue is in any case very complex as RAE/REF exercises can ironically promote a tool for change. For example, they improve the chances of management scholars to get an academic position in business schools, because they highly value publications in top journals (something that many experienced 'hero managers' fail to achieve). Therefore, a new door is opened for alternative views when some of those top journals publish papers by critical scholars.

Conclusion

This chapter has provided an overview of the role that business schools and consultancies play in the dissemination of managerial ideas. A brief history of both actors has been included, pointing at their functions as creators and disseminators of management knowledge as well as their involvement with Americanization. It has been argued that both institutions are essential to shaping views among managers and practitioners that would help to promote free market economics, individualism or competitiveness. These views were expressed clearly in the managerial discourses that formed the 'new spirit of capitalism', offering ideological justifications for the new organization of economy and labour under the post-Fordist regime. The influence of these values has become so strong that pro-managerial discourses have shaped the political, social, economic and organizational agendas, leaving little room for alternative voices.

Despite this clear ideological hegemony, recent events such as corporate scandals (the collapse of Enron being the most notable of these) and in particular the unethical practices of executives in the financial sector that erupted during the economic crisis of 2008 have helped damage the reputation of both institutions to some extent. Business schools and consultancies need to re-evaluate their current compromise with an Anglo-Saxon neoliberal agenda. These institutions should try to adapt themselves to a new scenario in which new sensibilities are likely to transform the ways in which the business world is understood. The current volatile scenario might also stimulate changes in public opinion, where the public could express its discontent with even the concept of management itself, thus offering an opportunity to develop new and more ethical approaches to organization analysis. Moreover, while drastic value changes in business schools and consultancies seem unlikely, perhaps we can still claim that the hegemony of the

Anglo-Saxon model is at stake. New economic powers are emerging, and their populations and executives have been raised with different values from those of the American Dream. There are also prospects for a possible European business school ethos in the making, different from that in the United States (Wedlin 2006). It is also interesting to notice how a critical current in organizational theory has gradually become institutionalized in some business schools, particularly in the United Kingdom, with an explicit critical and radical approach (e.g., Grey and Willmott 2005; Jones and O'Doherty 2005; Rowlinson and Hassard 2011). Therefore, important challenges to the current way that business schools and consultancies are developing and disseminating their innovations seem to be quite certain in the near future. However, the scenario remains undecided, and social struggles might play an important part in the way that management knowledge will be reconfigured in the near future.

Reflective questions

1. How many types of institutional isomorphism would exist, according to the theory developed by sociologists DiMaggio and Powell (1983)?
2. Which institution developed the first MBA programme?
3. List the stages that the so-called process of Americanization has followed.
4. What is controversial about the issue of the professionalization of managers and consultants?
5. Discuss the role of business schools and consultants in the development of pro-market values in society.

Recommended reading

- Abrahamson, E. (1991) 'Managerial fads and fashions: The diffusion and rejection of innovations'. *Academy of Management Review* 16(3): 586–612.
- Rodríguez Ruiz, Ó. and Martínez Lucio, M. (2010) 'The study of HRM in Spain: The Americanization of Spanish research and the politics of denial?'. *The International Journal of Human Resource Management* 21(1): 125–143.
- Rowlinson, M. and Hassard, J. (2011) 'How come the critters came to be teaching in business schools? Contradictions in the institutionalization of critical management studies'. *Organization* 18(5): 673–689.
- Whitley, R. (2008) 'Varieties of knowledge and their use in business and management studies: Conditions and institutions'. *Organization Studies* 29(4): 581–609.

References

Abrahamson, E. (1991) 'Managerial fads and fashions: The diffusion and rejection of innovations'. *Academy of Management Review* 16(3): 586–612.

Alonso, L. E. and Martínez Lucio, M. (eds.) (2006) *Employment Relations in a Changing Society: Assessing the Post-Fordist Paradigm.* Basingstoke: Palgrave Macmillan.

Alvesson, M. and Johansson, A. W. (2002) 'Professionalism and politics in management consultancy work'. In *Critical Consulting: New Perspectives on the Management Advice Industry*, edited by T. Clark and R. Fincham. Oxford: Blackwell.

Alvesson, M. and Willmott, H. (eds.) (1992) *Critical Management Studies.* London: Sage.

Amable, B. (2003) *The Diversity of Modern Capitalism.* Oxford: Oxford University Press.

Barley, S. and Kunda, G. (1992) 'Design and devotion: Surges of rational and normative ideologies of control in managerial discourse'. *Administrative Science Quarterly* 37: 363–399.

Boltanski, L. and Chiapello, È. (2005) *The New Spirit of Capitalism.* London: Verso.

Castells, M. (2000) *The Rise of the Network Society.* Oxford: Blackwell.

Clark, T. and Fincham, R. (eds.) (2002) *Critical Consulting: New Perspectives on the Management Advice Industry.* Oxford: Blackwell.

Clark, T. and Salaman, G. (1998) 'Telling tales: Management gurus and the construction of organizational identity'. *Journal of Management Studies* 35(2): 137–161.

Collins, D. (2000) *Management Fads and Buzzwords.* London: Routledge.

DiMaggio, P. and Powell, W. (1983) '"The iron cage revisited" institutional isomorphism and collective rationality in organizational fields'. *American Sociological Review* 48: 147–160.

Djelic, M.-L. (1998) *Exporting the American Model: The Postwar Transformation of European Business.* Oxford: Oxford University Press.

Du Gay, P. (1996) *Consumption and Identity at Work.* London: Sage.

Engwall, L. (2009) *Mercury Meets Minerva.* Oxford: Pergamon Press.

Fernández Rodríguez, C. J. and Gantman, E. (2011) 'Importers of management knowledge: Spain and Argentina in the 20th century (1955–2008)'. *Canadian Journal of Administrative Sciences* 28(2): 160–173.

Fournier, V. and Grey, C. (2000) 'At the critical moment: Conditions and prospects for critical management studies'. *Human Relations* 53(1):7–32.

Gantman, E. (2005) *Capitalism, Social Privilege and Managerial Ideologies.* Aldershot, UK: Ashgate.

Grey, C. (2005) *A Very Short, Fairly Interesting and Reasonably Cheap Book About Studying Organizations.* London: Sage.

Grey, C. and Willmott, H. (2005) *Critical Management Studies: A Reader.* Oxford: Oxford University Press.

Guillén, M. (1994) *Models of Management: Work, Authority and Organization in a Comparative Perspective.* Chicago: University of Chicago Press.

Hall, P. A. and Soskice, D. (2001) *Varieties of Capitalism: The Institutional Foundations of Comparative Advantage.* New York: Oxford University Press.

Harvey, D. (2005) *A Brief History of Neoliberalism.* Oxford: Oxford University Press.

Huczynski, A. (1993) *Management Gurus: What Makes Them and How to Become One.* London: Routledge.

Ibarra-Colado, E. (2006) 'Organization studies and epistemic coloniality in Latin America: Thinking otherness from the margins'. *Organization* 13(4): 463–488.

Jessop, R. (1995) 'The regulation approach, governance and post-Fordism: Perspectives on economic and political change'. *Economy and Society* 24(3): 307–333.

Jones, C. and O'Doherty, D. (eds.) (2005) *Manifestos for the Business School of Tomorrow*. Åbo, Finland: Dvalin Press.

Kieser, A. (2002) 'Managers or marionettes: Using fashion theories to explain the success of consultancies'. In *Management Consulting*, edited by M. Kipping and L. Engwall. Oxford: Oxford University Press, pp. 167–183.

Kipping, M. (1999) 'American management consulting companies in Western Europe, 1920–1990: Products, reputation, and relationships'. *Business History Review* 73(2): 190–221.

Kipping, M. (2011) 'Hollow from the start? Image professionalism in management consulting'. *Current Sociology* 59(4): 530–550.

Kipping, M. and Bjarnar, O. (eds) (1998) *The Americanization of European Business: The Marshall Plan and the Transfer of US Management*. London: Routledge.

Kipping, M. and Engwall, L. (eds.) (2002) *Management Consulting: Reference and Dynamics of a Knowledge Industry*. Oxford: Oxford University Press.

Lash, S. and Urry, J. (1987) *The End of Organized Capitalism*. Cambridge: Polity Press.

Mazza, C. and Álvarez, J. L. (2000) 'Haute couture and prêt-à-porter: The popular press and the diffusion of management practices'. *Organization Studies* 21(3): 567–588.

Micklethwait, J. and Wooldridge, A. (1996) *The Witch Doctors: Making Sense of the Management Gurus*. New York: Times Books.

Parker, M. (2002) *Against Management*. Cambridge: Polity Press.

Rassam, C. (1998) 'The management consultancy industry'. In *Management Consulting: A Handbook of Best Practice*, edited by P. Sadler. London: Kogan Page, pp. 3–30.

Rodríguez Ruiz, Ó. and Martínez Lucio, M. (2010) 'The study of HRM in Spain: The Americanization of Spanish research and the politics of denial?'. *The International Journal of Human Resource Management* 21(1): 125–43.

Rowlinson, M. and Hassard, J. (2011) 'How come the critters came to be teaching in business schools? Contradictions in the institutionalization of critical management studies'. *Organization* 18(5): 673–689.

Schröter, H. G. (2005) *Americanization of the European Economy: A Compact Survey of American Economic Influence in Europe since the 1880s*. Dordrecht: Springer.

Servan-Schreiber, J.-J. (1969) *The American Challenge*. London: Penguin.

Tietze, S. (2004) 'Spreading the management gospel—in English'. *Language and Intercultural Communication* 4(3): 175–189.

Wedlin, L. (2006) *Ranking Business Schools: Forming Fields, Identities and Boundaries in Management Education*. Cheltenham: Edward Elgar.

Whitley, R. (1984) 'The fragmented state of management studies: Reasons and consequences'. *Journal of Management Studies* 21(3): 331–348.

Whitley, R. (2008) 'Varieties of knowledge and their use in business and management studies: Conditions and institutions'. *Organization Studies* 29(4): 581–609.

Zeitlin, J. (2000) 'Introduction: Americanization and its limits: Reworking US technology and management in post-war Europe and Japan'. In *Americanization and Its Limits: Reworking US Technology and Management in Post-War Europe and Japan*, edited by J. Zeitlin and G. Herrigel. Oxford: Oxford University Press, pp. 1–50.

Three articles to be accessed by students

Ibarra-Colado, E. (2006) 'Organization studies and epistemic coloniality in Latin America: Thinking otherness from the margins'. *Organization* 13(4): 463–488.

Mazza, C. and Álvarez, J. L. (2000) 'Haute couture and prêt-à-porter: The popular press and the diffusion of management practices'. *Organization Studies* 21(3): 567–588.

Rowlinson, M. and Hassard, J. (2011) 'How come the critters came to be teaching in business schools? Contradictions in the institutionalization of critical management studies'. *Organization* 18(5): 673–689.

10 Developing contexts of human resource management and industrial relations: globalization and employment relations strategies and narratives

Naresh Kumar and Miguel Martínez Lucio

Learning objectives

- To understand the limitations of the discussion on developing countries and to appreciate the greater complexity of such countries
- To engage with the way the state plays a role in relation to multinational corporations in such contexts
- To use Malaysia as an example of proactive labour market strategies and state planning in relation to foreign direct investment and national training
- To outline some of the challenges in terms of employment relations and the way worker representation is developed

Introduction

There is an increasing trend among key texts on international human resource management (IHRM) to question whether developing countries should be dealt with as a national or regional context deserving special attention. At first glance, this may seem to be problematic as it appears to dismiss the realities and challenges of human resource management (HRM) and industrial relations (IR) in developing countries. It appears that when we think about the international dimension of these subjects, we should consider them in terms of transnational corporations and their impact across a range of contexts. However, this new trend is related to the difficulty of defining what a developing country is. In some cases, China is presented as developing, which is not always plausible, given the extent of its social and economic development. On the other hand, there is a concern that the use of binaries such as 'developing' and 'developed' ignores the more complex realities of the world in terms of the crisis among developed countries and the emergence of powerful developing countries such as India and Brazil. However, the term *developing* can still be used because of the ongoing income differentials; the dominance of specific types of multinational corporation (MNC) and the nature of their activities in low-income countries; the ongoing economic hierarchy between 'North' and 'South'; and the problematic political issues in relation to the nature of trade union and participatory systems in various developing contexts.

Many IHRM discussions may, in fact, conceal the specific challenges and dilemmas facing countries and their workforces in terms of the rapid and/or uneven economic and social changes that are taking place. What is more, they may remain silent on political issues and on questions of human rights. This silence may be driven by a particular view of management and economic development dominated by the politics of an Americanized, neoliberal/market economy or managerialist understandings of organizational change and social context.

This chapter aims to outline some of the debates concerning developing countries in relation to HRM and IR. It will show how such debates have been structured, and how changes since the 1990s, resulting from developments in foreign direct investment (FDI) and the role of MNCs, have introduced a new set of issues and dynamics. The chapter will then focus on a specific national context in terms of the impact of FDI and the way this has influenced both management and labour. The development of new forms of working and new groups of workers in internationalized sectors of the economy will be outlined, describing leading debates in the area. However, the chapter also aims to question the passivity implied in many of the dominant views of regulation, politics and participation in developing countries by arguing that national actors are highly significant in the development of the local economic context, albeit within a specific, normally marketized, context and framework. It will also show how the impact of developments such as FDI has actually contributed to new sets of debates and issues within such contexts concerning work and employment, as well as in management. Ethical issues have emerged in terms of work and employment change alongside social issues regarding the composition of the workforce, as well as regulatory dilemmas regarding managing international elite interests and those of local populations as economies and societies change. Furthermore, new agendas around employment representation and politics have not been far from the surface, as Chapter 14 outlines. This chapter therefore looks at two very different features of how employment relations systems are affected by internationalization and by state responses to it: first, we focus on how the state attempts to enhance the skills and 'pliability' of its workforce in relation to new forms of external investment and employment; second, we examine some dilemmas and issues that are emerging in terms of ambivalence towards collective worker representation. The chapter focuses on Malaysia as a national context which has been developing rapidly but which exhibits many of the positive and negative features of a country balancing economic and social demands in terms of HRM and industrial relations.

Understanding employment relations and the management of labour in developing countries

The question of development has been less central to the study of HRM and IR than one might imagine. The focus of many discussions has, until the past decade or so, been on so-called developed countries. The argument that developments in countries such as the United States or the United Kingdom need to be privileged rests on a series of assumptions about the dominance of the liberal market economy within management texts (see Chapter 8). First, these are economies that have developed market-oriented social and political structures, and where competition has led to a greater investment in management development and strategic innovation. Second, if one of the concerns of the study of employment, work and management is to seek best practice, then this is likely to be found within such national contexts. Third, where new forms of organizational innovation and change are seen in other contexts such as Japan (see Chapter 7 for a discussion of these developments linked to Japan), this can be attributed to the application of 'western' management thought, albeit within a distinct mediating context. Yet the problem with this approach and set of assumptions is that it supposes that employment practices and management strategies in developing countries can best be improved by mimicking and integrating those of developed countries, and that such practices are potentially transferable. Hence, there is a view of developing countries that stresses their passivity and fundamentally recipient status in organizational development and HRM change. Developing countries are seen as receivers and accommodators of international developments in terms of markets and organizational processes.

Developing nations are understood in terms of the dominance of industrial sectors such as agriculture and the public sector, which are renowned, albeit for quite different reasons, for being hampered by highly immobile bureaucracies and/or command-style management processes involving direct forms of supervision or results-related payments (Blunt and Jones 1992). Yet Jackson (2004: 229), in an important synthesis of the study of developing countries, tried to widen this view and explain a broader range of factors that are seen by many to constitute the core characteristics of developing countries and that inhibit development and change: authoritarian management, which can be explained by the political context of developing countries; a strong bureaucracy that emerges because of the importance of the state and formal interventions resulting from weak civil societies; a tendency to put the emphasis on inputs and direct control by management, rather than on outputs and quality, because of the limited nature of production processes and markets; the importance of informal and family links because of an absence of principles of equity in the labour market; a lack of worker involvement and a restrictive view of human resources; and a fundamental lack of management skills related to the absence of extensive education, among other factors. Many studies have focused on such features, seeing them as representative of a 'primitive' state of affairs within such countries. Moreover, they do so in many cases without explaining the colonial history of such contexts – as in the impact of the British or Belgian empires, say, in sustaining underdevelopment, or the impact of neocolonial actors such as the United States in focusing investment support on limited and primary sectors as in Guatemala. There is also the ongoing problem that many developing countries, as in Africa, for example, are studied in relation to the European and North American contexts – as if the developments in the Far East had not taken place and reference points for development were narrower (Kamoche 2002).

In addition, the political background is normally ignored in the study of HRM, and even part of IR, for example, the manner in which authoritarian settings can systematically suppress or inhibit the development of democratic voice mechanisms within industrial relations, and therefore inhibit traditions of social dialogue. The study of management and work in such circumstances is normally skewed, partly because of the need to sanitize and neutralize political discussion in the management classroom, placing the focus on matters of technique and 'best practice'.

Some try to remedy this by invoking the role of culture and the need to gain a broader understanding of a country's context and the possible influence on HRM developments and IR traditions. Within management and organizational studies, the use of aspects of Hofstede's work, such as *Culture's Consequences* (2001), continues to be invoked as a means of understanding the differences between cultures and nations in organizational terms: and even recently, it remains a point of entry for the comparative study of HRM (Marchington and Wilkinson 2008). Differences are measured in terms of the acceptance of hierarchy, risk aversion, individual and collective identity, and masculine versus feminine approaches. The accepted norm is that developing countries in the main are more hierarchical (or accepting of hierarchy), more masculine and in some cases more collectivist. That these terms are highly problematic is clear; however, the developing context is often seen as being locked into a particular cultural perspective: political and regulatory traditions are rarely accounted for in such views as Hofstede's (2001). Such explanations can run the risk of making social development seem difficult, or they may make the process of change in qualitative terms (e.g., the emergence of social and worker rights) appear to be less achievable. Countries appear to be complex and opaque in such approaches. Harvey (2002) warns us that the organizational and employment complexity of African nations, for example, may have been exacerbated by the impact of colonization and imperial control, which have disrupted ethnic communities and led to uneven urbanization and change. Hence, culturalist analysis might have limitations in explaining such contexts and understanding that cultures emerge from repression, resistance and change and are not static entities deeply embedded in general traits.

Others have tried to move away from characterizing cultural traits or economic customs and practices in a quixotic manner, and studied newly emerging centres of power such as in Latin America or the Middle East with a greater sensitivity to the actual context and the challenges of change (Vassolo et al. 2011). There is an increasing sensitivity – relatively speaking – in attempts to understand the role of political elites, economic/political networks, the informal economy, the impact of new forms of multinationals, human resource development gaps, and the impact of growing expectations and rights-related concerns. In addition, inter- and intra-regional collaboration between governments and social actors has emerged as of growing importance. In such approaches, developing countries appear to be more complex spaces, and more dynamic and changeable than traditionalist views would indicate. The way they interact with the global context is therefore deeper and richer than might be imagined from quasi-colonialist/managerial readings.

What is also becoming clear is that there is a need to view MNCs as more than just depositors of investment, and developers of technical and organizational knowledge, on the positive side; or, from a more critical perspective, as organizations that seek cost advantages and can do so with very little engagement with local states. The image of MNCs as being able to enter and leave such economies at will – exploiting their cost advantages in terms of both physical and human resources – is highly questionable (Lillie and Martínez Lucio 2011). In fact, in some cases, MNCs find themselves being forced to operate at a more 'sophisticated' political level, given a range of host country challenges: increasing political change in developing countries; greater awareness of qualitative issues at work such as workers' rights; the problem of developing local professional elites and their positions within new investment and employment networks; and greater governmental collaboration in a variety of regions. The social and learning agenda has shifted from the approach seen in the 1960s–80s, when investment was dominated primarily by a set of specific MNCs and national host countries. The politics of investment is more complex. Greater capacity within developing states has meant that the host country interaction with MNCs and international capital is changing.

Regardless of the positive impact on poverty generated by some aspects of FDI (Dollar and Krayy 2001), issues have emerged as a result of the rapid and uneven nature of economic change and its social consequences. The impact on women and children through their inclusion in the labour market within an unstable pattern of employment has generated increasing interest in health and safety issues, and a broad concern for both human and employment rights. Structural adjustment and privatization in developing countries has had a disproportionate impact on women as they attempt to combine a traditional role within a new employed role, normally within hidden economies (Pyle and Ward 2003). These increasing concerns with rights vary greatly, but the shift in concerns has led to a more complex set of debates with international corporate and political interests.

Much depends on the level of autonomy and power of independent social interests and groups such as trade unions or social movements within a nation. There remain enormous disparities in the manner in which organized labour influences social and political policy at work, yet the political and regulatory context can shape policies or create political concerns, as in Saudi Arabia, where the state regulation of employment quotas for foreign nationals and practices of segregation at work are highly significant. Traditions of labour regulation vary greatly in developing countries, from those where independent and free labour organization has been minimal (e.g., Colonel Gadaffi's Libya and Saudi Arabia) through to systems which, while being politically repressive, have put in place a semblance of minimal labour regulation to avoid the need for independent unions, as in Chile under the dictator Augusto Pinochet in the 1970s and 1980s. Then there are the countries where labour representation and regulation is quite extensive but under the tutelage of a centralized one-party state which dominates labour representation, as in China or Vietnam. Yet there are countries where industrial relations systems and trade union roles have been influenced by a colonial heritage with a particular model of industrial relations, that while being limited in terms of union influence do have a degree of independence and liberty (e.g., Malaysia).

And it is not solely in relation to organized labour representation and regulation that we may see considerable variety. Within developing countries, there are also changes in management circles. Increasing management education and rising professional expectations in relation to MNCs have begun to emerge, driven partly by exogenous factors (the increasing transnational orientation of MNCs' policies and staffing) and endogenous ones (the increasing presence of a professional middle class and the impact of new forms of management expectations). Zahra (2011) has argued that, in the Middle East, the growing clash between formal organizational cultures and traditional informal and hierarchical customs – coupled with major political change within both the state and society – means that the process of organizational change, greater external and internal investment and the systematic use of local resources will reveal a new set of political and academic agendas, as well as competing management views and values.

Hence, MNCs and investment within developing countries have contradictory effects and can lead to greater political learning and organizational tension. The issue of changing expectations and debates is not unilinear, leading to a certain pre-established outcome, rather it is disruptive in both positive and negative ways. In HRM and IR, we need to appreciate this dual effect of the impact of disruption and change. It unsettles communities in their rural or local contexts but also creates new communities and new struggles:

> The irony here is that at the same time as capital escapes regulatory contexts and national systems in search of increased value and surpluses, it also re-encounters regulatory systems. This creates a constant dilemma for capital in terms of escaping, encountering and rethinking relations within and between contexts. In a sense, however, focusing on the inevitability of re-regulation, and the sometimes high cost to capital of regulatory flux, misses the point.
>
> (Lillie and Martínez Lucio 2012: 77)

Hence, host countries at the local level may accommodate international capital and MNCs, but they can also create a degree of mutual dependency, as in the role of the state in areas such as labour market policy, learning and regulation, which facilitate the work of MNCs. The context of developing countries is somewhat passive – coming into itself only when MNCs appear to employ local resources (human, material and market) – yet over time these dynamics can become more complex and interactive.

It is for this reason that the state and social and economic actors within the national setting need to be seen as important to any attempt to understand how developing countries engage with international capital, develop their political space in relation to change and establish a range of 'supportive' practices and institutions. When discussing the state in a developing context, we see these more strategic roles emerge:

> Rather than simply retreating to the sidelines to function as the game's referee, the state must strategically co-ordinate the interaction between key economic actors in a way that will stimulate deep and crosscutting developmental linkages. These linkages are necessary to facilitate information flow, increase vested interests through participation (as opposed to simply consultation), and improve cross-checked monitoring and implementation – all while maintaining appropriate autonomy from distributional interests. But this new role for the state is also dramatically different from the theoretical role of the developmental state. Instead of simply directing investment and ameliorating risk, the state must now encourage, facilitate, and co-ordinate

the formation of *intangible* assets, which often requires more private-sector leadership.

(Ritchie 2002: 32)

The interaction between local institutions and processes of globalization is much more complex in terms of economic and political inputs (e.g., local state strategies on regional development zones) and social and political outcomes (e.g., the impact on local management traditions or the emergent politics of social rights and organization by groups such as women, both locally and internationally). A case study from Malaysia (see below) will highlight these complex processes and the tensions that can emerge.

Interpreting national contexts and the politics of industrial relations in the developmental context of Southeast Asia

International economic investment has begun to transform a range of national economies and the regulatory structures within them, and the sheer scale of this investment has been remarkable. The *World Investment Report 2013* by the United Nations Conference on Trade and Development (UNCTAD 2013) revealed that developing and transition economies absorbed more than half of global FDI inflows from 2010 to 2012 against a notable decrease in FDI inflows to developed countries. Total FDI inflows to Southeast Asia rose by 104% in 2010, reaching US$97,898 million, and this explains a fast recovery from the financial crisis of 2007–2008. The Association of Southeast Asian Nations (ASEAN) countries saw a significant influx of FDI in 2012, with Singapore being the largest recipient (US$56,651 million), followed by Indonesia (US$19,853 million), Malaysia (US$10,074 million), Vietnam (US$8,368 million), Thailand (US$8,607 million), the Philippines (US$ 2,797 million) and Cambodia (US$1,557 million). FDI has been seen as a key driver in promoting the economic growth of Asian countries. For example, the introduction of the Investment Incentive Act in 1968, the establishment of free trade zones in the early 1970s and the provision of export incentives in conjunction with the acceleration of open economies in the 1980s have encouraged MNCs to reposition their labour-intensive production to countries such as Malaysia since the late 1980s (Jomo 2007b; Ang 2008, 2009).

The Malaysian population was 27.9 million in 2009, of which 63.3% was urban. Being an emerging economy in Asia, Malaysia recorded a total labour force of 12,061,100 in 2009, with 63.1% being economically active in the working age population of 15 to 64 years (Government of Malaysia 2010). Employment in the different industrial sectors increased from 9.275 million in 2000 to 11.621

million in 2009. The average annual employment growth rate for the decade 2000 to 2009 was 2.8%. The average unemployment rate for the period 2000 to 2009 was 3.4%. Labour shortages have encouraged the influx of low-skilled foreign labour, which between 2000 and 2009 rose to 1.9 million (Government of Malaysia 2010: 234). Malaysia has recovered from the Asian economic and financial crisis of 1997 and appears to be heading towards a higher average level of income. Malaysia enjoyed high inflows of FDI in the 1980s and early 1990s compared with other countries in this region, since few countries have such flexible and attractive trade and investment policies as Malaysia. The dramatic economic transformations in Southeast Asia have led governments to develop and implement plans to attract high value-added FDI while competing with countries in the immediate region, and in South America and Eastern Europe. The UNCTAD (2013) report makes it clear that the strong FDI inflows into the Southeast Asian countries are a result of proactive policy efforts by the various governments to attract FDI inflows. Malaysia has implemented more liberalized economic policies similar to those of other ASEAN countries that facilitated the entry of transnational corporations (TNCs) and FDI inflows (World Bank 2011: 41). In addition, the country was ranked 12th in the World Bank's Ease of Doing Business Report 2013; while AT Kearney's Foreign Direct Investor Confidence Index 2012 placed Malaysia as the 10th best FDI destination (*The Star* 2013). However, FDI inflows to Malaysia in 2012 fell by 17.4% to US$10.1 billion compared to US$12.2 billion in 2011, as a result of the global slump in the manufacturing sector on which Malaysia depends for FDI (UNCTAD 2013).

It has been alleged that the increasing quantity of FDI and number of MNCs in developing countries has led to the emergence of some aspects of 'western' HRM policies and practices that could strengthen people management (Budhwar and Debrah 2001; Budhwar 2004; Rowley and Warner 2004). Since developing countries can have unique national manpower development policies and are at different stages of HRM practices, some maintain that local firms should emulate the best practices of western HRM that suit the local working culture, and the social, political and economic values of the country.

The case studies focus on Malaysia. The study will outline some of the ways in which the state and the industrial relations system engage with internationalization but also with related indigenous development. We look here at some of the formal strategies and rhetoric of developmental states. It will, however, be followed by an alternative reading of the way that the state and industrial relations strategies are developed to contain both workers' opinions and more positive possibilities for participation. There are various readings of how employment and HRM systems have developed. Readers need to be alert to the different narratives and interpretations that may exist.

Inward investment and economic development are engineered as much through local state policies as they are through external global economic trends

Case study: The state and industrial relations in Malaysia – Creating a context supportive of investment and support

Governments in Malaysia have argued since the early 2000s that knowledge, skills, abilities and other relevant competencies among the workforce are the key to succeeding in a competitive world. The wave of inward investment and the increasing internationalization of the economy have meant that the public authorities foster strategic reform initiatives on human capital and programmes aimed at accelerating the quality and performance of the Malaysian workforce.

The government has therefore begun to devote more resources to science and technology (S&T) and research and development (R&D), which are seen as vital for human resource development (HRD). In fact, the importance of HRD has been recognized and was given significant emphasis in Malaysia's earlier development plans (Malaysia Government 1991, 2001), though innovation capacity and patent production are still low (Wong 2011). Besides, poor performance culture and low productivity levels remain a focus of national political discourse (*The Star* 2013). Much is said formally about the priority given to education and training, which provides opportunities for academic pursuits and the advancement of knowledge, skills, abilities and other competencies as a way of boosting intellectual capital among the workforce and making Malaysia more competitive globally. Therefore, to assume a passive state role that only responds to and works around MNCs is ill-advised. The evolution of the country's development policies can be classified into the following major phases: the New Economic Policy (NEP), 1970–1990; the National Development Policy (NDP), 1991–2000; and the National Vision Policy (NVP), 2001–2010. The Third Outline Perspective Plan (OPP3), 2001–2010 was launched with a focus on building a 'resilient and competitive nation' and embodying the NVP to be implemented over a decade. The Economic Transformation Programme (ETP) was launched in 2010 to build on the policy directions, strategies and programmes of the 10th Malaysia Plan, 2010–2015. It also complements existing agendas, such as the Government Transformation Programme (GTP). Malaysia's global competitiveness is seen to depend heavily on new initiatives driven by the ETP and efficient development of human capital: these will be able, it was argued, to attract unremitting inflows of FDI. Hence, planning remains a central part of this logic of regulation.

The government also facilitated efforts in benchmarking and the adoption of best practices on human capital development from other countries as well as from international commitments and conventions. There has been much rhetoric and policy related to ensuring continuous employment and a smooth transition to an advanced level and quality of work among the workforce, and the Ministry of Human Resources (MOHR) officially released the National Action Plan for Employment (NAPE), 2008–2010 on 20 November 2008. The measures highlighted in NAPE were outlined in ten main areas: (1) active and preventive measures for the unemployed and the inactive; (2) promoting job creation and entrepreneurship; (3) promoting adaptability and mobility in the labour market; (4) promoting development of human capital and lifelong learning; (5) promoting active employment of older workers and the ageing; (6) strengthening gender equality in employment; (7) promoting the integration of special groups into the labour market; (8) ensuring decent wages; (9) transforming informal work into regular employment; and (10) overcoming regional and sectoral employment disparities (Ministry of Human Resources Malaysia 2009). In essence, NAPE is a national agenda that aims to provide direction and outline priorities for employment. Workers' rights in employment are seen as key priorities and given adequate emphasis to ensure that workers are not deprived of legal rights and benefits, though, as we shall see, the reality is more complicated. For example, the Human Resources Development Act of 1992, which came into force in January 1993, led to the establishment of the Human Resources Development Fund (HRDF), thus officially ending the training tax incentive scheme that had been in operation since 1987. The HRDF was administered by a Human Resources Development Council (HRDC) including representatives from the private sector and various government agencies, though the role of worker representatives was limited. The Human Resources Development Levy is a mandatory payment imposed by the government on specific groups of employers for the purpose of employee training and skills advancement. Eligible employers are required to contribute 1% of the monthly wages of each employee to the HRDF. The Minister of Human Resources is empowered to reduce or increase the specified levy rate from time to time, and to grant employers full or partial exemption from levy payments.

While evidence from surveys examined by the World Bank suggests that despite being efficient in reimbursing claims and making application procedures easy for employers to comply with, the training impact of the scheme appears to be modest (Tan 2001). Similar concerns surrounded the mandatory National Service Training Programme, or *Program Latihan Khidmat Negara* (PLKN), as provided for in the National Service Training Act, 2003. Young people aged 16 to 35 years are selected randomly from different ethnic groups and required to attend PLKN for three months to undertake four modules: (1) the physical module; (2) nation building; (3) character building; and (4) community service. Hence, the technical is combined with the cultural in such forms of state intervention, though the Auditor-General's report of December 2007 pointed out that many of the programme instructors were not well trained, the locations of the camps were unsuitable, the facilities were inadequate and rigid contracts caused government losses of up to RM110.1 million between 2004 and 2007 (*The Star* 2008). In addition, since 2004, sporadic serious incidents and accidents, including deaths of trainees (total fatalities at National Service camps since the programme's inception stand at 18 up to the time of writing), were highlighted by the local press (*The Sun* 2012).

The 'decent work' agenda has also been an increasing point of reference for the MOHR under its list of 'deliverables' within national developmental policies, and it links rhetorically at least to the statements of the International Labour Organization (ILO) in terms of working conditions. The MOHR's 'decent work' agenda is as follows (MOHR 2009):

1. To develop a workforce that is productive, informative, *disciplined*, caring and responsive to the changing labour environment towards increasing economic growth and hence creating more job opportunities.
2. To encourage and maintain conducive and *harmonious* industrial relations between employers, employees and trade unions for the nation's economic development and well-being of the people.
3. To uphold social justice and ensure *harmonious* industrial relations by solving industrial disputes between employers and employees.
4. To ensure that trade unions practice democracy, are *orderly* and responsible for helping to achieve the objective of industrial *harmony*.
5. To be the leader in the development of the nation's human resources.
6. To ensure the health and safety of the workforce.
7. To develop a skilled, knowledgeable and competitive workforce in an environment of *harmonious* industrial relations with social justice.

(Italics added by the authors.)

The development of a 'decent work' agenda has attempted to create a progressive counter-space within the state running alongside a narrative led by the Ministry of Higher Education on training. This emphasizes that technical and soft skills in particular are to be included in education and training programmes so as to increase the marketability of Malaysian graduates, and that higher learning institutions incorporate the following skills: communication skills; critical thinking and problem solving skills; life-long learning and information management; team work; entrepreneurship; professional ethics and morals; and leadership skills. The 'decent work' agenda also appears, however, to be linked to a more functional agenda of worker flexibility based on cultural and social pliability in the face of new employer needs and forms of inward investment fitting the more job-loading dimensions of lean production, for example. Much of the agenda is tied to a specific hierarchical and controlled view of work. In addition, there are concerns about access and equality issues across the different constituent populations of Malaysia, as it is a country with strongly embedded and large minority ethnic groups in the form of Indian and Chinese communities.

Questions

1. What are the main features of government policy in Malaysia with regard to creating a supportive environment for overseas investment in the country?
2. Why is the quality of working life an emergent issue in such contexts?
3. What might be the challenges in terms of such forms of state policy, and developments in terms of costs and expectations? How realistic might such initiatives be in the light of the pressures to contain labour costs as a result of the importance of FDI?
4. What are the particular views of employment and industrial relations that are embedded in this policy approach (e.g., the use of the terms *harmony and orderly*)?

and processes. Malaysia is an example of a nation that has begun to create a framework of skills development and 'national progress', which has helped to create a political and regulatory context that parallels and interacts with capital flows and changes. As MNCs seek environments with cost benefits in terms of labour, for example, or access points to new markets, they also draw a response from the institutions of the host country in which they are investing. In many cases, these are framed in a negative way, in that they create a context where MNCs may not be challenged by workers and their representatives, or where development zones are constructed in which worker rights are limited or suspended. Hence, in the case of Malaysia, there are other narratives that are more critical of the extent of state support.

Case study: The politics of industrial relations and worker rights in Malaysia – The reality of rights in Malaysia

While facing the Asian economic and financial crisis in 1997, Malaysia worked assertively towards a 'knowledge-based' economy with the aim of achieving the status of a newly industrialized country, which for some necessitates industrial harmony via a tripartite labour system. The Employment Act, 1955 (EA), Trade Unions Act, 1959 (TUA) and the Industrial Relations Act, 1967 (IRA) collectively form the basis of the industrial relations (IR) system in Malaysia. However, the Malaysian government receives constant criticism of its long-standing IR and labour laws, which, at the time of writing, have not been revised to accommodate current economic and workplace demands by employers (Arudsothy 1990; Arudsothy and Littler 1993; Jomo and Todd 1994; Rasiah 1995; Kuruvilla 1996; Sharma 1996; Anantaraman 1997; Ariffin 1997; Bhopal and Todd 2000; Ramasamy 2000; Todd and Peetz 2001; Ayadurai et al. 2002; Bhopal and Rowley 2002; Suhanah 2002; Mellahi and Wood 2004; Parasuraman 2004; Todd et al. 2004; Wu 2006; Aminuddin 2007). The Malaysian IR system has become increasingly more restrictive than pluralistic (Kuruvilla and Arudsothy 1995), based on a system of state–employer domination (Kuruvilla and Venkataratnam 1996), and repressive confrontation rather than being accommodating and cooperative (Sharma 1996). Todd and Peetz (2001) maintain it is a 'controlled' rather than a 'commitment-based' structure delineated by the early British colonial government and maintained by Malaysia since independence. Deficiencies in the democratization of labour legislation have apparently worked against the achievement of collaborative workplace relations. Anantaraman (1997) and Suhanah (2002) argue that Malaysian labour policies since 1958–1970, when the emphasis was on import substitution industrialization (ISI), encapsulated in relevant laws, threaten cooperative IR as the government attempts to turn Malaysia into a fully industrialized country by 2020. The government viewed the growth of manufacturing for export purposes as a central feature of economic development, allowing for strong competition among the Asian newly industrializing economies (NICs). Thus, the nature of IR policies appeared to be a form of 'controlled pluralism' based on significant state control aimed at avoiding industrial conflict in the interests of accelerating the industrialization process (Jomo 2007a, 2007b; Kuruvilla and Arudsothy 1995).

The Department of Trade Union Affairs (DTU) governs trade unions and deals with issues such as registration, internal organization, the election of officers, union finances and, in particular, specifies unions' rights, powers, duties and responsibilities. However, certain acts strictly forbid unions from representing workers from different establishments, trades, occupations or industries.

The Department of Industrial Relations (IRA) *regulates relations between employers, workers and their trade unions, and aims at the prevention and settlement of any trade disputes and related matters.* Workers have the right to form or join trade unions, with the exception of members of the police, the prison service, the armed forces and public sector employees employed in a confidential or security capacity. The IRA grants the director general absolute authority to determine the classifications of employees, and prohibits the formation of unions in 'pioneer industries'. Indeed, the focal point of criticism in labour studies is that the director general (previously the Registrar of Trade Unions) allowed in-house unions (enterprise unions) to represent workers in the electronics sector after unremitting pressure from international bodies, but exercised arbitrary power to prevent the formation of a national trade union in the electronics sector (unlike their counterparts in the electrical industries) since it comes under the 'pioneer status' consistent with the government's pursuit of a low-cost export-oriented strategy (Jomo 2007a; Jomo and Todd 1994; Kuruvilla and Arudsothy 1995). Furthermore, workers in 'pioneer status' industries were prohibited from having their terms determined by bargaining beyond the minimum standards stipulated in the Employment Act, 1955: this undermines the efforts of unionization in such companies (Peetz and Todd 2001). For some employees, the provisions of the Employment Act, 1955 guarantee their minimum employment protection and benefits, so the attractiveness of trade union membership is questionable. However, while the IRA consents to collective bargaining, its scope is limited to the provision of training, the annual review of wages and the development of performance-based remuneration systems. The Malaysian labour laws seem to some extent to be more favourable to employers than to unions or employees, and discourage genuine employee participation in workplace decision making at the in-house or enterprise level (Anantaraman 1997; Ariffin 1997; Suhanah 2002; Parasuraman 2004; Todd et al. 2004). Wad (2001: 4) views in-house unions as 'weak, management-controlled lapdogs, more or less unable to defend and improve employees' rights and interests, and that do not provide for concomitant wage and productivity increases'.

Hence, the way that the industrial relations environment has been constructed, and the way unions have been constrained, means that the positive features of dialogue, mutual gains and more inclusive HR strategies may not easily be developed (Kumar et al. 2013). The development of a fair and inclusive workplace may be also hampered by the limits on union renewal and the lack of external support for it. (For a more developed discussion of these issues see the source for this case – Kumar et al. 2013.)

Conclusion

The case of Malaysia therefore raises particular issues and concerns about the role of the state and the nature of industrial relations within such contexts. In a leading intervention, Bhopal and Rowley argue that the national state is a key mediating factor that is central to the narrative of investment, human resource management and labour related issues:

> The oppression of labour is not simply something desired *per se* by dependent states in all circumstances. The State has other considerations, which can give rise to concessions to labour. Yet, the degree of dependence on capital may determine the ability of the State to pursue a policy designed to meet its internal needs. If dependent states are less able to determine their labour policies owing to MNCs, the implication for those advocating trade/aid and labour rights links is that they need to address the fact that labour suppression may be the result of the actions of MNCs and inactions of states. The complicity of capital and its home state needs to be at the centre of any discussion on human rights and trade. A failure to do this not only leaves dependent developing countries caught between a 'rock and a hard place' (economic sanctions and failure to attract FDI), but fails to identify the role of home and dependent host states in the inherent contradictions between capital and labour.
>
> (Bhopal and Rowley 2002: 1181–1182)

The importance of the way the state therefore acts as a dimension of the globalization of capital is key. The question of globalization is not purely an economic or cultural phenomenon but is a process of interactions (albeit increasingly accelerated ones) between local organizations, regulatory bodies and transnational corporations and networks. What is more, the manner in which the local context responds in terms of HR and IR policies constitutes a complex set of political factors.

The state also has to deal with contradictory outcomes and the manner in which expectations and the understanding of rights change as a result of globalization. Even if only rhetorically, the state and the political elites have to balance a range of competing interests and social developments as investment regimes impact and change the way that people work and live. The Malaysian state is caught between developing supporting mechanisms in terms of training and investment strategies while also creating some semblance of order and supposed equity in what it does. It is likely that in a developmental context, there is a tension between the softer human development aspects and the harder positions on worker rights and forms of representation, and the contradictions between these may play themselves out and create a new set of issues and political dynamics.

Reflective questions

1. What opportunities may MNCs bring to a context of economic development?
2. How can governments and social actors ensure that these benefits are built upon and consolidated in relation to work and employment?
3. What are the main problems that MNCs may bring in terms of dependency or the nature of the work they develop?
4. What are the issues that may emerge in terms of worker rights and representation?

Recommended reading

- Harvey, M. (2002) 'Human resource management in Africa: Alice's adventures in wonderland'. *The International Journal of Human Resource Management* 13(7): 121–134.
- Kuruvilla, S. and Venkataratnam, C. S. (1996) 'Economic development and industrial relations: The case of South and Southeast Asia'. *Industrial Relations Journal* 27(1): 9–23.
- Kumar, N., Martínez Lucio, M. and Che Rose, R. (2013) 'Workplace industrial relations in a developing environment: Barriers to renewal within unions in Malaysia'. *Asia Pacific Journal of Human Resources*, 51(1): 22–44.
- Rasiah, R. (1995) 'Labour and industrialization in Malaysia'. *Journal of Contemporary Asia* 25(1): 73–92.
- Rowley, C. and Warner, M. (2004) 'Big business in Asia'. *Asia Pacific Business Review* 10(4): 485–496.

References

Aminuddin, M. (2007) *Malaysian Industrial Relations and Employment Law*, 6th edn. Kuala Lumpur: McGraw-Hill.

Anantaraman, A. (1997) *Malaysian Industrial Relations: Law and Practice*. Serdang, Malaysia: Universiti Putra Malaysia Press.

Ang, J. B. (2008) 'Determinants of foreign direct investment in Malaysia'. *Journal of Policy Modelling* 30: 185–189.

Ang, J. B. (2009) 'Financial development and the FDI–growth nexus: The Malaysian experience'. *Applied Economics* 41: 1595–1601.

Ariffin, R. (1997) 'Changing employment structures and their effects on industrial relations in Malaysia'. *The Economic and Labour Relations Review* 8(1): 44–56.

Arudsothy, P. (1990) 'The state and industrial relations in developing countries: The Malaysian situation'. *ASEAN Economic Bulletin* 6(3): 307–328.

Arudsothy, P. and Littler, C. (1993) 'State regulation and union fragmentation in Malaysia'. In *Organised Labour in the Asia-Pacific Region: A Comparative Study of Trade Unions in Nine Countries*, edited by S. Frenkel. Ithaca, NY: ILR Press, pp. 107–130.

Ayadurai, D., Yahaya, J. and Zainuddin, S. (2002) 'Malaysia'. In *The Handbook of Human Resource Management Policies and Practices in Asia Pacific Economies*, vol. 1, edited by M. Zanko. Northampton, UK: Edward Elgar.

Bhopal, M. and Rowley, C. (2002) 'The state in employment: The case of Malaysian electronics'. *The International Journal of Human Resource Management* 13(8): 1166–1185.

Bhopal, M. and Todd, P. (2000) 'Multinational corporations and trade union development in Malaysia'. In *Globalisation and Labour in the Asia Pacific Region*, edited by C. Rowley and J. Benson. London: Frank Cass, pp. 193–213.

Blunt, P. and Jones, M. L. (1992) *Managing Organisations in Africa*. Berlin: Walter de Gruyter.

Budhwar, P. (ed.) (2004) *Managing Human Resources in Asia-Pacific*. London: Routledge.

Budhwar, P. and Debrah, Y. A. (eds) (2001) *Human Resource Management in Developing Countries*. London: Routledge.

Dollar, D. and Krayy, A. (2001) *Trade, Growth and Poverty*. Washington, DC: World Bank.

Government of Malaysia (2010) *Tenth Malaysia Plan 2011–2015*. Putrajaya, Malaysia: Economic Planning Unit.

Harvey, M. (2002) 'Human resource management in Africa: Alice's adventures in wonderland'. *The International Journal of Human Resource Management* 13(7): 121–134.

Hofstede, G. (2001) *Culture's Consequences: Comparing Values, Behaviors, Institutions, and Organizations Across Nations*, 2nd edn. Thousand Oaks, CA: Sage.

Jackson, T. (2004) 'HRM in developing countries'. In *International Human Resource Management*, edited by A. W. Harzing and J. V. Russeveldt. London: Sage.

Jomo, K. S. (2007a) 'Industrialization and industry policy in Malaysia'. In *Malaysian Industrial Policy*, edited by K. S. Jomo. Singapore: NUS Press, pp. 1–34.

Jomo, K. S. (2007b) *Malaysian Industrial Policy*. Singapore: NUS Press.

Jomo, K. S. and Todd, P. (1994) *Trade Unions and the State in Peninsular Malaysia*. Kuala Lumpur: Oxford University Press.

Kamoche, K. (2002) 'Introduction: Human resource management in Africa' *International Journal of Human Resource Management* 13(7): 993–997.

Kumar, N., Martínez Lucio, M and Rose R. C. 'Workplace industrial relations in a developing environment: barriers to renewal within unions in Malaysia'. *Asia Pacific Journal of Human Resources* 51(1): 22–44.

Kuruvilla, S. (1996) 'Linkages between industrialisation strategies and industrial relations/ human resource policies: Singapore, Malaysia, the Philippines, and India'. *Industrial and Labour Relations Review* 49(4): 635–657.

Kuruvilla, S. and Arudsothy, P. (1995) 'Economic development strategy, government labour policy and firm-level industrial relations practices in Malaysia'. In *Employment*

Relations in the Growing Asian Economies, edited by A. Verma, T. A. Kochan and R. D. Lansbury. London: Routledge, pp. 158–193.

Kuruvilla, S. and Venkataratnam, C. S. (1996) 'Economic development and industrial relations: The case of South and Southeast Asia'. *Industrial Relations Journal* 27(1): 9–23.

Lillie, N. and Martínez Lucio, M. (2011) 'Rollerball and the spirit of capitalism: Competitive dynamics within the global context, the challenge to labour transnationalism, and the emergence of ironic outcomes'. *Critical Perspectives in International Business* 8(1): 74–92.

Malaysia Government (1991) *Second Outline Perspective Plan, 1991–2000*. Kuala Lumpur: National Printing Department.

Malaysia Government (2001) *The Third Outline Perspective Plan, 2001–2010*. Kuala Lumpur; National Printing Department.

Marchington, M. and Wilkinson, A. (2008) *Human Resource Management at Work*. London: CIPD.

Mellahi, K. and Wood, G. (2004) 'Human resource management in Malaysia'. In *Human Resource Management in Asia Pacific*, edited by P. S. Budhwar. London: Routledge.

Ministry of Human Resources Malaysia (2009) *Realizing Decent Work for Decent Life*. Malaysia: Ministry of Human Resources.

Parasuraman, B. (2004) *Malaysian Industrial Relations: A Critical Analysis*. Kuala Lumpur: Pearson Prentice Hall.

Peetz, D. and Todd, P. (2001) 'Otherwise you're on your own: Unions and bargaining in Malaysian banking'. *International Journal of Manpower* 22(4): 333–349.

Pyle, J. and Ward, K. (2003) 'Recasting our understanding of gender and work during global restructuring'. *International Sociology* 18(3): 461–489.

Ramasamy, P. (2000) Globalisation and Plantation Labour in Malaysia. Paper presented at seminar on Globalisation and Labour in Malaysia, Bangi, Malaysia, September.

Rasiah, R. (1995) 'Labour and industrialization in Malaysia'. *Journal of Contemporary Asia* 25(1): 73–92.

Ritchie, B. K. (2002) *Foreign Direct Investment and Intellectual Capital Formation in Southeast Asia*. Paris: OECD Development Centre, pp. 4–41.

Rowley, C. and Warner, M. (2004) 'Big business in Asia'. *Asia Pacific Business Review* 10(4): 485–496.

Sharma, B. (1996) *Industrial Relations in ASEAN: A Comparative Study*. Kuala Lumpur: International Law Book Services.

Suhanah, S. S. A. (2002) 'Law and labour market regulations in Malaysia: Beyond the new economy policy'. In *Law and Labour Market Regulation in East Asia*, edited by S. Cooney, T. Lindsey, R. Mitchell and Y. Zhu. London: Routledge.

Tan, H. (2001) The Malaysian Human Resource Development Fund: An Evaluation of Its Effects on Training and Productivity. Available at http://info.worldbank.org

The Star (Malaysia) (2008) 'NS deals led to RM110m loss'. 31 August.

The Star (Malaysia) (2013) 'ETP contributes to skilled workforce, but experts see need to improve work culture'. 2 May.

The Sun (Malaysia) (2012) 'Act to prevent deaths at NS camps: MP'. 20 April.

Todd, P. and Peetz, D. (2001) 'Malaysian industrial relations at century's turn: Vision 2020 or a spectre of the past?'. *The International Journal of Human Resource Management* 12(8): 1365–1382.

Todd, P., Lansbury, R. and Davis, E. M. (2004) 'Industrial relations in Malaysia: Some proposals for reform'. *Proceedings of the IIRA 5th Asian Regional Congress*, Korea Labour Institute, Seoul, South Korea.

UNCTAD (2011) *'Global Investment Trends Monitor'*. 17 January, Geneva: UNCTAD (www. unctad.org).

UNCTAD (2013) *The World Investment Report* Geneva: UNCTAD

Vassolo, R. S., De Castro, J. O. and Gomez-Mejia, L. R. (2011) 'Managing in Latin America: Common issues and a research agenda'. *Academy of Management Perspectives* 25(4): 22–36.

Wad, P. (2001) 'Transforming Industrial Relations: The Case of the Malaysian Auto Industry'. IIAS/IISG CLARA Working Paper No. 12, Amsterdam.

Wong, C.-Y. (2011) 'Rent-seeking, industrial policies and national innovation systems in Southeast Asian economies'. *Technology in Society* 33(3/4): 231–243.

World Bank (2011) *Malaysia Economic Monitor*. Washington DC: World Bank (www. worldbank.org/my), April.

Wu, M. A. (2006) *Industrial Relations Law of Malaysia*, 3rd edn. Kuala Lumpur: Longman.

Zahra, S. A. (2011) 'Doing research in the (new) Middle East: Sailing with the wind'. *Academy of Management Perspectives* 25(4): 1–16.

11 Migration and human resource management

Nathan Lillie, Erka Çaro, Lisa Berntsen and Ines Wagner

Learning objectives

- To understand the background of labour migration
- To understand the contemporary context of migration and the varieties of mobility
- To understand the role of MNCs and the impact of trade unions on the regulation and use of migrants
- To raise issues related to rights and decency at work in relation to migrants and their employment

Introduction

This chapter sets the scene for the understanding of labour mobility in time and in space from the perspective of international human resource management. Labour mobility and migration confront human resource managers with a number of unique challenges. Migration is the territorial movement of people, both temporary and permanent. Migration presents opportunities and challenges to managers and policy makers. For multinational firms, migrants represent an important source of skills, diversity and labour power. Multinational enterprises (MNEs) may have, or seek to recruit, employees who are immigrants, and to post employees internally to other countries. They may also engage multinational work groups from abroad through subcontractors or work agencies. Managing migrant workers presents challenges to human resource managers. The aim of this chapter is to give an understanding of what some of those challenges are, to introduce some of the concepts used by migration scholars to understand them and to illustrate how they apply in selected real-world examples.

People migrate for a variety of reasons. Academic work on migration studies often talks of 'push' and 'pull' factors that cause migration movements. Push factors are difficulties at home which create an incentive to leave, such as war, persecution and famine. Pull factors are incentives to go to a new location, such as good jobs, free farmland or the discovery of valuable resources such as gold. Labour migration can help to alleviate poverty and unemployment in depressed regions, while providing a source of manpower and skills for employers in regions of labour shortage. It can be a vehicle for transferring skills and practices internationally within firms, and between societies. Migration is also a source of social friction. It creates downward pressure on wages for native workers, and these workers may sometimes lose their jobs due to their being replaced by migrant workers. Migration is sometimes seen as a threat to national cohesion and security. Since access to social benefits in welfare states is often related to residence, governments attempt to control the amount and type of immigrants, usually to favour skilled migrants and to minimize demand on social welfare systems.

We start with a brief historical overview of the development of labour and migration since the late Middle Ages. Next, this chapter focuses in greater detail on the significance of migration in the contemporary world. First, we give an account of the main directions and scales of migration flows around the world. Second, we focus on different types of labour migration, stressing the significance of each type in shaping migrants' lives. We then present some of the most important migration policy issues and the main HRM issues raised by migration. Chief among these is the issue of diversity and multiculturalism (especially in the workplace): its causes, consequences and management. This section aims at detailing and understanding the experiences of labour migration in an increasingly mobile world (see Chapters 1 and 5). Finally, after the scenarios of the various migrant experiences are sketched, we end by describing some of the principal ways in which vulnerable migrants' rights are protected, focusing mainly on the trade union's role and functions.

Labour migration in history

The purpose of this section is to give an appreciation of the complex history of migration, and how deeply it has shaped and been shaped by the development of modern capitalism. Migration is not just a feature of the modern world, but rather has been around as long as there have been humans. From prehistoric times, people have moved in search of better hunting grounds or more suitable farmland, or because of competition and conflict with other groups. However, international migration in the modern definition is closely connected with the existence of the nation-states and the global economy, which developed since the end of the Middle Ages. This section will review some historical examples, in order to set the current situation in the context of its historical development. Push and pull factors are visible throughout history. On the one hand, people have fled wars and persecution, or made war and persecuted weaker groups to make new lands available for their settlement. On the other, people have sought out new economic opportunities, such as available farmland or industrial jobs at higher wages than those available at home. The cultural and ethnic makeup of modern-day societies reflects mass population movements of the past.

The early modern period from about 1500 to 1800 was characterized by migrant flows during Europe's initial period of colonial expansion. Europeans moved to North and South American colonies fleeing religious prosecution, often with the intention of settling and farming new land, usually after pushing out, exterminating or enslaving the previous occupants. Africans were brought by slave traders to work in plantations, mines, industry and as servants to the wealthy in the New World. Areas such as South Africa and Australia were also settled by Europeans in this period. Immigration was often forcibly resisted by people living in the colonized areas. Europeans who immigrated in this period usually did so as part of a colonial project, not integrating, but rather supplanting and/or dominating the native societies they encountered in their new homes.

Over the course of the 19th century, the emigration outflow from Europe continued, although many of the colonies became independent countries (such as the United States or Argentina), while others became established "white" settler dominions (such as Australia). Under French dominion, French and other European settlers settled in Algeria, becoming an important minority group there (which, on independence in 1962 was largely pushed out). Germans moved to German East Africa (present day Namibia), and British settlers established themselves in Kenya, Rhodesia and South Africa. Migration occurred within colonial empires – and also between the subject peoples under colonial rule. For example, under the British Raj, many Indians moved to the British colony in South Africa to work. In the 19th century, Chinese established enclave communities throughout Southeast Asia (Vandensbosch 1947), and also in the United States (Lee 2006). The vast colonial empires of the major European powers sometimes involved settlement, but always required administrators, and these would come from the colonizing power. Business entrepreneurs frequently followed, or even preceded the flag into the new colonial holdings of the European powers (for an account of colonialism in Africa, see, for example, Parkham 1992).

It was not only in moving to the New World and colonial empires that migration occurred. Industrialization in the 19th century brought millions of workers from rural areas to industrial centres in Western Europe. Lower travel costs and shorter travel times caused by railroads and other infrastructure improvements made mass migration possible (Bade 2003). The destinations included centres of coal and steel production as well as rapidly expanding urban industrial zones. For example, the industrial revolution in Britain required an ever-growing labour force that could not be met by the local population. British employers recruited workers from Ireland for the textile mills and building trades in cities such as Liverpool and Manchester (Castles and Kosack 1985).

In France, immigration was spontaneous and uncontrolled, and by 1886 there were more than a million migrants working mostly in agriculture and mining companies. In Germany, Polish and Italian workers came to work in construction and in the mines. Private recruitment agents facilitated labour migration because they could make a quick profit owing to the workers' weak negotiating position. Apart from low-skilled labour migration, highly skilled migrants were also on the move in 19th century Europe. Travelling craftsmen and merchants contributed to technology and skill transfer (Bade 2003). In contrast to low-wage labourers, they were invited to come to the host country and lived in good conditions. The migratory patterns that had developed in the 19th century were disrupted by the First World War. Men were called back to their home country for military service or munitions production. Owing to political tensions, many countries enacted tight immigration legislation, causing a halt to the free movement of workers throughout Europe. With the close of the 19th century, and into the 20th, countries began to institute increasing controls on who could cross their borders, settle and work. Passports and visas became increasingly important.

World Wars I and II, and the various conflicts between the wars, caused considerable migrant flows in the form of refugees and displaced people, but with the advent of peace and rapid economic growth in the post World War II period, economically focused migration came to dominate again. Europe's postwar reconstruction and subsequent economic growth prompted substantial inflows, often from the former colonies which became independent after World War II. France experienced immigration from francophone countries, particularly from Africa; Britain saw immigration from the Indian subcontinent, Africa and the Caribbean; and the Netherlands experienced repatriation and immigration of Moluks and Indonesians from its former Indonesian colony and in the 1970s immigration from its former colony Surinam. Sweden hosted substantial numbers of Finnish work migrants. Many European countries made use of migrant labour and guest worker programmes in the post World War II period, to fill jobs which increasingly prosperous western Europeans were no longer willing to do (Castles and Kosack 1985).

West Germany's guest worker programme provides a good example of how the guest worker programmes of the 1960s and 1970s functioned. The state and employers in West Germany started importing temporary labour as a solution to the growing labour shortage during the so-called post-war *Wirtschaftswunder* (economic miracle). Rapid industrial expansion and a shift to mass production (conveyor-line work, piece-work, and shift-work) required a large unskilled labour force as a key element in the post-war boom (Kindleberger 1967). The Federal Labour Office (*Bundesanstalt für Arbeit – BfA*) signed recruitment agreements for temporary employment with Italy, Spain, Greece, Turkey, Morocco, Portugal, Tunisia and Yugoslavia. The idea was to provide employers with relatively cheap, flexible and mobile labour for low-skilled, dirty and hard jobs that nobody else wanted to do. Employers requiring foreign labour had to pay a fee to the *BfA* and provide accommodation for the workers. Recruitment was based on a rotation system where mostly male migrants worked in Germany for a one- or two-year period and were then required to leave. Migrants were expected to not bring their families, not get involved in labour struggles and make few demands on social welfare systems (Castles 1986). The number of foreign workers increased from 95,000 in 1956 to 2.6 million by mid-1973 – the greatest labour migration anywhere in post-war Europe (Castles 1986). Yet, in 1973 the oil crisis caused a period of economic stagnation, high unemployment and an official halt to migrant entry to Germany. The German government expected migrants to leave after stopping recruitment, but many decided to stay and to reunite with their families in Germany. Employers were not in favour of mass repatriation. They feared labour shortages and upward pressure on wages. The former guest workers had become an integral part not only of the labour force but also of society.

Such immigration was not limited to Europe. In the United States, in the 20th century immigration was subject to increasing regulation compared to the 19th century. Mexican workers, however, continued to cross the border in substantial numbers, mainly to work in agriculture. Mexican migrant workers, working for wages well below what a native worker would accept, came to almost completely dominate wage work on industrial farms in the United States. In 1942, to allow US farmers to tap into the Mexican labour supply, the US and Mexican governments organized a guest-worker programme called the Bracero Program, which continued in various forms until 1964. The Bracero Program was an agreement between the US and Mexican government which allowed Mexicans to enter the United States for work (usually agricultural work). Wages were established by the agreement. The significant overhead involved in the programme often resulted in Mexican workers seeking illegal employment instead. With the ending of the Bracero Program, migration from Mexico and Latin America has continued, but quite often in illegal form, with poorly paid illegal immigrants making up a large part of the US workforce in certain industries, such as construction, meatpacking and agriculture.

Contemporary migration

The main migrant destination country in terms of absolute numbers is the United States, followed by the Russian Federation, Germany, Saudi Arabia and Canada (World Bank 2011). The main immigration countries relative to their total population are Qatar, Morocco, the United Arab Emirates, Kuwait and Andorra (World Bank 2011). In recent years, the Gulf countries (Kuwait, Qatar, Saudi Arabia, Bahrain and the United Arab Emirates) have experienced significant flows of immigrants from South and East Asia (World Bank 2011). According to the World Bank (2011), the largest migration corridor in the world continues to be the Mexico–United States corridor with 11.66 million migrants in 2011. In second place we find the migration corridors in the former Soviet Union, Russia–Ukraine. The migration corridor between Bangladeshi and India is in third place.

Within Europe, a new wave of migration started with the end of the communist regimes and demolition of the Iron Curtain between the East and West Europe (Philip 2001). Starting from the 1990s, there has been a surge of migration flows towards the United Kingdom, Spain, Italy and Germany, mainly from Eastern Europe; this accelerated with the accession of most of Eastern Europe to the EU in 2004 (2007 for Romania and Bulgaria) (IOM 2010).

Migration flows emerge within and between specific world regions following patterns driven by the factors which have been outlined above. Migration occurs everywhere in the world; limited space prevents us from discussing each migration flow in detail. However, in order to give a sense of how and why some particularly important flows have emerged, how they have been regulated and the policy issues which develop out of these, we present the cases of regional migration in the EU, and in Southeast Asia, as examples.

Regional migration in the EU

HRM across Europe is influenced by EU regulation, of which an important dimension is the free movement of labour. The Treaty of Rome introduced the principle of free movement of workers in 1957 to encourage cross-border mobility. Subsequent legislation, directives and European Court of Justice (ECJ) rulings added to the supranational legal regulation of the employment relationship in the EU. Since the accession of the Eastern European and Mediterranean island states in 2004 and 2007, transnational labour mobility from East to West accelerated. Workers can either take up work themselves or be sent by a firm as a posted worker to another EU member state. The rights of individual and posted workers are organized via different EU regulatory channels. Individual migrants fall under EU frameworks for labour mobility, while posted workers are regulated as dependents of the service providers they work for. Even though all foreign workers have to be treated equally within the EU, some workers have more rights than others. Individual labour migrants have the right to benefit from social security provisions in the host state, while posted workers remain insured in the home country (Dolvik and Visser 2009). This saves host country companies labour costs and encourages the employment of relatively inexpensive posted labour from underdeveloped regions. Posted workers are ensured key labour rights through the Posting of Workers Directive (PWD). Although originally intended by its drafters to allow host states to grand the migrant worker rights beyond the set expressed in the directive, the ECJ has since reinterpreted the directive as a comprehensive list of areas in which the host country can oblige foreign service providers to apply host country standards (Dolvik and Visser 2009). These decisions are highly controversial. Critics see this decision as placing fundamental workers' rights below the free movement of service providers in the EU (Dolvik and Visser 2009). Advocates of the court's approach see it as the logical extension of the free movement rights embedded in the EU's constitution.

Regional migration in Southeast Asia

Southeast Asia's migration flows are another example of a regional guest worker migration system with many similarities to the EU. Uneven development in the region means that some countries in the region (Singapore, Malaysia and Thailand) have become significantly wealthier than other countries in the region, motivating migration from other nearby countries. Indonesia and the Philippines, in particular, are important labour supplier countries. As is typical elsewhere, migrant jobs are usually in agriculture, domestic work (i.e., childcare and housework), construction, and sometimes manufacturing. Southeast Asian states administer strict guest worker programmes, with permission to reside tightly tied to employment, restricted length of stay so that workers must rotate back home frequently, and high administrative costs mostly borne by the migrant workers themselves. Recruitment agencies often charge fees as high as three months' salary for placements. Some restrictions go quite far in terms of limiting the personal freedom of the migrants. For example, Singapore restricts unskilled foreign work migrants from marrying a Singaporean national. Illegal migration is therefore also popular as a way of avoiding these costs and restrictions, although the legal risks, if caught, are high for migrants and employers alike. The situation for domestic workers has attracted criticism from human rights groups.

Labour migration

The attraction of economically developed places has always provided incentives for some people to move. When people move to new places looking for a job or better employment conditions, they are considered *labour migrants*. Throughout history, labour migration has been an important type of migration flow, but it has acquired greater importance today because of advances which facilitate easier, faster and cheaper movements around the globe (Hatton and Williamson 2005). These days, there are more than 100 million workers moving around the world, which constitutes 3% of the global labour force (Betts 2011). The main labour migration flows are directed from developing countries towards industrialized countries (32 million), from one developing country toward another (30 million) and flows among industrial countries (28 million) (IOM 2010). Labour migrants are often divided into high-skilled and low-skilled migrants.

High-skilled labour and low-skilled labour migration

High-skilled migrants are generally accepted to be migrants who possess at least a university degree or equivalent training and skills (Martin 2003). According to Regets (2007), high-skilled labour migration has expanded distinctly, in both the developed and developing countries, and has become an important element of national economic policies. Developing countries are trying to retain their highly skilled persons, while developed countries are trying to attract them away. Migration motivations may differ between high-skilled and low-skilled migrants. Although both push and pull factors are important, high-skilled migrants are attracted to destination countries by better employment prospects, higher salaries and opportunities to gain international experience, while low-skilled migrants are more often pushed from their countries of origin by low wages or unemployment. The out-migration of highly skilled and well-educated professionals from developing countries to more developed countries is a phenomenon known as *brain drain*. Brain drain has become a concern in many developing countries, such as in Africa, India and more recently Eastern Europe (Cohen 2008). Brain drain can sometime represent wastage, since the skills of migrants tend to be undervalued in host societies, because of discrimination, lack of knowledge of migrant source-country education systems and lack of official recognition of foreign certifications. As a result, highly educated migrants sometimes end up in unskilled jobs after migrating. This is often accepted by the migrant if the pay for the low-skilled job in a developed country is sufficiently higher than the pay for a high-skilled job in the migrant's home country.

Labour market segmentation and migrant workers

Migrants in host countries are often 'target earners' (Piore 1979). Target earners perceive their temporary jobs instrumentally, that is, solely as a way to earn money quickly. This is different from an understanding of work as a source of identity and social status, or as a rung on a career ladder (migrants' jobs and social positions in their home countries serve that purpose). They seek to save a certain amount of money to make an investment back home, whether it is to buy a business, or a house, or to pay for their children's education. This does not mean their plans cannot change – if, for example, they decide to settle.

Such 'target earning' workers commonly lack the motivation to organize to advance their conditions in foreign labour markets. This induces firms to treat low-skilled migrants as substitutable, disposable labour by employing them under exploitative employment conditions. According to segmentation theory, native workers refuse to accept such employment conditions and migrant workers are therefore seen as complementary rather than as substitutes for native workers: migrant workers simply realize a certain unfulfilled demand for labour. However, there are indications that firms sometimes use migrant workers not to complement but to substitute for their core labour force (Lillie 2012).

For a variety of reasons, migrants are often unable to enter employment on similar terms to native workers – even if they have a similar profile in terms of skill, experience and work ethic to native workers, they tend to be shunted into certain kinds of jobs. Low-skilled migrant workers often perform work under precarious working conditions. They are regularly subjected to underpayment, forced to work longer hours than overtime rules allow for and exposed to hazardous working conditions (see Chapter 4 on general payment issues). Lower segments of the labour market become the prerogative of migrant workers and other marginalized groups (Doeringer and Piore 1971; Piore 1979; Gordon, Edwards and Reich 1982; Rubery and Wilkinson 1994). This phenomenon is best explained by *labour market segmentation theory*, which holds that institutional barriers can segment labour markets, granting certain groups access only to specific segments of the labour market.

Segmentation theory assumes a dual labour market structure consisting of a capital-intensive, secure primary segment and a labour-intensive, insecure but flexible secondary labour market segment. The employment conditions under which many low-skilled migrants work are characteristic of the secondary labour market segment. This segmentation is driven by employers' demand for different types of labour: low-skilled and substitutable labour for the secondary segment, and workers with a certain level of training, skills and commitment for the primary segment. The primary labour segment functions as an internal market (i.e., within the firm), while market forces govern the employment relations in the secondary market. Employers' recruitment practices for jobs in the secondary segment rely more on market principles, offering less security, lower wages and poorer benefits (McGovern 2007).

Migration policy issues

Migration, being a dynamic phenomenon, requires diversified policy intervention in order to maximize its benefits and minimize the ill effects for countries both of origin and of destination as well as migrants themselves (IOM 2010).

National governments seek to control border access and residence rights of foreigners in order to minimize the number of people who can draw on government services and social security, to ensure cultural coherence, to keep out people who are thought to present security threats (such as criminals and/or foreign spies) and to regulate access to the labour market. Immigration policies often seek to encourage immigration by people with wealth or rare skills, while making it more difficult for those whose skills are in oversupply. Often, labour market access comes with the caveat that the migrant cannot expect to draw on public funds (e.g., in case of unemployment). Sometimes, as with the H1B visa programme in the United States for highly skilled migrants, visas are tied to a particular job, and if that job is lost the visa holder must leave the country.

Marriage and family reunification form a major channel for migration, and a way by which migrants taking advantage of high-skilled migrant programmes can bring their partners and children. Because of public perceptions that this avenue is often taken advantage of (e.g., via sham marriages), it is usually subject to various controls, tests and limitations. Another avenue is a blood tie with the country in question – Germany, Finland, Ireland and Israel, for example, are all countries which grant citizenship to people with ancestors with provable claims to that country's ethnicity.

Countries have made various agreements to permit migration between each other. For example, there has been free movement between the Nordic countries (Sweden, Norway, Finland, Denmark, Iceland and the Faroe Islands) since the 1950s. Particularly notable is the freedom of movement within the European Union, which allows citizens of any EU member state to take up residence in any other member state, on the same terms as citizens of that member state. Certain, allegedly temporary, restrictions were applied by some old EU members to the Eastern European states which joined the EU in 2004 (the Czech Republic, Estonia, Latvia, Lithuania, Hungary, Poland, Slovakia and Slovenia), and for a longer period upon those which joined in 2007 (Bulgaria and Rumania), but these are intended to be gradually phased out. Access of intra-EU migrants to social rights such as pensions, health insurance and unemployment insurance have been partially assured through mutual recognition, although there are still gaps in access in the system, which often disadvantage mobile workers in terms of benefits.

One major aspect of migration is its economic impact in both origin and destination countries/regions. Remittances, or money sent by migrants back to their home country/region, have an important economic impact (Castles and Miller 2009). In 2010, total global remittance flows were estimated to be more than $440 billion, which was an increase of 6% compared with 2009 (World Bank 2011). It is likely that actual remittances are much higher, taking into the consideration that remittances often flow through informal, undocumented channels (World Bank 2011; King et al. 2006).

HRM issues raised by migration

For HRM managers, migration presents challenges in terms of coping with immigration rules and regulations, international recruitment and recognition of diverse national educational and certification systems, diversity management and managing relationships between different nationalities on multinational work environments. In the international HRM literature, labour mobility is almost exclusively analysed in terms of expatriate managers, with most of the focus on why firms use expatriates, which selection procedures are best, how to best support expatriates and how to best make use of the skills they acquire in their international assignments (e.g., Harzing 2004). This intensive focus on expatriate managers ignores the fact that most employees are not managers, and expatriate managers represent only a very small proportion of total labour migration. More important are the challenges of diversity management and managing the relationships between multinational groups of workers.

Diversity and multiculturalism

With the number of international migrants increasing rapidly, workplaces around the world have become more diverse. Formerly homogenous workforces are being replaced by a mixture of ethnic and cultural groups. Flows of migrants are transforming societies, and this transformation is an ongoing subject of public and political debate (Legrain 2006). From the societal perspective, diversity offers benefits in terms of a variety of lifestyles, languages, ideas, styles and cultural norms. The acceptance and appreciation of cultural diversity is referred to as multiculturalism (Pharek 2000). Multiculturalism in business, education, social policy and culture is seen as a way of reducing intra-group conflict in diverse societies, and of harnessing the advantage diversity can bring (see Chapter 5 for more general diversity issues).

Diversity, multicultural and multilingual workforces and workplaces and the difficulties of managing these have become increasingly important. Diversity management is usually driven by legislative necessity, but many organizations have made a virtue of necessity and now realize its benefits in terms of tapping into diverse forms of knowledge and skills, which can come from hiring people with different backgrounds (Egan and Bendick 2003). A diverse and multicultural workplace is thought to bring benefits such as better decision making, greater creativity and innovation and more successful marketing to different types of customers (Cox 1991). However, diversity may also bring potential costs and challenges such as interpersonal conflict and communication breakdowns (Cox 1991), and if managed improperly, also lead to racism, sexism and ageism, which can create a hostile and non-productive environment (Parvis 2003).

However, multiculturalism and diversity are not accepted by some members of migration host societies. Some would seek to marginalize and stigmatize migrants, and to blame them as a source of economic problems (Castles and Miller 2009). Many countries have seen the rise of anti-immigration political parties and right-wing groups that seek to implement stricter immigration laws, and sometimes engage in violent anti-immigrant activities.

The potential costs and challenges of a multicultural environment might be greater with temporary migrant workers. In such cases, the problems that accompany multicultural environments, such as communication problems and group clusters according to nationalities, might persist not only in the workplace but also in their home environments. According to Parvis (2003) these challenges, if not detected, will lead to loss of innovative potential and ultimately to failure in the undertakings of an organization.

Managing multinational work environments

It is not uncommon to encounter work environments segmented by ethnicity, nationality and/or language. Certain types of jobs may be dominated by a certain national or ethnic group. At work sites where many different national groups of workers work side by side, management is often obliged to organize work groups according to language grouping. Although issues related to segmentation of labour markets resulting from labour migration have long been understood from a sociological perspective (Piore 1979), there have been few business and management studies on how to manage in such an environment.

Industries such as construction, shipbuilding, agriculture, domestic services and building maintenance, where subcontracting is common, use large numbers of migrant workers and experience ethnically segmented labour markets. Commonly, workers are recruited via work agencies or personal networks with good contacts to their home countries. Workers who speak the host society language well frequently become an interface point with management, taking on the role of foreman. These types of workers often progress into management or go into the labour-supply business, using personal contacts and local knowledge of home country and host society to match workers with available jobs. This type of recruitment is known as 'ganging' because migrants from a particular country work together with others from their home country, obviating the need to learn the local language or embed themselves in the local culture. In this way, it is possible to manage and coordinate very diverse groups of workers who do not share a common language.

Protecting migrant rights at the workplace

The fact that migrants are often not well integrated into host societies makes protection of migrant worker rights a matter of special concern. Added to this is the fact that they often work in secondary labour markets, where pay, conditions, job security and respect for worker rights are in general lower than in primary labour markets.

Efforts to protect migrant rights focus on making state enforcement of immigration rules more humane, promoting access of migrants to host-state services, fighting discrimination and racism and ensuring decent treatment in the workplace. State agencies which enforce immigration laws often take little account of the situation of the migrants, and the consequences of enforcement actions for them, their families and their employers. For example, a deportation can break up a family and leave dependants without means of support. There are many non-governmental organizations which help migrants access legal and other types of services; these sometimes represent any migrants who need assistance, or in other cases represent particular migrant communities. An example of the first would be Migrar, in Germany, which provides legal assistance and advice to illegal migrant workers. An example of the second type is the Federation of Poles in Britain, which has a cultural, social and community binding function, as well as representing the interests of Polish-born people living in the United Kingdom.

At the international level, the International Organization for Migration (IOM) is a UN agency set up to promote the rights of migrant workers. The IOM seeks to do this through advocating for good practices in the treatment of migrants, conducting research on migration, and providing technical assistance to countries in developing practices which protect the rights of migrants. The International Labour Organization (ILO) is another UN-associated agency, with a mandate to protect workers' rights. Despite the efforts of the IOM and the ILO, it cannot be said that there is an international consensus to protect migrant worker rights. States tend to place domestic economic interests and security policy higher on their priority list than the protection of foreign nationals working in their territory.

Case study: The Eemshaven, the Netherlands

The Eemshaven, an industrial area in the northern part of the Netherlands, was recently termed an 'energy port' because of the substantial investments in energy made in this region. Two large multinational enterprises have invested over 4 billion euros to build two energy centrals in the Eemshaven. The formerly Dutch company Nuon, now owned by the Swedish Vattenfall, invested an estimated 1.8 billion euros and the German company RWE invested up to 2.6 billion euros. The construction of these energy centrals requires an extensive labour force, which is principally from abroad. The construction of the Nuon multi-fuel power plant is managed by the Japan-based main contractor, Mitsubishi. RWE, in contrast, uses its own engineering team and manages predominantly foreign contractors to build its energy central. These foreign contractors generally bring their own foreign personnel with them. Still, a similar variety of foreign contractors, subcontractors and agencies is active at the Nuon construction site. However, Mitsubishi also hired Ballast Nedam, a large Dutch construction company that is primarily active in the Netherlands, to perform civil works.

All in all, a very transnational work force is building the energy centrals in the Eemshaven. At least 15 nationalities are employed on both sites, with people coming from, among others, Poland, Germany, Turkey, Italy, Portugal, Spain, France, Denmark, Hungary, Slovenia and Lithuania. During the main construction phase, around 2500 people will be working at the Nuon site and an estimated 3000 for RWE. There are no accurate numbers available, but the majority of workers employed at these sites are non-Dutch. The workers originating from a variety of countries are often unable to communicate with their co-workers on the worksite, as most of these workers only have basic foreign language skills. The official language of communication on the RWE site is German, while it is English on the Nuon site. Still, the language of communication usually varies between the different work groups. Most work teams are aligned on the basis of nationality, and therefore no, or only a very basic, understanding of English or German often suffices. The thousands of migrant workers are temporarily accommodated in the Groningen region that surrounds the Eemshaven. To this end, a number of temporary container hotels have been created, some of which can accommodate up to 1200 people at the same time.

Subcontracting practices are usually the norm at large construction sites. The Eemshaven is no exception to this, since there is a vast active presence of transnational subcontractors and agencies at the site. This obstructs transparency in the lengthy contracting chains and hinders effective union action against the 'real' employer. In addition, this paves the way for exploitative practices vis-à-vis migrant workers. In the Eemshaven, there are more than a few cases known where transnational subcontractors force their employees to work more hours than allowed according to Dutch regulations, and refuse to pay their workers overtime allowances. Effective union action to change the working conditions of migrant workers is quite complicated because of the great variety of employment practices used by the broad range of firms active at these transnational building sites.

Questions

1. Draft a convincing note to a manager of a construction contractor that is active in the Eemshaven explaining why it is more profitable to hire migrant workers via a (transnational) temp agency than to directly recruit domestic workers.
2. Does it sound like the Eemshaven is an example of good multicultural workplace practices? Why or why not? Would the project benefit from multicultural management, or does it not matter in the circumstances?
3. Apply the three dilemmas for trade unionism (see below) to the Eemshaven case.

Unions and migrants

Although trade unions usually start from an ideological basis of working class solidarity, their actual functioning as organizations is often closely tied to local communities, national identities or even ethnic backgrounds. These organic identities can serve as a source of strength for them, but this also means that they sometimes end up promoting a racist and insular discourse in response to migration – at least initially. According to Penninx and Roosblad (2000), unions face three main dilemmas in dealing with immigrant labour. First, unions need to decide whether to accept or oppose migration politically. Second, when (im) migrant workers have arrived, unions face the decision whether to seek to actively recruit and organize the migrants, including them as full members or to exclude them partly or completely from full union membership and not organize them. Virdee (2000) shows that over time, unions have evolved from policies of racist – sometimes even overt – exclusion of migrants to proactive policies of inclusion. Most unions have adopted a policy of formal inclusion, but the degree of inclusion differs, especially in terms of equal access to social and legal rights. Moreover, the degree of protection is often strongly related to a migrant's duration of stay as unions seem more inclined to take action in favour of permanent immigrants than to represent temporary labour migrants. Third, if unions opt for inclusion, they have to decide whether to advocate and implement special measures for (im)migrant workers or to maintain equal treatment for all workers. The different responses of unions in the United Kingdom and Denmark to diversity management provide an illustration of this last dilemma. Where the Danish unions were supportive of specific diversity policies, unions in the United Kingdom opposed specific measures to increase diversity in the workplace, because they believed it did not challenge the basis of race discrimination and thus in the longer term would not improve immigrants' labour market position (Wrench 2004).

Although many unions, especially in countries where immigration is a relatively new phenomenon, still struggle internally with racism and whether to include foreign-born workers as members (Lillie and Sippola 2011), for unions in countries where immigration has a longer history, the question is usually what sort of strategies are best for recruiting migrants, and to what extent there should be proactive policies favouring recruitment of minorities into leadership positions. Immigrant and migrant workers are, on average, more likely to perform casual, lower-paid jobs in sectors where unions have little or no influence. This complicates effective union action to change these workers' employment conditions. The most successful union campaigns targeting immigrant workers' problems combine strategic pressuring of employers by union officials with bottom-up rank-and-file mobilization. Bottom-up rank-and-file mobilization involves active agitation by the migrant workers themselves, often in the form of strikes and public demonstrations (Milkman 2006). The Southern California 1992 drywallers' strike to increase industry-wide wage levels is an example of a successful bottom-up grassroots organizing approach of Latino immigrant workers. This strike was initiated from below by Latino workers and received at a later stage material and moral support from established unions. Key to this campaign's success was the effective rank-and-file mobilization combined with the strategic professional union assistance that led to industry-wide organizing strongly embedded in the broader community (Milkman 2006). Employing staff from 'target' migrant groups is a common way to make a visible commitment to that minority, while also ensuring the necessary linguistic and cultural skills to organize and represent those workers. Some unions in the United Kingdom have had success with reserving elected seats for minority groups, to ensure a minimum level of representation in the union leadership. Seeking broad alliances has proved to be one of the more successful strategies used by unions to create a lasting change in working conditions of (im)migrant workers (see Wills 2009 or Fitzgerald and Hardy 2010 for interesting examples in the United Kingdom). Unions often are able to integrate 'settled' immigrant groups into their membership, but still struggle with more highly mobile migrants, who have no intention to settle (Greer, Ciupijus and Lillie 2013).

Conclusion

In this chapter, we have highlighted some of the issues, challenges and opportunities which labour migration presents for international human resource management. We have shown that labour migration is not a new phenomenon and has always played an important part in the capitalist world economy. In the past, as now, it has been motivated by a combination of push factors – factors which make the migrants' home location undesirable – and pull factors – factors which make the destination country desirable. Labour migrants are strategic in their migration, and often behave as 'target earners', particularly when they are temporary and less skilled. They are most often employed in secondary labour markets.

Employers find migrants useful either because less skilled migrants are less expensive than locals, or because they possess scarce skills, as in the case of highly skilled migrants. National migration policies tend to favour highly skilled migrants. Many countries make use of guest-worker policies, which allow migrants access to that country's labour market, but only in restricted ways, and seek to prevent the migrant from settling. The idea is to keep migrants in the secondary labour market, allowing them access to jobs which locals cannot fill (on the high-skill end) or do not want (on the low-skill end).

The challenge for managers is to take advantage of the skill and labour power of migrants, and the different perspectives they bring, while minimizing the tensions created by a diverse workforce, and avoiding falling foul of state policies designed to restrict migration. For unions, and others concerned with migrant rights and the effects of migration on labour markets, the challenge is to balance the interests of native members with the rights and interests of migrants.

Reflective questions

1. How has labour migration developed through history and what are the main economic factors affecting these changes? How has labour migration affected macroeconomic developments in the contemporary world?
2. What are the main characteristics of high-skilled and low-skilled labour migrants? Describe the main differences in terms of motivations and the integration process among these groups.
3. What are the main challenges and benefits of multicultural work environments for migrants? Describe and explain some effective ways to manage diversity in the work place (to maximize its benefits).
4. What is meant by the terms 'push' and 'pull' factors in migration studies?
5. What are the three dilemmas trade unions face in dealing with immigrant labour? Explain why these are dilemmas.
6. Based on the history of migration described in the chapter, do you think migration today is different from migration in the past, or is it just more of the same? Why?

> **Recommended reading**
>
> - Kamp, A. and Hagedorn-Rasmussen, P. (2004) Diversity management in a Danish context: Towards a multicultural or segregated working life? *Economic and Industrial Democracy* 25(4): 525–554, November.
> - Cheong, P. H., Edwards, R., Goulbourne, H. and Solomos, J. (2007) Immigration, social cohesion and social capital: A critical review. *Critical Social Policy* 27(1): 24–49, February.
> - Ludger, P. (2003) Labour migration, social incorporation and transmigration in the New Europe. The case of Germany in a comparative perspective. *Transfer: European Review of Labour and Research* 9(3): 432–451, August.

References

Bade, K. (2003) *Migration in European History*. Malden: Blackwell Publishing.

Betts, A. (2011) *Global Migration Governance*. Oxford: Oxford University Press.

Castles, S. (1986) 'The guest-worker in Western Europe – An obituary', *International Migration Review* 20(4), Special Issue: Temporary Worker Programs: Mechanisms, Conditions, Consequences, pp. 761–778.

Castles, S. and Kosack, G. (1985) *Immigrant Workers and Class Structure in Western Europe*. London: Oxford University Press.

Castles, S. and Miller, M. (2009) *The Age of Migration: International Population Movements in the Modern World* London: MacMillan.

Cohen, R. (2008) *Global Diasporas: An Introduction*. London and New York: Routledge.

Cox, T. Jr. (1991) 'The multicultural organization'. *Academy of Management Executive* 5(2): 34–47.

Doeringer, P. B. and Piore, M. J. (1971) *Internal Labor Markets and Manpower Analysis*. Lexington, MA: Heath.

Dolvik, J. E. and Visser, J. (2009) 'Free movement, equal treatment and workers' rights: Can the European Union solve its trilemma of fundamental principles?', *Industrial Relations Journal* 40(6): 491–509.

Egan, M. L. and Bendick, M. Jr. (2003) 'Workforce diversity initiative in U.S. multinational corporations in Europe', *Thunderbird International Business Review* 45(6): 701.

Fitzgerald, I. and Hardy, J. (2010) '"Thinking outside the box"? Trade union organizing strategies and Polish migrant workers in the United Kingdom', *British Journal of Industrial Relations* 48(1): 131–150.

Gordon, D. M., Edwards, R. and Reich, M. (1982) *Segmented Work, Divided Workers: The Historical Transformation of Labor in the United States*. Cambridge, New York: Cambridge University Press.

Greer, I., Ciupijus, Z. and Lillie, N. (2013) 'The European Migrant Workers Union and the barriers to transnational industrial citizenship', *European Journal of Industrial Relations* 19(1): 5–20.

Harzing, A.-W. (2004) 'Composing an international staff'. In *International Human Resource Management*, 2nd edition, A.-W. Harzing and J. van Ruysseveldt (eds.). London: Sage.

Hatton, T. and Williamson, J. (2005) *Global Migration and the World Economy*. Cambridge, MA: MIT Press.

IOM (International Organization for Migration) (2010) World Migration Report 2010. The Future of Migration: Building Capacities for Change, url: http://www.iom.ch/jahia/Jahia/about-migration/managing-migration/managing-migration-irregular-migration/cache/offonce/

Kindleberger, C. C. (1967) *Europe's Postwar Growth—The Role of Labor Supply*. Cambridge, MA: Harvard University Press.

King, R., Dalipaj, M. and Mai, N. (2006) 'Gendering migration and remittances: evidence from London and Northern Albania' *Population, Space and Place* 12(6): 409–434.

Lee, E. (2006) *At America's Gates: Chinese Immigration during the Exclusion Era, 1882–1943*. Chapell Hill: University of North Carolina Press.

Legrain, P. (2006) *Immigrants: Your Country Needs Them*. London: Little, Brown.

Lillie, N. (2006) *A Global Union for Global Workers: Collective Bargaining and Regulatory Politics in Maritime Shipping*. New York: Routledge.

Lillie, N. (2012) 'Subcontracting, posted migrants and labour market segmentation in Finland', *British Journal of Industrial Relations* 40(1): 148–167.

Lillie, N. and Sippola, M. (2011) 'National unions and transnational workers: the case of Olkiluoto 3, Finland', *Work, Employment and Society* 25(2): 1–17.

Martin, P. (2003) *Highly Skilled Labor Migration: Sharing the Benefits*. Geneva: ILO.

McGovern, P. (2007) 'Immigration, labour markets and employment relations: Problems and prospects', *British Journal of Industrial Relations* 45(2): 217–235.

Milkman, R. (2006) *L.A. Story: Immigrant Workers and the Future of the U.S. Labor Movement*. New York: Russell Sage Foundation.

Parkham, T. (1992) *The Scramble for Africa*. London: Abacus.

Parvis, L. (2003) 'Diversity and effective leadership in multicultural workplaces', *Journal of Environmental Health* 65(7): 37, 65, March.

Penninx, R. and Roosblad, J. (2000) *Trade Unions, Immigration and Immigrants in Europe, 1960–1993*. New York: Berghahn.

Pharek, M. (2000) *Rethinking Multiculturalism: Cultural Diversity and Political Theory*. Cambridge, MA: Harvard University Press.

Philip, M. (2001) 'International migration and the European Union, trends and consequences', *European Journal on Criminal Policy and Research* 9: 31–49.

Piore, M. J. (1979) *Birds of Passage: Migrant Labor and Industrial Societies*. Cambridge, New York: Cambridge University Press.

Regets, M. C. (2007) 'Research Issues in the International Migration of Highly Skilled Workers: A Perspective with Data from the United States'. Division of Science Resources Statistics, National Science Foundation Working Paper, SRS 07-203.

Rubery, J. and Wilkinson, F. (1994) *Employer Strategy and the Labour Market*. Oxford, New York: Oxford University Press.

Vandenbosch, A. (1947) 'The Chinese in South East Asia', *Journal of Politics* 9(1): 80–95.

Virdee, S. (2000) 'A Marxist critique of black radical theories of trade-union racism', *Sociology* 34(3): 545–565.

Wills, J. (2009) Subcontracted employment and its challenge to labor, *Labor Studies Journal* 34(4): 441–460.

World Bank (2011) 'Migration and Remittances Factbook 2011'. http://issuu.com/world.bank.publications/docs/9780821382189

Wrench, J. (2004) 'Trade union responses to immigrants and ethnic inequality in Denmark and the UK: The context of consensus and conflict', *European Journal of Industrial Relations* 10(1): 7–30.

12 Regulating work and employment internationally: the emergence of soft regulation

Robert MacKenzie and Miguel Martínez Lucio

Learning objectives

- To explain the meaning and development of regulation
- To outline the way regulation has been changing
- To discuss the ways in which multinational corporations are regulated in new and 'soft' ways in the international context
- To outline the dilemmas related to regulation in the transnational context

Introduction

This chapter addresses the notion of regulation and the transformation of regulation, in relation to work and the management of the employment relationship. We explore how we should understand the concept of regulation and why it is important for our understanding of the management of employment internationally. Regulation is often taken as being synonymous with the role of law and its enactment through institutions of the state; however, regulation is not solely about the government or the state but incorporates a range of players who shape the rules and processes influencing the firm and its decision making. This chapter will examine how political actors and institutions frame the rules and rights within the employment relationship. We will look beyond the nation-state and government to consider the various public, voluntary and private sector groups that may influence employment systems and their management in national and, increasingly, international contexts. There is a widening array of actors shaping the economic context of management, from fair-trade organizations, social lobbies and transnational governmental institutions such as the World Trade Organization (WTO). This broadening of the notion of regulation is essential if we are to understand the different players who shape the relations and rules of work, and the emergence of new actors and new regulatory spaces in which management may operate (MacKenzie and Martínez Lucio 2005). This chapter also explores the role of new actors such as international consultancies, accountancy firms and think tanks in propagating the agenda for regulatory change. Rising to view in the late 1970s, these bodies provided the intellectual imperative for the emerging neoliberal political agenda in the United Kingdom and the United States. Soon established as the new hegemonic project, the neoliberal agenda represented not just a critique of the role of regulatory actors but a challenge to the idea of regulation itself, albeit often narrowly defined in terms of 'hard' legalistic intervention. In their own terms, these actors have been successful in changing the nature of the debate, undermining the political appetite for 'hard' regulation. The catch-all vindication, globalization, fuelled the notion that, in addition to being illegitimate, national-level intervention was increasingly outmoded; hard regulation was bad for business but also bad for the national interests of countries wishing to attract crucial investment from MNCs. Yet the imperative for regulation cannot be removed; the political appetite for hard regulation may have diminished under ongoing ideological onslaught, but this has been transposed with a growing interest in new forms of 'soft regulation'. Current modes of thinking favour some re-regulation of MNCs and their employment practices, through establishing codes of practice and ethical agendas in the light of a greater interest in worker rights and social responsibility. Throughout the chapter, we will show how ideas and values that frame the economic and political context of MNCs are developed and often contested by a variety of actors and institutions.

Regulation and work

The purpose of regulation is to facilitate social and economic reproduction. The logic of reproduction is based on the establishment of order and regularity, in terms of establishing shared rules and sustaining consistent decision-making processes. Regulation offers some predictability regarding the conduct of agents operating within that environment. Whereas the development of standard expectations regarding the behaviour of others provides the basis for social and economic interaction and reproduction (MacKenzie and Martínez Lucio 2005), it does not imply that regulation is always effective in establishing a basis for economic activity (Jessop 1990; Peck 1996). Our understanding of regulation should go beyond viewing it as merely legal enactment (see MacKenzie and Martínez Lucio 2005; Martínez Lucio and Mackenzie 2004). Baldwin et al. (1998) argue that three key strands of thought on regulation can be detected. The first views regulation in terms of 'targeted rules' 'accompanied by some mechanism, typically a public agency, for monitoring and promoting compliance' (Baldwin et al. 1998: 3). A second view is to be found in the area of political economy, which conceptualizes regulation as the state and its attempt to manage the economy. However, a third view adopts a broader perspective, defining regulation to include 'all mechanisms of social control – including unintentional and non-state processes …' (ibid.: 4).

It has also been long recognized that regulation involves a variety of actors such as state institutions, trade unions, management networks, international state agencies and a range of social bodies such as international charities, to name some key examples (Regini 2000; MacKenzie and Martínez Lucio 2005; Martínez Lucio and MacKenzie 2004). Regulation also encompasses a variety of levels and relations between them. The regulatory roles of organized labour and organized capital, for instance, interrelate at various levels: from the national level apex organizations of national employer federations and trade union organizations; to regional or sectoral mechanisms; and down to the level of company and workplace relations between management and trade unions, which may also include less institutionalized, informal practices. The actual regulatory actors and the roles they play in the regulation of social and economic relationships vary according to the context. It is important to recognize, therefore, that the panoply of actors and levels reflects the coexistence of different types of regulation. Indeed, many insist that regulation has formal and informal qualities, reflected in the increasing array of actors involved (Picciotto 1999). Individuals and organizations may simultaneously be subject to a multiplicity of regulatory actors such as the state, employers and mechanisms of joint regulation, in addition to social agencies and institutions.

Regulatory change

Overall, from the mid 1940s until the late 1970s, most developed countries supported an interventionist role for the state and, whether effective or otherwise, encouraged systems of regulation through legislation or other institutionalized means (Esping Anderson 2000). Often associated with Keynesian models of state intervention in the management of the economy and the associated redistributive mechanisms of the Welfare State, this 'Golden Age' began to falter in the European context during the mid to late 1970s (see Jessop 2002: 55–79).

The critique made was that extensive state intervention in the economy, the increasing rigidity of labour market regulations in terms of hiring and firing workers, and the steadily increasing power of trade unions created an untenable inflationary situation. While much of this critique is disputed, the belief in structured and nationally based systems of regulation as a central feature of economic and social progress became tarnished (see Jessop 2002: 95–139; Hall 1988). What began to emerge from the mid to late 1970s is a political view of regulation per se as being costly and prohibitive for the firm and for society in general (Friedman 1968).

For some, this marketization represents an 'Americanization' of employment strategies (Guest 1990; Brewster 2004), where the role of regulation through the state and collective organization become secondary to management prerogative (Whitley et al. 2005). This model can be juxtaposed against a traditional European model where the state is more interventionist, and collective worker rights are more influential in terms of HRM practices and decision making (Communal and Brewster 2004).

The transmission of any new 'best practice' management approach ultimately relies upon the agency of management and other actors. The implementation of 'best practice', therefore, is essentially a political process – that is to say, it is based on struggles between actors, which are shaped by the power resources available to them. Competing views and divergent values pertaining to the market and the individual exist within the same firm, not only between management and the representatives of labour but also between different cohorts of management.

For example, stemming from developments associated with the Japanization debate, lean production and new techniques at work have been an important feature of change over recent decades, in UK workplaces and beyond. As Stewart (1996) argues, the associated organizational and employment changes were not the inevitable outcomes of objectively superior efficiencies associated with new management systems but rather were shaped by political debates and struggles between unions, employers and even academics (see Chapter 7). Furthermore, the practices of team working and quality management were to a significant degree crafted not just by overseas MNCs in the early 1990s but also by consultancy firms. The contribution of other actors was also highly significant, with a facilitating political context being shaped by the role of the right-wing think tanks in the United States (The Heritage Foundation founded in 1973) and the United Kingdom (Centre for Policy Studies founded by right-wing politicians Keith Joseph and Margaret Thatcher in 1974). These institutions, unaccountable to any electorate, were central to opposing, de-legitimizing and undermining state-led regulation (see Klein 2007: 50–51; Heller 2002; Legge 2002).

There was also the growth of business schools, which have propagated an increasingly neoliberal view of organizations and their purpose, supported by direct intervention from consultancy firms that research, motivate and legitimate organizational change (O'Shea and Madigan 1997). This has provided the new regulatory actors, be they state agencies or particular consultancy firms, with knowledge resources, technical abilities and competences, and the degree of legitimacy necessary for influencing the terminology and practices of new forms of management strategy (see Chapter 9). Yet these educational and knowledge-based spaces are changing and becoming the object of greater internal debate and challenge: the realities of what business schools 'do' can vary, especially in light of emergent albeit fragmented ethical agendas (Martínez Lucio 2007).

Even at the macro level of the global political scene, ideas of harder management-led HRM are propagated, both directly and indirectly. The World Bank and the IMF, as transnational and inter-state publicly funded bodies, have been crucial in extending the idea of free markets, greater competition and the importance of continuous labour market and organizational restructuring (Stiglitz 2006: 211–244; Klein 2007: 267–271). These agendas link with the harder and more performance-driven aspects of HRM (see Chapters 7 and 8).

Such approaches are forged through agency and political processes, and are not simply the natural or 'best' outcome in the light of the needs of the new global market. In the late 1970s, the political project of the new right in the United Kingdom and United States defined hegemonic views towards regulation for governments on either side of the Atlantic for the next three decades. Successive governments elected from either side of the respective political divides did not demur, whether owing to ideological commitment or political expediency. Indeed, it was not until the international economic crisis that emerged around 2008 that the recognized need for government intervention returned to the main-stream political narrative. Yet, despite being tarnished by the post-2008 economic crisis, neoliberalism still holds sway under the Conservative-led coalition gov-ernment in the United Kingdom, for example, with policy agendas dominated by public sector cuts, stimulating private sector growth through deregulation and encouraging people back to work through welfare reductions. However, this classic neoliberal prescription of state withdrawal coincides with levels of state intervention in the economy through the nationalization of key sections of the banking industry that are unprecedented in the neoliberal era. There is, therefore, a tension between the ongoing need for the state to resolve the economic crisis and the dismantling of particular state roles. Shoring up the economy through specific interventions in the banking sector has increased the financial burden on the state in the United States, United Kingdom, Spain, Greece and others, while attempts to cut public debt have redistributed the burden of the crisis, through swinging spending cuts to public sector investment and welfare.

The new tapestry of transnational regulation

Frameworks and soft law

Given the legitimacy and historical pre-eminence of the nation-state, the roles of national governments and government bodies have been central political influ-ences on firms and their HRM strategies. Extending beyond the nation-state, there has been a long standing tradition of international regulatory bodies. These organizations took on increased importance during the new wave of economic internationalization in the 1980s and the growing concern with setting minimum benchmarks for the treatment of workers. It is too early to talk of re-regulation of employment, given the weak and uneven nature of transnational regulatory bodies and the fact that the ideas underpinning them are not universally shared; the interaction of formal and informal regulatory processes around legal forms and codes of conduct is increasingly a part of modern business environments (Picciotto 1999). Codes of conduct, recommendations and resolutions over labour standards are often grouped together under the heading of 'soft law' (Regent 2003). Soft law may be seen as an approach to regulation that relies on influencing behaviour without being formally binding or backed by sanctions, but rather is traditionally reliant on peer review and monitoring by organizations such as the International Labour Organization (ILO) and Organisation for Economic Development and Cooperation (OECD), or even institutions of the EU (Borras and Jacobson 2004) for asserting any regulatory influence.

There is increasing interest in labour standards and the behaviour of employers from a range of bodies that are concerned with issues of malpractice, corruption and 'bad' employment practices. The ILO, the United Nations (UN) labour and work-related agency, was actually established as part of the UN's predecessor, the League of Nations, after the First World War (1919). The ILO historically outlined a basic body of labour codes and rights, which while often ignored were formally part of the system of inter-governmental relations. Over time, it has established more explicit sets of conventions and rules, and a vast array of research and educational activities that map and outline 'good' practices in relation to employment issues. The ILO sets the benchmarks against which firms and governments are measured in this area. Political sensitivities around issues such as child labour are directly informed by compliance with ILO standards. Furthermore, the ILO provides standards across the range of everyday employment issues which attract less media attention. Whether these standards are systematically developed or adhered to by member states is another issue; however, they constitute a part of the international dialogue on employment and human resource management.

The OECD has 30 members – mainly developed countries – which broadly share a free market and a liberal democratic philosophy. It has developed a range of economic and social agendas. In relation to MNCs, it has produced a set of guidelines establishing a series of principles on the approach of member states to MNCs and the behaviour of MNCs themselves. They cover a range of areas related to employment issues, through to corruption and investment matters. Bodies such as the World Bank and the WTO have also begun to address the issue of labour standards and the basic rights of labour organizations. While such bodies are mainly focused on the economic and developmental aspects of their affiliate nations, they do increasingly address employment and work-related issues, although their prescriptions tend to reflect a particular neoliberal orientation and vary in their social impact.

These international institutions provide a backdrop of minimum standards and benchmarks which do, on occasion, influence the way that firms behave in relation to their workforce. How much and how often they have an influence depends on the industrial sector and its traditions of labour organization. However, the main point is that there exists an array of bodies addressing international issues and cross-national labour standards, which impact upon employment relations and management at the transnational level. They have not possessed a strong regulatory and sanctioning role in many cases, but that does not detract from the fact that there is a tapestry of international labour bodies and HR influencing agencies that challenge the recent vogue for panegyrizing globalization.

Moreover, these developments are not always 'soft' or voluntary and may have the potential for sanctions and a more systematic regulatory process. In some regions of the world, countries are beginning to form more permanent systems of supranational economic and social governance. The most developed manifestation of this is the EU, a political structure unifying over 25 European nation-states to various degrees, which has a range of social and employment related rules and laws (see Chapter 1). This has included systematic frameworks of employee/human-resource-related regulations on issues such as mass redundancy, health and safety, working hours and discrimination. The European Works Councils Directive provides legislation on worker participation in MNCs, and represents the first supranational employment regulation within the EU. These are all developments that show the necessity of conceptualizing regulation within broader transnational frameworks.

Although hard regulation continues to play an important part in the influence the EU has over employment, political expediency in the post-Maastricht era has come to see an increasing emphasis being placed on soft regulation, and the pursuit of policy agendas through soft law (Boras and Jacobson 2004). With a long tradition within the EU (Borras and Jacobsson 2004), soft regulation may not be legally binding but nonetheless can be seen as having an actual impact – or regulatory bite – in terms of social and labour market policy, through the provision of normative frameworks that shape the conduct of political and social actors (Snyder 1994; Trubek and Trubek 2005). Since the impasse of the mid-1980s in the area of social and labour market policy, the EU has increasingly moved away from the top-down approach to regulation, driven by hard legislation and backed up by sanctions (Jespson and Pasqual 2005). Recognizing the need for a more participative approach, the European Commission developed its key mechanism for the application of soft regulation in the 'Open Method of Coordination'; this represented a more participative approach to regulation, engaging stakeholders from both community and national levels in the development of guidelines for achieving policy goals and benchmarks for measuring success (Scharpf 2002; Regent 2003; Watt 2004). Crucially, *plans* and *programmes* for policy responses to these EU level guidelines would be left to national actors to develop. Success would be assessed by benchmarking against other national cases (Arrowsmith et al. 2004), and failure to meet targets would not be met with sanctions; rather, any improvement would be encouraged through the sharing of good practice, although soft law proponents suggest that 'shaming' through peer reviews offers some form of sanction (Trubek and Trubek 2005). Originally developed in the late 1990s and unveiled at the Lisbon Summit of 2000 as a policy mechanism for implementing the European Employment Strategy, the Open Method of Coordination was subsequently rolled out to other policy areas, such as social exclusion and pensions.

The increased emphasis given to soft law is seen as politically expedient and offering the most binding approach to regulation possible in the post-Maastricht era (Watt 2004), offering sufficient ambiguity to facilitate interpretation into a wide range of policy outcomes and thus accommodate an increasingly diverse range of employment systems within an expanded EU. Alternatively, the increased emphasis given to soft law has been cited as contributing to fragmentation of the regulatory influence of the EU in the area of social and labour market regulation, promoting an inconsistency of application and exacerbating a downward pressure on standards (Gold 2009). The efficacy of soft law depends on the effective combination of a number of factors: politicians and social actors representing the interests of employers and labour, operating at the supranational, national and local level, engaging in social dialogue, providing guidelines and benchmarks for the development of policy, and asserting peer pressure to influence behaviour. As noted by Regent (2003), the soft law of the Open Method of Coordination is not targeted towards individuals but rather towards member states, which may choose to implement their policy response through hard law. The combination of 'hard' and 'soft' law, and the mechanisms that enforce or promote them, contribute to the panoply of multi-level governance within the EU, which in turn provides a unique supranational regulatory space within the broader picture of international regulation.

The developing tapestry of supranational, transnational and inter-nation state-based bodies is creating a framework of regulation affecting firms and their human resource practices. It is part of an evolving international dialogue on labour rights that has emerged since the end of the Second World War and is underpinned by the Universal Declaration of Human Rights (see Cassese 1992). There remains a great degree of cynicism regarding the development of such rights owing to the highly variable responses of national governments and multinational employers. There is also concern that the assertion of such rights favours the production regimes of developed countries and disadvantages developing countries, where competitive advantage based on low labour costs have become common government strategies for economic development.

Another school of thought in the form of the 'boomerang theory' is more optimistic and argues that governments which ignore the increasing establishment of international rights systems may be shamed and compelled in the longer term to subscribe to them (Risse et al. 1999). Even if this is symbolic in the first instance, over time it establishes expectations within countries, arising from unions or political bodies, as well as external pressure from international consumer groups, other nation-states (Norway, for example, has been highly active on such issues) and transnational inter-state organisations such as the EU.

Social responsibility

The developments described above dovetail with an increasing interest in social responsibility and ethics within human resource management (Pinnington et al. 2007) (see Chapter 9). In relation to major issues such as child labour there are emergent external pressures from NGOs such as Oxfam or War on Want. Movements such as 'Fairtrade', which campaigns for a decent wage for workers in the global agricultural sector, notably coffee, and in the textiles industry have provided a new reference point for ethically based regulation that is of growing importance.

The relationship between trade unions and NGOs highlights another important feature of the tapestry of regulation: the extent to which mechanisms of regulation are complementary or competing. There are positive examples of cooperation between NGOs and trade unions sharing information, drawing the attention of consumers to the working conditions under which goods are produced or even raising awareness of the benefits of unionization among hard-to-reach workers in MNC supply chains. The cooperative activities of trade unions and NGOs have been crucial in persuading organizations to sign up to voluntary codes of practice over their employment policies and have played an important role in policing adherence to such codes. More broadly, soft regulation or the implementation of soft law may often rely on the capacity of trade unions to influence the process, not necessarily through collective agreements – although these may play an important role – but also through the ongoing interaction between actors in the regulatory space they occupy at the level of the workplace or beyond. Even statutory interventions, such as Health and Safety regulations, can be seen to benefit in terms of their efficacy from the support of other mechanisms of regulation, in this case trade union health and safety representatives. In short, within the tapestry of regulation, different forms of regulation and a diverse range of regulatory actors may complement one another, or be seen to have complementarities in their regulatory impact. However, this may not always be the case, and regulatory actors may indeed compete or conflict with one another. In extreme cases, competition may result in more hostile developments where one actor seeks to displace or replace another, in effect colonizing the regulatory space in which they operate (MacKenzie and Martínez Lucio 2005; MacKenzie and Martínez Lucio forthcoming).

In terms of relations between trade unions and NGOs, the many examples of cooperation and complementarities of practice must be tempered by less frequent but important cautionary tales of actors set in competition. There are cases where employers promote a positive corporate image through endorsement by the Fair Trade movement while simultaneously engaging in anti-union activities in their production sites (Frundt 2007). Within the realm of joint regulation, developments in

Germany over recent years have seen increased tensions between the collective bargaining role of trade unions and the activities of works councils. These key mechanisms of regulation, which have successfully coexisted historically, now increasingly compete for influence in the workplace. The tensions between unions and works councils have been in no small part encouraged by employers seeking to promote an agenda of decentralization. Attempts to increase the role of works councils in localized bargaining is not so much the de-collectivization associated with decentralization in other countries, notably the United Kingdom, but can be seen as re-regulation through shifting the locus of collectivization. The growth in competition between traditionally mutually supportive regulatory actors has seen the increased colonization of the preserve of collective bargaining by works councils. Elsewhere, there are other examples of the displacement of regulatory actors and the colonization of regulatory space that has led to decollectivization. Indeed, the increased emphasis on self-regulation by corporate management can be seen as part of a process of displacing other regulatory actors including the state, international bodies promoting codes of conduct and, often through the rubric of strategic HRM practices promoting direct communication and employee participation, the role of trade unions.

Focusing on social issues and the rights to participation at work in MNCs (Wills 1998) has emerged as a renewed role for international trade union organizations such as the International Trade Union Congress. While these bodies have less resources than nation-states (Smith et al. 1998) and, indeed, compete with each other for scarce resources (Claude and Weston 1992), they do form part of the global set of institutions that contribute to the tapestry of regulation shaping the political and economic context in which IHRM exists (Lillie and Martínez Lucio, 2004). They play a regulatory role in terms of diffusing expert knowledge, and informing and educating public agencies and nation-states (Baehr 1999). They also constitute a counterpoint to the private and market-driven networks of consultancies and think tanks. These developments echo the interest in stakeholder theories of ethics in employment-related matters, which espouse a more pluralist understanding of voice and the role of different actors (Greenwood and De Cieri 2007). What is more, a range of informal and work-activist-based union networks have emerged, aimed at exchanging information on campaigns and coordinating across a range of disputes and mobilizations (Wills 1998). The politics of such networks has given rise to broad coalitions, combining trade unions with a diverse range of peace campaigners, environmentalist and anti-capitalist groups into movements that are both innovative and increasingly entrenched (Thomas 2007).

The Internet has provided a forum for discussion and a conduit for the transmission of critiques of MNCs and the articulation of alternative, progressive perspectives on consumption. Consumer groups are utilizing this medium to bring pressure to bear on the activities of MNCs and the ethicality of their approach to such issues as employment and sustainable resourcing. Whereas there may be a more individualist and consumerist orientation to contemporary capitalism (Alonso 2006), a new politics of consumption is emerging that places social and employment issues on the agenda.

Even business schools have begun to engage with new agendas around ethics and a growing interest in corporate social responsibility (CSR). In the UK context at least, control over the content and direction in which these agendas develop is becoming another politically contested terrain, counterposing mainstream managerial approaches and the more critical and progressive traditions that coexist in many business schools. Although interest in CSR tends to be dominated by concerns over environmental impact, which remain prone to the usual problems with self-regulation and suspicions of 'green-washing', there have been attempts to broaden the CSR agenda to include work and employment issues. Debates around Socially Responsible Restructuring, for example, have promulgated the need for employers to recognize their responsibilities towards employees made redundant through corporate restructuring and provide support and training to improve their chances of transition into employment elsewhere (Forde et al. 2009). This is a classic case where regulatory complementarities lead to more positive outcomes. Employers' self-regulation of Socially Responsible Restructuring is made more effective by the presence of joint regulation by trade unions and the involvement of the state through the statutory requirement of support for displaced workers in finding or preparing for new employment, or through the commitment to broader active labour market policies. The EU's Globalisation Adjustment Fund provides another layer of intervention and support for employees displaced in mass redundancy programmes, albeit essentially voluntaristic in terms of how it is activated.

These new dimensions of transnational regulation are a vital part of the environment that MNCs inhabit. Indeed, they encourage MNCs to internalize regulatory roles themselves, as they increasingly need to ethically police their organizations and create sustainable and legitimate operations.

Case study: Regulating labour standards – Types of social clauses

Part of the problem with international employment regulation is the lack of enforceability and the concern in various countries that such regulation can hamper economic development, and hence social development in the long term. The development of the social clause, which has been seen as one way of creating a framework for a greater commitment to dignity and fairness at work, has been the subject of much debate. According to Lim:

> In the context of international trade, a social clause essentially refers to a legal provision in a trade agreement aimed at removing the most extreme forms of labour exploitation in exporting countries by allowing importing countries to take trade measures against exporting countries which fail to observe a set of internationally agreed minimum labour standards ... While the focus is presently on trade measures, social clause provisions have been linked to non-trade

arrangements. For instance, the US Overseas Private Investment Corporation (OPIC), a government agency which offers insurance to US companies operating in developing countries, will withdraw its services from projects in countries not taking steps to adopt and implement laws that extend a set of internationally recognised labour standards. It has also been suggested that social clauses should also be added to development aid and loan programmes. At present, while the ILO actively promotes the ratification and supervision of Clauses, it cannot force compliance or impose financial, commercial or other sanctions; rather, it relies on persuasion and peer pressure to encourage States to meet their obligations. Nevertheless, despite not having a punitive enforcement mechanism, the ILO has in practice attained an influence that goes beyond legal formality.

(Lim, http://actrav.itcilo.org/actrav-english/telearn/global/ilo/
guide/hoelim.htm)

However, most social clauses appear to be voluntary and are rarely tied into trade agreements:

Human rights social movements have benefited from the ease of travel and communications of the last thirty years ... Nevertheless, as global communication erodes geographical remoteness, the universal principle of human rights becomes one upon which local actors can base their demands for justice. If the capitalist-owned mass media ignore a particular human right, the technology of global communications nevertheless allows its pursuit through the formation of independent media groups, chat rooms, and websites. Global consumer campaigns against abusive labour practices such as employment of child labour have been particularly successful. The Rugmark campaign, for example, tells consumers whether rugs they have purchased from Asia are made without child labour, exerting pressure for improved labour standards in producing countries such as Pakistan and Iran (Forsythe 2000; Pangalangan 2002). Retail companies are also susceptible to consumer pressure on human rights grounds, such as in the case of the Swiss grocery chain, Migros. Migros inserted a 'social clause' in its contract with Del Monte to ensure that working conditions on Del Monte's pineapple farms in the Philippines were above average (Pangalangan 2002). (Howard-Hassmann 2005: 19)

(Lim, http://actrav.itcilo.org/actrav-english/telearn/global/ilo/
guide/hoelim.htm)

This observation brings to our attention that even one of the more direct or interventionist of transnational regulatory levers relies on 'persuasion' and 'peer pressure' and is normally voluntarist in nature. What this means is that campaigning and communication are vital for the development of a robust system of regulation. In relation to peer pressure, it also means establishing benchmarks and mechanisms which highlight practices and literally shame those who do not abide by higher standards of employment rights and are not improving working conditions. Hence, the transnational system of regulation requires a strategic and networked-based approach. Enforcement is therefore based on public debates, popular boycotts, consumer actions, influencing key individuals and their reputations, and creating links with civil society organizations. This begins to necessitate a more plural and democratic view of regulation and of governance which brings the stakeholder closer to the centre of activity.

Questions

1. What are the features of the social clause as a strategy?
2. What may be the arguments against it?
3. What do social clauses represent as a new way of raising issues of dignity and rights within the world of employment?
4. Why do some use the term *soft regulation*?
5. What are the conditions for successful social clauses which are backed by trade agreements or company-specific codes?

Conclusion

The chapter has argued that the concept of regulation should be central to any discussion of employment relations and management at the transnational level. Regulation involves various levels and actors, and in any given context these will vary. There has also been a shift in the way regulation is viewed and who is involved in it. Where once stood the apparatus of the state and direct forms of intervention, there is now an even more complex scenario. While there has been a move towards more marketized economies where the remit of regulation is limited, this is only part of the story. First, such a shift towards a marketized and more individualistic perspective is itself the political product of a range of actors and knowledge networks – which can be prone to shifting economic and political contingencies, as witnessed in the clamour for regulatory responses to the emergent economic crisis in 2008–2009. Second, sustaining the hegemony of marketized perspectives has always been a contested process, and there is again increasing concern with the need to rebuild regulation and create a more effective platform for regulating international employment issues.

The current crisis and the nature of the political response to it will bring new challenges, as the project of re-regulation suggested earlier begins to come under pressure from a renewed assault on the state. The banking crisis and the manner in which the state institutions of various key developed nations – especially those within liberal market economies – have had to finance the sector means that the restructuring and containment of the state has become a central policy issue. This begins to restrict the role of the state and question the nature of regulation. The apparent reassertion of neoliberal ideology has meant that regulation is once more under pressure. However, it would be unwise to assume that the kinds of regulation we discuss in this chapter in relation to employment relations and management at the transnational level will be easily marginalized. The imperative for regulation will remain. The manner in which the social consequences and political outcomes of the crisis develop will require ever more strategic and innovative forms of state response (Rubery 2011).

The illusion that the emergence of market-oriented strategies would deliver a new world of autonomous managerial decision making has been shown to be questionable and surpassed by processes of re-regulation. There are competing views on how firms should conduct their HR strategies, and in the case of MNCs this has now become a question at the centre of a range of policy and social debates (see Klein 2007). The once-dominant view of the reassertion of the pre-rogative of management, as a new and invigorated actor that can assimilate many of the requirements of regulation and actually regulate in relation to the internal context of the firm, is highly problematic and contested. As MNCs develop their own specific forms of governance which are neither influenced by national systems of origin nor the contexts they operate in, it is becoming clear that there is an urgent need for new forms of global regulation. MNCs can create their own idiosyncratic management systems that are hybrids of what went before, but there are limits to the extent to which they can internalize their strategies to create systems that respond to internal business and operational requirements and minimize external regulatory influences.

Pressures remain in terms of national governments, transnational public bodies, transnational organizations, social movements, consumer organizations, and transnational trade unions structures and networks. This new environment is about setting standards and creating alternative visions of how people should be managed. This political dimension will be a global struggle of ideas about the way capitalism should be regulated, involving clusters of nation-states, national systems and international bodies and networks. Regulation, far from disappearing or being terminally weakened by the marginalization of nation-states, has become a significant and ever more complex reality. It would be too easy to dismiss this tapestry of often soft regulation, voluntary codes of practice and pressure groups as not being sufficiently coordinated, nor backed by meaningful sanctions, to provide an international equivalence to the regulatory role historically played by nation-states. Yet, given the obvious disparities in the geopolitical context, such direct comparisons become essentially meaningless. Regulation in the current global context involves a move towards combinations of actors at different levels: from nation-states, to transnational bodies (both regulatory and voluntary in character) and even social and private associations that lobby and highlight issues. Thus, both hard and soft forms of regulation will coexist and form the basis of a more complex system of international governance.

Reflective questions

1. What is regulation and what are its different components?
2. How has regulation changed and what have been the pressures on more direct forms of regulation?
3. What role have business schools played? Why do some see this role as negative?
4. What do we mean by soft regulation?
5. What are the major problems of soft regulation and more indirect forms of managing employers internationally?

Recommended reading

- Guest, D. (1990) 'Human resource management and the American dream'. *Journal of Management Studies* 27(4): 377–397.
- Mackenzie, R. and Martínez Lucio, M. (2005) 'The realities of regulatory change: Beyond the fetish of deregulation'. *Sociology* 39(3): 499–517.
- Rubery, J. (2011) 'Reconstruction amid deconstruction: Or why we need more of the social in European social models'. *Work, Employment and Society* 25(4): 658–674.

References

Alonso, L. (2006) 'The Fordist cycle and the genesis of the post-Fordist society'. In L. E. Alonso and M. Martínez Lucio (eds.), *Employment Relations in a Changing Society*. London: Palgrave.

Arrowsmith, J., Sisson, K., and Marginson, P. (2004) 'What can "benchmarking" offer the open method of co-ordination?'. *Journal of European Public Policy* 11(2): 311–328.

Baehr, P. R. (1999) *Human Rights: Universality in Practice*. Basingstoke: Macmillan.

Baldwin, R., Scott, C. and Hood, C. (1998) 'Introduction'. In R. Baldwin, C. Scott and C. Hood (eds.), *A Reader on Regulation*. Oxford: Oxford University Press.

Borras, S. and Jacobson, K. (2004) 'The open method of co-ordination and new governance patterns in the EU'. *Journal of European Public Policy* 11(2): 185–208.

Brewster, C. (2004) 'European perspectives on human resource management'. *Human Resource Management Review* 14(4): 365–382.

Cassese, D. (1992) 'The general assembly: Historical perspective 1945–1989'. In P. Ashton (ed.) *The United Nations and Human Rights: A Critical Appraisal*. New York: Cambridge University Press.

Claude, R. P. and Weston, B. H. (1992) 'International human rights: Overviews'. In R. P. Claude and B. H. Weston (eds.), *Human Rights in the World Community: Issues and Action*, 2nd edn. Philadelphia: University of Pennsylvania Press.

Esping Anderson, G. (2000) 'Who is harmed by labour market de-regulation?'. In G. Esping Anderson and M. Regini (eds.), *Why Deregulate Labour Markets*. Oxford: Oxford University Press.

Forde, C., Stuart, M., Gardiner, J., Greenwood, I., MacKenzie, R. and Perrett, R. (2009) 'Socially responsible restructuring in an era of mass redundancy'. Working Paper 5. Centre for Employment Relations Innovation and Change, Leeds University Business School.

Forsythe, D. (2000) *Human Rights in International Relations*. New York: Cambridge University Press.

Friedman, M. (1968) 'The role of monetary policy'. *American Economic Review* 58(March): 1–17.

Frundt, H. (2007) 'Organizing in the banana sector' In K. Bronfenbrenner (ed.), *Global Unions: Challenging Transnational Capital Through Cross-Border Campaigns*. Ithaca: Cornell University Press.

Gold, M. (2009) 'Overview of EU employment policy'. In M. Gold (ed.), *Employment Policy in the European Union: Origins Themes and Prospects*. Basingstoke: Palgrave Macmillan.

Greenwood, M. and De Cieri, H. (2007) 'Stakeholder theory and the ethicality of human resource management'. In A. H. Pinnington, R. E. Macklin and T. Campbell (eds.), *Human Resource Management: Ethics and Employment*. Oxford: Oxford University Press.

Guest, D. (1990) 'Human resource management and the American dream', *Journal of Management Studies* 27(4): 377–397.

Hall, S. (1988) *The Hard Road to Renewal*. London: Verso.

Howard-Hassmann, R. E. (2005) 'The second great transformation: Human rights leapfrogging in the era of globalization'. *Human Rights Quarterly* 27(1): 1–40.

Heller, F. (2002) 'What next? More critique of consultants, gurus and managers'. In T. Clark and R. Fincham (eds.), *Critical Consulting: New Perspectives on the Management Advice Industry*. Oxford: Blackwell.

Jepsen, M., and Pascual, A. S. (2005) 'The European Social Model: an exercise in deconstruction'. *Journal of European Social Policy* 15(3): 231–245.

Jessop, B. (2002) *The Future of the Capitalist State*. Cambridge: Polity.

Jessop, B. (1990) *State Theory*. Oxford: Polity.

Klein, N. (2007) *The Shock Doctrine*. London: Penguin.

Legge, K. (2002) 'On knowledge, business consultants and the selling of total quality management'. In T. Clark and R. Fincham (eds.), *Critical Consulting: New Perspectives on the Management Advice Industry*. Oxford: Blackwell.

Lillie, N. and Martínez Lucio, M. (2004) 'International trade union revitalization: The role of national union approaches'. In C. Frege and J. Kelly (eds.), *Labour Movement Revitalization in Comparative Perspective*. Oxford: Oxford University Press.

Lim, H. *The Social Clause: Issues and Challenges* http://actrav.itcilo.org/actrav-english/telearn/global/ilo/guide/hoelim.htm). Accessed May 20th 2013.

MacKenzie, R. and Martínez Lucio, M. (2005) 'The realities of regulatory change: Beyond the fetish of deregulation', *Sociology* 39(3): 499–517.

MacKenzie, R. and Martínez Lucio, M. (forthcoming) 'The colonisation of employment regulation and industrial relations? Dynamics and developments over five decades of change'. *Labor History*.

Martínez Lucio, M. (2007) 'Neoliberalismo y neoconservadurismo interrumpido? El porqué de la existencia de una tradición crítica en las escuelas de dirección de empresas británicas'. In C. Fernandez (ed.), *Estudios Sociales de la Organizacíon: El Giro PostModerno*. Madrid: Siglo VeintiUno.

Martínez Lucio, M. and MacKenzie, R. (2004) 'Unstable boundaries? Evaluating the "new regulation" within employment relations'. *Economy and Society* 33(1): 77–97.

O'Shea, J. and Madigan, C. (1997) *Dangerous Company: The Consulting Powerhouses and Businesses They Save and Ruin*. New York: Times Business.

Pangalangan, R. C. (2002) 'Sweatshops and international labor standards: Globalizing markets, localizing norms'. In A. Brysk (ed.), *Globalization and Human Rights*. Berkeley: University of California Press, pp. 98–114.

Peck, J. (1996) *Workplace: The Social Regulation of Labour Markets*. New York: Guildford.

Picciotto, S. (1999) 'Introduction: What rules for the world economy?'. In S. Picciotto and R. Mayne (eds.), *Regulating International Business: Beyond Liberalisation*. Basingstoke: Macmillan and Oxfam.

Pinnington, A. H., Mackin, R. E. and Campbell, T. (2007) 'Introduction'. In A. Pinnington, R. E. Macklin and T. Campbell, T. (eds.), *Human Resource Management: Ethics and Employment*. Oxford: Oxford University Press.

Regent, S. (2003) 'The open method of coordination: A new supranational form of governance?'. *European Law Journal* 9(2): 190–214.

Regini, M. (2000) 'The dilemmas of labour market regulation'. In G. Esping-Andersen and M. Regini (eds.), *Why Deregulate Labour Markets?*. Oxford: Oxford University Press.

Risse T., Ropp, S. C. and Sikkink, K. (eds.) (1999) *The Power of Human Rights: International Norms and Domestic Change*. Cambridge: Cambridge University Press.

Rubery, J. (2011) 'Reconstruction amid deconstruction: Or why we need more of the social in European social models'. *Work, Employment and Society* 25(4): 658–674.

Scharpf, F. (2002) 'The European social model: Coping with the challenges of legitimate diversity'. *Journal of Common Market Studies* 40(4): 645–670.

Smith, J., Pagnuncco, T. and Lopez, G. A. (1998) 'Globalising human rights: The work of transnational human rights NGOs in the 1990s'. *Human Rights Quarterly* 20(2): 379–412.

Snyder, F. (1994) *Soft Law and Institutional Practice in the European Community*. Netherlands: Springer.

Stewart, P. (1996) *Beyond Japanese Management*. London: Taylor & Francis.

Stiglitz, J. (2006) *Making Globalization Work*. London: Penguin.

Thomas, N. H. (2007) 'Global capitalism, the anti-globalisation movement and the Third World'. *Capital and Class* 92(Summer): 45–80.

Trubek, D. M. and Trubek, L. G. (2005) 'Hard and soft law in the construction of social Europe: The role of the open method of co-ordination'. *European Law Journal* 11(3): 343–364.

Watt, A. (2004) 'Reform of the European employment strategy after five years: A change of course or merely of presentation?'. *European Journal of Industrial Relations* 10(2): 117–137.

Whitley, R., Morgan, E. and Moen, E. (2005) *Changing Capitalisms? Internationalisation, Institutional Change and Systems of Economic Organization*. Oxford University Press: Oxford.

Wills, J. (1998) 'Taking on the CosmoCorps: Experiments in transnational labor organization'. *Economic Geography* 74: 111–130.

13 Globalization, multinational corporations and trade unions: creating new forms of international trade unionism and new forms of representation within multinational corporations

Miguel Martínez Lucio and Jeremy Waddington

Learning objectives

- To understand the development of trade unions in an international context
- To explain the manner in which they relate to the dynamics of globalization
- To focus on the new forms of worker representation that evolved in terms of European Works Councils as an example of transnational labour forums within companies
- To assess the nature of such developments and their impact

Introduction

The aim of this chapter is to allow readers to understand how unions are internationalizing through new global and transnational structures, which allow them to collaborate and develop strategies in innovative ways. In addition, the chapter highlights new dynamics in the way trade unions engage with multinational corporations (MNCs) through representative structures such as European Works Councils (EWCs).

This chapter therefore examines the way labour organizations, especially trade unions, have steadily internationalized in the past 20 years or so in terms of their structures and strategies. Globalization is normally viewed as a development that is associated with the internationalization of capital – as well as management – but increasingly we are witnessing a process of globalization in relation to the regulatory environment, social organizations and a range of political bodies. Trade unions as organizations aim to represent the workforce and its interests in relation to management, employers and the state. Primarily national in their focus, they have formed an essential, albeit variable, part of the process of employment regulation mediating and influencing change. A trade union may be defined as 'an organization whose membership consists of workers and union leaders, united to protect and promote their common interests. The principal purposes of a labour union are to (1) negotiate wages and working condition terms, (2) regulate relations between workers (its members) and the employer, (3) take collective action to enforce the terms of collective bargaining, (4) raise new demands on behalf of its members and (5) help settle their grievances' (Business Dictionary 2012). Trade unions can organize at the workplace, company, sector and national level as well as at the transnational level. Trade unions can also play a role in influencing state policies and political discourses.

The fundamental dilemma faced by trade unions is that their location in terms of national systems of employment and welfare has meant that their influence has focused primarily on national employers, management and the state. In some cases, their links with governments have assisted them in influencing the working conditions of workers through labour legislation and state intervention. However, the link with the state varies in its extent and depth – it depends on the political context and the national political system. Very often, trade unions organize to change or influence the state in addition to trying to change the agendas of management and employers.

In recent years, there has been a belief that trade unions have been unable to consistently keep up with the pace and impact of globalization – especially the increasing mobility of capital and the increasing power of MNCs, which are outside the control and influence of trade unions. This has meant that the influence of trade unions has waned. Trade unions appear to be *stuck* in a national mindset in terms of who they defend and how they defend them, leading to declining influence.

Hence, this chapter will start by outlining some of these experiences of decline, which in developed countries have been at their greatest in the liberal market economies (see Chapter 8 for a discussion of these systems). However, alongside considering renewal strategies within their national contexts (see Chapter 3 for a discussion of national systems), trade unionists have also looked to the international dimension in developing their structures and their strategies. In terms of their structures, trade unions have developed a more cohesive set of international organizational structures such as the International Trade Union Congress and the

European Trade Union Confederation, among others. In terms of trade unionists – the leaders, officials and activists of the trade union movement – there is also a range of informal and network based approaches (see Chapter 14 for a discussion of networking) and new forms of transitional coordination and networking. This chapter therefore focuses on the structural dimensions of international organization. Alongside these structures of trade union representation, there have also been ongoing attempts to create new forms of representation and agreements within the transnational corporations with the aim of creating frameworks which allow for a more open dialogue and social agenda to emerge, for example, EWCs, World Works Councils (WWCs) and International Framework Agreements. The second part of this chapter discusses these institutions and provides a case study illustrating these developments. This chapter focuses on the European Union owing to the experiments in worker representation within MNCs and the way in which this political space shows us some of the possibilities and limitations of international worker representation.

Reluctant internationalism and trade union decline?

Trade unions and trade union representatives can influence the working conditions of employees by negotiating with management on their behalf, lobbying and negotiating with governments and government departments on policies such health and safety at work, and mobilizing and protesting against employers and/ or governments, as with general strikes and demonstrations. Which vehicle of influence is used depends on the specific moment, political context and national climate towards unions and workers. The national contexts of trade unionism vary: in some cases, there is a broader orientation towards social dialogue on a wide range of issues between unions, employers and state institutions (e.g., Sweden and Finland); then there are systems where trade unions play a role in bargaining and dealing with management in establishing working conditions and pay rates but with less direct state involvement (e.g., the United Kingdom and the United States); through to systems where the influence of trade unions is limited to specific sectors or some leading companies (e.g., Hungary and Peru); and then on to systems where their influence is severely limited owing to the nature of the economy and/or the attitude of the governing parties and elites towards trade union and worker representation (e.g., Saudi Arabia).

Whatever the context, the concern is that trade unions have been locked in a national context. In addition, these national contexts have been undermined by increasing levels of internationalization of employers and corporate structures, while the international structures of trade unions have been relatively limited in scope. The history of the international labour movement is one of political difference and tensions regardless of the rhetoric of internationalism during the 20th century. It is important for any starting point in a discussion regarding labour internationalism that we exorcise ourselves of any optimistic views of the past based on some vision of a 'golden age' of unity and coherence which disappeared in the face of capitalist-led internationalization since the 1980s (see Hyman 2005a for such a discussion regarding labour unity generally). Wills (1998) points to the role of political differences in the way trade unions have developed internationally around competing agendas and structures. In understanding the role of trade unions internationally – Hyman (2005a) has argued – not only was there a competitive tension between what he calls the 'agitator' and 'bureaucratic' models, with the former preferring an anti-capitalist perspective and the latter a greater dialogue with employers and the state, there was also a third model, the 'labour diplomat' approach. Trade unionism internationally was therefore at times more akin to a diplomatic service internationally than a unified structure, and divided between different political perspectives throughout much of the 20th century.

However, these national anchors and links, along with the more symbolic nature of international action and coordination, have begun to reveal their limitations in a context of greater internationalization during the past 30 or so years as the geographic scale of capitalist production changes, linking transnational movements with ongoing segmentation (Gough 2004). Companies and managers relocate production processes to different jurisdictions, creating tensions between workers in different countries (Lillie 2006); hence, 'to maintain labour's organizational strength in the face of the shifting geography of capital, it would be necessary to constantly revise and renew union organizations and worker solidarities out of fragmented relations between dispersed groups of workers within firms and industries. Thus, as with the organization of work within a factory, the shifting geography of labour is influenced by management's imperatives for profitability and control' (Lillie and Martínez Lucio 2012).

Paralleling this narrative of greater capital and labour immobility, there has been a view that trade unions have had to engage more fully with:

- The production changes and new forms of working associated with a globalized context of new production regimes (see Chapter 7)
- More internationalized forms of production across boundaries
- New forms of social communication and organizing linked to the Internet and related technologies
- The challenges of organizing new groups of workers emerging from global change (see Martínez Lucio 2006)

Engaging with these developments requires greater coordination between different levels of trade union activity as the once 'closed' workplaces become increasingly exposed to international changes. Yet, these developments have generated new pressures on trade unions to respond and created new possibilities and responses. For example, new management techniques such as lean production have created an interest in worker organizations in terms of how workers are engaged with and respond to them (Martínez Lucio and Weston 1994). As management increasingly plays off one group of workers against another, workers and trade unionists may seek to gain more information on the company's international operations and structures. Hence, such management strategies across boundaries may bring tensions and differences, but they also give rise to new circuits of information and networking among trade union representatives across different countries. Within the space of transnational corporations, there are instances of cross-referencing and information sharing. As economic decision making becomes more visibly transnational, trade unionists on the ground and trade unions as organizations have begun to develop new forms of organizing across boundaries, as can be seen in the following case study.

Case study: A multinational and the strategy of whipsawing

Within Europe, a US MNC was seeking to change the manner in which it managed its workforce. There was a greater interest in developing new flexible ways of working and a new form of team working. The strategy pursued by the company had four dimensions in terms of how it attempted to use its greater mobility in international terms:

a. Generating plant consciousness by utilizing national and international divisions and tensions within unions across countries and plants: whipsawing strategies, based on dividing groups of workers across national and local lines
b. The systematic use of investment and disinvestment to reinforce this competition between plants
c. Redefining worker rights and expectations by building a closer link local between management and workers at the national plant levels as they competed with other plants in the company for investment
d. Creating an ideological framework to both condition and legitimize the implementation of change by referencing the pressures of competition and creating a greater sensitivity to business and corporate interests in unions

These four dimensions have been systematically present throughout the plants in question. It can therefore be argued that it is precisely because of the possibility and experiences of failure by management that multidimensional approaches to change are being adopted. However, certain developments can potentially undermine this type of management strategy and can indirectly provide opportunities for labour. Given the nature of these management strategies adopted by MNCs, with attempted convergence along the lines suggested earlier, new sites of labour mobilization can develop. With respect to the 'politics of investment', this has generated in the four dimensions a demand from labour for key company information. While they have been bombarded with a flow of specific technical company information, this has not satisfied the more general needs regarding the future strategy of the company. The strategy pursued by this company has fuelled this demand for information (a common outcome – Weston 1992), which in turn has given rise to a loose organizational network between certain unions (and their plant-based representatives) in different plants who have been exchanging information on production issues and investment. Furthermore, the strategy of management in 'building' and redefining industrial relations rights could open the door for alternative labour intervention as worker expectations may rise, especially with regards to worker participation at various levels of the company decision-making process. For example, attempts to involve worker representatives in matters relating to absenteeism and its possible diminution allowed labour in the German plant to broaden the agenda of such quality-led change to account for the health and safety aspects of this issue. In the case of the Spanish plant, rights and traditions relating to working time in the country led to conflict and even some concessions from management over weekend working. The management attempt to change working practices, therefore, continued to confront the reality of externally and historically constructed legacies of individual worker rights. In the British plant, agreed working practices are continually subjected to interpretation by union representatives in their attempt to condition developments. This has been facilitated by the unions' ability to highlight matters of autonomous worker representation in their relationships and negotiations with management.

These kinds of developments in the form of the demand for information, loose institutional networking and the increasing interest in worker rights are in many ways prompted and underpinned by the common elements within work organization which HRM-type strategies have developed. By developing standard techniques regarding production, time measurement, quality and a common ideological programme, a foundation for organized labour may be unknowingly constructed by management. This could facilitate an alternative convergence of interests and activities which may contradict or critically condition the eventual outcomes sought by management as workers and unions respond to issues such as performance management and challenge the related data.

Questions

1. What are the different methods by which MNCs attempt to change the working practices in their different subsidiaries?
2. What are the advantages and disadvantages of each approach?
3. What are the ways in which unions may be responding to this?

Source: Martínez Lucio and Weston (1994)

Transnational trade unionism as an emergent force and new organizational space

Such developments as outlined in the above case illustrate how new forms of international coordination between trade unionists based in different countries may emerge as a consequence of the nature of whipsawing and the use of investment strategies. There are a growing series of informal links and channels of communication between workplace representatives in the different national contexts of MNCs. There is a belief that there has been a series of political, social and environmental changes in the political ecology of industrial relations that have led to a 'new labour internationalism'. There are various features propelling a new labour internationalism which appears to be closer to social movements with their broader social and employment agendas, relatively less concerned with bureaucratic culture and more open in its geographical focus and concerns (Munck 2004). As Haworth summarized in discussing Levinson (1972): 'His argument was straightforward. Capital was internationalising and, consequently, the power of management was increasing. The trade union response had to match the scope and level of MNC power' (Haworth 2005: 189).

The impact of the internationalization of capital on trade unions has led to a need for new organizational approaches (Martínez Lucio and Weston 1995) and an increasing awareness of the *politics of production* based on the impact of global capitalist strategies within the labour process (Stewart 2006). As Herod (2009) points out, globalization brings a new set of links, spatial maps and connections. This has been sustained by social and technological developments. In terms of social developments, the emergence of social movements based around international labour and production issues challenged the form and content of international labour structures. Increasingly, there has been greater mobilization around broader issues of rights in employment (Hyman 2004), the exploitation of child labour by multinationals (Lavalette and Cunningham 2004), the desire for codes of conduct (O'Brien 2002) and the pressures emerging from what is labelled a renewed southern labour movement (Lambert 2002). For Wills (2000, 2001), this means finding new levels of trade union action both locally and globally: unions have to link the local into new global networks (Herod 2001).

In effect, there are new trade union logics of organization in the form of a 'network' trade union that is not based solely on traditional forms of bargaining logic and traditional forms of hierarchy – what Moody (1997) has been calling 'regulation from below' – where workers and activists organize at a grassroots level through networks and influence the agenda of MNCs and capital in general: 'Networking relates to communication rather than institutions ... This movement concerns itself with increasing access to the media, the right to communicate, diversity of expression, security and privacy' (Waterman 2001: 23–24). These new forms of organization are widely conceived of as networks, which are better placed to handle and react to environmental uncertainty than traditional, hierarchical organizations because in the case of unions, greater networking across boundaries is spurred on by technological developments of the Internet, which have provided greater impetus towards more flexible and networked forms of communication and exchange, and the possibility of greater liberty and creativity (Hyman 1999). The organizational impact of the Internet in opening up spaces for trade unionists to campaign on issues and to challenge corporate and even their union bureaucracies is increasingly apparent (Greene et al. 2003; Hogan 2006) – see Martínez Lucio (2010) for a discussion of the new internationalism in labour. These developments are sometimes undermined by problems of sustainability in terms of lacking organizational skills and resources – and inconsistent leadership – although some would argue that they represent a new alternative to the more formal structures of labour (Waterman 2001).

The more formal and organizational level of international trade unionism has witnessed the development of structures of representation, which have also engaged with the impact of globalization and capital mobility. Such trade union bodies develop strategies and programmes to support workers in various parts of the world and in transnational corporations who are deemed to be in need of greater regulation and rights.

The International Trade Union Confederation (ITUC), formed in 2006 from an amalgamation of previous world confederations of trade unions that had been initially politically opposed to one another, is an organization which brings together most national confederations of trade unions. The ITUC effectively seeks to act as the international voice for the working class by driving a set of campaigns on eliminating child labour, lobbying for the establishment of a charter for the rights of unprotected groups such as domestic workers and pushing for the right to 'decent work'. These campaigns focus on a range of international bodies with the aim of developing a coherent framework for regulations at the national and transnational level (see Chapter 12). They attempt to create a global and high-profile political dynamic that allows the issues to be raised and to be acted on – and this has been a focus of the work of this level of trade unionism in the context of globalization for some time (Gumbrell-McCormick 2000).

Such international trade union campaigns can often become disconnected and do not always influence the national contexts they are directed at owing to resistance among national governments or employers. These campaigns are also an attempt to create common approaches among trade unions that come from very different traditions in political and ideological terms, and whose influence in their own national contexts may vary tremendously. One can see the emergence of a transnational trade union elite through the ITUC or Global Union Federations for different sectors that create a series of common positions and policies, but in the process can become disconnected from the local realities of workers and their experiences by focusing on influencing international employers or regulatory bodies which are complex and slow in decision making.

At the continental level, there are cross-national trade union organizations such as the European Trade Union Confederation (ETUC), which brings together the vast majority of national unions across Europe. The organization views itself as the spokesperson for the European working class in relation to the European Union (EU) and its various governmental bodies (Hyman 2005b). The difference in the case of the ETUC is that it has a transnational regulatory and governmental body in the form of the EU it can lobby, negotiate and be represented on. Yet again – though – the need to deal with different views creates dilemmas 'because to most unions, the national level remains their basic terrain. Therefore, it is of crucial importance for any union's policy-making in the EU to map out exactly consensual perceptions and reform options among their homologues within the EU member states' (Busemeyer et al. 2007).

However, organizations such as the ITUC and the ETUC play a supporting role through training workers and their coordination and network initiatives in a range of transnational organizations (Pulignano 2009). They attempt to seek resources and expert knowledge – and economic information – that may assist international coordination efforts by trade unions in relation to specific firms such as General Motors, Axa and others.

The external regulatory space: transnational trade unions and the example of the European Works Council[1]

The development of EWCs represents an interesting example of how worker representatives may interact with each other across borders and consult or even negotiate within transnational corporations at higher decision-making levels. The adoption on 22 September 1994 of Council Directive 94/45/EC (hereinafter, the Directive) 'on the establishment of a EWC or a procedure in Community-scale undertakings or Community-scale groups of undertakings for the purposes of informing and consulting employees' was the first transnational legislation intended to promote employee participation in MNCs. The Directive set in train a process that has resulted in the establishment of more than 1200 EWCs and led to debates on the purpose and utility of EWCs. Although the Directive made no mention of trade unions and there was no explicit expectation that EWC representatives should be trade unionists, the Directive necessitated that trade union organizations act transnationally on four counts.[2] First, by definition, EWCs are transnational institutions that bring together representatives from the different countries within which MNCs operate. If trade union organizations are to provide training to EWC representatives and to support and coordinate EWC activities, it is necessary for them to act beyond national boundaries. Second, the terms of the Directive were welcomed by trade unionists but were viewed as being limited, with the consequence that transnational campaigning was required to lobby for a revision of the Directive, as was allowed by Article 15. Third, several aspects of the

Directive were not specified, in the expectation that they would be settled thorough negotiations between the parties within MNCs. As such, these aspects of the Directive were contested between employee representatives and managers, and thus promoted transnational trade union action towards reaching the most favourable outcome for the employees. Fourth, the activities of EWCs moved beyond the European and the information and consultation briefs specified in the Directive. In particular, some EWCs were transformed into WWCs, and others adopted a negotiation as well as an information and consultation role. In these circumstances, transnational trade union activity was thus extended beyond Europe, and the adoption of a negotiation function necessitated transnational activity to maintain trade union influence over the terms and conditions of employment.

As a result of these developments, the character and process of trade union internationalization was influenced as trade union organizations responded to the establishment of a new transnational industrial relations institution. This influence is traced in three stages. The first stage identifies the competing positions in the debate on the purposes of the Directive. The second stage examines the quality of information and consultation at EWCs and thus assesses how trade union organizations have been able to act transnationally to influence information and consultation practices. The third stage traces the development of European Framework Agreements (EFAs) and the activities of trade union organizations to exert influence on the process of their negotiation. Each of these stages identifies different aspects of trade union internationalization and illustrates how the establishment of EWCs promoted such internationalization.

Debate on the purpose of the Directive

Immediately following the adoption of the Directive, academic debate centred on the objectives identified for the Directive by the Commission and whether the content of the Directive was sufficiently robust to achieve them. In addition to the immediate purpose of creating transnational information and consultation rights, there were three interrelated objectives, each of which required transnational trade union activity. First, the Commission wished to promote greater transparency in the affairs of MNCs, particularly after the adoption of the Single European Act 1986, which stimulated a sharp rise in the rate of company restructuring. Second, the Commission took the view that managers of MNCs could circumvent nationally defined information and consultation rights. A transnational right to information and consultation would reduce the likelihood of such practices. Third, the Commission wished to promote institution building within industrial relations. By downplaying a statutory model in favour of negotiated arrangements in the Directive, transnational negotiations between employee representatives and central management were fostered, thus supplementing institution building with a transnational procedural dimension.

Adoption of the Directive stimulated a debate as to whether its provisions were sufficiently robust to enable the achievement of the objectives identified by the Commission. Critics of the Directive argued that it was 'neo-voluntarist' (Falkner 1996, 1998), was likely to lead to the erosion of national industrial relations standards (Streeck 1997) and might reinforce company-egoist tendencies, as there were insufficient links between EWCs and national institutions of information and consultation in the Directive (Keller 1995; Streeck 1998).[3] Those taking a more positive view of the Directive emphasized the impact of the intensification of cross-border cooperation on the scope of political action (Platzer 1998), and the possibility of extending the terms of the Directive, or the activities associated with it, by means of legal enactment or negotiations between the social partners at either inter-professional level or at EWCs established within MNCs (Bushak 1999; Carley 2001; Dølvik 1997).

Three interlinked issues underpinned the competing positions in this debate. First, critics of the Directive questioned whether the appropriate intensity of communication could be achieved, particularly as most early agreements and the terms attached to the Directive specified only one plenary meeting per year (Ramsay 1997). As a consequence of this infrequency of contact, critics argued that EWCs would be dominated by representatives from the same country of origin as the MNC (Streeck 1997). Proponents of the Directive acknowledged the challenges that arise from differences between representatives in terms of culture, language and industrial relations traditions, but envisaged that greater networking and dialogue between representatives of different countries would create a new dynamic through which transnational solidarity strategies might develop (Weston and Martínez Lucio 1998; Whittall 2000). A second area of contention focused on representation and articulation. Critics of the Directive argued that EWC representatives would be isolated from national structures of representation and that trade unions had neither the resources nor the political will to shift material and political resources to an appropriate level to co-ordinate and strategically link European with national structures and practices (Keller 1995; Schroeder and Weinert 2004). Those advocating the countervailing view envisaged trade union training and support as sufficient to mitigate the impact of isolation. For critics of the Directive, trade unions were central to EWC development, but were viewed as unlikely to meet the challenge, whereas proponents of the Directive envisaged trade union reform as being able to meet new demands. Third, critics of the Directive argued that its terms would generate a 'transnational micro-corporatism' as the isolation of the EWC from national collective bargaining arrangements might enhance company perspectives to the exclusion of a wider bargaining perspective (Schulten 1996; Martin and Ross 1998). In response, advocates of the Directive pointed to the role of the European trade Union Federations (ETUFs) in coordinating EWC activities and the linkages that could be developed between EWC activities and other elements of the European social dimension as encouraging developments towards an integrated European industrial relations system (Dølvik 2000; Marginson and Sisson 2004: 216–245).

The debate on the purpose of EWCs illustrated how the establishment of a new transnational industrial relations institution created circumstances that required more intense transnational activity by trade unionists if they were to exert influence on the development of the institution.

The quality of information and consultation

The argument now turns to the operational effect of the policies of trade union organizations. Survey data underpin the analysis.[4] The formal purpose of EWCs is the provision of information and consultation. The absence of a definition of information; the lack of guidelines regarding the form in which information should be provided; the lack of specificity regarding the timeliness of information and consultation; and the imprecise definition of consultation in the Directive ensure that the quality of information and consultation at EWCs is contested. Table 13.1 illustrates the quality of information and consultation as assessed by EWC representatives. The subject matter of information and consultation is divided into two parts. The issues in the top section of Table 13.1 are drawn from those specified in Paragraph 2 of the Subsidiary Requirements attached to the Directive. These items thus reflect the views of the Commission on the basic subject matter that should comprise a transnational information and consultation agenda. It is also important to examine whether EWC representatives have been able to extend agendas beyond the items found in the Subsidiary Requirements: that is, to introduce a trade union agenda to transnational practice. To test this proposition, the lower section of Table 13.1 includes some traditional trade union issues and items on which EU directives have been adopted, in part, as a result of trade union campaigns. These items are referred to as the extension agenda. The first four columns of Table 13.1 focus on the quality of information and consultation. Following earlier research, 'useful information' was defined in the questionnaire as appearing in an appropriate form, usually in writing; and at an appropriate time, allowing assessment of the information and the production of an appropriate response (Waddington 2003). The fifth column of Table 13.1 titled 'Disparity index' is calculated by subtracting the proportion of EWC representatives who were in receipt of 'useful information and consultation' from the proportion of EWC founding agreements current at the time of the survey that include the issue as an agenda item. As there are no data on the number of agreements that refer to parental leave, it was not possible to calculate a disparity index score for this item.

Most EWC representatives rate the information and, in particular, consultation, to be of modest quality For example, about one-third of EWC representatives report 'employment forecasts' and 'transfers/relocation' as items that had not appeared on the agenda at their EWCs. On average, respondents to the survey had attended between four and five plenary EWC meetings, suggesting that the

Table 13.1   Was the quality of the information and consultation adequate?

All EWC representatives

Issue	Not raised %	Raised, but useless information %	Useful information, but no consultation %	Useful information and consultation %	Disparity index
Economic and financial situation of the company	6.6	5.4	60.5	27.5	65.5
Corporate strategy and investment	9.7	5.1	57.3	27.9	52.1
Changes to working methods	44.5	11.3	29.1	15.1	58.9
Closures or cutbacks	20.6	7.8	44.4	27.2	54.8
Mergers, take-overs or acquisitions	19.6	7.0	55.4	18.1	69.9
New technology policy/ technological change	42.7	9.9	37.4	10.0	32.0
Reorganization of production	48.5	7.5	33.2	10.8	63.2
Transfers/relocation	35.1	6.5	40.9	17.5	65.5
Employment forecasts	33.3	10.1	42.7	13.9	77.1
Research and development policy	45.6	10.5	35.6	8.3	26.7
Vocational training	49.9	9.4	25.0	15.7	19.3
Equal opportunities	54.3	11.2	22.2	12.3	5.7
Health and safety	36.9	8.3	27.6	27.2	11.8
Environmental protection	43.4	9.6	28.2	18.9	19.1
Trade union rights	52.6	9.4	19.7	18.4	-3.4
Working time	59.0	8.9	21.1	10.9	-3.9
Profit sharing/ financial participation	66.7	6.8	18.1	8.4	-0.4
Parental leave	81.6	5.4	8.7	4.3	/

(N = 941)

non-appearance of these items is a medium-term phenomenon. EWC representatives who had served as national representatives for more than ten years, on average, before taking on European responsibilities and were experienced in negotiating, interpreting and implementing agreements appeared unable to secure the terms of EWC founding agreements in practice (Waddington 2011).

In the light of the limited coverage in EWC agreements of items from the extension agenda, it is no surprise that the 'not raised' results of these items tend to be high. For the same reason, the lower disparity index scores are not unexpected. It is noteworthy that EWC representatives have been successful in 'pushing through' several items from the extension agenda. More than 27% of EWC representatives, for example, report 'useful information and consultation' on 'health and safety'. Similarly, 'environmental protection' and 'vocational training' are items from the extension agenda on which EWC representatives report 'useful information and consultation' at comparable rates to several of the agenda items based on the Subsidiary Requirements. The disparity index scores are negative for three items from the extension agenda, 'working time', 'trade union rights' and profit sharing/financial participation', indicating that 'useful information and consultation' on these items occurs more frequently than they appear in EWC agreements and suggesting that these items have been pursued with particular vigour at a small number of EWCs (Waddington 2011).

In summary, EWCs are essentially institutions of information exchange rather than consultation, and the improving content of EWC agreements secured through the procedural centralization achieved by the ETUFs is not matched by the quality of information and consultation in practice. More positively, some representatives have been able to extend the agenda at EWCs beyond that mentioned in the Subsidiary Requirements to cover items of importance to a trade union agenda.

The limitations observed in the quality of information and consultation raise questions regarding the efficacy of the policies formulated through the ETUFs. Three of these policies are assessed here: maintaining high levels of unionization among EWC representatives, ensuring the presence of an EWC coordinator and encouraging the appointment of experts by the employees' side of the EWC.[5] Three points are apparent regarding the policies of the ETUFs. First, higher rates of unionization, the presence of an EWC coordinator and the appointment of an expert by the employees' side of the EWC are all associated with a higher quality of information and consultation. The policies of the ETUFs thus have a positive impact on the practices of EWCs. Second, it has been possible to limit the number of non-trade-unionists elected or appointed as EWC representatives. There is some variation by sector in unionization rates, however, with higher rates of unionization found in manufacturing and lower rates concentrated in areas of private sector services such as commerce, tourism and catering. This variation is consistent with overall patterns of unionization. Third, EWC coordinators are reported as present by fewer than 30% and experts by only 57.0% of EWC representatives. The policy of appointing EWC coordinators and experts results in a higher quality of information and consultation, but the implementation of the policies is partial.

Moving beyond the formal information and consultation agenda

Figure 13.1 shows the number and the content of EFAs concluded through EWCs. EWCs based in France, Germany, the Nordic countries and US-owned MNCs with regional management structures account for the vast majority of the agreements that have been concluded. Similarly, EFAs are concentrated in the engineering, energy and water supply, building, food and finance sectors. The tendency within EFAs is to outline the general principles that might be applied to the matter in question and to identify the parties charged with the responsibility of implementing and/or monitoring the agreed general principles. This can be illustrated by reference to restructuring, the issue dealt with most frequently by the texts of EFAs. Most texts that address restructuring outline the procedures for handling restructuring in terms of information, consultation and negotiation; and guarantees are laid down for adversely affected employees, which might refer to job security, maintenance of terms and conditions of employment, no compulsory redundancies and retraining. Furthermore, several texts on restructuring specify the role that the EWC or the select committee will undertake within these broadly defined procedures, thereby consolidating the position of the EWC.

Given the reluctance of managers to comply with the information and consultation requirements on restructuring, particularly regarding timeliness (Waddington 2011: 103), it is no surprise that restructuring is the issue that most frequently appears in EFAs. In practice, the negotiation function is used to strengthen the position of the EWC and to overcome some of the weaknesses of the Directive. Most of the remaining issues listed in Figure 13.1 reflect the broad range of industrial relations issues pertinent to MNCs. The key issue here, however, is that several EWCs have adopted a negotiation function, thereby moving beyond the formal information and consultatiion role, and have extended the agenda for the EWC beyond that mentioned in the Subsidiary Requirements. Furthermore, in engaging with ETUFs in the negotiation of transnational agreements, some EWCs have become more embedded in transnational union activities.

Analyses of EFAs are careful to point out that such agreements are not collective agreements in the sense of setting terms and conditions of employment, but are akin to rights agreements. Transnational negotiations conducted by EWC representatives at the company level, however, raise two strategic issues for labour. First, the substantive content included in the majority of EFAs does not impinge on what might be termed a traditional collective bargaining agenda, but issues such as bonus payments, financial participation and issues around stress in some of the EFAs on health and safety are not far removed from a collective bargaining agenda. In this context, the strategic issue for unions is to maintain the separation between collective agreements and EFAs. Second, transnational negotiations within MNCs are essential if labour is to influence managerial decision making within such companies, and EWCs are transnational,

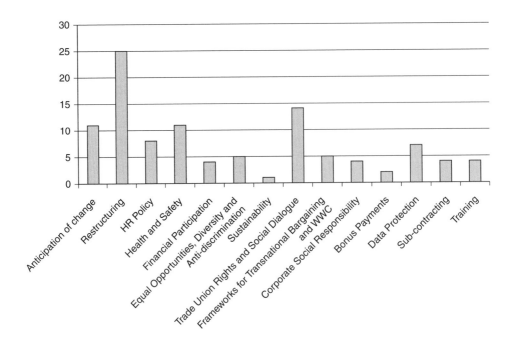

Figure 13.1 The content of European Framework Agreements.

representative institutions through which such negotiations may be conducted: yet, if EWCs were to conduct such negotiations independently of trade union organizations, the latter could be marginalized within the MNC. This concern is expressed most strongly in the Nordic countries, where some go as far as to define the negotiations function undertaken by EWCs as a 'threat to national industrial relations systems' (Dahlkvist 2007). In the light of this concern, it is no surprise that Nordic trade unions were influential in promoting the resolution adopted in December 2005 by the ETUC that called for transnational agreements to be signed only by trade union organizations (ETUC 2005: 199–122). While this call was rejected by UNICE (de Buck 2006), it indicates the concern within trade union organizations about the relationship between EWCs, negotiations and trade unions. The approaches taken by the European Metalworkers' Federation (EMF) are examined here to illustrate the issues.

Within the EMF, the EWC Task Force (from 2003, the Company Policy Committee) was assigned the responsibility of coordinating the conduct of EWC activities. This responsibility was expanded in the regulation of the negotiation function of EWCs, the details of which were influenced by the experience of handling successive restructuring events at General Motors Europe. In particular, the EMF Executive Committee agreed a 'policy approach towards socially responsible company restructuring' (EMF 2005), which was later supplemented by procedural regulations for all negotiations conducted at the MNC level (EMF 2006). The agreed approach places the onus on the EWC coordinator to initiate procedures within the EMF that effectively ensure articulation between EWCs and trade union organizations, while subordinating the former to the latter. Among the procedures to be followed are:

- The EWC select committee, EMF coordinator and representatives of the trade unions involved in the company should agree to commence negotiations, by means of a vote if the decision is contested. The EMF coordinator will inform the EMF Secretariat before negotiations commence, and the EMF Secretariat will keep the Executive Committee informed throughout the negotiation process.
- The mandate for negotiations is agreed on a case-by-case basis, but the negotiating team will comprise at least one representative of the EMF, and/or the EMF coordinator and/or a representative of the trade unions involved, one of whom will lead the negotiations.
- The negotiating team will present the draft agreement for approval to the trade unions involved in the company, a two-thirds majority in each country being required to ratify the agreement.
- The General Secretary, Deputy General Secretary or another person mandated by them shall sign the agreement on behalf of the trade unions involved in the MNC (EMF 2006).

By these means, the EMF wrested elements of control of the negotiation process within a company away from EWCs. In the specific case of agreements on, or in responding to, restructuring, the EMF recommends that preferably no negotiations will start, and certainly none will be concluded before a European trade union coordination group is established, comprising EWC representatives, members of the EMF Secretariat, the EMF coordinator, and one representative from each union with members in the MNC. In restructuring cases, therefore, the EMF approach is similar to that of UNI-Europa, where Trade Union Alliances are established. The impact of these measures on the pattern of signatories to texts is marked. Before 2005, eight of eleven texts were signed on behalf of EWCs. The three other texts were signed by both the EMF and the EWC at General Motors Europe. Experience of this approach underpinned the decisions taken by the EMF Executive Committee. In contrast, after the procedures were agreed, EWCs signed only two texts (Daimler Chrysler and EADS in 2006), both of which were signed under the mandate of the General Secretary of the EMF. All other texts were signed by the EMF. EWCs were thus constrained as the EMF assumed a more prominent position. The point remains, however, that the EMF attempted to regulate the negotiating function of EWCs through the introduction of the procedure.

Conclusion

This chapter has outlined the impact of globalization on trade unions as established organizations. The national context has always been the space within which trade unions have acted, given their tendency to mirror or react to the nation state and employers, and their pattern of historical development. As national systems have evolved and become increasingly more internationalized, trade unions find that they are confronted with a new set of challenges. These challenges come in the form of more mobile and internationalized corporations whose loyalty and links to national systems of regulation and politics have changed. Given the manner in which the defence of jobs and the desire to develop or sustain jobs within the national economic sphere has been a central feature of trade union organization, the development of transnational unions links and activities has been constrained on occasion.

However, over time the ongoing internationalization of production and capitalist organization, which has been paralleled by the development of new forms of communication and increasing international travel, has led to a greater level of international coordination and interaction among trade unionists. In some cases, as in the EU, such a development has been sustained by public funding as a way of creating a political counterbalance to the internationalization of companies. In this context, the development of participative forms such as EWCs within transnational corporations in the EU has created a new level of dialogue and influence for unions and workers. How effective or cohesive this has been is a matter of much conjecture, but the reality is that EWCs and WWCs are an intriguing and current feature of the new international employment relations landscape.

Paralleled by new forms of informal communication and coordination among worker representatives, and new international trade union structures, one could argue that the space of international employment relations is becoming a complex and increasingly organized space. It appears to be an arena with different actors and organizations that are more systematically beginning to question and engage in the politics of international production and investment.

Reflective questions

1. How are trade unions internationalizing?
2. Why are they becoming more concerned with their international strategies?
3. What may be the consequences of this for the management of work within MNCs?
4. What role do international forums play within MNCS where workers and their representatives have representatives such as EWCs?
5. What are the likely long-term impacts of EWCs and how may they develop as institutions?
6. What are the prospects for international trade union and worker representation and why?

Recommended reading

- Hyman, R. (2005) 'Trade unions and the politics of the European social model'. *Economic and Industrial Democracy*, 26(1): 9–40.
- Pulignano, V. (2009) 'International cooperation, transnational restructuring and virtual networking in Europe'. *European Journal of Industrial Relations*, 15(2): 187–205.
- Schroeder, W. and Weinert, R. (2004) 'Designing institutions in European industrial relations: A strong commission versus weak trade unions'. *European Journal of Industrial Relations*, 10(2): 199–217.
- Strange, G. (2007) 'From "embedded liberalism" to "negotiated openness": British trade unions and the European Union from the 1960s: A world-order approach'. *Capital and Class*, Special Issue: The Left and Europe, No. 93.
- Waddington, J. (2003) 'What do representatives think of the practices of European works councils? Views from six countries'. *European Journal of Industrial Relations*, 9(3): 303–325.

Notes

1. Much of the material for this section of the chapter is drawn from Waddington (2011). For a more detailed assessment of the arguments presented here, please refer to the original source.
2. The term 'trade union organizations' is used here to refer collectively to national trade unions or federations, national confederations, European Trade Union Federations and the European Trade Union Confederation.
3. Company-egoist tendencies refer to the preferences of some employee representatives who consider only the company within which they are employed, rather than the company in a wider context embracing industry, union policy and national industrial policy.
4. The survey comprised a postal questionnaire distributed by the ETUFs in the native language of the respondent and then returned to the author. A total of 3,705 questionnaires were distributed, of which 941 were returned (response rate: 25.4%). The EWC representatives who returned the questionnaire constituted about 1 in 19 of the entire population. The survey was conducted between late 2005 and 2008. The responses thus report the situation under Directive 94/45/EC rather than the recast Directive 2009/38/EC.
5. It is acknowledged that some EWC representatives may not be able to distinguish between an EWC coordinator and an expert, thereby introducing a degree of ambiguity into the survey results. As is discussed below, the efficacy of these measures and the coverage of the policies is not compromised by this ambiguity. The data reported in this paragraph are drawn from Waddington (2011) where the details about their compilation are available.

References

Busemeyer, M. R., Kellermann, C., Petring, A. and Stuchlík, A. (2007) *Overstretching Solidarity? Trade Unions' National Perspectives on the European Economic and Social Model*. International Policy Analysis Series, Friedrich Ebert Stiftung.

Bushak, W. (1999) 'Five years after: A look forward to the revision of the EWC directive'. *Transfer*, 5(3): 384–392.

Business Dictionary (2012) 'Trade Union'. http://www.businessdictionary.com/ definition/trade-union.html#ixzz1uHYaV4x0 accessed May 5th, 2012.

Carley, M. (2001) *Joint Texts Negotiated by European Works Councils*. Dublin: European Foundation for the Improvement of Living and Working Conditions.

Dahlkvist, A. (2007) 'European information and consultation as a threat to national industrial relations systems: The Swedish model of representation and the establishment of European Works Councils'. Paper presented at the *8th European Regional Congress of the International Industrial Relations Association*, Manchester, 3–6 September.

de Buck, P. (2006) *EWCs and Restructuring: The UNICE View*. European Works Council Bulletin, Issue 61, January/February, pp. 6–7.

Dølvik, J.-E. (1997) EWCS and the implications for Europeanisation of collective bargaining'. In J-E. Dølvik (ed.), *Redrawing Boundaries of Solidarity? ETUC, Social Dialogue and the Europeanisation of Trade Unions in the 1990s*. Oslo: Arena and FAFO, pp. 381–391.

Dølvik, J. E. (2000) 'Building regional structures: ETUC and the European Industry Federations'. *Transfer*, 6(1): 58–77.

EMF (2005) *EMF Policy Approach towards Socially Responsible Company Restructuring*. EMF Executive Committee, Luxembourg, 7 and 8 June. Brussels: European Metalworkers' Federation.

EMF (2006) *Internal EMF Procedure for Negotiations at Multinational Company Level*. EMF Executive Committee, Luxembourg, 13 and 14 June. Brussels: European Metalworkers' Federation.

ETUC (2005) *The Coordination of Collective Bargaining 2006*. Resolution adopted by the ETUC Executive Committee, Brussels, 5–6 December 2005, reproduced in ETUC (2006).

Falkner, G. (1996) 'European Works Councils and the Maastricht social agreement: Towards a new policy style'. *Journal of European Public Policy*, 3: 192–208.

Falkner, G. (1998) *EU Social Policy in the 1990s*. London: Routledge.

Gough, J. (2004) 'Changing scale as changing class relations: Variety and contradiction in the politics of scale'. *Political Geography*, 23: 185–211.

Greene, A. M., Hogan, J. and Greco, M. (2003) 'E-collectivism and distributed discourse: New opportunities for trade union democracy'. *Industrial Relations Journal* 34(4): 282–290.

Gumbrell-McCormick, R. (2000) 'Globalisation and the dilemmas of international trade unionism'. *Transfer*, 1: 29–42.

Haworth, N. (2005) 'You've got to admit it: It's getting better…: Organised labour and internationalization'. In B. Harley, J. Hyman and P. Thompson (eds.), *Participation and Democracy at Work*. London: Palgrave.

Herod, A. (2009) *Geographies of Globalisation*. Oxford: Blackwell.

Hogan, J. (2006) The Internet and the Politics and Processes of Trade Unionism. PhD Thesis. Leeds: University of Leeds.

Hyman, R. (1999) 'Imagined solidarities: Can trade union resist globalisation?' In P. Leisink (ed.), *Globalisation and Labour Relations*. Cheltenham: Edward Elgar.

Hyman, R. (2004) 'An emerging agenda for trade unions?' In R. Munck (ed.), *Labour and Globalisation: Results and Prospects*. Liverpool: Liverpool University Press, 2004, pp. 19–33.

Hyman, R. (2005a) 'Shifting dynamics in international trade unionism: Agitation, organisation, bureaucracy, diplomacy'. *Labor History*, 46(2): 137–154.

Hyman, R. (2005b) 'Trade unions and the politics of the European Social Model'. *Economic and Industrial Democracy*, 26(1): 9–40.

Keller, B. (1995) 'European integration, workers' participation and collective bargaining: A Euro-pessimistic view'. In B. Unger and F. van Waarden (eds.), *Convergence or Divergence? Internationalization and Economic Policy Responses*. Aldershot: Avebury, pp. 252–278.

Lavalette, M. and Cunningham, S. (2004) 'Globalisation and child labour: Liberation or anti-capitalism'. In R. Munck (ed.), *Labour and Globalisation*. Liverpool: Liverpool University Press.

Levinson, C. (1972) *International Trade Unionism*. London: Allen & Unwin.

Lillie, N. (2006) 'Globalization and class analysis: Prospects for labour movement influence in global governance'. *Industrielle Beziehungen*, 13(3): 223–237.

Lillie, N. and Martínez Lucio, M. (2012) 'Rollerball and the spirit of capitalism: Competitive dynamics within the global context, the challenge to labour transnationalism, and the emergence of ironic outcomes'. *Critical Perspectives on International Business*, 8(1), 74–92.

Marginson, P. and Sisson, K. (2004) *European Integration and Industrial Relations: Multi-Level Governance in the Making*. Basingstoke: Palgrave, MacMillan.

Martin, A. and Ross, G. (1998) 'European integration and the Europeanization of labor'. In E. Gabaglio and R. Hoffmann (eds.), *The ETUC in the Mirror of Industrial Relations Research*. Brussels: European Trade Union Institute, pp. 247–293.

Martínez Lucio, M. (2006) 'Trade unionism and the realities of change: reframing the language of change. In L.E. Alonso and M. Martínez Lucio (eds.), *Employment Relations in a Changing Society: Assessing the Post-Fordist Paradigm*. Basingstoke: Palgrave Macmillan, pp. 200–214.

Martínez Lucio, M. (2010) 'Dimensions of internationalism and the politics of the labour movement: Understanding the political and organisational aspects of labour networking and co-ordination'. *Employee Relations*, 32(6): 538–556.

Martínez Lucio, M. and Weston, S. (1994) 'New management practices in a multinational corporation: The restructuring of worker representation and rights?'. *Industrial Relations Journal*, June: 110–121.

Munck, R. (2004) 'Globalisation and labour transnationalism'. In R. Munck (ed.), *Labour and Globalisation*. Liverpool: Liverpool University Press.

O'Brien, R. (2002) 'The varied paths to minimum labour standards' south'. In J. Harrod and R. O'Brien (eds.), *Global Unions?* London: Routledge, pp. 221–234.

Platzer, H.-W. (1998) 'Industrial relations and European integration – patterns, dynamics and limits of transnationalization'. In W. Lecher and H-W. Platzer (eds.), *European Union – European Industrial Relations?* London: Routledge, pp. 81–117.

Pulignano, V. (2009) 'International cooperation, transnational restructuring and virtual networking in Europe'. *European Journal of Industrial Relations*, 15(2): 187–205.

Ramsay, H. (1997) 'Fool's gold? European works councils and workplace democracy'. *Industrial Relations Journal*, 28(4): 314–322.

Schroeder, W. and Weinert, R. (2004) 'Designing institutions in European industrial relations: A strong commission versus weak trade unions'. *European Journal of Industrial Relations*, 10(2): 199–217.

Schulten, T. (1996) 'European works councils: Prospects for a new system of European industrial relations.' *European Journal of Industrial Relations*, 2(3): 303–324.

Stewart, P. (2006) 'Individualism and collectivism in the sociology of the collective worker'. In L. E. Alonso and M. Martínez Lucio (eds.), *Employment Relations in a Changing Economy*. London: Palgrave.

Strange, G. (2007) 'From "embedded liberalism" to "negotiated openness": British trade unions and the European Union from the 1960s: A world-order approach'. *Capital and Class*, Special Issue: The Left and Europe, No. 93.

Streeck, W. (1997) 'Neither European nor works councils: A reply to Paul Knutsen'. *Industrial and Economic Democracy*, 18(2): 325–337.

Streeck, W. (1998) 'The internationalization of industrial relations in Europe: Prospects and problems'. *Politics and Society*, 26(4): 429–459.

Waddington, J. (2003) 'What do representatives think of the practices of European works councils? Views from six countries'. *European Journal of Industrial Relations*, 9(3): 303–325.

Waddington, J. (2011) *European Works Councils: A Transnational Industrial Relations Institution in the Making*. London: Routledge.

Waterman, P. (2001) Trade union internationalism in the age of Seattle. In P. Waterman and J. Wills (eds.), *Place, Space and the New Labour Internationalisms*. Oxford: Blackwell, pp. 8–32.

Weston, S. (1992) Trade Unions and Financial Information: A Review and Bibliography. Oxford University Discussion Paper.

Weston, S. and Martínez Lucio, M. (1998) 'In and beyond European works councils'. *Employee Relations*, 20(6): 551–564.

Whittall, M. (2000) 'The BMW European works council: A case for European industrial relations optimism?'. *European Journal of Industrial Relations*, 6(1): 61–83.

Wills, J. (1998) 'Taking on the CosmoCorps? Experiments in transnational labor organization'. *Economic Geography*, 74(2): 111–130.

Wills, J. (2001) 'Uneven geographies of capital and labour: The lessons of European works councils'. In P. Waterman and J. Wills (eds.), *Place, Space, and the New Labour Internationalisms*. Oxford: Blackwell.

14 Media, new union strategies and non-government organizations as global players: the struggle over representation and work

Steve Walker

Learning objectives

- To understand the role of different forms of media in relation to global employment issues
- To study the ways non-government organizations and trade unions have used the Internet to engage with multinational corporations and broaden the debate on their roles
- To appreciate the debates and engagements on questions of communication in relation to global employment issues

Introduction

The last quarter of a century has seen the rise of what Manuel Castells famously called the 'network society', in which the production of wealth has moved beyond the earlier industrial mode of capitalist production to what he terms an 'informational mode', represented by widespread changes in the nature and geographic distribution of work. These changes have affected not just corporations and governments, but also civil society; transnational networks of social movements, non-governmental organizations (NGOs) and trade unions have emerged, both responding to and shaping the contemporary world (Castells 2001). Of particular interest here is that actors within and beyond the traditional labour movement have used diverse networked technologies and organizational forms in responding to the changing structure of corporate organization and both governmental and non-governmental forms of work regulation. Labour's response has involved not just traditional trade unions but also, increasingly, collaboration with NGOs and wider social movements. The Internet is an important component of these developments, which have seen diverse actors within the wider labour movement using information and communication technologies (ICT) in widely differing ways, with similarly diverse effects.

This chapter discusses some of the dynamics in these changes. It is organized as follows: first, an introduction to this 'networked labour movement' focusing on the relationship between technology and organization. The subsequent discussion and examples are organized around three themes: the Internet as a resource for coordination, the Internet as a resource for campaigning and, briefly, ICT and the Internet as a site of conflict.

New strategies, new actors, new media

Unions and labour organizations do not use technologies such as the Internet in a vacuum; they use them as part of their wider attempts to respond to and influence the changing world around them. As is documented elsewhere in this book, the world of work has undergone a radical change over the last three decades. Many governments have used legislation to restrict the ability of unions to take industrial action; the composition of the workforce has changed; and work organization has been radically altered, not least as companies seek to exploit and respond to continuing technological change. Most notably, companies, their supply chains and financial markets have become increasingly integrated globally. In parallel, trade unions are adopting a range of alternative approaches to establishing and strengthening transnational and global levels of organization, including establishing links with anti-globalization, human rights and environmental social movements (Hogan et al. 2010). Contemporaneously with these developments we have seen the spread of the Internet; since Eric Lee's landmark book *The Labour Movement and the Internet*, published in 1997 (Lee 1997), a substantial literature has emerged documenting and analysing labour's use of the Internet to strengthen their international presence.

Before presenting some examples of how new media has been used in the labour movement, however, we need to stand back and look briefly at the wider picture. Technology in general and new media in particular does not simply cause particular things to happen, but is closely linked to the practices, organizations, relationships and ideas in which it is developed and used. Hence, in the context of trade unions, the use of ICT is intertwined with the evolving organization and practice of international labour in its responses to a rapidly changing, globalized world. Consequently, we need to briefly examine some of the contours of international trade unionism before considering the ways in which they and other actors have been using new media. Two broad areas are significant here; first, the diversity of national trade union organization and second, and perhaps more significantly, the organization of international labour.

The organization, culture and politics of trade unions vary widely between countries, reflecting, among other things, widely differing national histories and positions in the international division of labour. There is an extensive literature on 'comparative industrial relations' (see, for example, Hamman and Kelly 2008), which tends to emphasize these differences. This has been a particular area of interest in the context of the European Union, where there have been initiatives to strengthen links between unions from very different backgrounds. Two examples illustrate the differences. First, in Germany and some other north European countries, workers have legal rights to representation within companies through the mechanism of works councils (Betreibsrat), which have no corresponding mechanisms in the United Kingdom, the United States and many other countries. Second, trade unions themselves are organized differently; in Europe, some unions (e.g., in Italy and Spain) have been organized along political and confessional (religious) lines; along manual, 'white-collar' and educational lines (e.g., Sweden and Denmark) or in single, unitary confederations (e.g., Ireland and the United Kingdom). These, and many other, differences mean that assumptions about what trade unions are, what they do, and how they are organized can be misleading when workers based in one national setting try to build links with those from other countries.

Despite these differences, there has long been a practice of international labour organization; Marx's International Working Men's Association (widely known as the 'First International') was founded in 1864. The International Transport Workers' Federation, a global federation of unions organizing in the transport and logistics industries, was established in 1899, addressing the obvious international dimensions of workers' concerns in industries such as seafaring. The ITF is now one of a 'family' of Global Union Federations (GUFs, formerly known as International Trade Secretariats (ITS)), made up of trade unions across the world who organize workers in particular industrial sectors. These include IndustriALL[1] (mining, energy and manufacturing), Education International (school, college and university teachers) and Public Services International (public services and utilities). In turn, these GUFs are members of the International Trade Union Confederation (ITUC), along with national trade confederations.[2] In Europe (and particularly significantly in the European Union), the European Trade Union Confederation (ETUC) serves as analogue of the ITUC, bringing together the national union confederations within Europe and the European structures of the GUFs. The ETUC is also supported financially by the European Commission as a way of encouraging the representation of workers, interests within EU institutions. Since the 1970s, other organizations have also emerged which organize, represent or campaign for (what they believe to be) the interests of workers, particularly those in the developing world or at the margins of the established labour markets in the global North. Networks of campaigning NGOs such as the Clean Clothes Campaign concerned with the conditions of workers in the global textile supply chains; StreetNet, concerned with street workers; and the International Domestic Workers' Network (IDWN) have become increasingly influential. Relationships between such labour-oriented NGOs and international trade union organizations vary – in some cases, they work closely with GUFs, while in others relations may be quite hostile.

The preceding, very brief, excursion into the organization of labour and trade unions internationally provides the setting for a discussion of the role of new media in global labour organization. The potential of what we now call information and communication technologies (ICT) to sustain and perhaps extend such internationalism was noted in the early 1970s when some trade unions began to use them to compile and communicate information on the activities of global companies (Levinson 1972). During the 1980s, labour began more systematically to exploit the digital communications networks that were becoming available, for example, using e-mail to replace telex for international communications, or brokering access to the online business information databases. During the 1990s, like most parts of society, labour's use of the Internet and the Web became widespread. Digital communication became possible not just between organizational actors but increasingly among individual members and activists. However, despite many successes, early optimism about the ways in which the Internet would allow the transformation of labour organization, particularly at the international level, has been tempered by experience of the complexity involved. Issues such as language, technology access and the great diversity of national systems of industrial relations continue to pose obstacles to the establishment of a networked international labour organization (particularly in Europe) (Hodkinson 2009; Gill 2009; Walker and Creanor 2005). Nevertheless, websites and virtual organizations have emerged that make important contributions to sustaining international labour activity. Perhaps most notable is the LabourStart website (http://www.labourstart.org/), where an international network of volunteer correspondents and translators provide a news feed on labour issues around the world, via the website and social media sites such as Twitter and Facebook. LabourStart is an independent organization, but works closely with some GUFs and trade unions, and its news feed is carried on many union websites. The site has also been involved in the online presence of many campaigns (typically by facilitating protest e-mails to companies and governments) around the world (see Fougner and Kurtoglu 2011; Muir and Peetz 2010; Robinson 2006 for examples from Turkey, Australia and Eritrea).[3]

While the Internet allows trade unions to communicate more effectively both externally and with members and close allies, it is also closely associated with shifting dynamics within the labour movement itself. As access to the Internet has become increasingly widespread, so activists and union members have been able to coordinate their own activities independently of, and in some cases in opposition to, their union leadership; small, labour-oriented NGOs have been able to develop global reach; and the work of international labour bodies such as the GUFs is now more well known to union members.[4] Claims that the Internet allows union members to overthrow Michel's (1915) 'Iron Law of Oligarchy' (which argues that democratic organizations will tend over time to function for the benefit of full-time bureaucrats who have better access to informational and other resources than their members) are probably overstated (Greene et al. 2003). Union members have nevertheless used the Internet to challenge their leaderships, for example, through using the Web to campaign against allegedly corrupt senior officials. The most celebrated example of trade union activists' use of the Internet to sustain action in defiance of their own structures remains that of the Liverpool dockworkers' dispute of the mid-1990s (see below). These dynamics are more complex, though, than simply allowing a binary division between bureaucracy and membership as particular groups within each have exploited the technologies in differing ways. For example, among full-time trade union staff, educators, communication officers and ICT specialists have all incorporated the Internet into their activities in distinct ways (Martínez Lucio 2010).

Despite the obstacles and complexities, trade unions and organized labour more widely have, to use terminology from the social movement literature, used the Internet as part of broadening their 'action repertoires' in novel ways. We can distinguish three broad ways in which this has happened (Walker 2001; Van Laer and Van Aelst 2010). First, the Internet has been used as a resource for sustaining and coordinating organization, particularly at the international level, largely through improved 'internal' communications within and between unions. Second, the Internet has been used as a medium for campaigning by mobilizing wider support or raising public awareness of issues. Third, Internet resources can themselves be targets in direct conflict, as in cases of hacking or sabotage. While this final point is probably of least direct relevance to organized labour, various groups have sought to use such tactics against corporates and so is discussed briefly below. Of course, the distinction between these three areas is not clear-cut: winning enough public support in the form of sending protest e-mails, for example, might conceivably have the effect of degrading the performance of an adversary's e-mail infrastructure and blur the boundary between mobilizing support and direct conflict. They do, though, provide a useful way to think about how labour coordination and action repertoires have changed.

The following sections of this chapter are structured around these three themes: coordination, campaigning and conflict.

The Internet as a resource for coordinating and organizing

Widespread access to ICT has created opportunities for labour to establish new mechanisms for coordinating and organizing its activities, particularly in responding to global corporations and transnational dimensions of labour and workplace regulation. Trade unions have been confronted by global corporations who have played off employees in one country against those in another, for example, using the threat (and practice) of relocating work and jobs from one country to another as in the well-documented examples of General Motor's 2000 decision to close its Luton plant in the United Kingdom and Deutche Post's 2004 decision to close its DHL hub in Brussels, among many others. In the European Union, European Works' Councils[5] (EWCs) have provided resources and a particular focus for unions to coordinate their activities in larger corporations. These networks can be complex, involving unions in a dozen or more European countries, and contemporary ICT is essential to the effective ongoing exchange of information. Regular online communication, alongside face-to-face meetings, also has an important role in sustaining personal relationships that help to build a sense of common identity among participants (Whittal et al. 2009).

Through an influential educational project, the ETUC[6] supported online networks using e-mail, websites and online conferences/bulletin boards, along with training, to help European industry federations to communicate with and among their affiliates. While they largely used widespread technological infrastructures, the design and evolution of particular applications have varied significantly, reflecting the dynamics of the particular industrial sectors and the decisions of the EIFs and affiliates involved. Pulignano (2009) distinguished between informational and coordinative virtual networks in the project. Informational networks primarily gathered information in partially structured ways to build up a picture of the dynamics of a sector. For example, unions in the graphical industries used structured information gathered via questionnaires as a basis for analysing the industrial dynamics in particular areas (such as rotogravure printing) of the industry undergoing market consolidation and particularly rapid technological change. Coordinative networks, in contrast, developed shared or common responses between unions. For example, the European Metalworkers Federation (which became part of IndustriALL Europe in 2012) worked with its affiliates in GM to achieve a Europe-wide framework agreement, reflecting both the history and structure of the trade union organization in the automotive industry, and particular organizational and political decisions to 'regulate' the standards of EWC agreements agreed upon by affiliates. Importantly, the TRACE project highlighted that the mere availability of ICT is not of itself enough to generate effective transnational coordination; as well as sectoral dynamics and union policies, online networking in trade unions is subject to some of the social and organizational constraints on effective online work and collaboration that have been widely noted in the information systems and other fields (see, for example, Preece 2000).

Case study: European regulation, the 'Bolkestein directive' and service sector unions

UNI Europa is a European federation of 320 unions, in 50 countries, representing around 7 million workers in service industries. In 2004, the European Commission adopted a draft directive on services in the EU internal market, widely known as the 'Bolkestein directive'. The directive aimed to remove 'red tape' and to deregulate cross-border trade in services. Trade unions were concerned about several elements of the draft directive which took no account of differing service regulation and social provision among EU countries, and it specifically viewed labour law and collective agreements as forms of 'red tape'.

A central part of UNI Europa's response was to establish a network of affiliates to monitor the consequences of the directive across the EU and to strengthen UNI Europa's capacity to respond at the EU level, including piloting an online network. The network was based on collecting data using an online conference, primarily used by affiliates' policy officers. A particular problem that the unions were confronting was that although many affiliates had well-established networks and expertise in lobbying national policymakers, they were far less familiar with the arrangements for EU policymaking. The online network provided members with information updates which helped in national and European lobbying activities and access to the media. Following a sustained and coordinated campaign of lobbying Members of the European Parliament, in early 2006 the European Parliament voted by a large margin to exclude labour laws and collective rights from the agreement, along with other contentious elements. UNI Europa attributed this significant victory to the use of electronic networking, and the way it allowed anticipation of policy changes. Importantly, the network supported the development of new cooperative and open communication practices between national affiliates' policy officers across industrial sectors (see Kirton-Darling 2007).

Questions

1. What other successful examples are there of trade unions and others campaigning around decisions in intergovernmental bodies?
2. What difficulties would you expect to arise in coordinating action between trade unions operating in very diverse national industrial relations contexts?

Global supply chains pose new challenges for labour in gathering and interpreting information about complex corporate organizations and networks, and in coordinating its own responses. Organizing around these supply chains in consumer sectors such as textiles, cut flowers and foodstuffs involves working with organizations beyond the traditional labour movement to include, for example, consumer and advocacy NGOs. The emergence of 'corporate social responsibility' initiatives in which employers commit to ethical trading practices effectively provides a privatized form of regulation of working conditions in some global sectors, though one which is criticized by some in the labour movement as providing at best only weak forms of protection for workers in developing countries. Networks of NGOs and unions have emerged that seek to monitor the behaviour of large garment companies and organize in their supply chains. The Internet provides opportunities to strengthen and extend the coordination of such networks (e.g., Thorpe and Mather 2005), and new methods such as the 'mashups' of the open data movement, which bring together data from diverse external sources to generate new services and understandings of data, may provide new opportunities for labour organization over the coming years.

As noted in the preceding section, the Internet can also be exploited differently by different constituencies in the labour movement, changing internal power dynamics as well as the relationship between the labour movement and external actors. The example of the use of e-mail and the Internet by supporters of Liverpool dockworkers locked out by their employer in the 1990s, provides a graphic illustration of how these technologies can be used by workers to circumvent their union and speak directly with fellow workers and supporters around the world.

Case study: Liverpool dockers

In September 1995, dockworkers employed by Torside, a subcontractor to the Mersey Docks and Harbour Company (MDHC), were fired after protests about payment for working overtime. When workers employed by MDHC refused to cross the sacked workers' picket lines, they were also sacked and their jobs advertised within 24 hours. There followed a 28-month lockout. The dockers' union, the TGWU, did not make the strike official because the lockout was triggered by solidarity action illegal under UK law, and the union faced losing all its funds; the International Transport Workers' Federation (ITF), to which the TGWU was affiliated, was similarly hampered in providing support since they are based in London and covered by the same legislation. Consequently, the dockers adopted an independent strategy of building links with dockers elsewhere in the world who would be able to offer solidarity. Two International Days of Action were held during 1997, as dockers internationally expressed their support for the locked-out Liverpool workers through strikes, demonstrations and boycotts.

The dockers made extensive use of the Internet (Carter et al. 2003), making widespread use of e-mail and, in particular, pioneering the use of the Web at a time when the use of photographs and audio files of dockers' speaking were innovative techniques in representing the reality of dockers' experiences. The Internet was used to build connections with dockers around the world, most prominently in places such as South Africa and the United States, but including many other countries. They were able to do this despite a lack of support from their own union and from the ITF by establishing immediate connections with their peers internationally and being able to communicate news instantaneously around the world. This represented a radical new way of organizing, which many saw as a direct challenge to the authority of international union organizations. In the end, though, the dockers were defeated. Perhaps surprisingly, this experience, 15 years on, remains a classic example of the use of the Internet by trade unionists.

Questions

1. Are there other, more recent examples of the use of the Internet in coordinating international labour solidarity?
2. What other examples are there of trade union members' use of the Internet to circumvent or otherwise challenge their own trade unions?

The Internet as a medium for campaigning

The conventional mass media of television and newspapers have long had a reputation for presenting trade unions negatively, both in their coverage of labour issues and in their wider setting of the public agenda (e.g., Walton and Davis 1977; Walsh 1988). In response to this, unions developed strategies, including employing public relations officers, providing media training to officers and representatives and using paid advertising to try to engage more positively with the mass media to communicate both with members and with the wider public. The emergence of the Internet and the Web in the early 1990s promised the potential of direct, unmediated communications with both internal and external audiences. At a time when trade unions' ability to use traditional weapons in industrial conflict, such as strikes or working to rule, are for a range of reasons, diminished, the Internet offered ways to win wider public support and engage in new forms of communicative action. In an early example of what they termed 'cyberpicketing', the International Federation of Chemical, Energy, Mine and General Workers' Unions[7] (ICEM) supported US affiliates in dispute with tyre companies Bridgestone Firestone and Continental Tires by establishing campaign Web pages that parodied those of target companies and invited visitors to send messages of protest to the company management, to suppliers, corporate customers and investors (Walker 2001). In effect, the Web was used as a medium for a form of corporate campaigning that originated in the United States. This approach aims to generate widespread publicity for a dispute, and to draw in a company's suppliers and customers. At a time when it was unclear how the Internet would become significant, it was difficult to know the direct impact on the companies involved though they certainly attracted international attention to the disputes in the conventional media. Unions have continued to adopt this style of campaigning; in a more recent example, in 2012 the ITUC and two of the GUFs (the ITF and UNI Global) established a website to campaign in support of the right for employers in the DHL network of companies to join trade unions. While DHL, a global company headquartered in Germany, generally respects the right of its employees in the European Union to join a union, many employees elsewhere are denied the opportunity. The website (http://www.respectatdhl.org/) and associated social media sites provide news and briefings about the company and the campaign, and offer visitors the opportunity to download resources and join the campaign.

The Internet also allows workers to publicize their concerns independently of trade unions. The phenomenon of workplace blogging emerged since 2000 as a means for workers to document their working lives, overcome isolation and as an opportunity for what has been termed 'self-organised conflict expression' (Richards 2008: 96). Workers from a wide range of occupations, from sex workers to teachers, have used blogs in this way. Typically, such work bloggers are anonymous, not least because when identified many have been disciplined or sacked by their employers. In many cases, these blogs can be read as individual employees expressing individual resistance to situations that people find themselves in at work. The content may not be directly related to traditional industrial relations issues, but they are examples of workers gaining a voice about their workplaces and practices. These accounts are not typically linked explicitly to trade unions or other forms of organized labour, though bloggers often report feeling a sense of community with other (anonymous) bloggers from the same or similar industries. However, cases have arisen which conflate individual resistance and links to wider trade union organization, as in the case of Joe Gordon, the Waterstone blogger (see below).

Case study: Joe Gordon, the Waterstone blogger

In 2005, Joe Gordon, then an employee of the Waterstone's chain of booksellers for 11 years, was fired for making occasional satirical comments about the company on his personal blog, The Woolamalloo Gazette. His case was the first generally reported case of an employee losing their job as a direct result of blog postings and triggered widespread and generally supportive media comment about his right to free speech. His blog then became an organizing tool in his campaign, supported by his union the Retail Book Association (RBA), to win reinstatement.

Booksellers in general are particularly vulnerable to charges of denying free speech. Waterstone's was especially open to such charges, having run an advertising campaign along these lines some years earlier. Some novelists publicly supported Gordon in the media and on their own blogs, and Gordon publicized these statements through his own blog. The blog generated supportive comments from Brazil, Denmark and Norway, as well as, somewhat ironically, from China. Some anonymous contributors to the blog also identified themselves as Waterstone's employees and commented critically on working conditions in the company. An altered image of the Waterstone's logo, rendered as 'Bastardstone's', to use the contemporary term, went viral. During the campaign, Gordon also highlighted the continuing role of the RBA in supporting him. After four months, Gordon's appeal to Waterstone's for reinstatement was successful, though he had by that time taken up other employment.

Following the Gordon case, other bloggers have run into difficulties, and the Committee to Protect Bloggers was established (see http://committeetoprotectbloggers.org/), though it appears to have functioned only intermittently since. Since 2005, many companies have developed explicit policies about workplace blogging in an effort to control and contain their employees' public comments about the company. While individuals' blogging has not become a widespread feature of contention in the workplace, some trade union branches do use blogs as a way of communicating with their membership and with wider public audiences.

Questions

1. What more recent examples of workplace disputes arising from the use of blogs and social media can you find?
2. What issues do employers' guidelines on employees' use of social media address?

More recently, workers have begun using other social media to articulate their stories, for example, taking advantage of the decreasing cost and widespread availability of video cameras. In the United States, the Service Employees International Union (SEIU) has organized training in 'digital storytelling' methods for some of its members, with the aim of building links with other community organizations. Typically, over the course of a day-long workshop, participants are trained to write and record a brief script to produce a short video. Once posted on video-sharing sites, these can become powerful media, articulating workers' experiences directly to labour and other activists (see the accompanying Web resources for examples).

The Internet as a site of conflict

The Internet itself constitutes an arena of direct conflict; most obviously, there have been many examples of groups hacking their adversaries' websites. Although governments and corporations have increasingly identified this kind of activity as 'cyber-terrorism' and sought to isolate hackers from legitimate social protest, there have been recent examples of hacking against corporations in relation to social protest, most prominently by the Anonymous group of hackers.

The release of US intelligence data in late 2010 via the Wikileaks website (http://www.wikileaks.org) provided perhaps the highest-profile example of campaigners targeting corporate websites. As US politicians and others attacked Wikileaks for releasing the data, to the point of calling for the assassination of its founder Julian Assange, several US-based global corporations withdrew services to Wikileaks. Initially, companies such as Internet payment provider PayPal and the credit card company Visa cut the services which allowed people to make donations to Wikileaks, effectively isolating the website financially. As the Web traffic to the Wikileaks site grew massively, it was moved to Amazon's cloud computing infrastructure, which appeared to offer a way to maximize the reliability of the service. Under continued pressure in the United States, Amazon similarly withdrew their services from Wikileaks, significantly interfering with the operation of the website. In response, an unknown group of hackers known as Anonymous organized a 'distributed denial of service' (DDoS) attack flooding the websites of PayPal, Visa and Amazon (among others) with requests for Web pages. This had the effect of degrading, and ultimately denying, access to these companies' Web servers. However, by late 2011, the financial blockade was hindering Wikileaks' publication of leaked documents until the leaking of e-mails concerning the Syrian crisis in July 2012.

There is no evidence that organized labour in general, and trade unions in particular, have been involved in the kind of attack carried out by Anonymous, or any other form of hacking. Indeed, like other civil society websites (Zuckerman et al. 2010), labour movement sites appear more likely to be the target, rather than the originators, of such attacks; for example, the website of the UK Public and Commercial Services Union (PCS) was the target of such an attack from unidentified sources, disabling its website for 10 days in the run-up to its 2011 national conference.

These cyber attacks originate from more fluid and at least partially anonymous networked organizations such as the Anonymous group. They can, though, link with other forms of informal Internet-enabled anti-corporate campaigning organizations. By the time of the global economic downturn following the international banking crisis in 2008, sites like Facebook, YouTube, Twitter and the like had become pervasive media, allowing users to share information widely without reference to central authorities. Activists from outwith traditional labour organizations and NGOs have potential access to thousands of other activists using these tools to coordinate new protests. In the United Kingdom, the UK Uncut movement, started by a group of friends over a drink in a bar (Shepherd 2011), used Twitter and other social media to coordinate widespread protests against high street companies such as Vodafone, Boots and Barclays that they identified as having avoided tax payments, hence contributing to the need for large cuts in public spending. Similar campaigns emerged in the United States and elsewhere. Some activists from this milieu hacked the Vodafone's World of Difference website, which promotes the company's charitable and CSR activities, and posted messages demanding that the company pay its taxes (Taylor 2011). These campaigns not only make use of the Internet, but reflect what has been termed a 'culture 2.0' and 'subterranean politics' (Kaldor et al. 2012) in which activists outside traditional organizations of trade unions, NGOs and community organizations adopt both methods of organizing and values that are themselves closely linked to use of the Internet, such as a rejection of hierarchical forms of organization and links with the anti-copyright, open source values as embodied by, for example, the Pirate parties of Sweden, Germany and elsewhere.

Conclusion

The use of the Internet has opened up new action repertoires for trade unions, the wider labour movement and a range of new actors campaigning around corporate governance issues. This chapter has argued that, in three areas at least, Internet use by unions and others involves the interplay between evolving organizational forms and communications technologies in the relationship between labour and capital. The use of new communication technologies can be viewed as falling into three broad areas – (cross-border) coordination of labour activity, campaigning in the public arena and, to a much lesser degree among trade unions, as a site of conflict itself.

Technology is one of a range of factors at play, which also include state regulation (and differing national traditions thereof), corporate strategy, the global divisions of labour in different sectors and supply chains, the interplay of different organizational elements of the labour movement and organizational choices made by unions and other actors. As has been the case over most of the last 20 years, trade unions, and labour more widely, continue to use ICT in novel ways. We are perhaps beginning to see how the Internet has enabled new cultures, practices and organizational forms, most recently around the Web 2.0 family of social media. Peer production is allowing new actors to become involved in the organization of labour as in the involvement of NGOs in the formation of free (or at least, freer) trade unions in China (He and Xie, 2011); and individuals can give voice to their workplace grievances either with or without the support of traditional trade union organizations. As large parts of the economy become increasingly information-intensive, new methods of organizing and coordinating labour may become feasible. For example, the 'open data' movement, which to date has largely focussed on making government-held data sets freely available, may offer new ways of understanding the behaviour of complex corporate supply chains and networks, though there is little evidence to date of labour activists exploring such avenues. Whatever the technological details, it seems likely that workers and others will try to use new information and communication technologies as tools in workplace representation.

> **Reflective questions**
>
> 1. What other, more recent, examples of the use of the Internet in campaigning against corporations can you find? What actors and technologies are involved?
> 2. Do more recent examples of labour and social movement use of the Internet fit into one of the three categories suggested above?
> 3. What do you think will be the future developments in terms of campaigns around work on the Internet?

> **Recommended reading**
>
> - Earl, J. (2006) 'Pursuing social change online: The use of four protest tactics on the Internet.' *Social Science Computer Review*, 24(3), 362–377.
> - He, B. and Xie, Y. (2011) 'Wal-Mart's trade union in China.' *Economic and Industrial Democracy*, 33(3), 421–440.
> - Pulignano, V. (2009) 'International cooperation, transnational restructuring and virtual networking in Europe.' *European Journal of Industrial Relations*, 15(2), 187–205.

Notes

1. IndustriALL is the newest of the GUFs, established in 2012 by the merger of the International Metalworkers' Federation (IMF), the International Chemical, Energy, Mine and General Workers' Federation (ICEM) and the International Textile, Garment and Leather Workers Federation (ITGLWF).
2. Following the Second World War, in 1949 there was a historic, and debilitating, split in the international trade union movement between those aligned with the former Communist bloc unions in the West. Since the collapse of the Communist bloc the ITUC is now the pre-eminent international trade union organization. The former Communist-aligned World Federation of Trade Unions (WFTU) and its associated sectoral structures remain, though in a much weakened form.
3. Other examples of similar websites providing labour-oriented news and campaign support can be found in the online resources accompanying this chapter.
4. During the 1980s, a former general secretary of the Miners' International Federation (a forerunner of IndustriALL) and a long-standing activist in the then-militant South Yorkshire coalfield, remarked that he had only become aware that his union, the National Union of Miners (NUM),was affiliated to an international body after he was elected to the NUM National Executive.
5. European Works Councils (EWCs) cover about 60% of the EU workforce by companies employing more than 1,000 people in two or more EU countries. They are required by EU Directives as an information and consultation mechanism for companies with representatives for their workforces. For more information on EWCs, see the online resources accompanying this chapter.
6. TRACE (Trade Unions Anticipating Change in Europe) 2005–2007.
7. ICEM merged with other GUFs to create the IndustriALL GUF in 2012.

References

Carter, C., Clegg, S., Hogan, J. and Kornberger, M. (2003) 'The polyphonic spree: The case of the Liverpool Dockers.' *Industrial Relations Journal*, 34, 290–304.

Castells, M. (2001) *The Internet Galaxy*. Oxford: Oxford University Press.

Fougner, T. and Kurtoglu, A. (2011) 'Transnational labour solidarity and social movement unionism: Insights from and beyond a women workers' strike in Turkey.' *British Journal of Industrial Relations*, 49: 353–375.

Gill, L. (2009) 'The limits of solidarity: Labor and transnational organizing against Coca-Cola.' *American Ethnologist*, 36, 667–680.

Greene, A.-M., Hogan, J. and Grieco, M. (2003) 'E-collectivism and distributed discourse: New opportunities for trade union democracy.' *Industrial Relations Journal*, 34, 282–289.

Hamman, K. and Kelly, J. (2008) 'Varieties of capitalism and industrial relations.' In Blyton, P. et al. (eds.), *The SAGE Handbook of Industrial Relations*. SAGE: London, pp. 129–148.

Hodkinson, S. (2009) 'Internet campaigning across borders.' In Baringhorst, S., Kneip, V. and Niesyto, J. (eds.), *Political Campaigning on the Web*. Bielefeld, Germany: Transcript Verlag, pp. 147–171.

Hogan, J., Nolan, P. and Grieco, M. (2010) 'Unions, technologies of coordination, and the changing contours of globally distributed power.' *Labor History*, 51, 29–40.

Kaldor, M. et al. (2012) *The "Bubbling Up" of Subterranean Politics in Europe*. London School of Economics and Political Science.

Kirton-Darling, J. (2007) 'Anticipating and managing change in the services sectors: UNI Europa's network on services in the internal market.' *Transfer*, 2/70, 301–305.

Lee, E. (1997) *The Labour Movement and the Internet: The New Internationalism*. London: Pluto Press.

Levinson, C. (1972) *International Trade Unionism*. London: Allen & Unwin.

Martínez Lucio, M. (2010) 'Dimensions of internationalism and the politics of the labour movement: Understanding the political and organisational aspects of labour networking and co-ordination.' *Employee Relations*, 32, 538–556.

Martínez Lucio, M. and Walker, S. (2005) 'The networked union? The Internet as a challenge to trade union identity and roles.' *Critical Perspectives in International Business*, doi:10.1108/17422040510595645.

Michels, R. (1915) *Political Parties: A Sociological Study of the Oligarchical Tendencies of Modern Democracy*. New York: The Free Press.

Muir, K. and Peetz, D. (2010) 'Not dead yet: The Australian union movement and the defeat of a government.' *Social Movement Studies*, 9(2), 215–228.

Preece, J. (2000) *Online Communities: Designing Usability, Supporting Sociability*, Chichester, UK: John Wiley & Sons.

Pulignano, V. (2009) 'International cooperation, transnational restructuring and virtual networking in Europe.' *European Journal of Industrial Relations*, 15, 187–205.

Richards, J. (2008) '"Because I need somewhere to vent": The expression of conflict through work blogs'. *New Technology, Work and Employment*, 23, 95–110.

Robinson, B. (2006) 'Cybersolidarity: Internet-based campaigning and trade union internationalism.' In *International Federation for Information Processing—Social Inclusion:*

Societal and Organizational Implications for Information Systems. Boston, MA: Springer, pp. 123–135.

Shepherd, J. (2011) NUS President says non-violent tactics of UK Uncut should be model for students, *The Guardian*, 9th August available at: http://www.guardian.co.uk/education/2011/aug/09/nus-president-student-protests

Taylor, M. (2011) UK Uncut Hacks into Vodafone website, *The Guardian*, 10th March available at: http://www.guardian.co.uk/uk/2011/mar/10/uk-uncut-hacks-vodafone-website

Thorpe, V. and Mather, C. (2005) ITGLWF 'Targeting Multinationals' Project Assessment. ITGLWF.

Van Laer, J. and Van Aelst, P. (2010) 'Internet and social movement action repertoires.' *Information, Communication and Society*, 13, 1146–1171.

Walker, S. (2001) 'Pay us our wages! Information warfare and industrial conflict in a global economy.' *Southern Review: Communication, Politics and Culture*, 34(3), 55–70.

Walker, S. and Creanor, L. (2005) 'Crossing complex boundaries: Transnational online education in European trade unions.' *Journal of Computer Assisted Learning*, 21, 343–354.

Walsh, G. (1988) 'Trade unions and the media.' *International Labour Review*, 127, 205–220.

Walton, P. and Davis, H. (1977) 'Bad news for trade unionists.' In Beharrall, P. and Philo, G. (eds.), *Trade Unions and the Media*. London: MacMillan Press.

Whittal, M., Knudsen, H. and Huijgen, F. (2009) 'European works councils: Identity and the role of information and communication technology.' *European Journal of Industrial Relations*, 15, 167–185.

Zuckerman, E., Roberts, H., Mcgrady, R., York, J. and Palfrey, J. (2010) *Distributed Denial of Service Attacks Against Independent Media and Human Rights Sites*. The Berkman Center for Internet & Society at Harvard University.

Conclusion:
Contested spaces, globalization and the new politics of regulation

Miguel Martínez Lucio

The delivery of the manuscript of this book coincided with the death of over 1000 textile workers in Bangladesh when their place of work collapsed around them. The building had extra floors which were not part of the original planning request, and the workforce were told that regardless of serious cracks that were appearing throughout the building they were to go to work. Many were making clothes that would end up being sold through a global chain of purchasers and suppliers; the basis of these transactions was mainly to reduce costs. This illustrates how the human tragedies we see in relation to work throughout the world remain wedded to the way the economic system is globalizing. It is an indication of the nature of international economic relations.

We live in an uncertain age where models of employment relations and the practice of management are changing. The impact of globalization is resulting in a range of contradictory and uneven effects. While many people are being included in the market economy – and in the new global flows of capital and labour – their inclusion does not always lead to increased job enhancement and empowerment. The upbeat discourse of human resource management and the new individualism are sometimes purely rhetoric with little concern regarding the broader social agenda. We are seeing a rush to find 'best practices' and 'excellence' in how organizations develop and are managed. There is a new market for ideas and a range of examples and strategies – case studies – that are transmitted by multinational corporations (MNCs), consultancies and business schools. Government agencies seek to convince employers and organizations to mimic and use the practices of what are perceived to be 'winners' and 'success stories': the 'heroic' is the order of the day (see Chapter 9). In the 1980s, this was the 'Japanese way' in the United Kingdom, while in the last ten years it has been the

American business culture in such countries as Malaysia. This cross-referencing and learning increasingly seems to steer in a particular North American direction regardless of the emergence of major economies such as Brazil, China and India. Yet tensions are surfacing as to how a new global model appears regardless of the ideological leanings of leading business schools and consultancies. Students of globalization and the international dimensions of work and management need to be increasingly alert to the subliminal dimension of their education and development. The new global order is more contested and open to political questions than one would imagine.

We are also becoming aware of competing narratives of globalization and their impact. For some, this marks the age of new individualized and market-based ethics and behaviour which will re-mould the way we work and create a new dynamic force for change, while for other these changes are having significant effects in the dis-embedding of communities and the massive erosion of working standards. From child labour in the Far East, to concerns with the marginal position of migrant communities in the UAE, through to the new challenges women face in Africa, globalization is bringing contradictory signs of progress and poverty. An issue that is becoming of grave concern is how globalization appears to be linked to increasing informalization of the economy and employment: the growth of submerged economic activity and of organized crime. The movement of goods, capital and people has an increasingly hidden element. Globalization appears to be linked to deregulation and to such developments as outsourcing, which create hidden spaces where workers toil in inhuman conditions. International 'industries' in prostitution, drugs, armaments and undocumented labour constitute a world which runs parallel to and even interacts with the internationalization of business.

The general impact of MNCs is the subject of extensive discussion, but what is emerging is the challenge of managing greater movement, mobility and tension in their internal organizational spaces and the external arenas they engage in. They are finding that while they are a catalyst for change they are also themselves caught up in the new developments. When one looks closely at debates on diversity, payment systems, training and production processes within MNCs and their operations, one can see that at the heart of this is the impossibility of control and the fundamental challenge of creating consistent and coherent systems of management and representation. The need to develop diversity management programmes or clear compensation packages is not about seeking 'one best way' – although often that is what is driving many individuals and their projects – but it is a reflection of the need to respond to increasing contradictions and tensions that emerge from a new type of MNC which operates through more integrated systems and has a more diverse workforce. The racially hierarchical nature of MNCs is being challenged as seen in the legal cases brought against Japanese MNCs by African Americans in the United States and against the brushing out of visible ethnic minorities in the posters advertising a US MNC in Poland. MNCs are now increasingly contested spaces.

Much is said about the fact that the nation-state has been left behind in controlling MNCs, that the international regulatory bodies such as the International Labour Organization are fundamentally weak and rely on soft regulation, and that unions and non-government organizations such as charities rely mainly on shaming MNCs into 'doing the right thing'. However, environments are changing and evolving in nuanced ways: over time more coordinated actors and players are appearing in the international employment relations arenas that are beginning to learn to work more consistently, building alliances with each other, with the aim of conditioning and shaping global capitalism. The response by companies to these new pressures has been to construct corporate social responsibility strategies. These are often just a marketing device rather than a serious shift in the values and beliefs of MNCs. However, the development of these strategies does suggest that there is a perceived need to engage with a social approach to work because of these external pressures. The current economic crisis in various parts of the globe may weaken regulators as they deal with the debt of financial and other capitalist interests, but the question of what MNCs do and who they do it too is now an issue of debate and concern.

Innovation and change in the regulation of MNCs is ongoing, and how this develops in the future will require further research. New players are entering the field, and they are engaging more systematically with international capitalist organizations. Much may depend on how key countries such as China, Brazil, Russia, India and others begin to contribute to the new politics of regulation.

Index